ORACLE® *Oracle Press*™

Oracle9*i* JDBC™ Programming

Jason Price

McGraw-Hill/Osborne

New York Chicago San Francisco
Lisbon London Madrid Mexico City Milan
New Delhi San Juan Seoul Singapore Sydney Toronto

McGraw-Hill/Osborne
2600 Tenth Street
Berkeley, California 94710
U.S.A.

To arrange bulk purchase discounts for sales promotions, premiums, or fund-raisers, please contact **McGraw-Hill**/Osborne at the above address. For information on translations or book distributors outside the U.S.A., please see the International Contact Information page immediately following the index of this book.

Oracle9*i* JDBC™ Programming

1234567890 CUS CUS 0198765432

ISBN 0-07-222254-9

Publisher
Brandon A. Nordin

Vice President & Associate Publisher
Scott Rogers

Acquisitions Editor
Lisa McClain

Project Editor
Katie Conley

Acquisitions Coordinator
Athena Honore

Technical Editor
Kuassi Mensah

Copy Editor
Sally Engelfried

Proofreader
Deidre Dolce

Indexer
Irv Hershman

Computer Designers
Lucie Ericksen, Elizabeth Jang

Illustrators
Michael Mueller, Lyssa Wald

Series Design
Roberta Steele

Cover Designer
Greg Scott

This book was composed with Corel VENTURA™ Publisher.

This book is dedicated to my late mother,
Patricia Ann Price.

About the Author

Jason Price is a product manager at Oracle Corporation, where he was previously a senior member of technical staff. Jason has contributed to many of Oracle's products, including the database, the application server, and several of the CRM applications. Prior to joining Oracle, Jason worked at Logica PLC in London, England, where he was employed as a technical consultant and software engineer. Jason is an Oracle Certified Database Administrator and Application Developer and has over ten years of experience in the software industry. This is Jason's second book; his first was *Java Programming with SQLJ* (O'Reilly, 2001). Jason has also written many articles on Java programming with the Oracle database for O'Reilly's ONJava.com website.

Jason holds a Bachelor of Science degree (with honors) in physics from the University of Bristol, England.

Contents at a Glance

v

PART IV
Performance

PART V
Appendixes

Contents

PART I
Basic JDBC Programming

PART II
Advanced JDBC Programming

PART IV

Performance

PART V

Appendixes

Acknowledgments

Thanks to the wonderful people at McGraw-Hill/Osborne, including Lisa McClain, Athena Honore, and Katie Conley.

Thanks to Kuassi Mensah at Oracle Corporation for his thorough technical review, and to Ekkehard Rohwedder and Ashok Banergee for answering my questions and providing additional insights into Oracle's implementation of JDBC.

Introduction

J ava has taken its place as the cornerstone of enterprise development. You can run Java in the mid-tier and the back-end of a three-tier enterprise system, as well as in the browser. The Oracle database is one of the most widely used databases, and the Oracle9*i* Application Server (Oracle9*i* AS) has a growing share of the application server market. You can access a database from a Java program using the Java Database Connectivity (JDBC) API, which is a standard supported by all major database vendors, including Oracle Corporation.

In this book, you'll learn how to:

- Use standard JDBC, as well as the extensions developed by Oracle Corporation for use with the specific features of the Oracle database.

- Use Oracle9*i*AS Containers for J2EE (OC4J), which allows you to run components such as Enterprise JavaBeans (EJB), servlets, and JavaServer Pages (JSP). OC4J is at the heart of the Oracle9*i* Application Server (Oracle9*i*AS).

- Use Oracle JDeveloper, which is a graphical integrated development environment that allows you to develop and debug and Java programs.

- Develop Java stored programs, which are an alternative to writing business logic in Oracle's proprietary PL/SQL procedural language.

- Use relational databases, as well as use the object-relational features of the Oracle database.

If you don't know the Oracle database, you'll also learn the basics in this book. You'll find a wealth of programming examples that accompany the exposition of JDBC, along with scripts that create the various database schemas used in this book. The programs and database scripts have been tested with the Oracle8*i* database

(8.1.6 and 8.1.7), along with Oracle9*i* (9.0.1). Two scripts also illustrate some of the latest Oracle9*i* database features, and are designed to run against an Oracle9*i* database.

Part I: Basic JDBC Programming

Chapter 1   Introduction to JDBC
In this chapter, you'll learn what software you need to install and configure to develop and run Java programs containing JDBC statements. You'll also see an example program that performs a simple database operation using JDBC, and you'll compile and run this example program. In addition, you'll be introduced to Oracle's JDeveloper tool, which is a graphical integrated development environment that allows you to develop, compile, run, and debug Java programs.

Chapter 2   Introduction to Databases and Oracle
You'll explore databases and Oracle in this chapter, and you'll be introduced to the Structured Query Language (SQL) that allows you to access a database. You'll also see a simple database that is used to hold data for an example online store. You'll explore Oracle's proprietary procedural programming language, known as PL/SQL, which adds a programming layer around SQL and allows you to define procedures and functions in the database.

Chapter 3   The Basics of JDBC Programming
In this chapter, you'll learn the details of the various Oracle JDBC drivers that may be used to connect to an Oracle database. Next, you'll get into the details of writing a JDBC program: importing the JDBC packages, registering the Oracle JDBC drivers, opening a database connection, and performing SQL statements to retrieve, add, modify, and delete rows from database tables.

Part II: Advanced JDBC Programming

Chapter 4   Advanced Result Sets
You'll learn how you can move backward and forward through rows in a result set, as well as jump to any row. You'll also learn how result sets can be sensitive to changes in the database.

Chapter 5   PL/SQL and JDBC
In this chapter, you'll learn how to call PL/SQL procedures and functions using JDBC.

Chapter 6   Database Objects

Object-oriented programming languages such as Java and C++ allow you to define classes; these classes act as "templates" from which you can create objects. Classes define attributes and methods; attributes are used to store an object's state, and methods are used to model an object's behaviors. With the release of the Oracle8*i* database, objects became available within the database, and they contain even more features in Oracle9*i*. You'll learn how to create and use object types in this chapter.

Chapter 7   Collections

The Oracle8*i* database introduced two new database types known as *collections*: *varrays* and *nested tables*. A varray is similar to an array in Java; you can use a varray to store an ordered set of elements in the database. A nested table is a table that is embedded within another table. You'll learn how to create and use collection types in this chapter.

Chapter 8   Large Objects

After the release of Oracle8 (and all subsequent releases of the database), a new class of types known as *large objects* (LOBs) was introduced. LOBs may be used to store binary data, character data, and references to external files. LOBs can store up to 4 gigabytes of data and enable you to meet the demands of today's multimedia intensive applications and websites. In this chapter, you'll learn how to use LOBs.

Chapter 9   Advanced Transaction Control

Today's databases can handle many users and programs accessing the database at the same time, each potentially running their own transactions in the database. The database software must be able to satisfy the needs of all these concurrent transactions, as well as maintain the integrity of rows stored in the database tables. You can control the level of isolation that exists between your transactions and other transactions that may be running in the database using JDBC, and you'll learn how to do that in this chapter.

Part III: Deploying Java

Chapter 10   Java Stored Procedures and Triggers

The Oracle9*i* and 8*i* databases come with an integrated Java Virtual Machine known as the *Oracle JVM*. The Oracle JVM allows you to deploy and run Java programs from within the database, with such programs being known in official Oracle parlance as *Java stored procedures*. Java stored procedures provide an alternative to writing your business logic in PL/SQL. Triggers enable you to write code that is run automatically by the database when a certain event occurs. You'll learn about Java stored procedures and triggers in this chapter.

Chapter 11   Oracle9*i*AS Containers for J2EE (OC4J)

You can run Java 2 Enterprise Edition (J2EE) components using Oracle9*i*AS Containers for J2EE (OC4J). OC4J allows you to run J2EE components like Enterprise JavaBeans (EJB), servlets, and JavaServer Pages (JSP). You can then use JDBC statements within these components to access the database. In this chapter, you'll be introduced to OC4J, and you'll see how to deploy and run a servlet, a JSP, and an EJB using OC4J.

Part IV: Performance

Chapter 12   Connection Pooling and Caching

In this chapter, you'll learn how using a pool of connections to a database can improve the performance of your programs. You'll also see how you can set up and use cached database connections to further boost your program's performance.

Chapter 13   Performance Tuning

In this final chapter, you'll learn some of the standard JDBC performance tuning techniques, along with the Oracle performance extensions. Typically, the Oracle performance extensions offer an edge over standard JDBC.

Part V: Appendixes

Appendix A   Oracle and Java Type Mappings

This appendix contains three tables that document the mappings between the Oracle database types and the compatible Java types.

Appendix B   Oracle Java Tools Reference

This appendix documents the syntax and command-line options for the Oracle Java tools used in this book.

Appendix C   Selected JDBC Interface and Class Reference

This appendix documents selected JDBC interfaces and classes.

Appendix D   JNDI and Data Sources
The Java Naming and Directory Interface (JNDI) is an API that provides naming and directory functionality to your Java programs. Using JNDI with JDBC is very useful because it allows you to register, or *bind*, data sources and look up those data sources in your program without having to provide the exact database connection details. This appendix shows you how to use JNDI with JDBC data sources.

Intended Audience

If you're a Java programmer who needs to write programs that access an Oracle database, you need to read this book. If you're a technical manager who needs a comprehensive introduction to JDBC, you will also find this book extremely valuable. A working knowledge of the Java language is assumed. No prior knowledge of the Oracle database is assumed: you can find everything you need to know to understand this book in Chapter 2. No prior knowledge of JDBC is assumed: this book will teach you everything you need to know to become an expert in JDBC, including how to use the Oracle extensions to JDBC.

Retrieving the Examples

All the code, scripts, and other files for this book can be downloaded from the Oracle Press website at **www.OraclePressBooks.com**. Everything is contained in a ZIP file. Once you've downloaded this file, you open it using WinZip and select the Extract option from the Actions menu. This will create a directory named JDBC, with the following three subdirectories:

- **programs**   Contains the programs.
- **sample_files**   Contains the sample files used in Chapter 8.
- **sql**   Contains the SQL*Plus scripts used to create the database schemas.

PART
I

Basic JDBC
Programming

CHAPTER
1

Introduction to JDBC

ava has established itself as a lynchpin in enterprise computing. You can use Java with all the main computing platforms without modifying your Java code when you move from one platform to another. Another lynchpin is the Oracle database, which acts as the repository for an enterprise's data. The Java Database Connectivity (JDBC) API is the glue that allows Java to access a database. You can use standard JDBC to access many different databases, including the Oracle database. However, the Oracle database contains a number of unique features that you can only take advantage of by using Oracle's extensions to standard JDBC. In this book, you'll learn standard JDBC, as well as the Oracle extensions. The Oracle extensions allow you to leverage JDBC to the maximum when using an Oracle database and when the Oracle extensions are tuned for high performance.

In this chapter, you'll learn what software you need to install and configure to develop and run Java programs containing JDBC statements. You'll also see an example program that performs a simple database operation using JDBC, and you'll compile and run this example program. You'll be introduced to Oracle's JDeveloper tool, a graphical integrated development environment that allows you to develop, compile, run, and debug Java programs. Even if you don't have access to JDeveloper, you'll be able to see what this tool offers from my descriptions and screen shots.

Software Requirements

Prior to running the examples in this book, you'll need to install the following software on your development machine:

- A version of the Sun Microsystems Java Development Kit (JDK)
- The Oracle Client software, along with the Oracle JDBC drivers

You can download the JDK and view full installation instructions from Sun's Java website at `http://java.sun.com`. This site also contains all the reference materials for Java and JDBC. You should take the time to find and examine this material, including the JDBC API documentation.

You can download trial versions of Oracle software (including the Oracle9*i* database and JDeveloper) from the Oracle Technology Network (OTN) website at `http://otn.oracle.com`. The Oracle Client software also comes with the database software, but you can install it separately when you run the Oracle Universal Installer. You can also obtain documentation for Oracle products from the OTN website.

In addition, you'll need to have access to a machine running the following software:

- Oracle9*i* database (version 9.0.1 or higher) or the Oracle8*i* database (version 8.1.6 or higher). If you want use the additional database object and collection enhancements in Oracle9*i* that I cover in Chapters 6 and 7, you'll need access to an Oracle9*i* database. If you only have access to an Oracle8*i* database, you'll still be able to use objects and collections but not the additional enhancements made in Oracle9*i*.

■ Oracle Net, which is used to connect to a database.

■ Oracle9*i*AS Containers for J2EE, known as OC4J (version 9.0.2 or higher). At the time of writing, OC4J was available from OTN as a separate download, but you may need to obtain the entire Oracle9*i* Application Server to get OC4J by the time you read this. I'll describe the details of installing and using OC4J in Chapter 11.

The Oracle database, Oracle Net, and OC4J don't necessarily have to be on your local machine on which you do your development—they can be running on a machine anywhere on your network. Typically, your organization will have a person known as a *database administrator* (DBA) who is responsible for setting up and administering databases. If you don't know much about databases, you should get to know your DBA. You'll learn the basics of databases in the next chapter.

The versions of the JDK and Oracle JDBC drivers that you use are important: they must be compatible with each other and the database you use. You should check the documentation and readme files to find out which versions of the JDK and Oracle JDBC drivers are supported with which database. OTN has information on compatible software versions.

TIP
You should typically use the latest version of the JDK and Oracle JDBC drivers regardless of the database you are using, but check the documentation just to make sure they are compatible.

In this book, I used the following software and versions:

■ Java 2 Standard Edition JDK (1.3.1_01)

■ Oracle Client software and Oracle JDBC drivers (9.0.1)

■ Oracle9*i* (9.0.1) and Oracle8*i* (8.1.6 and 8.1.7) databases

■ Oracle Net (9.0.1)

■ Oracle9iAS Containers for J2EE (9.0.2)

■ Oracle9i JDeveloper (beta)

You don't actually need JDeveloper, but it is a very useful tool for developing and debugging Java programs. You'll learn more about JDeveloper later in this chapter.

The Oracle Client Software

The directory where you installed the Oracle Client software on your machine is known as the `ORACLE_HOME` directory. This directory contains various subdirectories, one of which is the `BIN` directory, which contains the Oracle executable programs; another is the `jdbc` directory, which contains the following:

■ A text file named `Readme.txt`. You should open and read this file; it contains important information on the Oracle JDBC drivers such as new features supported and installation information.

■ A directory named `doc`, which has a ZIP file that contains the Oracle JDBC API reference documentation. *Make sure you extract the contents of this ZIP file and study this reference material.* As you become proficient with Oracle JDBC, you'll find this reference material invaluable.

■ A directory named `demo`, which has a ZIP file that contains sample Java programs from Oracle.

■ A directory named `lib`, which contains a number of ZIP and Java Archive (JAR) files. I'll talk more about these files in the next section.

Configuration

Once you've downloaded and installed the required software, your next step is to configure your machine to develop and run Java programs containing JDBC. You must set four environment variables on your machine:

■ `ORACLE_HOME`

■ `JAVA_HOME` (and `J2EE_HOME` if you're using Java 2 Enterprise Edition)

■ `PATH`

■ `CLASSPATH` (and `J2EE_CLASSPATH` if you're using Java 2 Enterprise Edition)

If you're using Unix or Linux, you'll also need to set the additional `LD_LIBRARY_PATH` environment variable. You'll learn how to set these environment variables in the following sections.

Setting the ORACLE_HOME Environment Variable

The ORACLE_HOME directory is the directory where you installed the Oracle software, and you'll need to set an environment variable named ORACLE_HOME on your machine that specifies this directory.

Setting an Environment Variable with Windows 2000

To set an environment variable in Windows 2000, you first need to open the Environment Variables dialog. To do this, perform the following steps:

1. Open the Control Panel.

2. Double-click System. This displays the System Properties dialog.

3. Select the Advanced tab from the System Properties dialog.

4. Click the Environment Variables button. This displays the Environment Variables dialog.

Check if there's currently an ORACLE_HOME system variable defined, and if so, check that it's set to the directory where you installed the Oracle software. If there's no ORACLE_HOME defined, go ahead and create one by clicking the New button in the System Variables area. Figure 1-1 shows the Environment Variables dialog with a setting for ORACLE_HOME (on my machine it's set to F:\oracle\Oracle90).

Setting an Environment Variable with Unix or Linux

To set an environment variable in Unix or Linux, you'll need to add additional lines to a special file, and the file you need to modify depends on which shell you're using. If you're using the Bourne or Korn shell, you add the following lines to your .profile file using the following syntax:

```
ORACLE_HOME=install_directory
export ORACLE_HOME
```

You replace install_directory with the directory where you installed the Oracle software. If you're using the Bash shell with Linux, you use the same syntax but add the lines to your .bash_profile file. For example:

```
ORACLE_HOME=/usr/local/oracle
export ORACLE_HOME
```

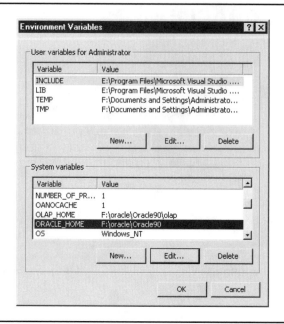

FIGURE 1-1.   *The Environment Variables dialog with a setting for*
ORACLE_HOME

If you're using the C shell, you add the environment variable to your `.login`
file using the following syntax:

 `setenv ORACLE_HOME` *install_directory*

For example:

 `setenv ORACLE_HOME /usr/local/oracle`

Setting the JAVA_HOME Environment Variable

The JAVA_HOME environment variable specifies the directory where you
installed your JDK. For example, if you installed the JDK in the `F:\jdk1.3.1_01`
directory, you need to set your JAVA_HOME variable to that directory using the
steps I showed you in the previous section.

NOTE
If you're using Java 2 Enterprise Edition, you need
to also set J2EE_HOME to the directory where you
installed J2EE. Refer to Sun's documentation for
further installation details.

Setting the PATH Environment Variable

The PATH environment variable contains a list of directories. When you enter a command using your operating system command line, the machine searches the directories in your PATH for the executable specified in your command. You'll probably already have a PATH set to some directories on your machine, and you need to add the following two directories to your existing PATH:

- The bin subdirectory of the directory where you installed the JDK

- The BIN subdirectory of the directory where you installed the Oracle software

For example, if you installed the JDK on Windows 2000 in the F:\jdk1.3.1_01 directory, and you installed the Oracle software in F:\oracle\Oracle90, you would add F:\jdk1.3.1_01\bin;F:\oracle\Oracle90\BIN to your PATH. Notice the semicolon (;) that separates the two directories. To set the PATH in Windows 2000, use the same steps I showed you earlier.

To add to an existing PATH in Unix or Linux, you need to modify the appropriate file for your shell. For example, if you're using the Bash shell with Linux, add lines to your .bash_profile file that are similar to the following:

```
PATH=$PATH:$JAVA_HOME/bin:$ORACLE_HOME/BIN
export PATH
```

Notice the colon (:) that separates the directories.

Setting the CLASSPATH Environment Variable

The CLASSPATH environment variable contains a list of locations where Java class packages are found. A location can be a directory name or the name of a ZIP file or JAR file containing classes. The ORACLE_HOME\jdbc\lib directory contains a number of ZIP files; which ones you add to your CLASSPATH depends on what JDK you're using and what features you need:

- If you're using JDK 1.2.x (or higher), add classes12.zip to your CLASSPATH. If you need National Language support, also add nls_charset12.zip to your CLASSPATH.

- If you're using JDK 1.1.x, add classes111.zip to your CLASSPATH. If you need National Language support, also add nls_charset11.zip to your CLASSPATH.

- If you need to use the Java Transaction API (JTA), add jta.zip to your CLASSPATH; the jta.zip file is located in the ORACLE_HOME\jdbc\lib directory.

■ If you need to use the Java Naming and Directory Interface (JNDI), add `jndi.zip` to your `CLASSPATH`; `jndi.zip` is also located in the `ORACLE_HOME\jdbc\lib` directory.

In Chapter 6, you'll be using SQLJ to translate and compile a SQLJ file into a Java class file. I'll talk more about SQLJ in Chapter 6, but in preparation you'll need to add `translator.zip` and `runtime.zip` to your `CLASSPATH`. Both of these files are located in the `ORACLE_HOME\sqlj\lib` directory.

NOTE
You also need to add the current directory to your CLASSPATH. You do this by adding a period (.) to your CLASSPATH. That way, the classes in your current directory will be found by Java when you run your programs.

A typical `CLASSPATH` for Windows 2000 might be

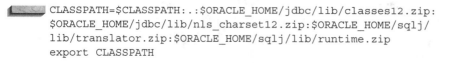

```
.;F:\oracle\Oracle90\jdbc\lib\classes12.zip;F:\oracle\
Oracle90\jdbc\lib\nls_charset12.zip;F:\oracle\Oracle90\sqlj\
lib\translator.zip;F:\oracle\Oracle90\sqlj\lib\runtime.zip;
```

If you're using Windows 2000, use the steps described earlier to set your `CLASSPATH`. If you're using Linux, you should add lines to your `.bash_profile` file similar to the following:

```
CLASSPATH=$CLASSPATH:.:$ORACLE_HOME/jdbc/lib/classes12.zip:
$ORACLE_HOME/jdbc/lib/nls_charset12.zip:$ORACLE_HOME/sqlj/
lib/translator.zip:$ORACLE_HOME/sqlj/lib/runtime.zip
export CLASSPATH
```

NOTE
If you're using Java 2 Enterprise Edition, you'll also need to set J2EE_CLASSPATH. Refer to Sun's documentation for further installation details.

Setting the LD_LIBRARY_PATH Environment Variable on Unix or Linux

If you're using Unix or Linux, you'll also need to set the `LD_LIBRARAY_PATH` environment variable to `$ORACLE_HOME/lib`. This directory contains shared libraries that are used by the JDBC OCI driver.

Your First JDBC Program

In this section, you'll see a simple program that connects to a database, displays the username used for the connection, and displays the current date and time retrieved from the database. The source code file for this program is FirstExample.java.

NOTE
Like all the programs in this book, the FirstExample.java file is located in the programs directory that was created when you extracted the ZIP file you downloaded for this book. That ZIP file contains all the programs, scripts, and other files used in this book. Instructions for downloading and extracting the ZIP file were given in the introduction to this book.

Example Program: FirstExample.java

I'll list the FirstExample.java program and then briefly describe what the main program statements do. Don't worry too much about the details of this program for now—you'll learn the details in Chapter 3. The FirstExample.java program source code is as follows:

```
/*
  FirstExample.java connects to the database as the "scott"
  user; the program then retrieves this username along with
  the current date and time from the database
*/

// import the standard JDBC package
import java.sql.*;

public class FirstExample {

  public static void main (String args []) {

    // declare Connection and Statement objects
    Connection myConnection = null;
    Statement myStatement = null;

    try {

      // register the Oracle JDBC drivers
      DriverManager.registerDriver(
        new oracle.jdbc.OracleDriver()
```

```
            );

            // create a Connection object, and connect to the database
            // as scott using the Oracle JDBC Thin driver
            myConnection = DriverManager.getConnection(
              "jdbc:oracle:thin:@localhost:1521:ORCL",
              "scott",
              "tiger"
            );

            // create a Statement object
            myStatement = myConnection.createStatement();

            // create a ResultSet object, and populate it with the
            // result of a SELECT statement that retrieves the
            // user and sysdate variables from the database via
            // the dual table - the executeQuery() method of the
            // Statement object is used to perform the SELECT
            ResultSet myResultSet = myStatement.executeQuery(
              "SELECT user, sysdate " +
              "FROM dual"
            );

            // retrieve the row from the ResultSet using the
            // next() method
            myResultSet.next();

            // retrieve the user from the row in the ResultSet using the
            // getString() method
            String user = myResultSet.getString("user");

            // retrieve the sysdate from the row in the ResultSet using
            // the getTimestamp() method
            Timestamp currentDateTime =
              myResultSet.getTimestamp("sysdate");

            System.out.println("Hello " + user +
              ", the current date and time is " + currentDateTime);

            // close this ResultSet object using the close() method
            myResultSet.close();

          } catch (SQLException e) {

            System.out.println("Error code = " + e.getErrorCode());
            System.out.println("Error message = " + e.getMessage());

          } finally {
```

```
try {

  // close the Statement object using the close() method
  if (myStatement != null) {
    myStatement.close();
  }

  // close the Connection object using the close() method
  if (myConnection != null) {
    myConnection.close();
  }

} catch (SQLException e) {

  System.out.println("Error code = " + e.getErrorCode());
  System.out.println("Error message = " + e.getMessage());

  }

 }

} // end of main()

}
```

Let's examine these program lines. The first thing this program does is to import the standard JDBC package:

```
import java.sql.*;
```

The java.sql package contains the various standard classes and interfaces required to access a database. Importing this package saves having to explicitly identify the JDBC classes used later in the code.

Next, the program's main() method declares JDBC Connection and Statement objects, named myConnection and myStatement respectively, and sets them to null:

```
Connection myConnection = null;
Statement myStatement = null;
```

The Connection and Statement classes are part of the java.sql package. If the import statement was left out at the start, I would have to explicitly identify this package in front of the class name in these declarations (java.sql.Connection, for example). As you'll see shortly, the Connection object is used to access the database, and the Statement object is used to represent a Structured Query Language (SQL) statement. As you'll learn in Chapter 2, SQL is the standard language for accessing information stored in a database.

The Try and Catch Block

Next, a `try` block is opened. The main database operations are placed within this `try` block If any errors occur within the `try` block when the program is run, they are passed to the `catch` block after the `try` block. The `catch` block in this program handles `SQLException` objects—these objects hold the details of any database error—and the code in the `catch` block displays the error code and message if a `SQLException` object is thrown by the `try` block.

   Let's examine the statements in the `try` block. First, the Oracle JDBC drivers are registered using the `DriverManager.registerDriver()` method:

```
DriverManager.registerDriver(
   new oracle.jdbc.OracleDriver()
);
```

   You use an Oracle JDBC driver to make the connection with a database. Next, the connection to the database is made using the `DriverManager.getConnection()` method:

```
myConnection = DriverManager.getConnection(
   "jdbc:oracle:thin:@localhost:1521:ORCL",
   "scott",
   "tiger"
);
```

   The first parameter specifies the JDBC driver to use in the connection, along with the details of the database you want to connect to. The second and third parameters specify the database username and password that you want to connect to the database as. In the previous example, the connection to a database running on the machine identified as `localhost` is attempted, with an Oracle System Identifier (SID) of `ORCL`, using the Oracle JDBC Thin driver (you'll learn about the various drivers in Chapter 3). The connection is made with the database username `scott` with the password `tiger`.

NOTE
The `scott` user is one of the sample users that comes with example Oracle databases. Check with your DBA if this user exists in your database. If not, ask your DBA for an alternative username and password. Also, if you don't have a database with a SID of `ORCL` running on your local machine, along with an Oracle Net listener waiting for connection requests on port 1521, you'll need to speak with your DBA to find an appropriate database to use.

Going back to the previous example, the Connection object returned by the call to getConnection() is stored in myConnection. The connection to a database is made through Oracle Net, which should be up and running before you attempt to run this program.

The next statement in the program creates a Statement object using a call to myConnection.createStatement(), storing the returned Statement object in myStatement:

```
myStatement = myConnection.createStatement();
```

As I mentioned, a Statement object is used to represent a SQL statement. To retrieve information from the database, you use the SQL SELECT statement. You can send a SELECT statement to the database using a Statement object's executeQuery() method; this method sends the statement to the database, the database then retrieves the requested information and returns the results. These results are returned in a JDBC ResultSet object, which you can then store and access in your program. For example, the following statement calls the executeQuery() method for myStatement, sending a SELECT statement to the database requesting the name of the user making the request along with the current date and time; the returned ResultSet is stored in myResultSet:

```
ResultSet myResultSet = myStatement.executeQuery(
    "SELECT user, sysdate " +
    "FROM dual"
);
```

Notice that the SELECT statement retrieves the user and sysdate from the dual table. As you'll learn in the next chapter, the dual table is a table that is always present in the database, and you can use it to select Oracle database built-in variables. Two of these variables are user and sysdate; user contains the name of the user accessing the database, and sysdate contains the current date and time set in the database. So, the SELECT statement used in the example returns the username, along with the current date and time. These values are then returned and stored in myResultSet.

ResultSet objects store information in the form of rows, and myResultSet contains one row. You access a row in a ResultSet using the next() method, and the following statement in the program calls myResultSet.next():

```
myResultSet.next();
```

As you'll learn in Chapter 3, you retrieve values from a ResultSet using get methods, and the following program statements retrieve the user and sysdate values from `myResultSet` and store them in `String` and JDBC `Timestamp` objects respectively:

```
String user = myResultSet.getString("user");
Timestamp currentDateTime =
  myResultSet.getTimestamp("sysdate");
```

The program then displays these values:

```
System.out.println("Hello " + user +
  ", the current date and time is " + currentDateTime);
```

The last statement in the `try` block closes `myResultSet` using the `close()` method:

```
myResultSet.close();
```

Closing `myResultSet` schedules it for garbage collection. You should always close `ResultSet` objects once you're finished with them.

The Finally Block

The `finally` block of the program's `main()` method is always executed before the program terminates, and in this program the `finally` block closes the `myStatement` and `myConnection` objects using the `close()` method if the objects are not `null`—meaning that if they've been set earlier in the `try` block, they will be closed.

Compiling and Running FirstExample.java

To compile `FirstExample.java`, you should first go to the command-line prompt of your operating system and change directories to the `programs` directory. Once in the `programs` directory, you compile `FirstExample.java` using the Java compiler (`javac`) by entering the following command:

```
javac FirstExample.java
```

To run the `FirstExample.class` file, you enter the following command:

```
java FirstExample
```

Sample output from the program is as follows:

```
Hello SCOTT, the current date and time is 2002-03-13 18:38:20.0
```

Of course, your date and time will be different from mine.

If the Program Fails to Compile

If you haven't set the CLASSPATH environment variable properly, you'll get the following error message when trying to compile the FirstExample.java program:

```
FirstExample.java:22: cannot resolve symbol
symbol  : class OracleDriver
location: package jdbc
        new oracle.jdbc.OracleDriver()
                        ^

1 error
```

You should check the setting for your CLASSPATH environment variable—it's likely your CLASSPATH is missing the Oracle JDBC classes ZIP file (classes12.zip, for example). I showed you how to set the CLASSPATH in the section entitled "Setting the CLASSPATH Environment Variable." Check your setting and try compiling the program again.

If the Program Fails to Run

If the program fails with the following error code and message, it means the scott user with a password of tiger doesn't exist in your database:

```
Error code = 1017
Error message = ORA-01017: invalid username/password; logon denied
```

If you get this error, ask your DBA for a suitable username and password.

The program may also be unable to find your database, in which case you'll get the following error:

```
Error code = 17002
Error message = Io exception: The Network Adapter could not establish
 the connection
```

Typically, there are two reasons why you might get this error:

■ There is no database running on your localhost machine with the Oracle SID of ORCL.

■ Oracle Net is not running, or is not listening for connections on port 1521.

You should once again check with the DBA to resolve this issue.

Oracle JDeveloper

Oracle's JDeveloper tool allows you to develop, debug, and deploy many types of Java programs, including standalone programs, Enterprise JavaBeans (EJB), servlets, JavaServer Pages (JSP), CORBA objects, and applets. In this section, you'll learn the basics of JDeveloper; specifically, I'll take you through creating a workspace and project, adding `FirstExample.java` to that project, running this program, and then using JDeveloper's debugging facilities. Even if you don't have JDeveloper, you'll be able to see what's going on in the various screen shots shown in this section.

Creating a New Workspace and Project

Start JDeveloper using Windows. Your screen should appear similar to that shown in Figure 1-2.

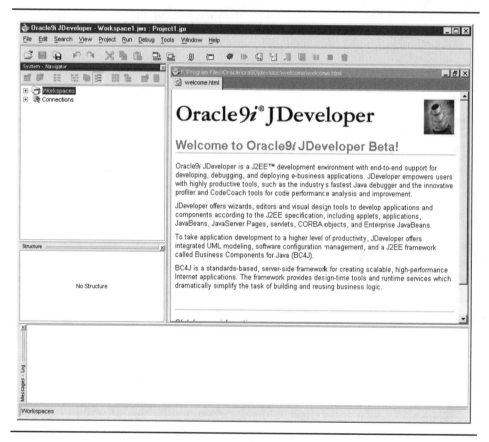

FIGURE 1-2. *JDeveloper start screen*

All of your work in JDeveloper is organized into a *workspace*, which consists of one or more *projects*. Any programs you develop are associated with a project. Access to all of JDeveloper's functions is done through the menu bar at the top of screen; you can also access the most frequently used functions with the toolbar underneath the menu bar. In addition, there are many keyboard shortcuts you can use to perform tasks; you'll learn some of them shortly.

To create a new workspace, select New from the File menu. This opens the New dialog from which you can create many different categories of items. Since you're going to create a workspace, under Categories, select Projects, and under Items, select Workspace, as shown in Figure 1-3.

Click OK, which takes you to the New Workspace dialog. Leave the entries in this dialog at their default settings, as shown in Figure 1-4. Notice that the workspace file name is set to `Workspace1.jws`.

Click OK, which takes you to the New Project dialog. Once again, leave the entries in this dialog at their default settings, as shown in Figure 1-5. Notice that the project file name is set to `Project1.jpr`.

Click OK, which displays `Workspace1.jws` and `Project1.jpr` in the Workspaces node of the System Navigator shown in the top left of the JDeveloper screen. Click `Project1.jpr`, as shown in Figure 1-6.

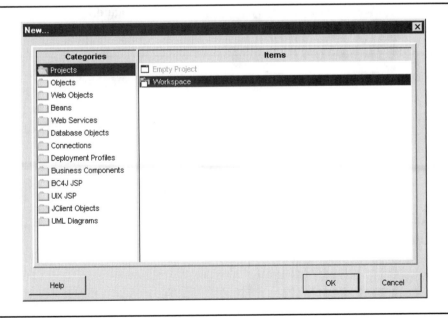

FIGURE 1-3.   *The New dialog, creating a Workspace*

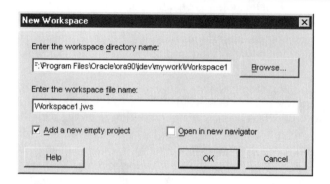

FIGURE 1-4. *The New Workspace dialog with its default settings*

Adding FirstExample.java to the Project

Next, you'll add `FirstExample.java` to your new project. From the Project menu, select Add to Project. This opens the Add to Project dialog, from which you can add files to your project. In this dialog, you navigate to your `programs` directory and select `FirstExample.java`, as shown in Figure 1-7.

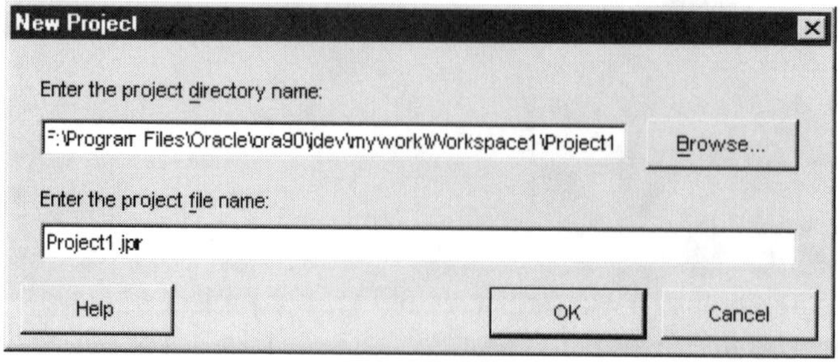

FIGURE 1-5. *The New Project dialog with its default settings*

FIGURE 1-6. *JDeveloper with the new workspace and project displayed in the System Navigator*

Click Open to add the `FirstExample.java` file to your project. You'll then be prompted to update the source path by the Add Project Source Path dialog, as shown in Figure 1-8.

Click Yes to add the `programs` directory to your project source path. JDeveloper will then add and display the code for `FirstExample1.java` to your project, as shown in Figure 1-9.

Notice that the `FirstExample1.java` code appears in the tab to the right, and that the `FirstExample1.java` file name is added below the `Project1.jpr` file

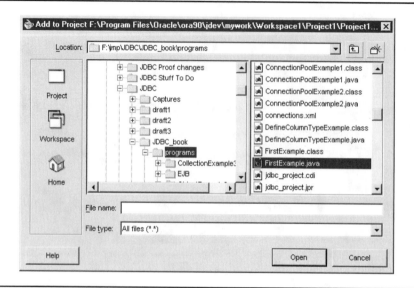

FIGURE 1-7. *Selecting FirstExample.java using the Add to Project dialog*

name in the System Navigator. Below the System Navigator, the program structure for `FirstExample.java` is displayed; this shows the class name, along with any methods defined in the class (in this case, only one method is defined in the `FirstExample` class: `main()`).

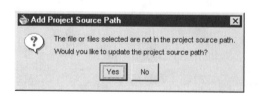

FIGURE 1-8. *Updating the project path using the Add Project Source Path dialog*

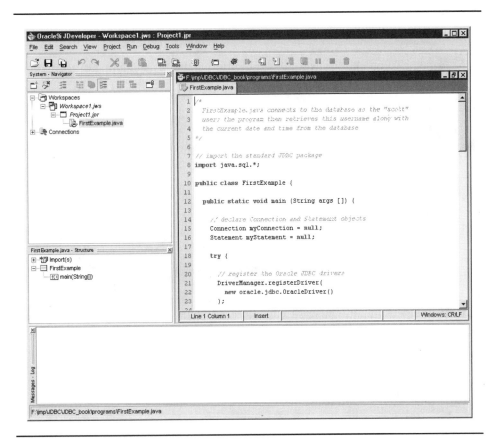

FIGURE 1-9. *FirstExample.java added to the project*

Adding the Oracle JDBC Library to the Project and Compiling and Running FirstExample.java

Because FirstExample.java contains JDBC statements, you'll need to add the Oracle JDBC library to the project libraries. To do this, select Project Settings from the Project menu and add the Oracle JDBC library to the Development Libraries, as shown in Figure 1-10.

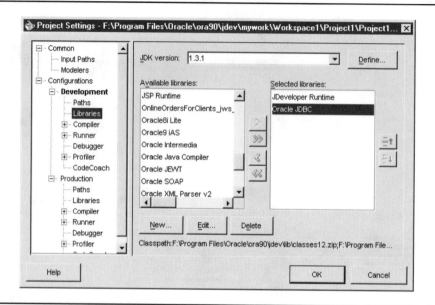

FIGURE 1-10. *Adding the Oracle JDBC library to the development libraries using the Project Settings dialog*

Click OK. To compile `FirstExample.java`, select Make `Project1.jpr` from the Project menu.

TIP
You can also compile your project with the keyboard shortcut CTRL-F9.

To run `FirstExample.java`, select Run `Project1.jpr` from the Run menu.

TIP
You can also run your project with the keyboard shortcut F11.

This runs `FirstExample1.java`, and its output is displayed at the bottom of the screen, as shown in Figure 1-11.

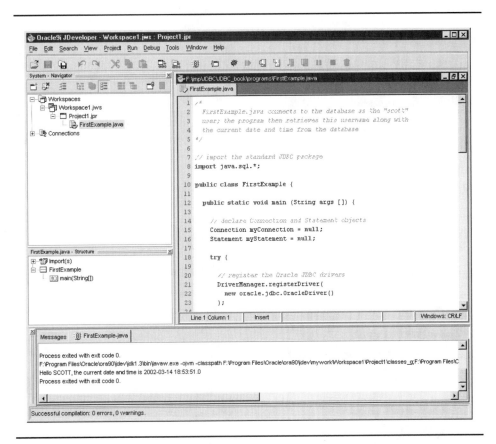

FIGURE 1-11. *The output from FirstExample.java*

Debugging FirstExample.java

You'll now learn the basics of JDeveloper's debugger. The debugging process starts by you setting a *breakpoint* in your code; breakpoint causes the execution of your program to stop at that point when you run the debugger. You can set a breakpoint in JDeveloper by clicking to the right of the code line in your program. Go ahead and set a breakpoint by clicking on line 15 of the code for FirstExample.java—this displays a dot to the right of the code line, as shown in Figure 1-12.

To start the debugger, select Debug Project1.jpr from the Debug menu.

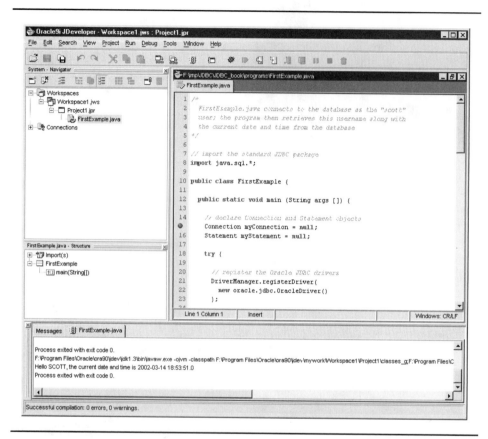

FIGURE 1-12. *Setting a breakpoint*

TIP
*You can also start the debugger with the keyboard
shortcut* SHIFT-F9.

When program control reaches your breakpoint at line 15, program execution
is suspended. You can then view the values of your program's variables and objects
in the area to the bottom right of the screen. To step over a code line, use the Step
Over button in the toolbar or press F8.

NOTE
You can step into a method using the Step Into
button or pressing F7. You can step out of a method
using the Step Out button or pressing SHIFT-F7.

Step over the lines of code by pressing F8 until you reach line 62, as shown in
Figure 1-13. As you're doing this, notice how the variable and object values change
in the bottom right of the JDeveloper screen. Also notice that the output from the
program is shown in the bottom left.

This section has only scratched the surface of JDeveloper. I encourage you to
spend time learning the features of this great tool.

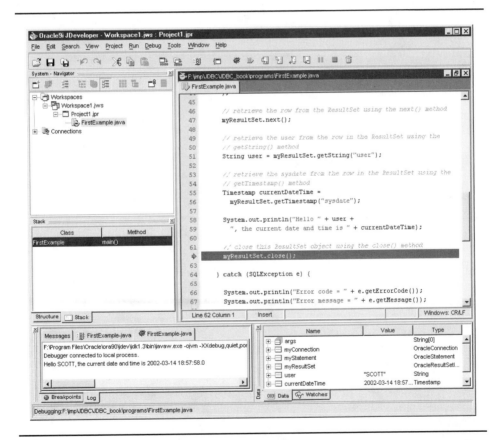

FIGURE 1-13. *Output from the debugger*

CHAPTER
2

Introduction to Databases and Oracle

I n this chapter, I'll teach you the basics of relational databases and the Structured Query Language (SQL), the standard language used to interact with a database. In addition, I'll introduce you to Oracle's PL/SQL programming language, which adds a programming framework around SQL. Of course, relational database theory, SQL, and PL/SQL are very large subjects, and I won't attempt to cover every aspect of these topics. My intention is to provide you with enough information for you to be productive with SQL and PL/SQL and enable you to understand the rest of this book.

There are many great books that can give you a more thorough education in these topics; for database theory, I recommend *An Introduction to Database Systems* by C. J. Date (Addison-Wesley, 1999). For SQL, I recommend *Oracle8i: The Complete Reference* by Kevin Loney and George Koch (McGraw-Hill/Osborne, 2000). For PL/SQL, I recommend *Oracle9i PL/SQL Programming* by Scott Urman (McGraw-Hill/Osborne, 2001).

What Is a Relational Database?

The concept of a relational database is not new: it was originally developed back in 1970 by Dr. E. F. Codd, and he laid down the theory of relational databases in his seminal paper entitled "A Relational Model of Data for Large Shared Data Banks" published in *Communications of the ACM* (Association for Computing Machinery), Vol. 13, No. 6, June 1970.

The basic concepts of a relational database are fairly easy to understand. A *relational database* is a collection of related information that has been organized into structures known as *tables*. Each table contains *rows* that are further organized into *columns*. These tables are stored in the database in structures known as *schemas*, which are areas where database users may store their tables. Each user may also choose to grant permissions to other users to access their tables.

Most of us are familiar with data being stored in tables—stock prices and train timetables are sometimes organized into tables. An example used in one of the schemas in this book is a table that records customer information for a hypothetical store. This table consists of columns containing the customer's first name, last name, date of birth (dob), and phone number:

```
first_name last_name  dob         phone
---------- ---------- ----------- -----------
John       Brown      01-JAN-1965 800-555-1211
Cynthia    Green      05-FEB-1968 800-555-1212
Steve      White      16-MAR-1971 800-555-1213
Gail       Black                  800-555-1214
Doreen     Blue       20-MAY-1970
```

Notice from this table that Gail Black's date of birth is unknown, as is Doreen Blue's phone number—any database should be able to support values that might be unknown. This table could be stored in a variety of forms: a piece of paper in a filing cabinet or ledger or in the file system of a computer, for example. An important point to note is that the *information* that makes up a database (in the form of tables) is different from the system used to access that information. The system used to access a database is known as a *database management system*.

In the case of a database consisting of pieces of paper, the database management system might be a set of alphabetically indexed cards in a filing cabinet; for a database accessed using a computer, the database management system is the software that manages the files stored in the file system of the computer. The Oracle database is one such piece of software; other examples include SQL Server, DB2, and MySQL.

Of course, every database must have some way to get data in and out of it, preferably using a common language understood by all databases. Today's database management systems implement a standard language known as the *Structured Query Language*, or SQL. Among other things, SQL allows you to retrieve, add, update, and delete information in a database.

Structured Query Language (SQL)

The Structured Query Language (SQL) is the standard language designed to access relational databases. SQL is pronounced either as the word "sequel" or as the letters "ess-que-ell." I'll give you a brief history lesson on the development of SQL: SQL is based on the groundbreaking work of Dr. E. F. Codd, with the first implementation of SQL being developed by IBM in the mid-1970s. IBM was conducting a research project known as System R, and SQL was born from that project. Later in 1979, a company then known as Relational Software Inc. (known today as Oracle Corporation) released the first commercial version of SQL. SQL is now fully standardized and recognized by the American National Standards Institute (ANSI). You can use SQL to access an Oracle database, SQL Server, DB2, and MySQL, to name just a few of the many database systems that support SQL.

The syntax used by SQL is quite easy to learn and master, and the fastest way to learn it is to look at some examples, which you'll see shortly. There are several types of SQL statements; the two most commonly used types are:

- *Data Manipulation Language* (DML) statements

- *Data Definition Language* (DDL) statements

DML statements allow you to retrieve, add, modify, and delete rows stored in tables. DDL statements are used to create database users, tables, and many other types of database structures that make up a database.

There are many ways to run SQL statements and get results back from the database, but the main thrust of this book is how to run SQL statements using JDBC. Some other ways to run SQL include programs written using Oracle Forms and Reports. SQL statements may also be embedded within programs written in other languages, such as Oracle's Pro*C, which allows you to add SQL statements to a C program. Oracle also has a tool called SQL*Plus that allows you to enter SQL statements using the keyboard or to supply a file that contains SQL statements and run those statements. SQL*Plus enables you to conduct a "conversation" with the database because you can enter SQL statements and view the results returned by the database.

SQL*Plus

There are two versions of SQL*Plus: the Windows version and the command-line version (which may be used in any operating system which Oracle supports). If you're at all familiar with the Oracle database, then the chances are that you're already somewhat familiar with SQL*Plus. If you're not, don't worry, you'll see it's easy to use, and the examples in this chapter illustrate the use of SQL*Plus. To start the Windows version of SQL*Plus, click the Start button and select Programs | Oracle | Application Development | SQL*Plus. To start the command-line version of SQL*Plus, use the sqlplus command.

The examples in this book use a number of different database schemas, one of which is the store_user schema. The file store_user.sql is a SQL*Plus script that you can download from this book's website; it contains the DDL and DML statements you use to create and populate the store_user schema. If you are not already familiar with the Oracle database and SQL*Plus, ask your database administrator (DBA) to run this script for you. The following section describes how to run the store_user.sql script using SQL*Plus.

Running the store_user.sql Script

To run the store_user.sql script using SQL*Plus, follow these steps:

1. Start the SQL*Plus tool.

2. Enter **system** as the user name and enter **manager** as the password (the default password for the system user). If that is not the correct password, ask your DBA for the password, or have your DBA run the script for you.

3. Run the store_user.sql script from SQL*Plus using the @ command. To do this in Windows, you use the @ command with the following format:

   @ *directory_path*\store_user.sql

   where *directory_path* is the directory and path where you previously saved the store_user.sql script. For example, if you saved that script in a directory named SQL on the C partition of your Windows file system, then you would enter the following:

```
@ C:\SQL\store_user.sql
```

If you are using Unix (or Linux), and you saved the script in a directory named SQL on the tmp file system, for example, then you would enter the following:

```
@ /tmp/SQL/store_user.sql
```

NOTE
Windows uses backslash characters (\) in directory paths, while Unix and Linux use forward slash characters (/).

If you want to, take a look at the store_user.sql script, but don't worry too much about the details of the statements contained in this file—you'll learn the details of the various DDL and DML statements in the following sections of this chapter.

Data Definition Language (DDL) Statements

As I mentioned earlier, *Data Definition Language* (DDL) statements are used to create users and tables, plus many other types of structures in the database. In this section, I'll show you how to use DDL statements to create the database user and tables for the store_user schema. The example statements shown here are the same as those contained in the store_user.sql script: you don't have to type the statements in yourself, just run the script as I described earlier.

The following sections describe how to create a database user, followed by the commonly used data types used in the Oracle database, and finally the various tables used for a hypothetical store that sells books, videos, DVDs, and CDs.

Creating a Database User
To create a user in the database, you use the CREATE USER statement. The simplified syntax for the CREATE USER statement is as follows:

```
CREATE USER user_name IDENTIFIED BY password;
```

The syntax elements are as follows:

- **user_name**   The name you assign to the database user
- **password**   The password for that database user

For example, the following CREATE USER statement creates the user store_user, with the password being set to store_password:

```
CREATE USER store_user IDENTIFIED BY store_password;
```

Next, if you want the user to be able to do things in the database, then that user must be granted the necessary *permissions* to do those things. In the case of store_user, that user must be able to log into the database (which requires the connect permission) and create things like database tables (which requires the resource permission). Permissions are granted by a privileged user (the system user, for example) using the GRANT statement. The following example grants the connect and resource permissions to store_user:

```
GRANT connect, resource TO store_user;
```

Once a user has been created, the database tables and other database objects can be created in the associated schema for that user. For most of the examples in this book, I've chosen to implement a simple store that sells books, videos, CDs, and DVDs; these tables will be created in the schema of store_user. Before I get into the details of the tables required for the store, you need to understand a little bit about the commonly used Oracle database types that are used to define the database columns.

Common Oracle Database Types

While there are many types that may be used to handle data in an Oracle database, the most commonly used types are as follows:

- **CHAR(length)**   Stores strings of a fixed length. The length parameter specifies the length of the string. If a string of a smaller length is stored, then it is padded with spaces at the end. For example, CHAR(2) may be used to store a fixed length string of two characters; if C is stored using this definition, then a single space is added at the end. CA would be stored as is with no padding.

- **VARCHAR2(length)**   Stores strings of a variable length. The length parameter specifies the maximum length of the string. For example, VARCHAR2(20) may be used to store a string of up to 20 characters in length. No padding is used at the end of a smaller string.

- **DATE**   Stores dates and times. It stores all four digits of a year, along with the month, the day, the hour (in 24-hour format), the minute, and the second. The DATE type may be used to store dates and times between January 1, 4712 B.C. and December 31, 4712 A.D. The default format for the output of columns defined using the DATE type is DD-MON-YY, where

DD is the day, MON is the first three letters of the month (in uppercase), and YY is the last two digits of the year. The default format for dates may be changed by the DBA.

- **INTEGER**   Stores integer numbers. An integer number doesn't contain a floating point: it is a whole number, such as 1, 10, and 115, for example.

- **NUMBER(precision, scale)**   Stores floating point numbers but may also be used to store integer numbers. *Precision* is the maximum number of digits (in front of and behind of a decimal point, if used) that may be used for the number. The maximum precision supported by the Oracle database is 38. *Scale* is the maximum number of digits to the right of a decimal point (if used). If neither precision nor scale are specified, then any number may be stored up to a precision of 38 digits—numbers that exceed precision are rejected by the database. The following table illustrates a few examples of how numbers are stored in the database:

Format	Number Supplied	Number Stored
NUMBER	1234.567	1234.567
NUMBER(6, 2)	123.4567	123.457
NUMBER(6, 2)	12345.67	Exceeds precision; rejected by the database

The store_user Tables

In this section, I'll show you how the tables for the store_user schema are created. The store_user schema will hold the details of the hypothetical store and will need to hold the following information:

- Customer details
- Types of products sold
- Product details
- A history of the products purchased by the customers

Four tables will be used to store the product, customer, and sales information for our store:

- **customers**   Stores customer details
- **product _types**   Stores the types of products stocked by the store

■ **products**   Stores product details

■ **purchases**   Stores which products were purchased by which customers

In the next sections, I'll describe the details of the four store tables, and I'll show you the CREATE TABLE statements included in the store_user.sql script that create these tables.

The customers Table   The customers table is used to store the details of the customers of the hypothetical store. The following items are to be stored in this table for each one of the store's customers:

■ First name

■ Last name

■ Date of birth (dob)

■ Phone number

Each of these items requires a column in the customers table, which is created by the store_user.sql script using the following CREATE TABLE statement:

```
CREATE TABLE customers (
    id          INTEGER CONSTRAINT customers_pk PRIMARY KEY,
    first_name  VARCHAR2(10) NOT NULL,
    last_name   VARCHAR2(10) NOT NULL,
    dob         DATE,
    phone       VARCHAR2(12)
);
```

As you can see, the customers table contains five columns, one for each item in the previous list, and an extra column named id. The following list contains the details of each of these columns:

■ **id**   A unique integer for each row in the table. Each table should have one or more columns that uniquely identifies each row in the table and is known as that table's *primary key*. The CONSTRAINT clause for the id column indicates that this is the table's primary key. A CONSTRAINT clause is used to restrict the values stored in a table or column and, for the id column, the PRIMARY KEY keywords indicate that the id column must contain a unique number for each row. You can also attach an optional name to a constraint, which must immediately follow the CONSTRAINT keyword—in this case, the name of the constraint is customers_pk. When a row is added to the customers table, a unique value for the id column must be given, and the Oracle database will prevent you from adding a row with the same primary key value—if you try to do so, you will get an error from the database.

■ **first_name** Stores the first name of the customer. You'll notice the use of the NOT NULL constraint—this means that a value must be supplied for this column. The default constraint is NULL, meaning that you don't have to supply a value.

■ **last_name** Stores the last name of the customer. This column is NOT NULL, and therefore you must supply a value.

■ **dob** Stores the date of birth for the customer. Notice that a NOT NULL constraint is not specified for this column, therefore the default NULL is assumed, and a value is optional.

■ **phone** Stores the phone number of the customer. This is an optional value.

The store_user.sql script populates the customers table with the following rows:

```
     id first_name last_name  dob        phone
---------- ---------- ---------- --------- -----------
      1 John       Brown      01-JAN-65 800-555-1211
      2 Cynthia    Green      05-FEB-68 800-555-1212
      3 Steve      White      16-MAR-71 800-555-1213
      4 Gail       Black                800-555-1214
      5 Doreen     Blue       20-MAY-70
```

Notice that customer #4's date of birth is null, as is customer #5's phone number. I'll show you how to add more rows to this table later in the section on DML.

The product_types Table   The product_types table is used to store the names of the product types that may be stocked by the store. This table is created by the store_user.sql script using the following CREATE TABLE statement:

```
CREATE TABLE product_types (
    id   INTEGER CONSTRAINT product_types_pk PRIMARY KEY,
    name VARCHAR2(10) NOT NULL
);
```

The product_types table contains the following two columns:

■ **id** Uniquely identifies each row in the table; the id column is the primary key for this table. Each row in the product_types table must have a unique integer value for the id column.

- **name** Contains the product type name. It is a NOT NULL column, and therefore a value must be supplied.

The store_user.sql script populates this table with the following rows:

```
       id name
---------- ----------
        1 Book
        2 Video
        3 DVD
        4 CD
```

This defines four product types for the store: book, video, DVD, and CD. Each product stocked by the store may be of one of these types.

The products Table The products table is used to store detailed information about the products sold. The following pieces of information are to be stored for each product:

- Product type

- Name

- Description

- Price

The store_user.sql script creates the products table using the following CREATE TABLE statement:

```
CREATE TABLE products (
  id          INTEGER
    CONSTRAINT products_pk PRIMARY KEY,
  type_id     INTEGER
    CONSTRAINT products_fk_product_types
    REFERENCES product_types(id),
  name        VARCHAR2(30) NOT NULL,
  description VARCHAR2(50),
  price       NUMBER(5, 2)
);
```

The columns in this table are as follows:

- **id** Uniquely identifies each row in the table. This column is the primary key of the table.

- **type_id** Associates each product with a product type. This column is a reference to the id column in the product_types table and is known as a *foreign key* because it references a column in another table. The table containing the foreign key (the products table) is known as the *detail* or *child* table, and the table that is referenced (the product_types table) is known as the *master* or *parent* table. When you add a new product, you should also associate that product with a type by supplying the product type id number in the type_id column. This type of relationship is known as a *master-detail* or *parent-child* relationship.

- **name** Stores the product name.

- **description** Stores an optional description of the product.

- **price** Stores an optional price for a product. This column is defined as NUMBER(5, 2)—the precision is 5, and therefore a maximum of five digits may be supplied for this number. The scale is 2—and therefore two of those maximum five digits may be to the right of the decimal point.

The following is a selection of the rows that are stored in the products table, populated by the store_user.sql script:

id	type_id	name	description	price
1	1	Modern Science	A description of modern science	19.95
2	1	Chemistry	Introduction to Chemistry	30
3	2	Supernova	A star explodes	25.99
4	2	Tank War	Action movie about a future war	13.95

The first row in the products table has a type_id of 1, which means that this product represents a book. The type_id value comes from the product_types table, which uses an id value of 1 to represent books. The second row also represents a book, but the third and fourth rows represent videos.

The purchases Table   The purchases table stores the purchases made by a customer. For each purchase made by a customer, the following information is to be stored:

- The product id

- The customer id

- The number of units of the product purchased (quantity)

The store_user.sql script uses the following CREATE TABLE statement to create the purchases table:

```
CREATE TABLE purchases (
  product_id   INTEGER
    CONSTRAINT purchases_fk_products
    REFERENCES products(id),
  purchased_by INTEGER
    CONSTRAINT purchases_fk_customers
    REFERENCES customers(id),
  quantity     INTEGER NOT NULL,
  CONSTRAINT   purchases_pk PRIMARY KEY (product_id, purchased_by)
);
```

The columns in this table are as follows:

- **product_id**   The id of the product that was purchased. This must match a value in the id column for a row in the products table.

- **purchased_by**   The id of a customer who made the purchase. This must match a value in the id column for a row in the customers table.

- **quantity**   The number of units of the product that were purchased.

The purchases table has a constraint named purchases_pk that spans multiple columns in the table. The purchases_pk constraint is also a PRIMARY KEY constraint and specifies that the table's primary key consists of two columns: product_id and purchased_by. The combination of the two values in these columns must be unique for each row in the table.

The following is a subset of the rows that are stored in the purchases table, populated by the store_user.sql script:

```
product_id purchased_by   quantity
---------- ------------ ----------
         1            1          1
         2            1          3
         1            4          1
         2            2          1
         1            3          1
```

As you can see, the combination of the values in the `product_id` and `purchased_by` columns is unique for each row.

Data Manipulation Language (DML) Statements

As I mentioned earlier, *Data Manipulation Language* (DML) statements are used to retrieve, add, modify, and delete rows stored in database tables. There are four basic DML statements:

- ■ **SELECT**   Retrieves rows
- ■ **INSERT**   Adds rows
- ■ **UPDATE**   Modifies rows
- ■ **DELETE**   Removes rows

In the following sections, I'll describe each of these statements and illustrate examples of such statements using the `store_user` schema. Specifically, I'll describe the following:

- ■ `SELECT` statements that retrieve rows from only one table
- ■ Restricting rows retrieved by a `SELECT` statement using the SQL `WHERE` clause
- ■ Using the SQL operators to perform pattern matching, range matching, and selecting null values
- ■ Using the SQL logical operators to perform logical operations in a SQL statement
- ■ Sorting rows using the `ORDER BY` clause
- ■ `SELECT` statements that retrieve rows from multiple tables
- ■ Adding rows using the `INSERT` statement
- ■ Modifying rows using the `UPDATE` statement
- ■ Removing rows using the `DELETE` statement
- ■ How the Oracle database maintains integrity of the stored information
- ■ How transactions are implemented in the Oracle database (transactions are logical units of work)
- ■ Row identifiers, or ROWIDs, the physical addresses of rows stored in a table

First off, I'll describe single-table `SELECT` statements.

Single-Table SELECT Statements

The SELECT statement is used to retrieve information stored in the database. The SELECT statement has several forms involving differing degrees of complexity. In the simplest version of the SELECT statement, you specify the table from which to retrieve data, along with a list of columns to retrieve from that table. The examples in this section use SQL*Plus; if you wish to follow along with the examples, you can type the statements into SQL*Plus and run them.

The SELECT statement in the following example retrieves the id, first_name, last_name, dob, and phone columns from the customers table:

```
SQL> SELECT id, first_name, last_name, dob, phone
  2  FROM customers;
```

Immediately after the SELECT keyword, you supply the column names that you want to retrieve. After the FROM keyword, you supply the name of the table from which the columns are to be retrieved.

SQL*Plus, and indeed SQL itself, is not case sensitive, meaning that you can specify column names and table names using either lowercase or uppercase. However, it is better to stick to one style and use it consistently; this will make your SQL statements more readable. The examples in this book use uppercase for SQL keywords and built-in functions and lowercase for everything else. Also, the entry of SQL statements may be split over multiple lines, with SQL*Plus automatically numbering each line.

The SQL statement ends with a semicolon character (;). Notice that you don't tell the database management system software exactly how to access the information you want—you just tell it what you want and let the software worry about how to get it.

After you hit ENTER at the end of the SQL statement, the query is run and the results are returned to SQL*Plus for display on the screen, as shown in the following output:

```
        ID FIRST_NAME LAST_NAME  DOB        PHONE
---------- ---------- ---------- ---------- ------------
         1 John       Brown      01-JAN-65  800-555-1211
         2 Cynthia    Green      05-FEB-68  800-555-1212
         3 Steve      White      16-MAR-71  800-555-1213
         4 Gail       Black                 800-555-1214
         5 Doreen     Blue       20-MAY-70
```

As you can see, the Oracle database converts the column names in the output to uppercase. Also, by default, the Oracle database displays dates in the format DD-MON-YY, where DD is the day number, MON is the first three characters of the month (in uppercase), and YY is the last two digits of the year (although the Oracle database does store all four digits of the year). A DBA can change the default display format for dates.

Notice that customer #4's dob is not displayed, and nor is customer #5's phone number. These values are null in the table and are therefore not displayed by SQL*Plus.

You can select all the columns in a table by using the asterisk character (*) in the column select list. For example, the asterisk is used in the following SELECT statement to select all the columns from the customers table:

```
SQL> SELECT *
  2  FROM customers;

        ID FIRST_NAME LAST_NAME  DOB       PHONE
---------- ---------- ---------- --------- ------------
         1 John       Brown      01-JAN-65 800-555-1211
         2 Cynthia    Green      05-FEB-68 800-555-1212
         3 Steve      White      16-MAR-71 800-555-1213
         4 Gail       Black                800-555-1214
         5 Doreen     Blue       20-MAY-70
```

As you can see, all the columns in the customers table are displayed.

Restricting Rows Using the WHERE Clause

You can use the WHERE clause in a SELECT statement to restrict the rows returned from the database to only those that you are interested in. In the following example, the WHERE clause is used to retrieve the row from the customers table where the value stored in the id column is equal to 2:

```
SQL> SELECT *
  2  FROM customers
  3  WHERE id = 2;

        ID FIRST_NAME LAST_NAME  DOB       PHONE
---------- ---------- ---------- --------- ------------
         2 Cynthia    Green      05-FEB-68 800-555-1212
```

Notice that this example uses the equality operator (=) to select rows where the id column is equal to the value 2. There are many operators that you can use in a WHERE clause, as listed in the following table:

Operator	Description
=	Equal
<> or !=	Not equal
<	Less than

Operator	Description
>	Greater than
<=	Less than or equal
>=	Greater than or equal

The following SELECT statement retrieves the id, name, and price columns from the products table for all the rows where the id column is less than 4:

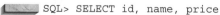

```
SQL> SELECT id, name, price
  2  FROM products
  3  WHERE id < 4;

        ID NAME                                     PRICE
---------- ------------------------------- ----------
         1 Modern Science                           19.95
         2 Chemistry                                   30
         3 Supernova                                25.99
```

Pattern Matching Using the SQL Operators

There are four SQL operators that may be used in a WHERE clause. The SQL operators allow you to limit rows based on pattern matching of strings, lists of values, ranges of values, and null values. The SQL operators are listed in the following table:

Operator	Description
LIKE	Matches patterns in strings
IN	Matches lists of values
BETWEEN	Matches a range of values
IS NULL	Matches null values

You can also use the NOT keyword to reverse the meaning of a SQL operator:

- NOT LIKE
- NOT IN
- NOT BETWEEN
- IS NOT NULL

The following sections cover the LIKE operator, the IN operator, and the BETWEEN operator, along with examples of their use.

The LIKE Operator　You can use the LIKE operator in a WHERE clause to select rows whose column values match a specified pattern. These patterns may be specified using a combination of normal characters and the following wildcard characters:

- **An underscore character (_)**　One character in a specified position

- **A percent character (%)**　Any number of characters beginning at the specified position

The following SELECT statement uses the LIKE operator with the pattern '_l%' applied to the last_name column of the customers table. The underscore character (_) before the l allows any one character in the first position of the column value, and the percent character (%) allows any characters to follow the l:

```
SQL> SELECT *
  2  FROM customers
  3  WHERE last_name LIKE '_l%';

        ID FIRST_NAME LAST_NAME  DOB        PHONE
---------- ---------- ---------- ---------- ------------
         4 Gail       Black                 800-555-1214
         5 Doreen     Blue       20-MAY-70
```

As you can see, two rows are selected by this query, and the values in the last_name column both have a l in the second position.

The following example uses NOT LIKE to reverse the rows retrieved by the previous query:

```
SQL> SELECT *
  2  FROM customers
  3  WHERE last_name NOT LIKE '_l%';

        ID FIRST_NAME LAST_NAME  DOB        PHONE
---------- ---------- ---------- ---------- ------------
         1 John       Brown      01-JAN-65  800-555-1211
         2 Cynthia    Green      05-FEB-68  800-555-1212
         3 Steve      White      16-MAR-71  800-555-1213
```

As expected, all rows other than the previous rows were retrieved.

If you need to perform a text match on the actual underscore or percent characters in a string, you can use the ESCAPE option. The following example retrieves the products whose name contains the string a_product:

```
SELECT name
FROM products
WHERE name LIKE '%a\_product%' ESCAPE '\';
```

The ESCAPE option specifies that the backslash character precedes any wildcard characters used with the LIKE operator—in this example, the underscore (_) is the wildcard used. The underscore is then used in the text match, rather than being treated as a wildcard character as would otherwise be the case.

The IN Operator   You can use the IN operator in a WHERE clause to select only those rows whose column value is in a list that you specify. The following SELECT statement uses the IN operator to retrieve rows from the customers table where the value in the id column is 2, 3, or 5:

```
SQL> SELECT *
  2  FROM customers
  3  WHERE id IN (2, 3, 5);

        ID FIRST_NAME LAST_NAME  DOB       PHONE
---------- ---------- ---------- --------- ------------
         2 Cynthia    Green      05-FEB-68 800-555-1212
         3 Steve      White      16-MAR-71 800-555-1213
         5 Doreen     Blue       20-MAY-70
```

Of course, NOT IN reverses the rows selected by IN—if IN were replaced by NOT IN for the previous example, all rows except those shown above would be retrieved.

The BETWEEN Operator   The BETWEEN operator may be used in a WHERE clause to select rows whose column value is inclusive within a specified range. The following example uses the BETWEEN operator to retrieve rows from the customers table where the id column is between 1 and 3:

```
SQL> SELECT *
  2  FROM customers
  3  WHERE id BETWEEN 1 AND 3;

        ID FIRST_NAME LAST_NAME  DOB       PHONE
---------- ---------- ---------- --------- ------------
         1 John       Brown      01-JAN-65 800-555-1211
         2 Cynthia    Green      05-FEB-68 800-555-1212
         3 Steve      White      16-MAR-71 800-555-1213
```

The range specified with the BETWEEN operator is inclusive so the rows where the id column is equal to 1, 2, or 3 are retrieved. As you'd expect, NOT BETWEEN reverses the rows retrieved.

The IS NULL Operator   When you select a column that contains a null value, you see nothing in that column. You saw this (or rather, *didn't* see it!) in the earlier examples of selecting rows from the customers table: customer #4 has a null value in the dob column, and customer #5 has a null value in the phone column.

You can check for null values using the IS NULL operator in a SELECT statement. In the following example, customer #4 is retrieved based on the fact that the dob column is null:

```
SQL> SELECT id, first_name, last_name, dob
  2  FROM customers
  3  WHERE dob IS NULL;

        ID FIRST_NAME LAST_NAME  DOB
---------- ---------- ---------- ---------
         4 Gail       Black
```

Similarly, in the following example, customer #5 is retrieved based on the fact that the phone column is null:

```
SQL> SELECT id, first_name, last_name, dob
  2  FROM customers
  3  WHERE phone IS NULL;

        ID FIRST_NAME LAST_NAME  DOB
---------- ---------- ---------- ---------
         5 Doreen     Blue       20-MAY-70
```

Since null values don't display anything, how do you tell the difference between a null value and a blank string if you retrieve all the rows? The answer is to use one of the built-in functions: NVL(). NVL() allows you to convert a null value into another value that you can actually read. NVL() accepts two parameters: a column (or more generally, any expression that returns a value), and the value that should be substituted if the first parameter is null. In the following example, NVL() is used to convert a null value in the phone column to the string 'Unknown phone number':

```
SQL> SELECT id, first_name, last_name,
  2  NVL(phone, 'Unknown phone number') AS PHONE
  3  FROM customers;

        ID FIRST_NAME LAST_NAME  PHONE
---------- ---------- ---------- --------------------
         1 John       Brown      800-555-1211
         2 Cynthia    Green      800-555-1212
```

```
3 Steve      White      800-555-1213
4 Gail       Black      800-555-1214
5 Doreen     Blue       Unknown phone number
```

In addition to using NVL() to convert string columns that contain null values, you can also use NVL() to convert number columns and date columns. In the following example, NVL() is used to convert a null value in the dob column to the date '01-JAN-2000':

```
SQL> SELECT id, first_name, last_name,
  2  NVL(dob, '01-JAN-2000') AS DOB
  3  FROM customers;

  ID FIRST_NAME LAST_NAME  DOB
---------- ---------- ---------- ---------
   1 John       Brown      01-JAN-65
   2 Cynthia    Green      05-FEB-68
   3 Steve      White      16-MAR-71
   4 Gail       Black      01-JAN-00
   5 Doreen     Blue       20-MAY-70
```

Notice that customer #4's date of birth is now displayed as '01-JAN-00'.

Logical Operators

There are three logical operators that may be used in a WHERE clause. The logical operators allow you to restrict rows based on logical conditions. The logical operators are listed in the following table:

Operator	Description
x AND y	Returns true when both x and y are true
x OR y	Returns true when either x or y are true
NOT x	Returns true if x is false, and returns false if x is true

The following example illustrates the use of the AND operator to retrieve rows from the customers table where *both* of the following conditions are met:

- The dob column is greater than 1-JAN-1970.

- The id column is greater than 3.

```
SQL> SELECT *
  2  FROM customers
  3  WHERE dob > '01-JAN-1970'
  4  AND id > 3;
```

```
    ID FIRST_NAME LAST_NAME  DOB        PHONE
---------- ---------- ---------- --------- ------------
     5 Doreen     Blue       20-MAY-70
```

The following example illustrates the use of the OR operator to retrieve rows from the customers table where *either* of the following conditions are met:

- The dob column is greater than 1-JAN-1970.

- The id column is greater than 3.

```
SQL> SELECT *
  2  FROM customers
  3  WHERE dob > '01-JAN-1970'
  4  OR id > 3;
```

```
    ID FIRST_NAME LAST_NAME  DOB        PHONE
---------- ---------- ---------- --------- ------------
     3 Steve      White      16-MAR-71 800-555-1213
     4 Gail       Black                800-555-1214
     5 Doreen     Blue       20-MAY-70
```

You can use the logical operators AND and OR to combine expressions in a WHERE clause.

NOTE
If you combine AND and OR in the same expression, the AND operator takes precedence over the OR operator (which means the AND operator is evaluated first). The comparison operators take precedence over AND. Of course, you can override these using parentheses.

The following example retrieves rows from the customers table where *either* of the following two conditions are met:

- The dob column is greater than 01-JAN-1968.

- The id column is less than 3 *and* the phone column has '1213' at the end.

```
SQL> SELECT *
  2  FROM customers
  3  WHERE dob > '01-JAN-1968'
  4  OR id < 3
  5  AND phone LIKE '%1213';
```

```
    ID FIRST_NAME LAST_NAME  DOB        PHONE
---------- ---------- ---------- --------- ------------
     2 Cynthia    Green      05-FEB-68 800-555-1212
     3 Steve      White      16-MAR-71 800-555-1213
     5 Doreen     Blue       20-MAY-70
```

As I mentioned, the AND operator takes precedence over OR, so you can think of the previous query as follows:

```
dob > '01-JAN-1968' OR (id < 3 AND phone LIKE '%1213')
```

Therefore, customers #2, #3, and #5 are displayed.

Sorting Rows Using the ORDER BY Clause

You use the ORDER BY clause to sort the rows retrieved from the database. The ORDER BY clause may specify one or more columns on which to sort the data and must follow the FROM clause or the WHERE clause (if a WHERE clause is supplied).

The following example uses the ORDER BY clause to sort the last_name column values from the customers table:

```
SQL> SELECT *
  2  FROM customers
  3  ORDER BY last_name;
```

```
    ID FIRST_NAME LAST_NAME  DOB        PHONE
---------- ---------- ---------- --------- ------------
     4 Gail       Black                 800-555-1214
     5 Doreen     Blue       20-MAY-70
     1 John       Brown      01-JAN-65 800-555-1211
     2 Cynthia    Green      05-FEB-68 800-555-1212
     3 Steve      White      16-MAR-71 800-555-1213
```

By default, the ORDER BY clause sorts the columns in ascending order (lower values appear first). You can use the DESC keyword to sort the columns in descending order (higher values appear first). You can also use the ASC keyword to explicitly specify an ascending sort—as I mentioned, this is the default, but you can still specify it.

The following example uses the ORDER BY clause to sort the first_name column values from the customers table in ascending order, followed by a sort on the last_name column values in descending order:

```
SQL> SELECT *
  2  FROM customers
  3  ORDER BY first_name ASC, last_name DESC;
```

```
    ID FIRST_NAME LAST_NAME  DOB        PHONE
---------- ---------- ---------- --------- ------------
     2 Cynthia    Green      05-FEB-68 800-555-1212
     5 Doreen     Blue       20-MAY-70
     4 Gail       Black                 800-555-1214
     1 John       Brown      01-JAN-65 800-555-1211
     3 Steve      White      16-MAR-71 800-555-1213
```

You can also use a column position number in the ORDER BY clause to indicate which column to sort: 1 means sort by the first column selected, 2 means sort by the second column, and so on. In the following example, column 1 (the id column) is used to sort the rows:

```
SQL> SELECT id, first_name, last_name
  2   FROM customers
  3   ORDER BY 1;

    ID FIRST_NAME LAST_NAME
---------- ---------- ----------
     1 John       Brown
     2 Cynthia    Green
     3 Steve      White
     4 Gail       Black
     5 Doreen     Blue
```

Multiple Table SELECT Statements

Most database schemas have more than one table, with those tables storing different aspects of an enterprise. Even our simple store has four tables: customers, product_types, products, and purchases, with each table representing a different aspect of the store. All the queries you've seen so far have involved only one database table from our store. However, you might want to get information in one go using more than one table; for example, you might want to get the name of the product type and display that name along with the name of the actual product itself.

Queries Involving Two Tables   Let's consider an example: assume we want to view the names of our products along with the name of the product type for each product in the same output. We know the name of the product is stored in the name column of the products table, and the product type name is stored in the name column of the product_types table. We also know that the products and product_types table are related to each other via the foreign key column type_id. Just to refresh your memory, the type_id column (the foreign key) points to the id column (the primary key) of the product_types table.

So, if we select the `type_id` and `name` columns from the `products` table
for product #1 we have the following:

```
SQL> SELECT type_id, name
  2  FROM products
  3  WHERE id = 1;

  TYPE_ID NAME
---------- ----------------------------
        1 Modern Science
```

And if we select the `name` column from the `product_types` table for the
product type with a `type_id` of 1 we have the following:

```
SQL> SELECT name
  2  FROM product_types
  3  WHERE id = 1;

NAME
----------
Book
```

From this, we know that product #1 represents a book. Nothing very complicated
so far, but what we really want is to view the product name and the product type
name on the same line. How do we do this?

The answer is to join the two tables in the query. To join two tables means that
you must specify both the tables in the query's FROM clause and then use related
columns (a foreign key from one table and the primary key from another table, for
example) from each table, along with an operator—equals (=) for example—in the
query's WHERE clause.

For our example, the FROM clause would be as follows:

```
FROM products, product_types
```

And the WHERE clause could be as follows:

```
WHERE type_id = id
```

But there's a problem with this WHERE clause: both `products` and `product_
types` contain a column named `id`. We know we want the `id` column from
the `product_types` table, but how do we indicate this in our WHERE clause?
One answer is to include the table name before the column name, so our WHERE
clause becomes:

```
WHERE type_id = product_types.id
```

I'll show you another way to indicate which table to use later. There's one more problem before we put our query together: how do we tell the database that we want the `name` columns from both the `product_types` and `product` tables? We can't just select the name column, since the database wouldn't know which one we meant! The answer is again to include the table names in the `SELECT` clause: `product_types.name` and `products.name`. This way, there's no confusion. Our `SELECT` clause becomes:

```
SELECT product_types.name, products.name
```

Let's put everything together into a complete query, and run that query in SQL*Plus:

```
SQL> SELECT product_types.name, products.name
  2  FROM products, product_types
  3  WHERE type_id = product_types.id;

NAME       NAME
---------- ------------------------------
Book       Modern Science
Book       Chemistry
Video      Supernova
Video      Tank War
Video      Z Files
Video      2412: The Return
DVD        Space Force 9
DVD        From Another Planet
CD         Classical Music
CD         Pop 3
CD         Creative Yell
```

Perfect! This is exactly what we wanted. Notice, however, that the product "My Front Line" is missing from the output; this product doesn't appear in the output because its `type_id` is null. You'll see how to include this row later in the section on outer joins.

If a join condition is missing, you will end up selecting all rows from one table joined to all the rows in the other table, a situation known as a *Cartesian product*. When this occurs, you may end up with a lot of rows being displayed. For example, assume you had one table containing 50 rows and a second table containing 100 rows. If you then select columns from those two tables without a join, you would get 5,000 rows returned. This is because each row from table one would be joined to each row in table two, which would yield a total of 50 multiplied by 100 rows, or 5,000 rows.

Table Aliases   I mentioned earlier that one way to qualify columns for queries that involve columns of the same name in different tables is to include the entire table name with the column. The previous example used the following query:

```
SELECT product_types.name, products.name
FROM products, product_types
WHERE type_id = product_types.id;
```

A better way is to use a table alias to "rename" the table referenced in a specific query, and include that alias when referencing columns. For example, let's use the alias "pt" for the product_types table, and an alias of "p" for the products table; when we do this, our query becomes

```
SELECT pt.name, p.name
FROM products p, product_types pt
WHERE p.type_id = pt.id;
```

Notice that the alias for each table is specified in the FROM clause after each table name and that the alias is used with each column reference. Just for good measure, I've also added the p alias to the type_id column; strictly speaking, that's not necessary, but it does make the query a little more understandable. Table aliases make your queries more readable, especially when you start writing longer queries.

Outer Joins   An outer join retrieves a row even when one of the columns in the join contains a null value. You use an outer join operator plus character in parentheses (+) on the opposite side of the join that contains the null.

Remember the query earlier that didn't show the "My Front Line" product because its type_id is null? You can use an outer join to get that row; notice that the outer join operator (+) is on the opposite side of the type_id column that contains the null:

```
SQL> SELECT pt.name, p.name
  2  FROM products p, product_types pt
  3  WHERE p.type_id = pt.id (+);

NAME        NAME
----------  -----------------------------
Book        Modern Science
Book        Chemistry
Video       Supernova
Video       Tank War
Video       Z Files
Video       2412: The Return
DVD         Space Force 9
DVD         From Another Planet
CD          Classical Music
```

```
CD          Pop 3
CD          Creative Yell

NAME        NAME
----------  -----------------------------
            My Front Line
```

Notice that the product with the null `type_id`, "My Front Line"—is now shown.

Queries Involving More Than Two Tables   Joins can be used to connect any number of tables together. Use the following formula to calculate the number of joins you will need in your `WHERE` clause:

> *Add all the number of tables used in your query and subtract one from this total; this is the number of joins you need in your* `WHERE` *clause.*

In the example shown earlier, there were two tables used in the query: `products` and `product_types`. Therefore, the number of joins required is 2 minus 1, or 1, and only one join is used in that example.

Now, let's consider a more complicated example that will involve four tables and therefore require three joins. Say we want to see the purchases each customer has made, as well as the customer's name (first and last), the name of the product they purchased, and the name of the product type.

In order to do this, we will need to use the `customers`, `purchases`, `products`, and `product_types` tables, and our joins will need to navigate the foreign key relationships between these tables. The following list shows this navigation using three steps:

1. To get the customer who made the purchase, join the `customers` and `purchases` tables using the `id` and `purchased_by` columns from those tables.

2. To get the product purchased, join the `products` and `purchases` tables using the `id` and `product_id` columns from those tables.

3. To get the product type name for the product, join the `products` and `product_types` tables using the `type_id` and `id` columns from those respective tables.

Using this navigation, the query may appear as follows:

```
SELECT c.first_name, c.last_name, p.name AS PRODUCT, pt.name AS TYPE
FROM customers c, purchases pr, products p, product_types pt
WHERE c.id = pr.purchased_by
AND p.id = pr.product_id
AND p.type_id = pt.id;
```

Notice that I've also renamed the heading for the product name to PRODUCT, and renamed the product type name to TYPE. The output of this query is as follows:

```
FIRST_NAME  LAST_NAME   PRODUCT                        TYPE
----------  ----------  -----------------------------  ----------
John        Brown       Modern Science                 Book
Cynthia     Green       Modern Science                 Book
Steve       White       Modern Science                 Book
Gail        Black       Modern Science                 Book
John        Brown       Chemistry                      Book
Cynthia     Green       Chemistry                      Book
Steve       White       Chemistry                      Book
Gail        Black       Chemistry                      Book
Steve       White       Supernova                      Video
```

Adding Rows Using the INSERT Statement

You use the INSERT statement to add new rows to a table. You can specify the following information in an INSERT statement:

- The table into which the row is to be inserted

- A list of columns for which you want to specify column values

- A list of values to store in the specified columns

When inserting a row, you need to supply a value for the primary key and all other columns that are defined as NOT NULL. You don't have to specify values for the other columns if you don't want to (they will be set to null if you don't specify a value). You can tell which columns are defined as NOT NULL using the SQL*Plus DESCRIBE command. The following example describes the customers table:

```
SQL> DESCRIBE customers
 Name                                      Null?    Type
 ----------------------------------------- -------- ------------
 ID                                        NOT NULL NUMBER(38)
 FIRST_NAME                                NOT NULL VARCHAR2(10)
 LAST_NAME                                 NOT NULL VARCHAR2(10)
 DOB                                                DATE
 PHONE                                              VARCHAR2(12)
```

As you can see the id, first_name, and last_name columns are NOT NULL, meaning that you must supply a value for these columns. The dob and phone columns don't require a value—you could omit the values if you wanted, and they would be set to null.

The following INSERT statement adds a row to the customers table. Notice that the order of values in the VALUES list matches the order in which the columns are specified in the column list. Also notice that the statement has two parts: the column list and the values to be added.

```
SQL> INSERT INTO customers (id, first_name, last_name, dob, phone)
  2  VALUES (6, 'Fred', 'Brown', '01-JAN-1970', '800-555-1215');

1 row created.
```

SQL*Plus responds that 1 row has been created. You can verify this by issuing a SELECT statement:

```
SQL> SELECT *
  2  FROM customers;

        ID FIRST_NAME LAST_NAME  DOB       PHONE
---------- ---------- ---------- --------- ------------
         1 John       Brown      01-JAN-65 800-555-1211
         2 Cynthia    Green      05-FEB-68 800-555-1212
         3 Steve      White      16-MAR-71 800-555-1213
         4 Gail       Black                800-555-1214
         5 Doreen     Blue       20-MAY-70
         6 Fred       Brown      01-JAN-70 800-555-1215
```

You may omit the column list when supplying values for each column. For example:

```
SQL> INSERT INTO customers
  2  VALUES (7, 'Jane', 'Green', '01-JAN-1970', '800-555-1216');
```

If you omit the column list, the order of the values you supply must match the order in which the columns are listed when you use the DESCRIBE command to describe the table.

You can specify a null value for a column using the NULL keyword. The following example specifies a null value for the dob and phone columns:

```
SQL> INSERT INTO customers
  2  VALUES (8, 'Sophie', 'White', NULL, NULL);
```

Of course, when you view this row using a query, you won't see a value for the dob and phone columns because they've been set to null values:

```
SQL> SELECT *
  2  FROM customers
  3  WHERE id = 8;
```

```
        ID FIRST_NAME LAST_NAME  DOB       PHONE
---------- ---------- ---------- --------- ------------
         8 Sophie     White
```

You can even copy rows from one table to another (as long as the number of columns and the column types match) using a query in the place of the column values in the INSERT statement. The following example uses a query to select the first_name and last_name columns for customer #1 and uses those columns in an INSERT statement:

```
INSERT INTO customers (id, first_name, last_name)
SELECT 11, first_name, last_name
FROM customers
WHERE id = 1;
```

Notice that the id for the new row is set to 11. This is because the id for each row in the customers table must be unique.

Modifying Rows Using the UPDATE Statement

You use the UPDATE statement to change rows in a table. Normally, when you use the UPDATE statement, you specify the following information:

- The table containing the row(s) that are to be changed

- A WHERE clause that specifies the row(s) that are to be changed

- A list of column names, along with their new values, specified using the SET clause

You can change one or more rows using the same UPDATE statement. If more than one row is specified, then the same change will be implemented for all of those rows. The following statement updates the last_name column to 'Orange' for the row where the id column equals 2:

```
SQL> UPDATE customers
  2   SET last_name = 'Orange'
  3   WHERE id = 2;

1 row updated.
```

SQL*Plus confirms that 1 row was changed, or updated. If the WHERE clause were omitted, then all the rows would be updated. Notice that the SET clause is used in the UPDATE statement to specify the column and the new value for that column. You can confirm that the previous UPDATE statement did indeed change customer #2's last name using the following query:

```
SQL> SELECT *
  2  FROM customers
  3  WHERE id = 2;

        ID FIRST_NAME LAST_NAME  DOB       PHONE
---------- ---------- ---------- --------- -----------
         2 Cynthia    Orange     05-FEB-68 800-555-1212
```

You can change multiple rows and multiple columns at the same time with an
UPDATE statement. The next example raises the price by 20 percent for all products
where the current price is greater than or equal to 20, and it changes the product
names to lowercase for those products at the same time:

```
SQL> UPDATE products
  2  SET
  3    price = price * 1.20,
  4    name = LOWER(name)
  5  WHERE
  6    price >= 20;

3 rows updated.
```

As you can see, three rows are updated by this statement. You can confirm this
using the following query:

```
SQL> SELECT id, name, price
  2  FROM products
  3  WHERE price >= (20 * 1.20);

        ID NAME                            PRICE
---------- ------------------------------ ----------
         2 chemistry                          36
         3 supernova                        31.19
         5 z-files                          59.99
```

Removing Rows Using the DELETE Statement

You use the DELETE statement to remove rows from a table. Generally, you should
specify a WHERE clause that limits the row(s) that you wish to delete—if you don't,
all the rows will be deleted! The following example uses a DELETE statement to
remove one row from the customers table (customer #2):

```
SQL> DELETE FROM customers
  2  WHERE id = 2;

1 row deleted.
```

SQL*Plus confirms that one row has been deleted.

Database Integrity

When using DML statements, the database ensures that the rows in the tables maintain their integrity, which means that any changes you make to the rows in the tables must always be in keeping with the primary key and foreign key relationships set for the tables. For example, the customers table's primary key is the id column, which means that every value stored in the id column must be unique. If you try to insert a row with a duplicate value for a primary key column, you will get the Oracle database error ORA-00001:

```
SQL> INSERT INTO customers (id, first_name, last_name, dob, phone)
  2  VALUES (1, 'Jason', 'Price', '01-JAN-60', '800-555-1211');
INSERT INTO customers (id, first_name, last_name, dob, phone)
*
ERROR at line 1:
ORA-00001: unique constraint (STORE.CUSTOMERS_PK) violated
```

Similarly, if you attempt to update a primary key value to a value that already exists in the table, you will get the same error:

```
SQL> UPDATE customers
  2  SET id = 1
  3  WHERE id = 2;
UPDATE customers
*
ERROR at line 1:
ORA-00001: unique constraint (STORE.CUSTOMERS_PK) violated
```

Foreign key relationships are also enforced by the database. A foreign key relationship is where a column from one table is referenced in another. For example, the type_id column in the products table references the id column in the product_types table using a foreign key relationship. Earlier, I mentioned that the product_types table is known as the *parent* table, and the products table is known as the *child* table because the type_id column in the products table is dependent on the id column in the product_types table. If you try to insert a row that specifies a nonexistent type_id for the id in the products table, you will get the Oracle database error ORA-02291, which means the parent key (the id column in the product_types table) for the foreign key relationship was not found. The following example shows this by attempting to insert a row into the products table with a nonexistent type_id:

```
SQL> INSERT INTO products (id, type_id, name, description, price)
  2  VALUES (13, 6, 'Test', 'Test', NULL);
INSERT INTO products (id, type_id, name, description, price)
*
```

```
ERROR at line 1:
ORA-02291: integrity constraint (STORE.PRODUCTS_FK_PRODUCT_TYPES) violated -
parent key not found
```

Similarly, attempting to update a `type_id` in the `products` table to a nonexistent `id` in the `product_types` table will generate the same error:

```
SQL> UPDATE products
  2   SET type_id = 6
  3   WHERE id = 1;
UPDATE products
*
ERROR at line 1:
ORA-02291: integrity constraint (STORE.PRODUCTS_FK_PRODUCT_TYPES) violated -
parent key not found
```

Also, attempting to delete a row in the parent table that already has dependent rows that reference it in a child table generates the Oracle database error ORA-02292, which means a child record was found. For example, if you attempt to delete the row with an `id` of 1 in the `product_types` table, you will get this error because the `products` table contains rows with `type_ids` equal to that value:

```
SQL> DELETE FROM product_types
  2   WHERE id = 1;
DELETE FROM product_types
*
ERROR at line 1:
ORA-02292: integrity constraint (STORE.PRODUCTS_FK_PRODUCT_TYPES) violated -
child record found
```

If the database were to allow this deletion, the child rows would be invalid because they wouldn't point to valid values in the parent table.

Database Transactions

A database *transaction* is a group of SQL statements that are considered to be a *logical unit of work*. You can think of a transaction as an inseparable set of SQL statements that should be made permanent in the database (or undone) as a whole. An example of this would be a transfer of money from one bank account to another: one UPDATE statement would subtract from the total amount of money from one account, and another UPDATE would add money to the other account. Both the subtraction and the addition must either be permanently recorded in the database, or they both must be undone—otherwise money will be lost, and that cannot be tolerated in any system. This simple example uses only two UPDATE statements, but a more realistic transaction may consist of many SELECT, INSERT, UPDATE, and DELETE statements.

To permanently record the results of the SQL statements in a transaction, you perform a *commit* using the SQL COMMIT statement. To undo the results of the SQL statements, you perform a *rollback* using the SQL ROLLBACK statement, which resets all the rows back to what they were originally.

If you've made any changes to the example tables, roll them back using the ROLLBACK statement now, as shown in the following example:

```
SQL> ROLLBACK;

Rollback complete.
```

Any changes you made prior to performing the rollback will be undone, as long as you haven't disconnected from the database beforehand. The contents of the customers and products tables should now be as they were before you made any changes. If you disconnected from the database before performing the rollback, don't worry: simply rerun the store_schema.sql script in SQL*Plus to recreate everything.

The following example adds a row to the customers table and then makes the change permanent by performing a commit:

```
SQL> INSERT INTO customers
  2  VALUES (6, 'Fred', 'Green', '01-JAN-1970', '800-555-1215');

1 row created.

SQL> COMMIT;

Commit complete.
```

The following example updates a row in the customers table and then undoes the change by performing a rollback:

```
SQL> UPDATE customers
  2  SET
  3    first_name = 'Edward'
  4  WHERE id = 1;

1 row updated.

SQL> ROLLBACK;

Rollback complete.
```

You can verify these statements using the following query:

```
SQL> SELECT *
  2  FROM customers;

        ID FIRST_NAME LAST_NAME  DOB       PHONE
---------- ---------- ---------- --------- ------------
         1 John       Brown      01-JAN-65 800-555-1211
         2 Cynthia    Green      05-FEB-68 800-555-1212
         3 Steve      White      16-MAR-71 800-555-1213
         4 Gail       Black                800-555-1214
         5 Doreen     Blue       20-MAY-70
         6 Fred       Green      01-JAN-70 800-555-1215
```

Notice that the result of INSERT statement that added customer #6 is indeed made permanent by the COMMIT and that the result of the UPDATE statement that changed the first name of customer #1 is undone by the ROLLBACK.

Starting and Ending a Transaction   As I mentioned, transactions are logical units of work you use to split up your database activities. A transaction has both a beginning and an end; it begins when one of the following events occurs:

- You connect to the database and perform the first DML statement.
- A previous transaction ends, and you enter another DML statement.

A transaction ends when one of the following events occurs:

- You perform a COMMIT or a ROLLBACK statement.
- You disconnect from the database. (By the way, if you exit SQL*Plus by entering the EXIT command, a COMMIT is automatically performed for you; otherwise, a ROLLBACK is automatically performed.)
- You perform a DDL statement to create or alter a database object.
- The server on which the database is running crashes.

It is considered poor practice not to explicitly commit or rollback your transactions once they are complete, so make sure you issue a COMMIT or ROLLBACK statement at the end of each of your transactions.

Concurrent Transactions   The Oracle database supports many users interacting with the database at the same time, each running their own transactions; this is known as *concurrent* transactions. If multiple database users are running transactions that affect the same tables, the effects of those transactions are separated from each other until a COMMIT is performed. The following sequence of events, based on two users accessing a single table, illustrates this concept:

1. User 1 performs a SELECT that retrieves all the rows in table 1.

2. User 2 performs an INSERT to insert a row in table 1 but doesn't perform a COMMIT.

3. User 1 performs another SELECT and retrieves the same rows as she in step 1.

4. User 2 finally performs a COMMIT.

5. User 1 performs another SELECT, and the results include the new row added by user 2.

This simple example illustrates that each user has their own transaction associated with their database session, and the effects of these transactions are only visible to other transactions after a COMMIT is performed (at least, this is the default behavior—I'll show you how you can change this in Chapter 9). In the example, user 2 adds a row to the table in step 2, but this row is not visible to user 1 until after user 2 performs a COMMIT in step 4.

Transaction Locking   To support concurrent transactions, the Oracle database must ensure that the data in the tables remains valid. It does this through the use of transaction isolation and *locks*. This may be understood by considering the following example, in which two users attempt to modify the same row in the same table:

1. User 1 performs an UPDATE to modify a row in a table but doesn't commit the transaction. She is said to have "locked" the row.

2. User 2 attempts to UPDATE the same row, but since this row is already locked by User 1, he is prevented from doing so. His UPDATE statement has to wait until User 1's transaction ends.

3. User 1 performs a COMMIT, freeing her lock on the row.

4. Users 2's UPDATE is performed, and he gets the lock on the row.

The point is that if a user attempts to modify the same row as another user at the same time, he must wait until the other user ends her transaction.

NOTE
The easiest way to understand default locking in the Oracle database is to remember this: readers don't block readers, writers don't block readers, and writers only block writers when they attempt to modify the same rows.

Savepoints   You can also set a *savepoint* at any point within a transaction. These allow you to rollback changes to that point. This might be useful if you have a very long transaction because if you make a mistake after you've set a savepoint, you don't have to rollback the transaction all the way to the start. You should use savepoints sparingly; you might be better off restructuring your transaction into smaller transactions instead. I'll show you an example of using a savepoint, but before we begin, let's check the details for product #1 and product #2:

```
SQL> SELECT id, price
  2  FROM products
  3  WHERE id IN (1, 2);

        ID      PRICE
---------- ----------
         1      19.95
         2         30
```

So far, so good: the price for product #1 is $30.00, and the price for product #2 is $19.95. Next, let's increase the price of product #1 by 20 percent:

```
SQL> UPDATE products
  2  SET price = price * 1.20
  3  WHERE id = 1;
```

Set a savepoint here named `save1`; this will allow us to rollback any further DML statements and preserve the previous UPDATE:

```
SQL> SAVEPOINT save1;

Savepoint created.
```

Next, let's increase the price of product #2 by 30 percent:

```
SQL> UPDATE products
  2  SET price = price * 1.30
  3  WHERE id = 2;
```

Let's check the prices of the two products, just to make sure everything's set as we expect:

```
SQL> SELECT id, price
  2  FROM products
  3  WHERE id IN (1, 2);

        ID      PRICE
---------- ----------
         1      23.94
         2         39
```

Everything looks good: product #1's price is 20 percent greater, and product #2's price is 30 percent greater. Okay, let's rollback the transaction to the savepoint established earlier:

```
SQL> ROLLBACK TO SAVEPOINT save1;
```

This should preserve the new price set for product #1, but it will rollback the price for product #2 back to its original price before we began because the savepoint was set before the change to product #2's price was made:

```
SQL> SELECT id, price
  2  FROM products
  3  WHERE id IN (1, 2);

        ID      PRICE
---------- ----------
         1      23.94
         2         30
```

These are the expected results: product #1's price is $23.94 (the new price—assuming products are priced in dollars) and product #2's price is back to the original price. Finally, rollback the entire transaction:

```
SQL> ROLLBACK;
```

This rolls back the changes all the way to the start of the transaction and undoes the change made to the price of product #1.

I'll return to the subject of database transactions in Chapter 9.

Row Identifiers (ROWIDs)

Each row in an Oracle database has a unique row identifier, or *ROWID*, which is used internally by the software to access the row. You can think of a ROWID as a pointer to the row. In Oracle9i/8i databases, a ROWID is an 18-digit number that is stored using base 64, and it contains the physical address of a row in the database.

You can view the ROWIDs for rows in a table by selecting the ROWID column in a query. This is known as a *virtual* or *pseudo* column because you didn't explicitly create it when creating a table. The query in the following example retrieves the ROWID and id columns from the customers table:

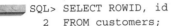

```
SQL> SELECT ROWID, id
  2  FROM customers;

ROWID                    ID
------------------ ----------
AAAF6xAABAAAHeyAAA        1
AAAF6xAABAAAHeyAAB        2
AAAF6xAABAAAHeyAAC        3
AAAF6xAABAAAHeyAAD        4
AAAF6xAABAAAHeyAAE        5
```

Notice that the values in the ROWID column are shown as base 64 numbers.

Oracle PL/SQL

Oracle added a procedural programming language known as PL/SQL (Procedural Language/SQL) to the database. PL/SQL is built on top of SQL and enables you to write programs that contain SQL statements. PL/SQL is a third-generation language, and contains the standard programming constructs you would expect from such a language, such as:

- Block structure
- Variables and types
- Conditional logic such as IF, THEN, ELSE, and ELSIF
- Loops
- Cursors that hold the results returned by a query
- Procedures
- Functions
- Packages, which may be used to group procedures and functions together in one unit

You can use PL/SQL to add business logic to the database. This centralized code may be called by any program that can access the database (including a JDBC program). PL/SQL is primarily used for adding procedures and functions to a database, and in Chapter 5 I'll show you how to call the example PL/SQL procedures, functions, and packages shown in this section using a JDBC program.

Later, in Chapter 10, I'll show you how to create PL/SQL *triggers*, blocks of code that are run (or *fired*) when a certain event occurs in the database.

Block Structure

PL/SQL programs are divided up into structures known as *blocks*, with each block containing PL/SQL program statements. A typical PL/SQL block has the following structure:

```
[DECLARE
  declaration_statements
]
BEGIN
  executable_statements
[EXCEPTION
  exception_handling_statements
]
END;
```

The declaration and exception blocks are optional, and the elements for the above syntax are as follows:

- **declaration_statements**   Contained within a declaration block, they declare the variables subsequently used in the rest of the block. These variables are local to that block, meaning that they cannot be referenced outside of that block. Declarations are always placed at the start of the block.

- **executable_statements**   The actual executable statements for the block; statements for performing loops, conditional logic, and so on.

- **exception_handling_statements**   Handle any errors that might occur due to the executable statements.

Every statement is terminated by a semicolon (;), and a block is terminated using the END keyword. Before I get into the details of PL/SQL, I want to show you a simple example so you get a feel for the language. The following PL/SQL example calculates the area of a rectangle:

```
DECLARE
  width INTEGER := 2;
  height INTEGER;
  area INTEGER;
BEGIN
  height := 3;
  area := width * height;
  DBMS_OUTPUT.PUT_LINE('Area = ' || area);
END;
/
```

As you can see, three INTEGER variables are declared: width, height, and area. The width variable is initialized to 2 when it is declared, and height is set to 3 later. The area variable is calculated by multiplying width by height. The call to the DBMS_OUTPUT.PUT_LINE() method displays the value set for the area variable on the screen (you must enter the command **SET SERVEROUTPUT ON** in SQL*Plus to see the output). The forward slash character (/) at the end executes the PL/SQL block. The following listing shows the block being entered and run in SQL*Plus:

```
SQL> SET SERVEROUTPUT ON
SQL> DECLARE
  2    width INTEGER := 2;
  3    height INTEGER;
  4    area INTEGER;
  5  BEGIN
  6    height := 3;
  7    area := width * height;
  8    DBMS_OUTPUT.PUT_LINE('Area = ' || area);
  9  END;
 10  /
Area = 6

PL/SQL procedure successfully completed.
```

Notice that the forward slash character is used at line 10 to run the PL/SQL.

Variables and Types

As I mentioned earlier, any variables declared within the DECLARE section of a PL/SQL block may only be referenced within that block. As you saw in the previous example, a variable declaration has both a name and a type. For example, the height variable was declared as:

```
height INTEGER;
```

The PL/SQL types are basically the same as the database column types. I showed you some of the more common database types earlier; in this example, the INTEGER type is used to declare the height variable.

The following example illustrates some more variable declarations that may be used to store the column values from the products table:

```
id          INTEGER;
type_id     INTEGER;
name        VARCHAR2(30);
description VARCHAR2(50);
price       NUMBER(5, 2);
```

You may also declare variables using the %TYPE keyword. This tells PL/SQL to use the same type as a specified column in a table. The following example uses %TYPE to declare a variable of the same type as the price column of the products table:

```
product_name products.price%TYPE;
```

Conditional Logic

You may use the IF, THEN, ELSE, ELSIF, and END IF keywords in PL/SQL for performing conditional logic. The following syntax illustrates the use of conditional logic:

```
IF condition1 THEN
    statements1
ELSIF condition2 THEN
   statements2
ELSE
   statements3
END IF;
```

The syntax elements condition1 and condition2 are Boolean expressions that evaluate to true or false. The syntax elements statements1, statements2, and statements3 are PL/SQL statements. This conditional logic flows as follows: if condition1 is true, statements1 is executed; if condition1 is false but condition2 is true, statements2 is executed; if neither condition1 nor condition2 are true, statements3 is executed.

You can also embed IF statements within another IF statement, as shown in the following example:

```
IF count > 0 THEN
   message := 'count is positive';
   IF area > 0 THEN
     message := 'count and area are positive';
   END IF
ELSIF count = 0 THEN
   message := 'count is zero';
ELSE
   message := 'count is negative';
END IF;
```

Loops

You may use a loop to run one or more statements multiple times. There are three types of loops in PL/SQL:

- **Simple loop**   Runs until you explicitly end the loop
- **WHILE loop**   Runs until a specified condition occurs
- **FOR loop**   Runs a predetermined number of times

The following sections cover the details of these loops.

Simple Loops

A simple loop runs until you explicitly end the loop. The syntax for a simple loop is as follows:

```
LOOP
   statements
END LOOP;
```

To end the loop, you use either an `EXIT` or `EXIT WHEN` statement. The `EXIT` statement ends a loop immediately, and the `EXIT WHEN` statement ends a loop when a specified condition occurs.

The following example shows a simple loop: a variable named `count` is initialized to 0 prior to the beginning of the loop, and the loop adds 1 to `count`. The loop exits when `count` is equal to 5 using an `EXIT WHEN` statement:

```
count := 0;
LOOP
  count := count + 1;
  EXIT WHEN counter = 5;
END LOOP;
```

The `EXIT WHEN` statement can appear anywhere in the loop code.

WHILE Loops

A `WHILE` loop runs until a specified condition occurs. The syntax for a `WHILE` loop is as follows:

```
WHILE condition LOOP
   statements
END LOOP;
```

The following example shows a `WHILE` loop:

```
count := 0;
WHILE counter < 6 LOOP
  count := count + 1;
END LOOP;
```

The loop runs until the variable `count` reaches 5.

FOR Loops

A FOR loop runs a predetermined number of times—you determine the number of times the loop runs by specifying the *lower* and *upper bounds* for a loop variable. This loop variable is then incremented (or decremented) each time around the loop. The syntax for a FOR loop is as follows:

```
FOR loop_variable IN [REVERSE] lower_bound..upper_bound LOOP
   statements
END LOOP;
```

The syntax elements are as follows:

- **loop_variable**   You may use a variable that already exists as the loop variable, or you can just have the loop create one for you (this occurs if the variable specified doesn't exist). The loop variable value is increased (or decreased if you use the REVERSE keyword) by 1 each time through the loop.

- **REVERSE**   Specifies that the loop variable value is to be decremented each time through the loop. The loop variable is initialized to the upper bound and is decremented by 1 until the loop variable reaches the lower bound. You must still specify the lower bound before the upper bound.

- **lower_bound**   This is the loop's lower bound. The loop variable is initialized to this lower bound as long as REVERSE is not used.

- **upper_bound**   This is the loop's upper bound. If REVERSE is used, the loop variable is initialized to this upper bound.

The following example shows a FOR loop; notice that the variable count2 isn't explicitly declared—the FOR loop automatically creates an INTEGER variable in this case:

```
FOR count2 IN 1..5 LOOP
   DBMS_OUTPUT.PUT_LINE(count2);
END LOOP;
```

If I had used REVERSE in this example, the loop variable counter would start at 5, be decremented by 1 each time through the loop, and end at 1.

Cursors

You use a PL/SQL cursor when you have a SELECT statement that returns more than one row from the database. You retrieve the rows into the cursor using your

`SELECT` statement and then fetch the rows from the cursor. There are five steps that you must follow when using a cursor:

1. Declare variables to store the column values from the `SELECT` statement.

2. Declare the cursor, specifying your `SELECT` statement.

3. Open the cursor.

4. Fetch the rows from the cursor.

5. Close the cursor.

I will now describe the details of these five steps.

Step 1: Declare the Variables to Store the Column Values

The first step is to declare the variables that will be used to store the column values. These variables must be compatible with the column types. I mentioned earlier that `%TYPE` is used to get the type of a column. If you use this when declaring your variables, your variables will always be of the correct type. The following example declares three variables to store the `id`, `name`, and `price` columns from the `products` table:

```
DECLARE
    id      products.id%TYPE;
    name    products.name%TYPE;
    price   products.price%TYPE;
```

Step 2: Declare the Cursor

A cursor declaration consists of a name that you assign to the cursor and the `SELECT` statement that you want to execute—this `SELECT` statement is not actually run until you open the cursor. The cursor declaration, like all other declarations, is placed in the declaration section.

The following example declares a cursor named `product_cursor` whose `SELECT` statement retrieves the `id`, `name`, and `price` columns from the `products` table:

```
CURSOR product_cursor IS
    SELECT
        id, name, price
    FROM
        products
    ORDER BY
        id;
```

Step 3: Open the Cursor

The next step is to open the cursor, which runs the SELECT statement. You open a cursor using the OPEN statement, which must be placed in the executable section of the block.

The following example opens product_cursor, and therefore also runs the SELECT statement that retrieves the rows from the products table:

```
OPEN product_cursor;
```

Step 4: Fetch the Rows from the Cursor

To read each row from the cursor, you use the FETCH statement. The FETCH statement reads the column values into the variables that you specify. The following example uses the FETCH statement to retrieve a row from product_cursor and stores the column values in the id, name, and price variables created earlier in step 1:

```
FETCH
    product_cursor
INTO
    id, name, price;
```

Of course, the cursor may contain many rows; therefore, a loop is required is to read each row in turn. To determine when the loop is to end, you can use the Boolean variable product_cursor%NOTFOUND—this variable is true when the FETCH statement has reached the end of the rows in the cursor, and there are no further rows to read. The following example shows a loop that reads each row from product_cursor:

```
LOOP

    FETCH
        product_cursor
    INTO
        id, name, price;

    -- exit the loop when there are no more rows, as indicated by
    -- the Boolean variable product_cursor%NOTFOUND (= true when
    -- there are no more rows)
    EXIT WHEN product_cursor%NOTFOUND;

    -- use DBMS_OUTPUT.PUT_LINE() to display the variables
    DBMS_OUTPUT.PUT_LINE(
        'id = ' || id || ', name = ' ||name ||
        ', price = ' || price
    );

END LOOP;
```

Notice that I've used `DBMS_OUTPUT.PUT_LINE()` to display the `id`, `name`, and `price` variables that were read for each row.

Step 5: Close the Cursor

Once you've finished with the cursor, the final step is to close the cursor using the `CLOSE` statement. Closing your cursors frees up system resources. The following example closes `product_cursor`:

```
CLOSE product_cursor;
```

The following section shows a complete example script that may be run using SQL*Plus; this script contains all of the five steps for using a cursor.

Complete Example: product_cursor.sql

The SQL*Plus script `product_cursor.sql` is available for download from this book's website and is as follows:

```
-- product_cursor.sql displays the id, name, and price columns
-- from the products table using a cursor

DECLARE

  -- step 1: declare the variables
  id    products.id%TYPE;
  name  products.name%TYPE;
  price products.price%TYPE;

  -- step 2: declare the cursor
  CURSOR product_cursor IS
    SELECT
      id, name, price
    FROM
      products
    ORDER BY
      id;

BEGIN

  -- step 3: open the cursor
  OPEN product_cursor;


  LOOP

    -- step 4: fetch the rows from the cursor
    FETCH
```

```
   product_cursor
INTO
   id, name, price;

-- exit the loop when there are no more rows, as indicated by
-- the Boolean variable product_cursor%NOTFOUND (= true when
-- there are no more rows)
EXIT WHEN product_cursor%NOTFOUND;

-- use DBMS_OUTPUT.PUT_LINE() to display the variables
DBMS_OUTPUT.PUT_LINE(
  'id = ' || id || ', name = ' ||name ||
  ', price = ' || price
);

END LOOP;

-- step 5: close the cursor
CLOSE product_cursor;

END;
/
```

To run this script, you should follow these four steps:

1. Start SQL*Plus.

2. Log into the database with the username store_user and the password store_password.

3. Enter the command **SET SERVEROUTPUT ON**. This causes the output from the calls to DBMS_OUTPUT.PUT_LINE() to appear on the screen.

4. Run the product_cursor.sql script, using the following command:

   @ c:\sql\product_cursor.sql

   (Of course, if you've saved the script in a different directory, you should use that directory in this command.)

The output from this script is as follows:

```
id = 1, name = Modern Science, price = 19.95
id = 2, name = Chemistry, price = 26.4
id = 3, name = Supernova, price = 22.87
id = 4, name = Tank War, price = 12.28
id = 5, name = Z Files, price = 43.99
id = 6, name = 2412: The Return, price = 13.16
id = 7, name = Space Force 9, price = 11.87
```

```
id = 8, name = From Another Planet, price = 11.43
id = 9, name = Classical Music, price = 9.67
id = 10, name = Pop 3, price = 14.07
id = 11, name = Creative Yell, price = 13.19
id = 12, name = My Front Line, price = 11.87
```

Procedures

You can create a procedure in PL/SQL that contains a group of SQL and PL/SQL statements. These procedures allow you to centralize your business logic in the database and may be used by any program that accesses the database. You can also create Java stored procedures in the database; I'll show you how to do that in Chapter 10.

You create a procedure in PL/SQL using the CREATE PROCEDURE statement. The syntax for the CREATE PROCEDURE statement is as follows:

```
CREATE [OR REPLACE] PROCEDURE procedure_name
[(parameter_name [IN|OUT|IN OUT] type [, ...])]
{IS|AS}
{
  body
};
```

The syntax elements are as follows:

- **procedure_name**   The name that you assign to the procedure.

- **parameter_name**   The name of a parameter to the procedure. A procedure may have more than one parameter.

- **IN|OUT|IN OUT**   The *mode* of the parameter. There are three parameter modes:

  - **IN**   The default mode for a parameter. This mode is specified for parameters that already have a value when the procedure is run and that value may not be changed in the body.

  - **OUT**   This mode is specified for parameters whose values are only set in the body.

  - **IN OUT**   This mode is specified for parameters that may already have a value when the procedure is called, but their value may also be changed in the body.

- **type**   The PL/SQL type of the parameter.

- **body**   This is the procedure body, and it contains the required SQL and PL/SQL statements to perform your task.

The following CREATE PROCEDURE statement defines a procedure named update_product_price(). This statement is also contained in the store_user.sql script that you should have already run. This procedure multiplies the price of a product by a factor—the product id and the factor are passed as parameters to the procedure. If the specified product doesn't exist, the procedure takes no action; otherwise, it updates the product price by the factor.

```
CREATE PROCEDURE update_product_price(

  p_product_id IN products.id%TYPE,
  p_factor     IN NUMBER

) AS

  product_count INTEGER;

BEGIN

  -- count the number of products with the
  -- supplied id (should be 1 if the product exists)
  SELECT
    COUNT(*)
  INTO
    product_count
  FROM
    products
  WHERE
    id = p_product_id;

  -- if the product exists (product_count = 1) then
  -- update that product's price
  IF product_count = 1 THEN
    UPDATE
      products
    SET
      price = price * p_factor;
    COMMIT;
  END IF;

END update_product_price;
/
```

As you can see from this listing, the procedure takes two parameters named p_product_id and p_factor. Notice that both of these parameters use the IN mode, which means their values cannot be changed in the body.

The declaration section contains an `INTEGER` variable named `product_count`:

```
product_count INTEGER;
```

The body of the procedure follows this declaration section, starting with `BEGIN`. The first statement in the body uses a `SELECT` statement that counts the number of products with the specified id, using the built-in `COUNT()` function:

```
-- count the number of products with the
-- supplied id (should be 1 if the product exists)
SELECT
  COUNT(*)
INTO
  product_count
FROM
  products
WHERE
  id = p_product_id;
```

NOTE
COUNT(*) counts all of the rows and returns the total.

If the product exists in the table, `product_count` will be set to 1; if the product doesn't exist, it will be 0. If the value in `product_count` is 1, the `price` column can be multiplied by `p_factor` using an `UPDATE` statement, and the change can be committed; otherwise, no action should be taken. The following statement does all of this:

```
-- if the product exists (product_count = 1) then
-- update that product's price
IF product_count = 1 THEN
  UPDATE
    products
  SET
    price = price * p_factor;
  COMMIT;
END IF;
```

Finally, the `END` keyword is used to mark the end of the procedure:

```
END update_product_price;
/
```

The repetition of the procedure name at the end is not required, but it is good programming practice to put it in.

Functions

A PL/SQL function is similar to a procedure, except that a function must return a value to the statement from which it is called. Functions may also be stored in the database, just like procedures. Together, stored procedures and functions are sometimes referred to as stored subprograms because they are, in one sense, small programs.

You create a function using the PL/SQL CREATE FUNCTION statement. The syntax for the CREATE FUNCTION statement is as follows:

```
CREATE [OR REPLACE] FUNCTION function_name
[(parameter_name [IN|OUT|IN OUT] type [, ...])]
RETURN type
{IS|AS}
{
  body
};
```

The syntax elements are as follows:

- **function_name**   The name that you assign to the function.

- **parameter_name**   The name of a parameter to the function. A function may have more than one parameter.

- **IN | OUT | IN OUT**   The *mode* of the parameter. There are three parameter modes:

  - **IN**   The default mode for a parameter. This mode is specified for parameters that already have a value when the function is called, and that value may not be changed in the body.

  - **OUT**   Specified for parameters whose values are only set in the body.

  - **IN OUT**   Specified for parameters that may already have a value when the function is called, but their value may also be changed in the body.

- **type**   The PL/SQL type of the parameter.

- **body**   The function body. It contains the required SQL and PL/SQL statements to perform your task. Unlike a procedure, the body for a function must return a value of the PL/SQL type specified in the RETURN clause.

The following CREATE FUNCTION statement creates a function named update_product_price_func(). This statement is also contained in the store_user.sql script. This function is similar to the procedure update_product_price() shown earlier, but this function returns the INTEGER value 1 if the specified product is not found. If the product is found, the value in the product's price column is once again multiplied by the specified factor, and the INTEGER value 0 is returned.

```sql
CREATE FUNCTION update_product_price_func(

  p_product_id IN products.id%TYPE,
  p_factor     IN NUMBER

) RETURN INTEGER AS

  product_count INTEGER;

BEGIN

  SELECT
    COUNT(*)
  INTO
    product_count
  FROM
    products
  WHERE
    id = p_product_id;

  -- if the product doesn't exist then return 0,
  -- otherwise perform the update and return 1
  IF product_count = 0 THEN
    RETURN 0;
  ELSE
    UPDATE
      products
    SET
      price = price * p_factor;
    COMMIT;
    RETURN 1;
  END IF;

END update_product_price_func;
/
```

The main thing to note about this function is that it returns an `INTEGER` value whose value depends on whether or not the product was found. Apart from that, it operates in a similar manner to the `update_product_price()` procedure described earlier.

Packages

In this final section, I'll discuss how you may group procedures and functions together into *packages*, which allow you to encapsulate related functionality into one self-contained unit. By modularizing your PL/SQL code in such a manner, you can potentially build up your own libraries of code that other programmers could reuse—and, at the very least, your code might be more readable.

Packages are typically made up of two components: a *specification* and a *body*. The package specification contains information about the package, and it lists the available procedures and functions. These are potentially available to all database users, so I'll refer to these procedures and functions as being *public* (although only users who have the rights to access your package can use it). The specification generally doesn't contain the code that makes up those procedures and functions—the package body contains the actual code.

The procedures and functions listed in the specification are available to the outside world, but any procedures and functions only contained in the body are only available within that body—they are *private* to that body. By using a combination of public and private procedures and functions, you can build up very complex packages whose complexity is hidden from the outside world. This is one of the primary goals of all programming: hide complexity from your users.

Creating a Package Specification

To create a package specification, you use the `CREATE PACKAGE` statement. The syntax for the `CREATE PACKAGE` statement is as follows:

```
CREATE [OR REPLACE] PACKAGE package_name
{IS|AS}
package_specification;
```

The syntax elements are as follows:

- **package_name**   The name that you assign to the package

- **package_specification**   The list of procedures and functions (along with any variables, type definitions, and cursors) that are available to your package users

The following example creates a package specification for a package named
`ref_cursor_package`:

```
CREATE OR REPLACE PACKAGE ref_cursor_package AS

  TYPE t_ref_cursor IS REF CURSOR;
  FUNCTION get_products_ref_cursor RETURN t_ref_cursor;

END ref_cursor_package;
/
```

You'll notice that this package defines a type named `t_ref_cursor`. PL/SQL
enables you to create your own types. The type `t_ref_cursor` uses the PL/SQL
REF CURSOR type; a `REF CURSOR` is similar to a pointer in the C programming
language, and it basically points to rows retrieved from the database using a PL/SQL
cursor. In the next section, I'll use a `REF CURSOR` to point to the result set returned
by a `SELECT` statement that retrieves rows from the `products` table using a
PL/SQL cursor. This is done using the function `get_products_ref_cursor()`,
which returns a variable of type `t_ref_cursor`.

Creating a Package Body
To create a package body, you use the CREATE PACKAGE BODY statement. The
syntax for the CREATE PACKAGE BODY statement is as follows:

```
CREATE [OR REPLACE] PACKAGE BODY package_name
{IS|AS}
package_body;
```

The syntax elements are as follows:

- **package_name**   The name of your package, which must match
  the package name previously set in your package specification

- **package_body**   The code for the procedures and functions (along
  with any variables and cursors)

The following example creates the package body for `ref_cursor_package`:

```
CREATE PACKAGE BODY ref_cursor_package AS

  -- function get_products_ref_cursor() returns a REF CURSOR
  FUNCTION get_products_ref_cursor
  RETURN t_ref_cursor IS
```

```
        products_ref_cursor t_ref_cursor;

    BEGIN

      -- get the REF CURSOR
      OPEN products_ref_cursor FOR
        SELECT
          id, name, price
        FROM
          products;

      -- return the REF CURSOR
      RETURN products_ref_cursor;

    END get_products_ref_cursor;

END ref_cursor_package;
/
```

The `get_products_ref_cursor()` function opens a cursor and retrieves the `id`, `name`, and `price` columns from the `products` table The reference to this cursor (the REF CURSOR) is then returned by the function. This REF CURSOR may then be accessed to read the column values, and I'll show you how to do that using JDBC in Chapter 5.

You can also implement stored procedures and functions using Java, and I'll talk about that in Chapter 10.

CHAPTER
3

The Basics of JDBC Programming

n this chapter, I'll discuss the basics of JDBC programming—JDBC stands for *Java Database Connectivity*. First, I'll cover the details of the various Oracle JDBC drivers that may be used to connect to an Oracle database, then I'll get into the details of writing a JDBC program. These details include: importing the JDBC packages, registering the Oracle JDBC drivers, opening a database connection, and performing SQL DML statements to retrieve, add, modify, and delete rows from database tables.

I'll also cover how to use the various Java types to get and set column values in the database, including how to handle numbers and database NULL values in your Java programs. In addition, I'll show you how to perform transaction control statements and SQL DDL statements and how to handle database exceptions that may occur when your Java programs are run.

In the final part of this chapter, I'll introduce you to Oracle's extensions to JDBC, which allow you to gain access to all of the data types supported by an Oracle database. The Oracle extensions also contain a number of Oracle-specific performance enhancements.

Throughout this chapter, you'll see examples of JDBC and complete Java programs that illustrate the points covered.

Okay, let's dive in, starting with a discussion of the Oracle JDBC drivers.

The Oracle JDBC Drivers

In this section, I'll discuss the various Oracle JDBC drivers that enable the JDBC statements in a Java program to access an Oracle database. It is through a JDBC driver that your JDBC statements access a database. There are four Oracle JDBC drivers:

- Thin driver
- OCI driver
- Server-side internal driver
- Server-side Thin driver

The following sections describe each of these drivers in detail.

The Thin Driver

The Thin driver has the smallest footprint of all the drivers, meaning that it requires the least amount of system resources to run, and it is written entirely in Java. If you are writing a Java applet, you should use the Thin driver. The Thin driver may also be used in stand-alone Java applications and may be used to access all versions of the Oracle database. The Thin driver only works with TCP/IP and requires that Oracle Net be up and running; for details on Oracle Net, speak with your DBA or consult the Oracle Net documentation. The Thin driver is written entirely in Java and is known as a *type 4* driver. It uses the TTC protocol to communicate with the Oracle database.

NOTE
You don't have to install anything on the client computer to use the Thin driver and therefore you can use it for applets.

The OCI Driver

The OCI driver requires more resources than the Thin driver but generally has better performance than the Thin driver. The OCI driver is suitable for programs deployed on the middle tier—a web server, for example. You may not use the OCI driver in applets. The OCI driver is a *type 2* driver, meaning that it is not written in Java alone and contains code written in C.

NOTE
The OCI driver requires that you install it on the client computer and is therefore not suitable for applets.

The OCI driver has a number of additional performance enhancing features, including advanced connection pooling facilities. You'll learn more about performance tuning later in Part 4 of this book. The OCI driver replaces the older OCI7 and OCI8 drivers that were used to access Oracle7 and Oracle8/8*i* databases. If you have any programs that use those drivers, they will still work with Oracle9*i*, but they are depreciated, and so you should modify your programs to use the OCI driver instead. The OCI driver works with all versions of the database and works with all of the supported Oracle Net protocols.

The Server-Side Internal Driver

The server-side internal driver provides direct access to the database, and is used by the Oracle JVM to communicate with that database. As you'll learn in Chapter 10, the Oracle JVM is a Java Virtual Machine that is integrated with the database—you can load a Java class into the database, and then publish and run methods contained in that class using the Oracle JVM.

The Server-Side Thin Driver

The server-side Thin driver is also used by the Oracle JVM, and provides access to remote databases. Like the Thin driver, this driver is also written entirely in Java.

Importing the JDBC Packages

In order for your programs to use JDBC, you must import the required JDBC packages into your Java programs. There are two sets of JDBC packages: the standard JDBC packages from Sun Microsystems and Oracle's extension packages. The standard JDBC packages enable your Java programs to access the basic features of most databases, including the Oracle database, SQL Server, DB2, and MySQL. The Oracle extensions to JDBC enable your programs to access all of the Oracle specific features, as well as the Oracle specific performance extensions. I'll talk about some of the Oracle-specific features later in this chapter, and I'll talk about the Oracle performance extensions in Part 4. As this book progresses, I'll introduce you to more of the Oracle extensions.

To use JDBC in your programs you should import the `java.sql.*` packages, as shown in the following `import` statement:

```
import java.sql.*;
```

Of course, importing `java.sql.*` imports *all* of the standard JDBC packages. As you become proficient in JDBC, you'll find that you don't always need to import all the classes: you can just import those packages that your program actually uses.

Registering the Oracle JDBC Drivers

Before you can open a database connection, you must first register the Oracle JDBC drivers with your Java program. As I mentioned earlier, the JDBC drivers are the software "glue" that allow your JDBC statements to actually access the database.

There are two ways to register the Oracle JDBC drivers: the first is to use the `forName()` method of the class `java.lang.Class`, and the second is to use the `registerDriver()` method of the JDBC `DriverManager` class. The following example illustrates the use of the `forName()` method:

```
Class.forName("oracle.jdbc.OracleDriver");
```

The second way to register the Oracle JDBC drivers is to use the `registerDriver()` method of the `java.sql.DriverManager` class, as shown in the following example:

```
DriverManager.registerDriver(new oracle.jdbc.OracleDriver());
```

Once you have registered the Oracle JDBC drivers, you can open a connection to a database.

If you are using the Oracle8i JDBC drivers, you will need to import the `oracle.jdbc.driver.OracleDriver` class and then register an instance of that class:

```
import oracle.jdbc.driver.OracleDriver;

DriverManager.registerDriver(
  new oracle.jdbc.driver.OracleDriver()
);
```

NOTE
As of JDBC 2.0, a more standardized way of using the JDBC drivers is through data sources, which I'll discuss later in this chapter.

Opening a Database Connection

Before you can perform any SQL statements in your Java programs, you must first open a database connection. There are two main ways to open a database connection. The first way is to use the `getConnection()` method of the `DriverManager` class. The second way uses an Oracle data source object, which must first be created and then connected to. Using an Oracle data source employs a standardized way of setting database connection details, and an Oracle data source object may be used with the *Java Naming and Directory Interface* (JNDI). I'll discuss data sources and JNDI in Appendix D.

I'll describe both of these ways to open a database connection in the following sections, starting with the first way—which uses the `getConnection()` method of the `DriverManager` class.

Connecting to the Database Using the getConnection() Method of the DriverManager Class

The `getConnection()` method accepts three parameters: a database username, a password, and a database URL. The `getConnection()` method returns a JDBC `Connection` object, which should be stored in your program so it may be referenced later. The syntax of a call to the `getConnection()` method is as follows:

```
DriverManager.getConnection(URL, username, password);
```

The syntax elements are as follows:

- **URL**   This is the database that your program connects to, along with the JDBC driver you want to use. See the following section, "The Database URL," for details on the URL.

- **username**   This is the name of the database user that your program connects as.

- **password**   This is the password for the username.

The following example shows the get Connection() method being used to connect to a database:

```
Connection myConnection = DriverManager.getConnection(
    "jdbc:oracle:thin:@localhost:1521:ORCL",
    "store_user",
    "store_password"
);
```

In this example, the connection is made to a database running on the machine identified as localhost with an Oracle System Identifier (SID) of ORCL, using the Oracle JDBC Thin driver. The connection is made with the username store_user and the password store_password. The Connection object returned by the call to getConnection() is stored in myConnection. I'll use the Oracle JDBC Thin driver for most of the program examples in this book. The connection to a database is made through Oracle Net, which should be up and running.

The Database URL

The database URL specifies where the database your program connects to is located. The structure of the database URL is dependent on the vendor who provides the JDBC drivers. In the case of Oracle's JDBC drivers, the database URL structure is as follows:

```
driver_name:@driver_information
```

The syntax elements are as follows:

- **driver_name**   The name of the Oracle JDBC driver that your program uses. This may be set to one of the following:

  - **jdbc:oracle:thin**   The Oracle JDBC Thin driver

  - **jdbc:oracle:oci**   The Oracle JDBC OCI driver

  - **jdbc:oracle:oci8**   The Oracle JDBC OCI8 driver

  - **jdbc:oracle:oci7**   The Oracle JDBC OCI7 driver

■ **driver_information** The driver-specific information required to connect to the database. This is dependent on the driver being used. In the case of the Oracle JDBC Thin driver, the driver-specific information may be specified in the following format:

■ **host_name:port:database_SID** For the Oracle JDBC Thin driver

For all the Oracle JDBC drivers, including the Thin driver and the various OCI drivers, the driver-specific information may also be specified using Oracle Net keyword-value pairs, which may be specified in the following format:

```
(description=(address=(host=host_name)(protocol=tcp)(port=port))
(connect_data=(sid=database_SID)))
```

The syntax elements are as follows:

■ **host_name** The name of the machine on which the database is running.

■ **port** The port number on which the Oracle Net database listener waits for requests; 1521 is the default port number. Your DBA can provide the port number.

■ **database_SID** The Oracle SID of the database instance to which you want to connect. Your DBA can provide the database SID.

For the Oracle OCI driver, you may also use an Oracle Net TNSNAMES string (for more information on this, speak with your DBA or consult the Oracle documentation that describes Oracle Net).

The following example shows the getConnection() method being used to connect to a database using the Oracle OCI driver, with the driver-specific information specified using Oracle Net keyword-value pairs:

```
Connection myConnection = DriverManager.getConnection(
  "jdbc:oracle:oci:@(description=(address=(host=localhost)" +
    "(protocol=tcp)(port=1521))(connect_data=(sid=ORCL)))",
  "store_user",
  "store_password"
);
```

As you can see, in this example a connection is made to a database running on the machine identified as localhost, with an Oracle SID of ORCL, using the Oracle OCI driver. The connection to the database is made with the username store_user, with a password of store_password. The Connection object returned by the call to getConnection() is stored in myConnection.

Connecting to the Database Using an Oracle Data Source

You can also use an Oracle *data source* to connect to a database. An Oracle data source uses a more standardized way of supplying the various parameters to connect to a database than the previous method that used the DriverManager.getConnection() method. In addition, an Oracle data source may also be registered with JNDI. Using JNDI with JDBC is very useful because it allows you to register, or *bind*, data sources, and then *lookup* those data sources in your program without having to provide the exact database connection details. Thus, if the database connection details change, only the JNDI object must be changed. I'll discuss data sources and JNDI in Appendix D. Data sources are also used with connection pooling and caching, which are performance enhancing features that I'll cover in Chapter 12.

There are three steps that must be performed to use an Oracle data source:

1. Create an Oracle data source object of the oracle.jdbc.pool.OracleDataSource class.

2. Set the Oracle data source object attributes using the set methods.

3. Connect to the database via the Oracle data source object using the getConnection() method.

The following sections describe these three steps.

Step 1: Create an Oracle Data Source Object

The first step is to create an Oracle data source object of the oracle.jdbc.pool.OracleDataSource class. The following example creates an OracleDataSource object named myDataSource (you may assume that the oracle.jdbc.pool. OracleDataSource class has been imported):

```
OracleDataSource myDataSource = new OracleDataSource();
```

Once you have your OracleDataSource object, the second step is to set that object's attributes using the set methods.

Step 2: Set the Oracle Data Source Object Attributes

Before you can use your OracleDataSource object to connect to a database, you must set a number of attributes in that object to indicate the connection details using various set methods defined in the class. These details include items like the database name, the JDBC driver to use, and so on. Each one of these details has a corresponding attribute in an `OracleDataSource` object.

The `oracle.jdbc.pool.OracleDataSource` class actually implements the `javax.sql.DataSource` interface provided with JDBC. The `javax.sql.DataSource` interface defines a number of attributes, which are listed in Table 3-1. This table shows the name, description, and type of each attribute.

The `oracle.jdbc.pool.OracleDataSource` class provides an additional set of attributes, which are listed in Table 3-2.

You may use a number of methods to read from and write to each of the attributes listed in Tables 3-1 and 3-2. The methods that read from the attributes are known as *get* methods, and the methods that write to the attributes are known as *set* methods.

The set and get method names are easy to remember: take the attribute name, convert the first letter to uppercase, and add the word "set" or "get" to the beginning.

Attribute Name	Attribute Description	Attribute Type
databaseName	The database name (Oracle SID).	String
dataSourceName	The name of the underlying data source class.	String
description	Description of the of the data source.	String
networkProtocol	The network protocol to use to communicate with the database. This only applies to the Oracle JDBC OCI drivers, and defaults to "tcp". For further details, see the Oracle Net documentation provided by Oracle Corporation.	String
password	The password for the supplied username.	String
portNumber	The port on which the Oracle Net listener waits for database connection requests. The default is 1521. For further details, see the Oracle Net documentation.	int
derverName	The database server machine name (TCP/IP address or DNS alias).	String
user	The database username.	String

TABLE 3-1. *DataSource Attributes*

Attribute Name	Attribute Description	Attribute Type
driverType	The JDBC driver to use. If you are using the server-side internal driver, this is set to "kprb", and the other settings for the attributes are ignored.	String
url	May be used to specify an Oracle database URL, which can be used as an alternative to setting the database location. See the section earlier on database URLs for details.	String
tnsEntryName	May be used to specify an Oracle Net TNSNAMES string, which can also be used to specify the database location when using the OCI drivers.	String

TABLE 3-2. *OracleDataSource Attributes*

For example, to set the database name (stored in the databaseName attribute), you use the setDatabaseName() method; to get the name of the database currently set, you use the getDatabaseName() method. There is one exception to this: there is no getPassword() method that you can call; this is for security reasons—you don't want someone to be able to get your password programmatically!

Most of the attributes are Java String objects, so most of the set methods accept a single String parameter, and most of the get methods return a String. The exception to this is the portNumber attribute, which is an int. Therefore, its set method, setPortNumber(), accepts an int, and its get method, getPortNumber(), returns an int.

The following examples illustrate the use of the set methods to write to the attributes of the OracleDataSource object myDataSource that was created earlier in Step 1:

```
myDataSource.setServerName("localhost");
myDataSource.setDatabaseName("ORCL");
myDataSource.setDriverType("oci");
myDataSource.setNetworkProtocol("tcp");
myDataSource.setPortNumber(1521);
myDataSource.setUser("scott");
myDataSource.setPassword("tiger");
```

The next examples illustrate the use of some of the get methods to read the attributes previously set in myDataSource:

```
String serverName = myDataSource.getServerName();
String databaseName = myDataSource.getDatabaseName();
String driverType = myDataSource.getDriverType();
String networkProtocol = myDataSource.getNetworkProtocol();
int portNumber = myDataSource.getPortNumber();
```

Once you've set your OracleDataSource object attributes, you can use it to connect to the database.

Step 3: Connect to the Database via the Oracle Data Source Object

The third step is to connect to the database via the OracleDataSource object. You do this by calling the getConnection() method using your OracleDataSource object. The getConnection() method returns a JDBC Connection object, which must be stored.

The following example shows how to call the getConnection() method using the myDataSource object populated in the previous step:

```
Connection myConnection = myDataSource.getConnection();
```

The Connection object returned by getConnection() is stored in myConnection. You can also pass a username and password as parameters to the getConnection() method, as shown in the following example:

```
Connection myConnection = myDataSource.getConnection(
  "store_user", "store_password"
);
```

In this case, the username and password will override the username and password previously set in myDataSource. Therefore, the connection to the database will be made using the username of store_user with a password of store_password, rather than scott and tiger, which were previously set in myDataSource.

Once you have your Connection object, you can use it to create a JDBC Statement object.

Creating a JDBC Statement Object

Before you can issue SQL statements using JDBC, you need to create a JDBC Statement object of the class java.sql.Statement. A Statement object is used to represent a SQL statement, such as a DML statement (SELECT, INSERT,

UPDATE, or DELETE) or a DDL statement (such as CREATE TABLE). I will discuss issuing both DML and DDL statements later in this chapter.

To create a Statement object, you use the createStatement() method of a Connection object. In the following example, a Statement object named myStatement is created using the createStatement() method of the myConnection object that was created earlier:

```
Statement myStatement = myConnection.createStatement();
```

Depending on the SQL statement you want to perform, you will use a different method in the Statement class to run the SQL. If you want to perform a SELECT statement, you use the executeQuery() method. If you want to perform an INSERT, UPDATE, or DELETE statement, you use the executeUpdate() method. If you don't know ahead of time which type of SQL statement is to be performed, you can use the execute() method, which may be used to perform SELECT, INSERT, UPDATE, or DELETE statements. You may also use the execute() method to perform DDL statements, as I'll show you later in this chapter.

There is another JDBC class that may be used to represent a SQL statement: the PreparedStatement class. This offers more advanced functionality than the Statement class; I will defer discussion of the PreparedStatement class until after I have discussed the use of the Statement class.

Once you have a Statement object, you're ready to issue SQL statements using JDBC.

Retrieving Rows from the Database

As I discussed in the previous chapter, the SQL SELECT statement is used to retrieve information from the database. To perform a SELECT statement using JDBC, you should use the executeQuery() method of your Statement object, which accepts a Java String containing the text for the SELECT statement.

Now, because a SELECT statement may return more than one row, the executeQuery() method returns an object that stores the row(s) returned by your SELECT statement. This object is known as a JDBC *result set* and is of the java.sql.ResultSet class. When using a ResultSet object to read rows from the database, there are three steps you should follow:

1. Create a ResultSet object and populate it using a SELECT statement.

2. Read the column values from the ResultSet object using get methods.

3. Close the ResultSet object.

I will now walk you through an example that uses a `ResultSet` object to retrieve the rows from the `customers` table. This example will illustrate the use of these three steps.

Step 1: Create and Populate a ResultSet Object

You must first create a `ResultSet` object and populate it using a `SELECT` statement that retrieves the required rows from the database. The following example creates a `ResultSet` object named `customerResultSet` and populates it using a `SELECT` statement that retrieves the `id`, `first_name`, `last_name`, `dob`, and `phone` columns for each row in the `customers` table:

```
ResultSet customerResultSet = myStatement.executeQuery(
  "SELECT id, first_name, last_name, dob, phone " +
  "FROM customers"
);
```

Notice that this statement uses the `executeQuery()` method of the `myStatement` object. After this statement has been run, the `ResultSet` object will contain the column values for the rows retrieved by the `SELECT` statement. The `ResultSet` object may then be used to access the column values for the retrieved rows. In this example, `customerResultSet` will contain the five rows retrieved from the `customers` table. Of course, a `ResultSet` object may also be used to store one row.

Because the `executeQuery()` method accepts a Java `String`, you can build up your SQL statements when your program actually runs. This means that you can do some fairly powerful things in JDBC. For example, you could have the user of your program type in a string containing a `WHERE` clause for a `SELECT` statement when they run your program, or even enter the whole `SELECT` statement. The following example shows a `WHERE` clause being set and added to the query executed by another `ResultSet` object:

```
String whereClause = "WHERE id = 1";
ResultSet customerResultSet2 = myStatement.executeQuery(
  "SELECT id, first_name, last_name, dob, phone " +
  "FROM customers " +
  whereClause
);
```

You're not limited to building up `SELECT` statements dynamically: you can build up other SQL statements in a similar manner.

Step 2: Read the Column Values from the ResultSet Object

To read the column values for the rows stored in a `ResultSet` object, the `ResultSet` class provides a series of get methods. Before I get into the details of these get methods, you need to understand how the data types used to represent values in Oracle may be mapped to compatible Java data types.

Oracle and Java Types

In the previous chapter, I described the main types used by Oracle. These types may be used to define columns in a table and may also be used in PL/SQL programs. The Oracle types include the following:

- **CHAR** Stores fixed-length strings
- **VARCHAR2** Stores variable-length strings
- **DATE** Stores dates
- **INTEGER** Stores integer numbers
- **NUMBER** Stores floating-point numbers and may also be used to store integer numbers

A Java program, of course, uses a different set of types from the Oracle types to represent values. Fortunately, the types used by Oracle are compatible with certain Java types. This allows Java and Oracle to interchange data stored in their respective types. The following table shows one set of compatible type mappings:

Oracle Type	Java Type
CHAR	String
VARCHAR2	String
DATE	java.sql.Date java.sql.Time java.sql.Timestamp
INTEGER	short int long
NUMBER	float double java.math.BigDecimal

From this table, you can see that an Oracle `INTEGER` is compatible with a Java `int`. (I'll talk about the other numeric types later in this chapter in the section "Handling Numbers.") This means that the `id` column of the `customers` table (which is defined as an Oracle `INTEGER`) may be stored in a Java `int` variable. Similarly, the `first_name`, `last_name`, and `phone` column values may be stored in Java `String` variables.

The Oracle `DATE` type stores a year, month, day, hour, minute, and second. You may use a `java.sql.Date` object to store the date part of the `dob` column value and a `java.sql.Time` variable to store the time part. You may also use a `java.sql.Timestamp` object to store both the date and time parts of the `dob` column. Later in this chapter, I'll discuss the `oracle.sql.DATE` type, which is an Oracle extension to the JDBC standard and provides an alternative to storing dates and times.

The `id`, `first_name`, `last_name`, `dob`, and `phone` columns are retrieved by the `SELECT` statement in the previous section, and the following examples declare Java variables and objects that are compatible with those columns:

```
int id = 0;
String firstName = null;
String lastName = null;
java.sql.Date dob = null;
String phone = null;
```

The `int` and `String` types are part of the core Java language, while `java.sql.Date` is part of JDBC and is an extension of the core Java language. JDBC provides a number of such types that allow Java and a relational database to exchange data. However, JDBC doesn't cover types that handle all of the types used by Oracle, one example of which is the `ROWID` type described in the previous chapter—you must use the `oracle.sql.ROWID` type to store an Oracle `ROWID`.

To handle all of the Oracle types, Oracle provides a number of additional types, which are defined in the `oracle.sql` package. Also, Oracle has a number of types that may be used as an alternative to the core Java and JDBC types, and in some cases these alternatives offer more functionality and better performance than the core Java and JDBC types. I'll talk more about the Oracle types defined in the `oracle.sql` package later in this chapter.

The previous table only shows a subset of the compatible Java and Oracle type mappings. You can view the entire type mapping tables for Java and Oracle in Appendix A. That appendix covers the core Java types, the JDBC types, and the Oracle-specific types.

Now that you understand a little bit about compatible Java and Oracle types, let's continue with the discussion on using the get methods to read column values.

Using the Get Methods to Read Column Values

As I mentioned earlier, the get methods are used to read values stored in a
ResultSet object. The name of each get method is simple to understand: take the
name of the Java type you want the column value to be retuned as and add the
word "get" to the beginning. For example, use getInt() to read a column value
as a Java int, and use getString() to read a column value as a Java String.
To read the value as a java.sql.Date, you would use getDate(). Each get
method accepts one parameter: an int representing the position of the column in
the original SELECT statement, or a String containing the name of the column.
Let's examine some examples based on the earlier example that retrieved the
columns from the customers table in the customerResultSet object.

To get the value of the id column, which was the first column specified in the
earlier SELECT statement, you use getInt(1). You can also use the name of
the column in the get method, so you could also use getInt("id") to get the
same value.

TIP
*Using the column name rather than the column
position number in a get method makes your code
easier to read.*

To get the value of the first_name column, which was the second
column specified in the earlier SELECT statement, you use getString(2) or
getString("first_name"). You use similar method calls to get the last_name
and phone column values because those columns are also text strings. To get the
value of the dob column, you could use getDate(4) or getDate("dob").

To actually read the values stored in a ResultSet object, you must call the
get methods using that ResultSet object. Table C-1 in Appendix C shows all of
the get methods for a ResultSet object.

Because a ResultSet object may contain more than one row, JDBC provides
a method named next() that allows you to step through each row stored in a
ResultSet object. You must call the next() method to access the first row in
the ResultSet object, and each successive call to next() steps to the next row.
When there are no more rows in the ResultSet object to read, the next()
method returns the Boolean false value.

Okay, let's get back to our example: we have a ResultSet object named
customerResultSet that has five rows containing the column values retrieved
from the id, first_name, last_name, dob, and phone columns in the
customers table. The following example shows a while loop which reads the

column values from `customerResultSet` into the `id`, `firstName`, `lastName`, `dob`, and `phone` variables and objects created earlier, the contents of which are displayed:

```
while (customerResultSet.next()) {
   id = customerResultSet.getInt("id");
   firstName = customerResultSet.getString("first_name");
   lastName = customerResultSet.getString("last_name");
   dob = customerResultSet.getDate("dob");
   phone = customerResultSet.getString("phone");

   System.out.println("id = " + id);
   System.out.println("firstName = " + firstName);
   System.out.println("lastName = " + lastName);
   System.out.println("dob = " + dob);
   System.out.println("phone = " + phone);
} // end of while loop
```

When there are no more rows to read from `customerResultSet`, the `next()` method returns `false` and the loop terminates. You'll notice that the example passes the name of the column to be read to the get methods, rather than numeric positions. Also, I've copied the column values into Java variables and objects; for example, the value returned from `customerResultSet.getInt("id")` is copied to `id`, for example. You don't have to do that copy: you could simply use the get method call whenever you need the value. However, it is generally better if you copy it to a Java variable or object because it will save time if you use that value more than once, and it makes your code more readable.

Step 3: Close the ResultSet Object

Once you've finished with your `ResultSet` object, you must close that `ResultSet` object using the `close()` method. The following example closes `customerResultSet`:

```
customerResultSet.close();
```

> **NOTE**
> *It is important that you remember to close your*
> *ResultSet object once you've finished with it; this*
> *ensures that it is scheduled for garbage collection.*

Now that you've seen how to retrieve rows, I will now show you how to add rows to a database table using JDBC.

Adding Rows to the Database

As you saw in the previous chapter, you use the SQL INSERT statement to add rows to a table. There are two main ways you can perform an INSERT statement using JDBC:

- Use the executeUpdate() method defined in the Statement class.

- Use the execute() method defined in the PreparedStatement class. (I will discuss this class later in this chapter.)

The examples in this section illustrate how to add a row to the customers table. The id, first_name, last_name, dob, and phone columns for this new row will be set to 6; Jason; Price; February 1, 1969; and 800-555-1216, respectively.

To add this new row, I'll use the same Statement object declared earlier (myStatement), along with the same variables and objects that were used to retrieve the rows from the customers table in the previous section. First off, I'll set those variables and objects to the values that I want to set the database columns to in the customers table:

```
id = 6;
firstName = "Jason";
lastName = "Price";
dob = new java.sql.Date(69, 1, 1);
phone = "800-555-1216";
```

NOTE
Month numbers start at 0 and therefore the month of 1 is February.

When you attempt to specify a date in a SQL statement, you should convert it to a format that Oracle can understand using the TO_DATE() built-in Oracle function. TO_DATE() accepts a string containing a date, along with the format for that date. You'll see the use of the TO_DATE() function in the following example. In fact, you don't even need to use a java.sql.Date object to represent a date: you could just use a Java String containing the appropriate information. Later in this chapter, I'll discuss the Oracle JDBC extensions, and you'll see an additional—and superior—way of representing Oracle specific dates using the oracle.sql.DATE type.

Okay, we're ready to perform an INSERT to add the new row to the customers table. The myStatement object is used to perform the INSERT statement, setting the id, first_name, last_name, dob, and phone column values equal to the values previously set in id, firstName, lastName, dob, and phone:

```
myStatement.executeUpdate(
  "INSERT INTO customers " +
  "(id, first_name, last_name, dob, phone) VALUES (" +
  id + ", '" + firstName + "', '" + lastName + "', " +
  "TO_DATE('" + dob + "', 'YYYY, MM, DD'), '" + phone + "')"
);
```

Notice the use of the TO_DATE() function to convert the contents of the dob object to an acceptable Oracle date. Once this statement has completed, the customers table will contain the new row.

Modifying Rows in the Database

You use the SQL UPDATE statement to modify existing rows in a table. Just as with performing an INSERT statement with JDBC, you can use the executeUpdate() method defined in the Statement class or the execute() method defined in the PreparedStatement class. Use of the PreparedStatement class is covered later in this chapter.

The following example illustrates how to modify the row in the customers table where the id column is equal to 1:

```
first_name = "Jean";
myStatement.executeUpdate(
  "UPDATE customers " +
  "SET first_name = '" + firstName + "' " +
  "WHERE id = 1"
);
```

Once this statement has completed, customer #1's first name will be set to "Jean".

Deleting Rows from the Database

You use the SQL DELETE statement to delete existing rows from a table. You can use the executeUpdate() method defined in the Statement class or the execute() method defined in the PreparedStatement class.

The following example illustrates how to delete customer #5 from the customers table:

```
myStatement.executeUpdate(
  "DELETE FROM customers " +
  "WHERE id = 5"
);
```

Once this statement has completed, the row for customer #5 will have been removed from the `customers` table.

Handling Numbers

This section describes the issues associated with storing numbers in your Java programs. You learned in the previous chapter that Oracle is capable of storing numbers with a precision of up to 38 digits. In the context of number representation, precision refers to the accuracy with which a floating-point number may be represented in a digital computer's memory. The 38 digits of precision offered by Oracle enables you to store very large numbers in the database.

That's fine when working with numbers in the database, but as you have seen, Java uses its own set of types to represent numbers. Therefore, you must be careful when selecting the Java type that will be used to represent numbers in your programs—especially if those numbers are going to be stored in a database.

To store integers in your Java program, you can use the `short`, `int`, `long`, or `java.math.BigInteger` types, depending on how big the integer you want to store is and how much memory space you want to use. The following table shows the number of bits used to store `short`, `int`, and `long` types, along with the low and high values supported by each type:

Type	Bits	Low Value	High Value
short	16	−32768	32767
int	32	−2147483648	2147483647
long	64	−9223372036854775808	9223372036854775807

To store floating-point numbers in your Java programs, you can use the `float`, `double`, or `java.math.BigDecimal` types. The following table shows the same columns as the previous table for the `float` and `double` types, along with the precision supported by each of these types:

Type	Bits	Low Value	High Value	Precision
float	32	−3.4E+38	3.4E+38	6 digits
double	64	−1.7E+308	1.7E+308	15 digits

As you can see, a `float` may be used to store floating-point numbers with a precision of up to six digits, and a `double` may used for floating-point numbers with a precision of up to 15 digits. If you have a floating-point number that requires more than 15 digits of precision for storage in your Java program, you can use the `java.math.BigDecimal` type; this type can store an arbitrarily long floating-point number.

In addition to these types, you can also use the Oracle JDBC extension type
`oracle.sql.NUMBER`; this type allows you to store numbers with up to 38 digits
of precision. I'll talk more about the `oracle.sql.NUMBER` type later in this chapter.

Let's take a look at some examples of using the various integer and floating-point
types to store the `id` and `price` column values for a row retrieved from the
`products` table. Assume that a `ResultSet` object named `productResultSet`
has been populated with the `id` and `price` columns for a row from the `products`
table. The `id` column is defined as a database `INTEGER`, and the `price` column
is defined as a `NUMBER`. The following examples create variables of the various
integer and floating-point types and retrieve the `id` and `price` column values into
those variables:

```
short idShort = productResultSet.getShort("id");
int idInt = productResultSet.getInt("id");
long idLong = productResultSet.getLong("id");
float priceFloat = productResultSet.getFloat("price");
double priceDouble = productResultSet.getDouble("price");
java.math.BigDecimal priceBigDec =
  productResultSet.getBigDecimal("price");
```

Notice the use of the different get methods to retrieve the column values as
the different types, the output of which is then stored in a Java variable of the
appropriate type.

Handling Database Null Values

In the previous chapter, I described how columns in a database table may be defined
as being `NULL` or `NOT NULL`. `NULL` indicates that the column may store a `NULL`
value; `NOT NULL` indicates that the column cannot contain a `NULL` value. A `NULL`
value means that the value is unknown. When a table is created in the database
and you don't specify that a column is `NULL` or `NOT NULL`, Oracle assumes you
mean `NULL`.

The Java object types, such as `String`, may be used to store database `NULL`
values. When a `SELECT` statement is used to retrieve a column that contains a
`NULL` value into a Java `String`, that `String` will contain a Java `null` value.
For example, the phone column (defined as a `VARCHAR2`) for customer #5 is `NULL`,
and the following statement uses the `getString()` method to read that value
into a `String` named phone:

```
phone = customerResultSet.getString("phone");
```

Once the statement is run, the phone Java `String` will contain the Java
`null` value.

That's fine for NULL values being stored in Java objects, but what about the Java numeric, logical, and bit type types? If you retrieve a NULL value into a Java numeric, logical, or bit variable—int, float, boolean, and byte, for example—that variable will contain the value zero. To the database, zero and NULL are different values: zero is a definite value, NULL means the value is unknown. This causes a problem if you want to differentiate between zero and NULL in your Java program.

There are two ways to get around this problem:

■ You can use the wasNull() method in the ResultSet. The wasNull() method returns true if the value retrieved from the database was NULL; otherwise, the method returns false.

■ You can use a Java *wrapper class*. A wrapper class is a Java class that allows you to define a *wrapper object*, which can then be used to store the column value returned from the database. A wrapper object stores database NULL values as Java null values, and non-NULL values are stored as regular values.

Let's take a look at an example that illustrates the use of first technique, using product #12 from the products table. This row has a NULL value in the type_id column, and this column is defined as a database INTEGER. Also, assume that a ResultSet object named productResultSet has been populated with the id and type_id columns for product #12 from the products table. The following example uses the wasNull() method to check if the value read for the type_id column was NULL:

```
System.out.println("id = " + productResultSet.getInt("id"));
System.out.println("type_id = " + productResultSet.getInt("type_id"));
if (productResultSet.wasNull()) {
  System.out.println("Last value read was NULL");
}
```

Because the type_id column contains a NULL value, wasNull() will return true, so the string "Last value was NULL" would be displayed for that row.

Before I show you an example of the second method that uses the Java wrapper classes, I need to explain what these classes actually are. The wrapper classes are defined in the java.lang package, with the following seven wrapper classes being defined in that package:

■ java.lang.Short

■ java.lang.Integer

- `java.lang.Long`

- `java.lang.Float`

- `java.lang.Double`

- `java.lang.Boolean`

- `java.lang.Byte`

Objects declared using these wrapper classes may be used to represent database NULL values for the various types of numbers, as well as for the `Boolean` type. When a database NULL is retrieved into a wrapper object, it will contain the Java null value. The following example declares a `java.lang.Integer` named `typeId`:

```
java.lang.Integer typeId;
```

A database NULL may then be stored in `typeId` using a call to the `getObject()` method, as shown in the following example:

```
typeId = (java.lang.Integer) productResultSet.getObject("type_id");
```

The `getObject()` method returns an instance of the `java.lang.Object` class and must be cast into an appropriate type, in this case, to a `java.lang.Integer`. Assuming this example reads the same row from `productResultSet` as the previous example, `getObject()` will return a Java null value, and this value will be copied into `typeId`. Of course, if the value retrieved from the database had a value other than NULL, `typeId` would contain that value; for example, if the value retrieved from the database was 1, then `typeId` would contain the value 1.

You can also use a wrapper object in a JDBC statement that performs an INSERT or UPDATE to set a column to a regular value or a NULL value. If you want to set a column value to NULL using a wrapper object, you would set that wrapper object to null and use it in an INSERT or UPDATE statement to set the database column to NULL. For example, the following statement sets the `price` column for product #12 to NULL using a `java.lang.Double` object that is set to null:

```
java.lang.Double price = null;
myStatement.executeUpdate(
  "UPDATE products " +
  "SET price = " + price + " " +
  "WHERE id = 12"
);
```

Controlling Database Transactions

In the previous chapter, I explained the concept of database transactions and how to use the SQL COMMIT statement to permanently record the results of any INSERT, UPDATE, and DELETE statements you issue. I also showed you how to use the ROLLBACK statement to undo any changes made to table rows in a database transaction. The same concepts apply to SQL statements executed using JDBC.

By default, the results of your INSERT, UPDATE, and DELETE statements executed using JDBC are immediately committed. This is known as *auto-commit* mode.

NOTE
Generally, using auto-commit mode is not the preferred way of committing changes because it is counter to the idea of considering transactions as logical units of work. With auto-commit mode, all statements are considered as individual transactions, and this is usually an incorrect assumption. Also, auto-commit mode may cause your SQL statements to take longer to complete, due to the fact that each statement is always committed.

Fortunately, you can enable or disable auto-commit mode using the setAutoCommit() method of the Connection class, passing it a Boolean true or false value. The following example disables auto-commit mode for the Connection object named myConnection, which was created earlier:

```
myConnection.setAutoCommit(false);
```

Should you wish to, you can enable auto-commit mode using setAutoCommit(true). Once auto-commit has been disabled, you can commit your transaction changes using the commit() method of the Connection class, or you can rollback your changes using the rollback() method. In the following example, the commit() method is used to commit any changes made to the database using the myConnection object:

```
myConnection.commit();
```

In the next example, the rollback() method is used to rollback any changes made to the database:

```
myConnection.rollback();
```

If auto-commit has been disabled and you close your `Connection` object, an implicit commit is performed. Therefore, any DML statements you have performed up to that point and haven't already committed will be committed automatically.

Performing Data Definition Language Statements

As I discussed in the previous chapter, the SQL Data Definition Language (DDL) statements are used to create database users, tables, and many other types of structures that make up a database. DDL consists of statements such as `CREATE USER`, `ALTER USER`, `CREATE TABLE`, `ALTER TABLE`, `DROP TABLE`, and so on.

Performing DDL statements using JDBC may be performed using the `execute()` method of the `Statement` class. In the following example, the `CREATE TABLE` statement is used to create a table named `addresses`, which may be used to store customer addresses:

```
myStatement.execute(
  "CREATE TABLE addresses (" +
  "  id INTEGER CONSTRAINT addresses_pk PRIMARY KEY," +
  "  customer_id INTEGER CONSTRAINT addresses_fk_customers " +
  "    REFERENCES customers(id)," +
  "  street VARCHAR2(20) NOT NULL," +
  "  city VARCHAR2(20) NOT NULL," +
  "  state CHAR(2) NOT NULL" +
  ")"
);
```

As I also mentioned in the previous chapter, performing a DDL statement results in an implicit commit being issued. Therefore, if you've performed any noncommitted DML statements prior to a issuing DDL statement, then those DML statements will also be committed.

Handling Exceptions

As you learned in Chapter 1, when an error occurs in either the database or the JDBC driver, a `java.sql.SQLException` will be raised. The `java.sql.SQLException` class is a subclass of the `java.lang.Exception` class. For this reason, you must either place all your JDBC statements within a `try/catch` statement, or your code must throw a `java.sql.SQLException`. When such an exception occurs, Java attempts to locate the appropriate handler to process the exception.

If you include a handler for a `java.sql.SQLException` in a `catch` clause, then, when an error occurs in either the database or the JDBC driver, Java will move to that handler and run the appropriate code that you've included in that `catch` clause. In this code, you can do things like display the error code and error message, which will help you determine what caused the error.

The following `try/catch` statement contains a handler for any `java.sql.SQLExceptions` that may occur in the try statement:

```
try {
    ...
} catch (SQLException e) {
    ...
}
```

The `try` statement will contain your JDBC statements that may cause a `java.sql.SQLException`, and the `catch` clause will contain your error handling code.

The `java.sql.SQLException` class defines four methods that are useful for finding out what caused the exception to occur:

- **getErrorCode()**   In the case of errors that occur in the database or the JDBC driver, this method returns the Oracle error code, which is a five-digit number.

- **getMessage()**   In the case of errors that occur in the database, this method returns the error message, along with the five-digit Oracle error code. In the case of errors that occur in the JDBC driver, this method returns just the error message.

- **getSQLState()**   In the case of errors that occur in the database, this method returns a five-digit code containing the SQL state. In the case of errors that occur in the JDBC driver, this method doesn't return anything of interest.

- **printStackTrace ()**   This method displays the contents of the stack when the exception occurred. This information may further assist you in finding out what went wrong.

The following `try/catch` statement illustrates the use of these four methods:

```
try {
    ...
} catch (SQLException e) {

    System.out.println("Error code = " + e.getErrorCode());
    System.out.println("Error message = " + e.getMessage());
    System.out.println("SQL state = " + e.getSQLState());
    e.printStackTrace();

}
```

If your code throws a java.sql.SQLException, rather than handling it locally as just shown, Java will search for an appropriate handler in the calling procedure or function until one is found. If none are found, the exception will be handled by the default exception handler, which displays the Oracle error code, the error message, and the stack trace.

Closing Your JDBC Objects

In the examples shown in this chapter, I've created a number of JDBC objects: a Connection object named myConnection, a Statement object named myStatement, and two ResultSet objects named customerResultSet and productResultSet. As I mentioned earlier in the section on result sets, ResultSet objects should be closed when they are no longer needed using the close() method. Similarly, you should also close any Statement and Connection objects when those objects are no longer needed.

In the following example, the myStatement and myConnection objects are closed using the close() method:

```
myStatement.close();
myConnection.close();
```

 Generally, you should close your Statement and Connection objects in a finally clause. Any code contained in a finally clause is guaranteed to be run, no matter how control leaves the try statement. If you want to add a finally clause to close your Statement and Connection objects, those objects should be declared before the first try/catch statement used to trap exceptions. The following example shows how to structure the main() method so that the Statement and Connection objects may be closed in a finally clause:

```
public static void main (String args []) {

  // declare Connection and Statement objects
  Connection myConnection = null;
  Statement myStatement = null;

  try {

    // register the Oracle JDBC drivers
    DriverManager.registerDriver(
      new oracle.jdbc.driver.OracleDriver()
    );

    // connect to the database as store_user
    // using the Oracle JDBC Thin driver
```

```
    myConnection = DriverManager.getConnection(
      "jdbc:oracle:thin:@localhost:1521:ORCL",
      "store_user",
      "store_password"
    );

    // create a Statement object
    myStatement = myConnection.createStatement();

    // more of your code goes here
    ...

  } catch (SQLException e) {
    e.printStackTrace();
  } finally {

    try {

      // close the Statement object using the close() method
      if (myStatement != null) {
        myStatement.close();
      }

      // close the Connection object using the close() method
      if (myConnection != null) {
        myConnection.close();
      }

    } catch (SQLException e) {
      e.printStackTrace();
    }

  }
} // end of main()
```

Notice that the code in the `finally` clause checks to see if the `Statement` and `Connection` objects are not equal to `null` before closing them using the `close()` method. If they are equal to `null`, there is no need to close them. Because the code in the `finally` clause is the last thing to be run and is guaranteed to be run, the `Statement` and `Connection` objects are always closed if required, regardless of what else happens in your program. You should use this technique in your own programs. For the sake of brevity, only the first two programs featured in this book use a `finally` clause to close the `Statement` and `Connection` objects.

You have learned how to write JDBC statements that connect to a database, run DML and DDL statements, control transactions, handle exceptions, and close JDBC objects. The following section contains a complete program that illustrates the use of these aspects of JDBC.

Example Program: BasicExample1.java

The program `BasicExample1.java`, shown in the following listing, is a complete Java program that uses JDBC to access the database tables owned by `store_user`. This program, like all the other programs used in this book, may be downloaded from this book's website. The program performs the following tasks:

1. Imports the JDBC packages

2. Registers the Oracle JDBC drivers

3. Creates `Connection` and `Statement` objects

4. Connects to the database as the `store_user` database user using the Oracle JDBC Thin driver

5. Adds a new row to the `customers` table using an `INSERT` statement

6. Updates customer #1's first name using an `UPDATE` statement

7. Deletes customer #5 using a `DELETE` statement

8. Creates and populates a `ResultSet` object using a `SELECT` statement that retrieves the column values for all the rows from the `customers` table

9. Reads the values from the `ResultSet` object using the get methods and stores those values for subsequent display

10. Closes that `ResultSet` object

11. Performs a rollback to undo the changes made to the `customers` table

12. Creates and populates another `ResultSet` object with the id, type_id, and `price` columns for product #12 (which has a database `NULL` value in the type_id column) retrieved from the `products` table

13. Reads and displays the column values for that product using the get methods, checks the type_id column using the `wasNull()` method, stores the value for the type_id column in a `java.lang.Integer` wrapper object (wrapper objects store database `NULL` values as Java `null` values), and uses various numeric variables to retrieve and display the id and `price` column values

14. Closes that `ResultSet` object

15. Creates a new table named `addresses` using the SQL DDL `CREATE TABLE` statement

16. Drops the `addresses` table using the `DROP TABLE` statement

17. Closes the `Statement` and `Connection` objects in a `finally` clause

```java
/*
  BasicExample1.java shows how to:
  - import the JDBC packages
  - load the Oracle JDBC drivers
  - connect to a database
  - perform DML statements
  - control transactions
  - use ResultSet objects to retrieve rows
  - use the get methods
  - perform DDL statements
*/

// import the JDBC packages
import java.sql.*;

public class BasicExample1 {

  public static void main (String args []) {

    // declare Connection and Statement objects
    Connection myConnection = null;
    Statement myStatement = null;

    try {

      // register the Oracle JDBC drivers
      DriverManager.registerDriver(
        new oracle.jdbc.OracleDriver()
      );

      // create a Connection object, and connect to the database
      // as store_user using the Oracle JDBC Thin driver
      myConnection = DriverManager.getConnection(
        "jdbc:oracle:thin:@localhost:1521:ORCL",
        "store_user",
        "store_password"
      );

      // disable auto-commit mode
      myConnection.setAutoCommit(false);

      // create a Statement object
      myStatement = myConnection.createStatement();
```

```java
// create variables and objects used to represent
// column values
int id = 6;
String firstName = "Jason";
String lastName = "Red";
java.sql.Date dob = new java.sql.Date(69, 1, 1);
java.sql.Time dobTime;
java.sql.Timestamp dobTimestamp;
String phone = "800-555-1216";

// perform SQL INSERT statement to add a new row to the
// customers table using the values set in the previous
// step - the executeUpdate() method of the Statement
// object is used to perform the INSERT
myStatement.executeUpdate(
  "INSERT INTO customers " +
  "(id, first_name, last_name, dob, phone) VALUES (" +
  id + ", '" + firstName + "', '" + lastName + "', " +
  "TO_DATE('" + dob + "', 'YYYY, MM, DD'), '" + phone + "')"
);
System.out.println("Added row to customers table");

// perform SQL UPDATE statement to modify the first_name
// column of customer #1
firstName = "Jean";
myStatement.executeUpdate(
  "UPDATE customers " +
  "SET first_name = '" + firstName + "' " +
  "WHERE id = 1"
);
System.out.println("Updated row in customers table");

// perform SQL DELETE statement to remove customer #5
myStatement.executeUpdate(
  "DELETE FROM customers " +
  "WHERE id = 5"
);
System.out.println("Deleted row row from customers table");

// create a ResultSet object, and populate it with the
// result of a SELECT statement that retrieves the
// id, first_name, last_name, dob, and phone columns
// for all the rows from the customers table  - the
// executeQuery() method of the Statement object is used
// to perform the SELECT
ResultSet customerResultSet = myStatement.executeQuery(
```

```
    "SELECT id, first_name, last_name, dob, phone " +
    "FROM customers"
  );
  System.out.println("Retrieved rows from customers table");

  // loop through the rows in the ResultSet object using the
  // next() method, and use the get methods to read the values
  // retrieved from the database columns
  while (customerResultSet.next()) {
    id = customerResultSet.getInt("id");
    firstName = customerResultSet.getString("first_name");
    lastName = customerResultSet.getString("last_name");
    dob = customerResultSet.getDate("dob");
    dobTime = customerResultSet.getTime("dob");
    dobTimestamp = customerResultSet.getTimestamp("dob");
    phone = customerResultSet.getString("phone");

    System.out.println("id = " + id);
    System.out.println("firstName = " + firstName);
    System.out.println("lastName = " + lastName);
    System.out.println("dob = " + dob);
    System.out.println("dobTime = " + dobTime);
    System.out.println("dobTimestamp = " + dobTimestamp);
    System.out.println("phone = " + phone);
  } // end of while loop

  // close this ResultSet object using the close() method
  customerResultSet.close();

  // rollback the changes made to the database
  myConnection.rollback();

  // create numeric variables to store the id and price columns
  short idShort;
  int idInt;
  long idLong;
  float priceFloat;
  double priceDouble;
  java.math.BigDecimal priceBigDec;

  // create another ResultSet object and retrieve the
  // id, type_id, and price columns for product #12 - this row
  // has a NULL value in the type_id column
  ResultSet productResultSet = myStatement.executeQuery(
    "SELECT id, type_id, price " +
    "FROM products " +
    "WHERE id = 12"
  );
  System.out.println("Retrieved row from products table");
```

```java
while (productResultSet.next()) {
  System.out.println("id = " + productResultSet.getInt("id"));
  System.out.println("type_id = " + productResultSet.getInt("type_id"));

  // check if the value just read by the get method was NULL
  if (productResultSet.wasNull()) {
    System.out.println("Last value read was NULL");
  }

  // use the getObject() method to read the value, and convert it
  // to a wrapper object - this converts a database NULL value to a
  // Java null value
  java.lang.Integer typeId =
    (java.lang.Integer) productResultSet.getObject("type_id");
  System.out.println("typeId = " + typeId);

  // retrieve the id and price column values into
  // the various numeric variables created earlier
  idShort = productResultSet.getShort("id");
  idInt = productResultSet.getInt("id");
  idLong = productResultSet.getLong("id");
  priceFloat = productResultSet.getFloat("price");
  priceDouble = productResultSet.getDouble("price");
  priceBigDec = productResultSet.getBigDecimal("price");
  System.out.println("idShort = " + idShort);
  System.out.println("idInt = " + idInt);
  System.out.println("idLong = " + idLong);
  System.out.println("priceFloat = " + priceFloat);
  System.out.println("priceDouble = " + priceDouble);
  System.out.println("priceBigDec = " + priceBigDec);
} // end of while loop

// close this ResultSet object
productResultSet.close();

// perform a SQL DDL CREATE TABLE statement to create a new table
// that may be used to store customer addresses
myStatement.execute(
  "CREATE TABLE addresses (" +
  "  id INTEGER CONSTRAINT addresses_pk PRIMARY KEY," +
  "  customer_id INTEGER CONSTRAINT addresses_fk_customers " +
  "    REFERENCES customers(id)," +
  "  street VARCHAR2(20) NOT NULL," +
  "  city VARCHAR2(20) NOT NULL," +
  "  state CHAR(2) NOT NULL" +
  ")"
);
```

```
    System.out.println("Created addresses table");

    // drop this table using the SQL DDL DROP TABLE statement
    myStatement.execute("DROP TABLE addresses");
    System.out.println("Dropped addresses table");

  } catch (SQLException e) {

    System.out.println("Error code = " + e.getErrorCode());
    System.out.println("Error message = " + e.getMessage());
    System.out.println("SQL state = " + e.getSQLState());
    e.printStackTrace();

  } finally {

    try {

      // close the Statement object using the close() method
      if (myStatement != null) {
        myStatement.close();
      }

      // close the Connection object using the close() method
      if (myConnection != null) {
        myConnection.close();
      }

    } catch (SQLException e) {
      e.printStackTrace();
    }

  }
 } // end of main()
}
```

To compile `BasicExample1.java`, type the following command at your operating system command prompt:

```
javac BasicExample1.java
```

Once this command has completed, you can run the resulting executable class file named `BasicExample1.class` using the following command:

```
java BasicExample1
```

You should get the following output:

```
Added row to customers table
Updated row in customers table
Deleted row row from customers table
Retrieved rows from customers table
id = 1
firstName = Jean
lastName = Brown
dob = 1965-01-01
dobTime = 00:00:00
dobTimestamp = 1965-01-01 00:00:00.0
phone = 800-555-1211
id = 2
firstName = Cynthia
lastName = Green
dob = 1968-02-05
dobTime = 00:00:00
dobTimestamp = 1968-02-05 00:00:00.0
phone = 800-555-1212
id = 3
firstName = Steve
lastName = White
dob = 1971-03-16
dobTime = 00:00:00
dobTimestamp = 1971-03-16 00:00:00.0
phone = 800-555-1213
id = 4
firstName = Gail
lastName = Black
dob = null
dobTime = null
dobTimestamp = null
phone = 800-555-1214
id = 6
firstName = Jason
lastName = Red
dob = 1969-02-01
dobTime = 00:00:00
dobTimestamp = 1969-02-01 00:00:00.0
phone = 800-555-1216
Retrieved row from products table
id = 12
type_id = 0
Last value read was NULL
```

```
typeId = null
idShort = 12
idInt = 12
idLong = 12
priceFloat = 13.49
priceDouble = 13.49
priceBigDec = 13.49
Created addresses table
Dropped addresses table
```

Prepared SQL Statements

When you send a SQL statement to the database, the database software reads the SQL statement and verifies that it is correct. This is known as *parsing* the SQL statement. The database software then builds a plan, known as the *execution plan*, to actually run the statement. So far, all the SQL statements sent to the database through JDBC have required a new execution plan to be built; this is because each SQL statement sent to the database has been different.

Suppose you had a Java application that was performing the same INSERT statement repeatedly—an example might be loading many new products to our example store, a process that would require adding lots of rows to the products table using INSERT statements. Let's consider an example that would actually do this. Assume that a class named Product has been defined as follows:

```
class Product {
  int id;
  int typeId;
  String name;
  String description;
  double price;
}
```

The following code creates an array of five Product objects. Because the products table already contains rows with id values from 1 to 12, the id attributes of the Product objects start at 13:

```
Product [] productArray = new Product[5];
for (int counter = 0; counter < productArray.length; counter ++) {
  productArray[counter] = new Product();
  productArray[counter].id = counter + 13;
  productArray[counter].typeId = 1;
  productArray[counter].name = "Test product";
  productArray[counter].description = "Test product";
  productArray[counter].price = 19.95;
} // end of for loop
```

To add the rows to the `products` table, we'll use a `for` loop that contains a JDBC statement to perform an `INSERT` statement, and the column values will come from `productArray`:

```
Statement myStatement = myConnection.createStatement();
for (int counter = 0; counter < productArray.length; counter ++) {
  myStatement.executeUpdate(
    "INSERT INTO products " +
    "(id, type_id, name, description, price) VALUES (" +
    productArray[counter].id + ", " +
    productArray[counter].typeId + ", '" +
    productArray[counter].name + "', '" +
    productArray[counter].description + "', " +
    productArray[counter].price + ")"
  );
} // end of for loop
```

Each iteration through the loop results in an `INSERT` statement being sent to the database. Because the string representing each `INSERT` statement contains different values, the actual `INSERT` sent to the database is slightly different each time. This means that the database creates a different execution plan for every `INSERT` statement—very inefficient.

You'll be glad to know that JDBC provides a better way to run such SQL statements. Instead of a using a JDBC `Statement` object to run your SQL statements, you can use a JDBC `PreparedStatement` object. A `PreparedStatement` object allows you to perform the same basic SQL statement but supply different values for actual execution of that statement. This is more efficient because the same execution plan is used by the database when the SQL statement is run. The following example creates a `PreparedStatement` object containing an `INSERT` statement similar to the one used in the previous loop:

```
PreparedStatement myPrepStatement = myConnection.prepareStatement(
  "INSERT INTO products " +
  "(id, type_id, name, description, price) VALUES (" +
  "?, ?, ?, ?, ?"
  ")"
);
```

There are two things you should notice about this example:

- The `prepareStatement()` method is used to specify the SQL statement.

- Question mark characters (?) are used to indicate the positions where you will later provide variables to be used when the SQL statement is actually run.

The positions of the question marks are important: they are referenced according to their position, with the first question mark being referenced using number 1, the second as number 2, and so forth.

The process of supplying Java variables to a prepared statement is known as *binding* the variables to the statement, and the variables themselves are known as *bind variables*. To actually supply variables to the prepared SQL statement, you must use *set* methods. These methods are similar to the get methods that I've already discussed in the section on result sets, except that set methods are used to supply variable values, rather than read them.

For example, to bind a Java int variable named intVar to the id column in the PreparedStatement object previously created, you use setInt(1, intVar). The first parameter indicates the numeric position of the question mark (?) in the string previously specified in the prepareStatement() method call. For this example, the value 1 corresponds to the first question mark, which supplies a value to the id column in the INSERT statement. Similarly, to bind a Java String variable named stringVar to the name column, you use setString(3, stringVar), because the third question mark corresponds to the name column. Table C-5 of Appendix C shows all of the set methods available to a PreparedStatement object.

The following example features a loop that shows the use of set methods to bind the attributes of the Product objects in productArray to the PreparedStatement object; notice that the execute() method is used to actually run the SQL statement:

```
for (int counter = 0; counter < product_array.length; counter ++) {
  myPrepStatement.setInt(1, productArray[counter].id);
  myPrepStatement.setInt(2, productArray[counter].typeId);
  myPrepStatement.setString(3, productArray[counter].name);
  myPrepStatement.setString(4, productArray[counter].description);
  myPrepStatement.setDouble(5, productArray[counter].price);
  myPrepStatement.execute();
} // end of for loop
```

Once this code has completed, the products table will contain five new rows.

To set a database column to NULL using a PreparedStatement object, you may use the setNull() method. For example, the following statement sets the description column to NULL:

```
myPrepStatement.setNull(4, java.sql.Types.VARCHAR);
```

The first parameter in the call to setNull() is the numeric position of the column you want to set to NULL; the second parameter is an int that corresponds to the database type of the column that is to be set to NULL. This second parameter should be specified using one of the constants defined in the java.sql.Types class. For a VARCHAR2 column (the description column is defined as a VARCHAR2), you should use java.sql.Types.VARCHAR. Table C-7 in Appendix C shows all the constant names and the corresponding database types in java.sql.Types.

The program BasicExample2.java contains the statements shown in this section, but the listing for that program is omitted from this book for brevity. That program is available in the program directory where you unzipped the ZIP file for this book.

The Oracle JDBC Extensions

As I mentioned earlier, the Oracle extensions to JDBC contain packages and interfaces that enable you to access all of the data types provided by Oracle, along with Oracle-specific performance extensions. I'll discuss the Oracle performance extensions in Part 4.

This section introduces you to the classes and interfaces in the Oracle JDBC packages and covers how to access some of the Oracle-specific types using the Oracle JDBC extensions. This section doesn't cover *all* of the Oracle types: I'll cover handling of strings, numbers, dates, and row identifiers in this section, and handling of other Oracle specific types will be covered in later chapters.

There are two JDBC extension packages supplied by Oracle:

- **oracle.sql**   Contains the classes that support all the Oracle types

- **oracle.jdbc**   Contains the interfaces that support access to an Oracle database

These packages may be used with JDK 1.2.x or above, and they are compliant with the JDBC 2.0 standard. If you are using JDK 1.1.x, you must use the oracle.jdbc2 package, which contains the interfaces that are equivalent to the JDBC 2.0 interfaces.

To import the Oracle JDBC packages into your Java programs, you may add the following import statements to your program (assuming you are using JDK 1.2.x or above):

```
import oracle.sql.*;
import oracle.jdbc.*;
```

Of course, you don't have to import all the packages: you could just import the classes and interfaces you actually use in your program. In addition, you should still import the java.sql packages you reference in your program. In the following sections, I'll discuss the key features of the oracle.sql and oracle.jdbc packages.

The oracle.sql Package

The oracle.sql package contains the classes that support all of the Oracle types. Using objects of the classes defined in this package to access database columns is more efficient than using regular Java objects. This is because the database column values don't need to be converted to an appropriate base Java type first. Also, using a Java float or double to represent a floating-point number may result in a loss of precision for that number. If you use an oracle.sql.NUMBER object, your numbers never lose precision.

TIP
If you are writing a program that moves a lot of data around in the database, you should use the oracle.sql.* classes.

All of the oracle.sql.* classes extend the oracle.sql.Datum class, which contains the functionality that is common to all the classes. The following table shows a subset of the oracle.sql classes, along with the mapping to the compatible Oracle database types (Table A-5 in Appendix A shows the entire table for all the classes):

Class	Database Type
oracle.sql.NUMBER	INTEGER
	NUMBER
oracle.sql.CHAR	CHAR
	VARCHAR2
	NCHAR
	NVARCHAR2
oracle.sql.DATE	DATE
oracle.sql.ROWID	ROWID

From this table, you can see that an oracle.sql.NUMBER object is compatible with a database column defined using the INTEGER or NUMBER type, and a VARCHAR2 column is compatible with an oracle.sql.CHAR object. Notice that an oracle.sql.CHAR object is also compatible with the NCHAR and NVARCHAR2 database types. These types allow you store multibyte character sets in the database (for full details on how Oracle may be used with such types, refer to the *Oracle9i Globalization Support Guide* published by Oracle Corporation). As discussed in the previous chapter, the ROWID pseudo-column contains the physical address of a table row in the database. You can use an oracle.sql.ROWID object to store that.

Objects declared using the `oracle.sql.*` classes store the data as byte arrays—also known as *SQL format*—and don't reformat the data retrieved from the database. This means that no information is ever lost due to conversion into a core Java type. Each of the classes provides a `getBytes()` method that returns the binary data stored in an `oracle.sql` object as a byte array, and a `toJdbc()` method that returns the binary data as a compatible Java type. The only exception to this is an `oracle.sql.ROWID`, for which `toJdbc()` just returns another `oracle.sql.ROWID` object.

Each class also provides methods to convert their SQL format data to a core Java type. For example, `stringValue()` returns the value as Java `String`, `intValue()` returns a Java int, `floatValue()` returns a `float`, `doubleValue()` returns a `double`, `bigDecimalValue()` returns a `java.math.BigDecimal`, `dateValue()` returns a `java.sql.Date`, and so forth. You use these methods when you want to store the SQL format data in a core Java type or output the SQL data on the screen.

As you will learn shortly, the `OraclePreparedStatement` class, which is defined in the `oracle.jdbc` package, contains a number of set methods that may be used to specify column values using `oracle.sql.*` objects. The `OracleResultSet` class defines a number of get methods that may be used to read column values as `oracle.sql.*` objects.

Each of the `oracle.sql.*` classes contains a constructor that may take a byte array as input, or, as you will more frequently use, a Java variable or object. The following sections describe the details of using the `oracle.sql` classes shown in the previous table in your Java programs.

The oracle.sql.NUMBER Class

The `oracle.sql.NUMBER` class is compatible with the database `INTEGER` and `NUMBER` types, and may be used to represent a number with up to 38 digits of precision. The following example creates an `oracle.sql.NUMBER` object named `id`, which is set to the value 6 using the constructor:

```
oracle.sql.NUMBER id = new oracle.sql.NUMBER(6);
```

You can read the value stored in `id` using the `intValue()` method, which returns the value as a Java int. For example:

```
int idInt = id.intValue();
```

You can also set an `oracle.sql.NUMBER` object to a floating-point number. The next example passes the value 19.95 to the constructor of an `oracle.sql.NUMBER` object named `price`:

```
oracle.sql.NUMBER price = new oracle.sql.NUMBER(19.95);
```

You can read the floating-point number stored in `price` using the `floatValue()`, `doubleValue()`, and `bigDecimalValue()` methods, which return a Java `float`, `double`, and `bigDecimal` respectively. You can also get the value truncated to an `int` using `intValue()`, so `19.95` would be returned as `19`. The following examples show the use of these four methods:

```
float priceFloat = price.floatValue();
double priceDouble = price.doubleValue();
java.math.BigDecimal priceBigDec = price.bigDecimalValue();
int priceInt = price.intValue();
```

Also, the `stringValue()` method returns the value as a Java `String`:

```
String priceString = price.stringValue();
```

The oracle.sql.CHAR Class

The `oracle.sql.CHAR` class is compatible with the database CHAR, VARCHAR2, NCHAR, and NVARCHAR2 types. Both the Oracle database and the `oracle.sql.CHAR` class contain globalization support for many different languages. For full details of the various languages supported by Oracle, see the *Oracle9i Globalization Support Guide* published by Oracle Corporation.

When you retrieve character data from the database into an `oracle.sql.CHAR` object, the Oracle JDBC driver constructs and returns that object using either the database character set, WE8ISO8859P1 (ISO 8859-1 West European), or UTF8 (Unicode 3.0 UTF-8 Universal).

If you are creating your own `oracle.sql.CHAR` object for storage in the database, there are restrictions on which character set you may use, depending on the database column type that the object will be stored in. If you are storing your `oracle.sql.CHAR` object in a CHAR or VARCHAR2 column, you must use US7ASCII (ASCII 7-bit American), WE8ISO8859P1 (ISO 8859-1 West European), or UTF8 (Unicode 3.0 UTF-8 Universal). If you are storing your `oracle.sql.CHAR` object in an NCHAR or NVARCHAR2 column, you must use the character set used by the database.

When creating your own `oracle.sql.CHAR` object, there are two steps you must follow:

1. Create an `oracle.sql.CharacterSet` object containing the character set you wish to use.

2. Create an `oracle.sql.CHAR` object using the previous `oracle.sql.CharacterSet` object to specify the character set.

The following sections describe the details of these steps.

Step 1: Create an oracle.sql.CharacterSet Object

The following example creates an `oracle.sql.CharacterSet` object named `myCharSet`:

```
oracle.sql.CharacterSet myCharSet =
    CharacterSet.make(CharacterSet.US7ASCII_CHARSET);
```

The `make()` method accepts an `int` that specifies the character set to use. In this case, the constant `US7ASCII_CHARSET` (defined in the `oracle.sql.CharacterSet` class) is used to specify that the US7ASCII character set is to be used. Other values include `UTF8_CHARSET` (for UTF8), and `DEFAULT_CHARSET` (for the character set used by the database).

Step 2: Create an oracle.sql.CHAR Object

The following example creates an `oracle.sql.CHAR` object named `firstName`, using the `myCharSet` object created in the previous step:

```
oracle.sql.CHAR firstName = new oracle.sql.CHAR("Jason", myCharSet);
```

The `firstName` object is populated with the string "Jason". You can read the value stored in `firstName` using the `stringValue()` method, which returns the value as a Java `String`. For example:

```
String firstNameString = firstName.stringValue();
System.out.println("firstNameString = " + firstNameString);
```

This will display `firstNameString = Jason`.

Similarly, the following example creates another `oracle.sql.CHAR` object named `lastName`:

```
oracle.sql.CHAR lastName = new oracle.sql.CHAR("Price", myCharSet);
```

You can also display the value in an oracle.sql.CHAR object directly, (rather than first storing it in a Java `String`) as shown in the following example:

```
System.out.println("lastName = " + lastName);
```

This statement will display the following:

```
lastName = Price
```

The oracle.sql.DATE Class

The `oracle.sql.DATE` class is compatible with the database `DATE` type. The following example creates an `oracle.sql.DATE` object named `dob`:

```
oracle.sql.DATE dob = new oracle.sql.DATE("1969-02-01 13:54:12");
```

Notice that the constructor may accept a string in the format YYYY-MM-DD HH:MI:SS, where YYYY is the year, MM is the month, DD is the day, HH is the hour, MI is the minute, and SS is the second. You can read the value stored in dob as a Java String using the stringValue() method, as shown in the following example:

```
String dobString = dob.stringValue();
```

In this case, dobString will contain 2/1/1969 13:54:12—notice the change in the date format to MM/DD/YYYY HH:MI:SS.

You can also pass a java.sql.Date object into the oracle.sql.DATE constructor, as shown in the following example:

```
oracle.sql.DATE anotherDob = new oracle.sql.DATE(new java.sql.Date(69, 1, 1));
```

So, in this example, anotherDob will contain the oracle.sql.DATE 1969-02-01 00:00:00. Notice that the month is February, not January. This is because java.sql.Date objects start month numbering at 0 for January.

The oracle.sql.ROWID Class

The oracle.sql.ROWID class is compatible with the database ROWID type. The following example creates an oracle.sql.ROWID object named rowid:

```
oracle.sql.ROWID rowid;
```

Because the ROWID pseudo-column in the database contains the internal address of a row and is set directly by the Oracle database, you should only retrieve values from the database into an oracle.sql.ROWID object. I'll show you how to do that shortly.

The oracle.jdbc Package

The classes and interfaces of the oracle.jdbc package allow you to read and write column values in the database using objects declared using the oracle.sql.* classes. The oracle.jdbc package also contains a number of performance enhancements specifically for use with an Oracle database, which I'll talk about in Part 4 of this book. In this section, I'll introduce you to the contents of the oracle.sql package, and show you how to create a row in the customers table. Then I'll show you how to read that row using the oracle.sql.* objects created in the previous section.

The Classes and Interfaces of the oracle.jdbc Package

The following table outlines the classes and interfaces of the oracle.jdbc package:

Name	Class or Interface	Description
OracleDriver	Class	Implements `java.sql.Driver`. You input an object of this class when registering the Oracle JDBC drivers in your programs using the `registerDriver()` method of the `java.sql.DriverManager` class.
OracleConnection	Interface	Implements `java.sql.Connection`. This interface extends the standard JDBC connection functionality to use `OracleStatement` objects, plus Oracle performance extensions.
OracleStatement	Interface	Implements `java.sql.Statement` and is the superclass of the `OraclePreparedStatement` and `OracleCallableStatement` classes. This interface supports Oracle performance extensions on a per-statement basis.
OraclePreparedStatement	Interface	Implements `java.sql.PreparedStatement`, and is the superclass of `OracleCallableStatement`. This interface supports Oracle performance extensions on a per-statement basis, plus various set methods for binding `oracle.sql.*` objects.
OracleCallableStatement	Interface	Implements `java.sql.CallableStatement`. This interface contains various get and set methods for binding `oracle.sql.*` objects. I'll show an example that uses this interface in Chapter 5.
OracleResultSet	Interface	Implements `java.sql.ResultSet`. This interface contains various get methods for binding `oracle.sql.*` objects. I'll show an example that uses this interface in Chapter 5.
OracleResultSetMetaData	Interface	Implements `java.sql.ResultSetMetaData`. This interface contains methods for retrieving meta data about Oracle result sets, like the column names and types. I'll discuss metadata in Chapter 4.
OracleDatabaseMetaData	Class	Implements `java.sql.DatabaseMetaData`. This class contains methods for retrieving meta data about the Oracle database, like the software version. I'll discuss meta data in Chapter 4.
OracleTypes	Class	Defines integer constants that are used by JDBC to identify database types. This class duplicates the standard `java.sql.Types` class, along with the new constants for the Oracle types.

In the following sections, I'll show you how to use an OraclePreparedStatement object, then add a row to the customers table, and then finally use an OracleResultSet object to read that row.

Using an OraclePreparedStatement Object

The OraclePreparedStatement interface implements java.sql.PreparedStatement. I described the use of a java.sql.PreparedStatement object to add a row to a table earlier in the section "Prepared SQL Statements." If you need a refresher on this use of such objects, I suggest you take a look at that section before proceeding.

In the previous section, I showed you how to create the following four objects using the classes in the oracle.sql package:

■ An oracle.sql.NUMBER object named id, which was set to 6

■ An oracle.sql.CHAR object named firstName, which was set to "Jason"

■ Another oracle.sql.CHAR object named lastName, which was set to "Price"

■ An oracle.sql.DATE object named dob, which was set to "1969-02-01 13:54:12"

To use these objects directly in a SQL DML statement, you must use an OraclePreparedStatement object, which contains set methods that are capable of handling oracle.sql.* objects. The following example creates an OraclePreparedStatement named myPrepStatement, which will be used to add a row to the customers table using the id, firstName, lastName, and dob objects:

```
OraclePreparedStatement myPrepStatement =
  (OraclePreparedStatement) myConnection.prepareStatement(
    "INSERT INTO customers " +
    "(id, first_name, last_name, dob, phone) VALUES (" +
    "?, ?, ?, ?, ?" +
    ")"
  );
```

Notice that I've used the JDBC Connection object created earlier named myConnection, and I've cast the JDBC PreparedStatement object returned by the prepareStatement() method to an OraclePreparedStatement object, which is stored in myPrepStatement. Also, I want to specify a value for the phone column using the fifth '?' character, even though I haven't created a corresponding oracle.sql.* object. I'm going to specify a database NULL value for this column shortly.

The next step is to bind the `oracle.sql.*` objects to `myPrepStatement` using the set methods. This involves assigning values to the placeholders marked by '?' characters in `myPrepStatement`. Just as you use set methods like `setInt()`, `setFloat()`, `setString()`, and `setDate()` to bind Java variables to a `PreparedStatement` object, you also use set methods to bind `oracle.sql.*` objects to an `OraclePreparedStatement` object. These get methods include `setNUMBER()`, `setCHAR()`, and `setDATE()`. Table C-6 in Appendix C shows the various set methods for an `OraclePreparedStatement` object.

The following examples illustrate how to bind the `id`, `firstName`, `lastName`, and `dob` objects to `myPrepStatement` using the appropriate set methods:

```
myPrepStatement.setNUMBER(1, id);
myPrepStatement.setCHAR(2, firstName);
myPrepStatement.setCHAR(3, lastName);
myPrepStatement.setDATE(4, dob);
```

To specify a database `NULL` value for the phone column (which corresponds to the fifth '?' in `myPrepStatement`), I will use the `setNull()` method:

```
myPrepStatement.setNull(5, OracleTypes.CHAR);
```

The `int` constant `OracleTypes.CHAR` is used to specify that the database column type is compatible with the `oracle.sql.CHAR` type. The phone column is defined as a database `VARCHAR2`, which is compatible with `oracle.sql.CHAR`. Table C-8 in Appendix C shows the extended constants defined in the `OracleTypes` class.

The only thing left to do now is to run the `INSERT` statement using the `execute()` method:

```
myPrepStatement.execute();
```

This adds the row to the `customers` table.

Using an OracleResultSet Object

The `OracleResultSet` interface implements `java.sql.ResultSet` and contains get methods that are capable of handling `oracle.sql.*` objects. In this section, I'll show you how to use an `OracleResultSet` object to retrieve the row previously added to the `customers` table in the previous step.

The first thing we need is a JDBC `Statement` object, through which a SQL statement may be run:

```
Statement myStatement = myConnection.createStatement();
```

Next, the following example creates an `OracleResultSet` object named `customerResultSet`, which is populated with the `ROWID`, `id`, `first_name`, `last_dob`, and `phone` columns for product #6:

```
OracleResultSet customerResultSet =
  (OracleResultSet) myStatement.executeQuery(
    "SELECT ROWID, id, first_name, last_name, dob, phone " +
    "FROM customers " +
    "WHERE id = 6"
  );
```

I defined five `oracle.sql.*` objects earlier: `rowid`, `id`, `firstName`, `lastName`, and `dob`. These objects may be used to hold the first five column values. In order to store the `phone` column, which contains a database `NULL` value, I'll create another `oracle.sql.CHAR` object using the `myCharSet` `CharacterSet` object created earlier object:

```
oracle.sql.CHAR phone = new oracle.sql.CHAR("", myCharSet);
```

An `OracleResultSet` object contains a number of get methods to return the various `oracle.sql.*` objects. You use `getCHAR()` method to get an `oracle.sql.CHAR`, `getNUMBER()` to get an `oracle.sql.NUMBER`, `getDATE()` to get an `oracle.sql.DATE`, and so forth. Table C-3 in Appendix C lists the various get methods for an `OracleResultSet` object.

The following example uses a `while` loop, which uses the appropriate get methods to copy the column values into the `rowid`, `id`, `firstName`, `lastName`, `dob`, and `phone` objects; to display the values, the example uses calls to the `stringValue()` method to convert the `rowid`, `id`, and `dob` objects to Java `String` values. For the `firstName`, `lastName`, and `phone` objects (which are already strings), the example simply uses these objects directly in the `System.out.println()` calls:

```
while (customerResultSet.next()) {
    rowid = customerResultSet.getROWID("ROWID");
    id = customerResultSet.getNUMBER("id");
    firstName = customerResultSet.getCHAR("first_name");
    lastName = customerResultSet.getCHAR("last_name");
    dob = customerResultSet.getDATE("dob");
    phone = customerResultSet.getCHAR("phone");

    System.out.println("rowid = " + rowid.stringValue());
    System.out.println("id = " + id.stringValue());
    System.out.println("firstName = " + firstName);
    System.out.println("lastName = " + lastName);
    System.out.println("dob = " + dob.stringValue());
    System.out.println("phone = " + phone);
} // end of while loop
```

You have now seen how to use the Oracle JDBC extension packages to add and retrieve a database row. The following section contains a complete program that illustrates the use of these Oracle JDBC extensions.

Example Program: BasicExample3.java

The program `BasicExample3.java`, shown in the following listing, is a complete Java program that uses the Oracle JDBC extensions to add a row to the `customers` table and retrieve and display that row's column values. The program performs the following tasks:

1. Imports the Oracle JDBC extension packages

2. Creates an `oracle.sql.NUMBER` object named `id` and sets it to 6

3. Creates two `oracle.sql.CHAR` objects named `firstName` and `lastName` and sets them to "Jason" and "Price"

4. Creates an `oracle.sql.DATE` object named `dob` and sets it to "1969-02-01 13:54:12"

5. Creates an `OraclePreparedStatement` object named `myPrepStatement`, which contains an INSERT statement to add a row to the `customers` table

6. Binds the `id`, `firstName`, `lastName`, and `dob` objects to `myPrepStatement`,and sets the phone column to NULL using the `setNull()` method

7. Executes `myPrepStatement`, which adds the row to the `customers` table

8. Creates and populates an `OracleResultSet` object named `customerResultSet` with the ROWID, `id`, `first_name`, `last_name`, `dob`, and `phone` columns for the new row retrieved from the `customers` table

9. Uses a `while` loop to retrieve the column values into the `oracle.sql.*` objects and displays their values

10. Closes the various JDBC objects

```
/*
  BasicExample3.java shows how to use the Oracle JDBC extensions
   to add a row to the customers table, and then retrieve that row
*/

// import the JDBC packages
import java.sql.*;
```

```java
// import the Oracle JDBC extension packages
import oracle.sql.*;
import oracle.jdbc.*;

public class BasicExample3 {

  public static void main (String args []) {

    try {

      // register the Oracle JDBC drivers
      DriverManager.registerDriver(
        new oracle.jdbc.OracleDriver()
      );

      // create a Connection object, and connect to the database
      // as store_user using the Oracle JDBC Thin driver
      Connection myConnection = DriverManager.getConnection(
        "jdbc:oracle:thin:@localhost:1521:ORCL",
        "store_user",
        "store_password"
      );

      // disable auto-commit mode
      myConnection.setAutoCommit(false);

      // create an oracle.sql.NUMBER object
      oracle.sql.NUMBER id = new oracle.sql.NUMBER(6);
      int idInt = id.intValue();
      System.out.println("idInt = " + idInt);

      // create two oracle.sql.CHAR objects
      oracle.sql.CharacterSet myCharSet =
        CharacterSet.make(CharacterSet.US7ASCII_CHARSET);
      oracle.sql.CHAR firstName = new oracle.sql.CHAR("Jason", myCharSet);
      String firstNameString = firstName.stringValue();
      System.out.println("firstNameString = " + firstNameString);
      oracle.sql.CHAR lastName = new oracle.sql.CHAR("Price", myCharSet);
      System.out.println("lastName = " + lastName);

      // create an oracle.sql.DATE object
      oracle.sql.DATE dob = new oracle.sql.DATE("1969-02-01 13:54:12");
      String dobString = dob.stringValue();
      System.out.println("dobString = " + dobString);

      // create an OraclePreparedStatement object
      OraclePreparedStatement myPrepStatement =
        (OraclePreparedStatement) myConnection.prepareStatement(
          "INSERT INTO customers " +
```

```java
      "(id, first_name, last_name, dob, phone) VALUES (" +
      "?, ?, ?, ?, ?" +
      ")"
  );

// bind the objects to the OraclePreparedStatement using the
// appropriate set methods
myPrepStatement.setNUMBER(1, id);
myPrepStatement.setCHAR(2, firstName);
myPrepStatement.setCHAR(3, lastName);
myPrepStatement.setDATE(4, dob);

// set the phone column to NULL
myPrepStatement.setNull(5, OracleTypes.CHAR);

// run the PreparedStatement
myPrepStatement.execute();
System.out.println("Added row to customers table");

// retrieve the ROWID, id, first_name, last_name, dob, and
// phone columns for this new row using an OracleResultSet
// object
Statement myStatement = myConnection.createStatement();
OracleResultSet customerResultSet =
  (OracleResultSet) myStatement.executeQuery(
    "SELECT ROWID, id, first_name, last_name, dob, phone " +
    "FROM customers " +
    "WHERE id = 6"
  );
System.out.println("Retrieved row from customers table");

// declare an oracle.sql.ROWID object to store the ROWID, and
// an oracle.sql.CHAR object to store the phone column
oracle.sql.ROWID rowid;
oracle.sql.CHAR phone = new oracle.sql.CHAR("", myCharSet);

// display the column values for row using the
// get methods to read the values
while (customerResultSet.next()) {
  rowid = customerResultSet.getROWID("ROWID");
  id = customerResultSet.getNUMBER("id");
  firstName = customerResultSet.getCHAR("first_name");
  lastName = customerResultSet.getCHAR("last_name");
  dob = customerResultSet.getDATE("dob");
  phone = customerResultSet.getCHAR("phone");

  System.out.println("rowid = " + rowid.stringValue());
  System.out.println("id = " + id.stringValue());
  System.out.println("firstName = " + firstName);
```

```
      System.out.println("lastName = " + lastName);
      System.out.println("dob = " + dob.stringValue());
      System.out.println("phone = " + phone);
    } // end of while loop

    // close the OracleResultSet object using the close() method
    customerResultSet.close();

    // rollback the changes made to the database
    myConnection.rollback();

    // close the other JDBC objects
    myPrepStatement.close();
    myConnection.close();

  } catch (SQLException e) {

    System.out.println("Error code = " + e.getErrorCode());
    System.out.println("Error message = " + e.getMessage());
    System.out.println("SQL state = " + e.getSQLState());
    e.printStackTrace();

  }
 } // end of main()
}
```

The output from this program is as follows:

```
idInt = 6
firstNameString = Jason
lastName = Price
dobString = 2/1/1969 13:54:12
Added row to customers table
Retrieved row from customers table
rowid = 4141414636784141424141486579414146
id = 6
firstName = Jason
lastName = Price
dob = 2/1/1969 13:54:12
phone = null
```

PART

II

Advanced
JDBC Programming

CHAPTER
4

Advanced Result Sets

I n the previous chapter, I introduced you to JDBC result sets and showed you how to use them to read rows stored in a database table. In JDBC 1.0, you could only move forward one row at a time in a result set. With the introduction of JDBC 2.0, a new class of result sets known as *scrollable* result sets were added to the JDBC standard. Scrollable result sets allow you to move backwards as well as forwards through rows in a result set. Scrollable result sets also allow you to jump to any row directly, using either the actual row number stored in the result set (known as the *absolute* row number), or a row number *relative* to the current row.

Result sets can also be used to add, update, or delete rows in the underlying database table that was used for the query that populated it. These are known as *updatable* result sets.

Scrollable result sets can also be sensitive to certain changes made to the database rows that were originally used to populate it. This means that you can create a result set that can see certain changes in the database. These are known as *sensitive* scrollable result sets.

In the first part of this chapter, I'll discuss the basics of scrollable result sets. I'll show you how to create a scrollable result set and how to navigate the rows in such a result set. In the second part, I'll discuss updatable result sets and the visibility of database changes to result sets, including sensitive scrollable result sets. Finally, in the last part of this chapter, I'll discuss result set and database *meta data*. Meta data includes information about the columns and the database being accessed by a result set and a database connection. Meta data is useful for determining things like the underlying database type of the columns being accessed and the version of the database.

Scrollable Result Sets

Before I get into the details of scrollable result sets, you need to understand that they can decrease performance of your program: only use a scrollable result set if you absolutely need to.

The process of creating a scrollable result set actually begins when you create a statement. In the previous chapter, I showed you how to create a JDBC `Statement` object, which allows you to run SQL statements. Once you have your `Statement` object, you can create `ResultSet` objects. Let's look at an example. Assume we already have a `Connection` object named `myConnection` that has opened a connection to the database using the `store_user` database user. The following example creates a `Statement` object named `myStatement`, which specifies that any `ResultSet` objects created from it are to be scrollable and read-only:

```
Statement myStatement = myConnection.createStatement(
    ResultSet.TYPE_SCROLL_INSENSITIVE,
    ResultSet.CONCUR_READ_ONLY
);
```

Notice that the `createStatement()` method accepts two parameters: the result set type and the result set concurrency. The result set *type* determines whether your `ResultSet` objects created from the `Statement` object are scrollable or not and, if they are scrollable, whether they are sensitive to changes in the database. The result set type may be specified using one of the following `int` constants defined in the `ResultSet` class:

- **ResultSet.TYPE_FORWARD_ONLY** Specifies that the `ResultSet` objects are not scrollable. This is the default.

- **ResultSet.TYPE_SCROLL_INSENSITIVE** Specifies that the `ResultSet` objects are scrollable but not sensitive to changes in the database.

- **ResultSet.TYPE_SCROLL_SENSITIVE** Specifies that the `ResultSet` objects are scrollable and are also sensitive to changes in the database. (I'll talk about sensitive result sets and visibility of database changes later in this chapter.)

The result set *concurrency* determines whether or not your `ResultSet` objects can modify the rows in the database and may be specified using one of the following `int` constants, also defined in the `ResultSet` class:

- **ResultSet.CONCUR_READ_ONLY** Specifies that the `ResultSet` objects can not make changes to the database. This is the default.

- **ResultSet.CONCUR_UPDATABLE** Specifies that the `ResultSet` objects may make changes to the database.

As this chapter progresses, I'll show you how to combine certain result set types and concurrencies. Depending on your exact requirements, you should pick the appropriate settings for your result sets.

Going back to the earlier example that created the `Statement` object named `myStatement`, you can see that it allows you to create `ResultSet` objects that are scrollable but insensitive to database changes, and it is read-only (it cannot make changes to the database). The following example creates a `ResultSet` object that uses the result set type and concurrency previously set for `myStatement`:

```
ResultSet customerResultSet = myStatement.executeQuery(
    "SELECT id, first_name, last_name, dob, phone " +
    "FROM customers " +
    "ORDER BY id"
);
```

This example used a `Statement` object to create the `ResultSet` object; you can also create scrollable result sets using a `PreparedStatement` object. As I discussed in the previous chapter, a `PreparedStatement` object allows you to bind different variable values to the same SQL statement and therefore use the same execution plan created by the database. The following examples create a `PreparedStatement` object named `myPrepStatement`, which retrieves rows from the `customers` table where the `id` column is less than or equal to a bind parameter set to 5; the example then creates a `ResultSet` object (also named `customerResultSet`), which executes the query:

```
// create a PreparedStatement object
PreparedStatement myPrepStatement = myConnection.prepareStatement(
  "SELECT id, first_name, last_name, dob, phone " +
  "FROM customers " +
  "WHERE id <= ?" +
  "ORDER BY id",
  ResultSet.TYPE_SCROLL_INSENSITIVE,
  ResultSet.CONCUR_READ_ONLY
);

// bind the value 5 to the first int parameter in the PreparedStatement,
// this sets the WHERE clause to "WHERE id <= 5" in the query
myPrepStatement.setInt(1, 5);

// execute the query, storing the rows retrieved from the query
// scrollable ResultSet object
ResultSet customerResultSet = myPrepStatement.executeQuery();
```

I'll use the `customerResultSet` created in this example in the rest of this section. This result set will contain the five rows from the `customers` table after these statements have been run.

NOTE
If you are using the Oracle JDBC drivers with JDK 1.1.x, you must use the `OracleResultSet` class instead of the `ResultSet` class to get the constants for defining your result sets. For example, you would use `OracleResultSet.TYPE_SCROLL_INSENSITIVE` rather than `ResultSet.TYPE_SCROLL_INSENSITIVE`.

Navigating a Scrollable Result Set

In the previous chapter, I showed you how to navigate a result set using the next ()
method, which moves you through each row one at a time. With a scrollable result
set, you can use many more methods to navigate the rows in a more flexible manner.
The following list summarizes these methods, including the next () method:

- **next()**   Navigates to the next row stored in a result set. If there is no row
  to move forward to in the result set, this method returns the Boolean false
  value; otherwise, it returns true.

- **previous()**   Navigates to the previous row. If there is no row to move back
  to, this method returns false; otherwise, it returns true.

- **first()**   Navigates to the first row. If there are no rows in the result set, this
  method returns false; otherwise, it returns true.

- **last()**   Navigates to the last row. If there are no rows in the result set, this
  method returns false; otherwise, it returns true.

- **beforeFirst()**   Navigates to a position before the first row. If there are no
  rows in the result set, calling this method has no effect.

- **afterLast()**   Navigates to a position after the last row. If there are no rows
  in the result set, calling this method has no effect.

- **absolute(int rowNumber)**   Navigates to the row specified by rowNumber,
  which may be any expression that evaluates to a Java int value. The first
  row in the iterator has a row number of 1. If you attempt to navigate to a
  row before the first row, calling this method is the same as calling the
  beforeFirst () method. Similarly, attempting to navigate to a row after
  the last row is the same as calling the afterLast () method. If you pass a
  negative row number to absolute (), it will navigate to a row counting
  the back from the last row. If there are no rows in the result set, this method
  returns false; otherwise, it returns true.

- **relative(int relativeRowNumber)**   Navigates to a row relative to the
  current row. The row to navigate to is specified by relativeRowNumber,
  which may be any expression that evaluates to a Java int value. The
  relative row number can be positive, specifying a row after the current row,
  or negative, specifying a row before the current row. If you attempt to navigate
  to a row before the first row, calling this method is the same as a call to the
  beforeFirst () method. Similarly, attempting to navigate to a row after
  the last row is the same as calling the afterLast () method. If there are no
  rows in the result set, this method returns false; otherwise, it returns true.

The following example uses a `while` loop to navigate and display the five rows stored in `customerResultSet` in reverse order. Notice the use of the `afterLast()` and `previous()` methods.

```
customerResultSet.afterLast();
while (customerResultSet.previous()) {
  System.out.println("id = " +
    customerResultSet.getInt("id"));
  System.out.println("first_name = " +
    customerResultSet.getString("first_name"));
  System.out.println("last_name = " +
    customerResultSet.getString("last_name"));
  System.out.println("dob = " +
    customerResultSet.getString("dob"));
  System.out.println("phone = " +
    customerResultSet.getString("phone"));
} // end of while loop
```

The next example navigates to row #3 using the `absolute()` method:

```
customerResultSet.absolute(3);
```

If you pass a negative number to `absolute()`, it will navigate to a row counting the back from the last row. For example, the following navigates to row #4 by passing −2 to the `absolute()` method:

```
customerResultSet.absolute(-2);
```

NOTE
absolute(-1) is equivalent to `last()`.

The next example navigates to row #2 by navigating back two rows relative to the current row (which is row #4):

```
customerResultSet.relative(-2);
```

NOTE
You cannot use relative positioning from before the first row or after the last row. If you try to, you will cause a SQL exception.

Determining the Position in a Scrollable Result Set

When using the scrollable result set methods to navigate rows, you might lose track of where you are. You can check your current position in a result set using the following methods:

■ **getRow()**   Returns an int containing the current row. If there is no current row, the method returns 0.

■ **isFirst()**   Returns true if the current row is the first row; otherwise, the method returns false.

■ **isLast()**   Returns true if the current row is the last row; otherwise, the method returns false.

■ **isBeforeFirst()**   Returns true if the position is before the first row; otherwise, the method returns false.

■ **isAfterLast()**   Returns true if the position is after the last row; otherwise, the method returns false.

In the following example, the beforeFirst() method is used to navigate to a position before the first row, then the isBeforeFirst() method is used to check the condition (returns true because it is indeed before the first row); finally, the getRow() method is called within a println() call to display the returned value (displays 0 because there is no valid current row):

```
customerResultSet.beforeFirst();
if (customerResultSet.isBeforeFirst()) {
  System.out.println("Current row = " + customerResultSet.getRow());
}
```

In the next example, the first() method is used to navigate to the first row, and then the getRow() method is used to display the current row (displays 1 for the first row):

```
customerResultSet.first();
System.out.println("Current row = " + customerResultSet.getRow());
```

The following section contains a complete program that illustrates the use of scrollable result sets.

Example Program: AdvResultSetExample1.java

The program AdvResultSetExample1.java, shown in the following listing, is a complete Java program that illustrates the use of a scrollable result set to navigate the five rows retrieved from the customers table. This program performs the following tasks:

1. Creates a PreparedStatement object named myPrepStatement, which retrieves the five rows from the customers table. This object uses the TYPE_SCROLL_INSENSITIVE and CONCUR_READ_ONLY constants, defined in the ResultSet class, to specify that any result set objects will be scrollable, will be insensitive to database changes, and will be read-only.

2. Creates a ResultSet object named customerResultSet into which the five rows from the customers table are retrieved.

3. Navigates the rows in customerResultSet in reverse order using the afterLast() and previous() methods.

4. Uses the absolute(), relative(), first(), and beforeFirst() methods to navigate the rows and uses the isBeforeFirst() and getRow() methods to determine the position.

```
/*
  AdvResultSetExample1.java shows how to use
  an insenstive scrollable result set
*/

// import the JDBC packages
import java.sql.*;

public class AdvResultSetExample1 {

  public static void main (String args [])
  throws SQLException {

    // register the Oracle JDBC drivers
    DriverManager.registerDriver(
      new oracle.jdbc.OracleDriver()
    );

    // create a Connection object, and connect to the database
    // as store_user using the Oracle JDBC Thin driver
    Connection myConnection = DriverManager.getConnection(
      "jdbc:oracle:thin:@localhost:1521:ORCL",
```

```java
  "store_user",
  "store_password"
);

// create a PreparedStatement object from which an insensitive
// scrollable ResultSet object will be created
PreparedStatement myPrepStatement =
  myConnection.prepareStatement(
  "SELECT id, first_name, last_name, dob, phone " +
  "FROM customers " +
  "WHERE id <= ?" +
  "ORDER BY id",
  ResultSet.TYPE_SCROLL_INSENSITIVE,
  ResultSet.CONCUR_READ_ONLY
);

// bind the int value 5 to the PreparedStatement object
myPrepStatement.setInt(1, 5);

// create a ResultSet object
ResultSet customerResultSet = myPrepStatement.executeQuery();

// display the rows in the ResultSet in reverse order
System.out.println("Customers in reverse order");
customerResultSet.afterLast();
while (customerResultSet.previous()) {
  System.out.println("id = " +
    customerResultSet.getInt("id"));
  System.out.println("first_name = " +
    customerResultSet.getString("first_name"));
  System.out.println("last_name = " +
    customerResultSet.getString("last_name"));
  System.out.println("dob = " +
    customerResultSet.getString("dob"));
  System.out.println("phone = " +
    customerResultSet.getString("phone"));
} // end of while loop

// navigate to row #3
System.out.println("Going to row #3");
customerResultSet.absolute(3);
System.out.println("id = " + customerResultSet.getInt("id"));

// navigate back two rows to row #1
System.out.println("Going back two rows");
```

```
customerResultSet.relative(-2);
System.out.println("id = " + customerResultSet.getInt("id"));

// navigate before first row
customerResultSet.beforeFirst();
if (customerResultSet.isBeforeFirst()) {
  System.out.println("Before first row");
  System.out.println("Current row = " +
    customerResultSet.getRow());
}

// navigate to the first row
System.out.println("Going to first row");
customerResultSet.first();
System.out.println("Current row = " +
  customerResultSet.getRow());

// close the ResultSet object using the close() method
customerResultSet.close();

// close the other JDBC objects
myPrepStatement.close();
myConnection.close();

  } // end of main()
}
```

The output from this program is as follows:

```
Customers in reverse order
id = 5
first_name = Doreen
last_name = Blue
dob = 5/20/1970 0:0:0
phone = null
id = 4
first_name = Gail
last_name = Black
dob = null
phone = 800-555-1214
id = 3
first_name = Steve
last_name = White
dob = 3/16/1971 0:0:0
phone = 800-555-1213
id = 2
```

```
first_name = Cynthia
last_name = Green
dob = 2/5/1968 0:0:0
phone = 800-555-1212
id = 1
first_name = John
last_name = Brown
dob = 1/1/1965 0:0:0
phone = 800-555-1211
Going to row #3
id = 3
Going back two rows
id = 1
Before first row
Current row = 0
Going to first row
Current row = 1
```

Updatable Result Sets

Updatable result sets allow you to make changes to rows in the database. In the previous section, I mentioned that the *concurrency* parameter controls whether or not a result set is updatable; this parameter is set when creating a statement. The following int constants are defined in the ResultSet class and are used to indicate the result set concurrency:

- **ResultSet.CONCUR_READ_ONLY**   Specifies that the ResultSet objects cannot make changes to the database. This was used to create the ResultSet objects in the previous section.

- **ResultSet.CONCUR_UPDATABLE**   Specifies that the ResultSet objects may make changes to the database: these are updatable result sets.

The following example creates a Statement object using the ResultSet.CONCUR_UPDATABLE constant for the second parameter:

```
Statement myStatement = myConnection.createStatement(
    ResultSet.TYPE_SCROLL_INSENSITIVE,
    ResultSet.CONCUR_UPDATABLE
);
```

Notice that this example also uses the ResultSet.TYPE_SCROLL_ INSENSITIVE constant—this means that a result set created from this Statement object will be scrollable, but insensitive to any database changes. I'll talk about the sensitivity of a result set to database changes shortly. You can also specify forward-only updatable result sets by using the `ResultSet.TYPE_FORWARD_ONLY` constant, but this means you can only use the `next()` method to navigate the rows in those result sets.

Next, the following statement creates a `ResultSet` object, named `customerResultSet`, and populates it with five rows retrieved from the `customers` table:

```
ResultSet customerResultSet = myStatement.executeQuery(
  "SELECT id, first_name, last_name, dob, phone " +
  "FROM customers"
);
```

There are a number of limitations for the query used with an updatable result set:

- You can only use a single table.

- You must select the table's primary key column and all the other NOT NULL columns.

- You cannot use an ORDER BY clause.

- You must only select column values.

- You cannot use SELECT *. You must either specify the columns individually or use a table alias such as SELECT customers.* FROM customers.

In the following sections, I'll show you how to use an updatable result set to update, delete, and insert rows.

Updating a Row

In the previous chapter, I showed you some of the set methods that may be used to specify column values in a prepared statement. In an updatable result set, you use update methods to specify column values, and these methods are used in a similar manner to the set methods used in a prepared statement. You can see all of the update methods for a `ResultSet` object in Table C-2 of Appendix C; you can see all of the update methods for an `OracleResultSet` object in Table C-4.

You may use the `updateString()` method to update a CHAR or VARCHAR2 column; `updateDate()` to update a DATE column; `updateInt()` to update an INTEGER column; `updateDouble()` to update a NUMBER column, and so forth.

The update methods accept two parameters:

- **The column to be updated** This is specified using either a number representing the position or the column name.

- **The new value** This is specified using any expression that evaluates to the appropriate Java type for the update method.

For example, let's assume we want to update the customer in row #2 and set the first name to "Greg". The first thing to do is to navigate to row #2 in `customerResultSet`:

```
customerResultSet.absolute(2);
```

Next, because the `first_name` column is defined using the database VARCHAR2 type, we'll use the `updateString()` method. The column is specified using the `String` "first_name", and the new value is set using a Java `String` containing "Greg":

```
String newFirstName = "Greg";
customerResultSet.updateString("first_name", newFirstName);
```

Of course, we could have just set the new value using a literal value, as shown in the following example:

```
customerResultSet.updateString("first_name", "Greg");
```

The following example updates the `dob` column using the `updateDate()` method:

```
java.sql.Date dob = new java.sql.Date(69, 1, 1);
customerResultSet.updateDate("dob", dob);
```

NOTE
You cannot modify the primary key column using an update method.

If you want to undo your changes, you can use the `cancelRowUpdates()` method; this method sets the values for that row back to their original state.

At this point, the changes made to the row using the update methods are only made in the result set object itself: they are not changed in the database yet. You can, however, still use the get methods to inspect the current values set for that row in the result set. For example, the following statement will display "Greg":

```
System.out.println(customerResultSet.getString("first_name"));
```

Once you're finished with your changes to the current row, you need to send them to the database using the `updateRow()` method:

```
customerResultSet.updateRow();
```

The updateRow() method sends an appropriate SQL UPDATE statement to the database containing the new column values. Once the updateRow() method has been called, the UPDATE statement forms part of the current database transaction and may be committed using the commit() method of the JDBC Connection object (or rolled back using the rollback() method). The following example commits the row changes:

```
myConnection.commit();
```

NOTE
You cannot use the cancelRowUpdates() *method to undo changes once you've called the* updateRow() *method. You can only use the* rollback() *method to undo changes at that point.*

If you've left auto-commit in its enabled default setting for the Connection object, your changes will automatically be committed. Generally, as I discussed in the previous chapter, you should disable auto-commit so that you can control the transaction.

Deleting a Row

You can delete the current row being processed in an updatable result set using the deleteRow() method. The following example navigates to row #5 using the absolute() method and then deletes that row using the deleteRow() method:

```
customerResultSet.absolute(5);
customerResultSet.deleteRow();
```

The deleteRow() method sends an appropriate SQL DELETE statement to the database. Once the deleteRow() method has been called, the DELETE statement forms part of the current database transaction and may be committed using the commit() method of the Connection object (or rolled back using the rollback() method).

Conflicts When Updating and Deleting Rows Using an Updatable Result Set

When you populate a result set using a SELECT statement, the rows returned by that statement are not "locked" by the database, meaning that other transactions may alter those rows after your result set has read them. Result sets identify rows using row identifiers (row identifiers are physical pointers to rows in the database; see Chapter 2 for more details).

Because the rows are not locked, this means that if you update or delete a row using your result set, your changes will overwrite anyone else's changes (as long as that row identifier is still valid). Overwriting someone else's changes is not good from a database transaction standpoint.

Fortunately, there's a solution to this problem: you can use the FOR UPDATE clause with a SELECT statement to lock the rows retrieved. In the following example, the FOR UPDATE clause is used to lock the rows retrieved from the customers table:

```
ResultSet customerResultSet = myStatement.executeQuery(
   "SELECT id, first_name, last_name, dob, phone " +
   "FROM customers " +
   "FOR UPDATE"
);
```

Although this prevents any conflicts, there is a downside: the FOR UPDATE clause locks the rows for the duration of your transaction. This means that no one else can write to the rows until your transaction ends—although the rows can always be read.

Inserting a Row

Inserting a new row using an updatable result set is slightly more complicated than updating or deleting a row. First, you must call the moveToInsertRow() method to create a blank row in the result set:

```
customerResultSet.moveToInsertRow();
```

This creates a new row in customerResultSet. To set the column values for the new row, you must use the update methods that were described in the previous section. The following examples use update methods to set the column values for the new row:

```
customerResultSet.updateInt("id", 6);
customerResultSet.updateString("first_name", "Jason");
customerResultSet.updateString("last_name", "Price");
customerResultSet.updateDate("dob", dob);
```

You must set values for the primary key and other NOT NULL columns using the update methods. For columns that are defined as NULL in the database table, you don't have to provide values (if you don't provide values, they will be set to NULL). You'll notice I didn't set the phone column in the previous example, so when the row is inserted into the database, the phone column will be NULL for that row.

To send the new row to the database, you use the insertRow() method:

```
customerResultSet.insertRow();
```

The `insertRow()` method sends an appropriate SQL `INSERT` statement to the database. Once the `insertRow()` method has been called, the `INSERT` statement forms part of the current database transaction and may be committed using the `commit()` method of the `Connection` object (or rolled back using the `rollback()` method).

You can start inserting a new row from any point when processing a result set. You don't even have to read a row before inserting a new row, but you do need to perform a query to populate the result set. If you did read a row prior to performing the insert, then you can return to that row using the `moveToCurrentRow()` method. For example, say you had just navigated to row #2 in the result set and then called the `moveToInsertRow()` method and inserted a new row. Once you finish inserting that row, you could return to row #2 by calling `moveToCurrentRow()`.

The following section contains a complete program that illustrates the use of an updatable result set.

Example Program: AdvResultSetExample2.java

The program `AdvResultSetExample2.java`, shown in the following listing, illustrates the use of an updatable result set that retrieves the five rows from the `customers` table and then updates a row, deletes a row, and inserts a row in the `customers` table. The program performs the following tasks:

1. Creates an updatable scrollable insensitive result set named `customerResultSet`, which is populated with the five rows from the `customers` table.

2. Updates the first name and dob of the customer in row #2 using the `updateString()` and `updateDate()` methods.

3. Displays the new first name and dob values using the `getString()` methods.

4. Inserts a new row into `customerResultSet` using the `moveToInsertRow()` method and sets the column values using the appropriate update methods. The `insertRow()` method is then used to insert the row into the `customers` table.

5. Deletes row #5 from the `customers` table using the `deleteRow()` method.

6. Displays the rows in `customerResultSet`.

```
/*
  AdvResultSetExample2.java shows how to use
  an updatable result set
*/
```

```java
// import the JDBC packages
import java.sql.*;

public class AdvResultSetExample2 {

  public static void main (String args [])
  throws SQLException {

    // register the Oracle JDBC drivers
    DriverManager.registerDriver(
      new oracle.jdbc.OracleDriver()
    );

    // create a Connection object, and connect to the database
    // as store_user using the Oracle JDBC Thin driver
    Connection myConnection = DriverManager.getConnection(
      "jdbc:oracle:thin:@localhost:1521:ORCL",
      "store_user",
      "store_password"
    );

    // disable auto-commit mode
    myConnection.setAutoCommit(false);

    // create a Statement object from which an updatable
    // ResultSet object will be created
    Statement myStatement = myConnection.createStatement(
      ResultSet.TYPE_SCROLL_INSENSITIVE,
      ResultSet.CONCUR_UPDATABLE
    );

    // create a ResultSet object
    ResultSet customerResultSet = myStatement.executeQuery(
      "SELECT id, first_name, last_name, dob, phone " +
      "FROM customers"
    );
    System.out.println("Retrieved rows from customers table");

    // update row #2's first name and dob
    System.out.println("Updating the first_name and dob for row #2");
    customerResultSet.absolute(2);
    String newFirstName = "Greg";
    customerResultSet.updateString("first_name", newFirstName);
    java.sql.Date dob = new java.sql.Date(69, 1, 1);
    customerResultSet.updateDate("dob", dob);
    customerResultSet.updateRow();

    // display the new first name and dob
```

```
      System.out.println("first_name = " +
        customerResultSet.getString("first_name"));
      System.out.println("dob = " +
        customerResultSet.getString("dob"));

      // insert a new row
      System.out.println("Inserting new row");
      customerResultSet.moveToInsertRow();
      customerResultSet.updateInt("id", 6);
      customerResultSet.updateString("first_name", "Jason");
      customerResultSet.updateString("last_name", "Price");
      customerResultSet.updateDate("dob", dob);
      customerResultSet.insertRow();
      customerResultSet.moveToCurrentRow();

      // delete row #5
      System.out.println("Deleting row #5");
      customerResultSet.absolute(5);
      customerResultSet.deleteRow();

      // display the rows in the ResultSet
      System.out.println("Rows in customerResultSet");
      customerResultSet.beforeFirst();
      while (customerResultSet.next()) {
        System.out.println("id = " +
          customerResultSet.getInt("id"));
        System.out.println("first_name = " +
          customerResultSet.getString("first_name"));
        System.out.println("last_name = " +
          customerResultSet.getString("last_name"));
        System.out.println("dob = " +
          customerResultSet.getString("dob"));
        System.out.println("phone = " +
          customerResultSet.getString("phone"));
      } // end of while loop

      // rollback the changes made to the database
      myConnection.rollback();

      // close this ResultSet object using the close() method
      customerResultSet.close();

      // close the other JDBC objects
      myStatement.close();
      myConnection.close();

    } // end of main()
  }
```

The output from this program is as follows:

```
Retrieved rows from customers table
Updating the first_name and dob for row #2
first_name = Greg
dob = 2/1/1969 0:0:0
Inserting new row
Deleting row #5
Rows in customerResultSet
id = 1
first_name = John
last_name = Brown
dob = 1/1/1965 0:0:0
phone = 800-555-1211
id = 2
first_name = Greg
last_name = Green
dob = 2/1/1969 0:0:0
phone = 800-555-1212
id = 3
first_name = Steve
last_name = White
dob = 3/16/1971 0:0:0
phone = 800-555-1213
id = 4
first_name = Gail
last_name = Black
dob = null
phone = 800-555-1214
```

What Database Changes does a Result Set "See"?

In this section, I'll discuss what database changes a result set "sees" when changes are made to the column values for rows that were initially read from the database. What do I mean by "see"? By this, I mean what value a get method returns if the column value originally read from the database by that result set is changed.

Changes to column values can be made by two sources:

■ **Updatable result set changes**   I'll refer to these changes as *internal*, because they are changes that are made using the update methods by that result set.

■ **Other database transactions that may be performing inserts, updates, or deletes that change the rows originally read by the result set**   I'll refer to these changes as *external*, because they are changes that are made outside of the result set.

In addition, the external changes seen by a result set are also affected by the transaction isolation level (I'll talk about this topic in Chapter 9). For now, I'll assume the default transaction isolation level is used, which means that only database changes that have been committed have the possibility of affecting the rows seen by a result set.

Depending on the type of the result set (forward only, scrollable insensitive, or scrollable sensitive), that result set may see different rows than those originally read if there have been internal and/or external changes. The following table shows how the three types of result sets are affected by internal and external changes to rows:

Result set type	Sees internal updates	Sees internal deletes	Sees internal inserts	Sees external updates	Sees external deletes	Sees external inserts
Forward only	Yes	No	No	No	No	No
Scrollable insensitive	Yes	Yes	No	No	No	No
Scrollable sensitive	Yes	Yes	No	Yes	No	No

As you can see from this table, a forward only result set can only see internal updates; a scrollable insensitive result set can only see internal updates and deletes; and a scrollable sensitive result set can only see internal updates and deletes and external updates. Notice that only one external change is seen, an external update, and only by a scrollable sensitive result set. Also, internal inserts aren't seen by any result set type.

The refreshRow() Method

Now, the previous table shows the default visibility for the result sets: you can actually override them by refreshing the current row in the result set using the `refreshRow()` method. This method reads the column values for that row again from the database. The `refreshRow()` method works with updatable scrollable insensitive and sensitive result sets.

NOTE
You cannot use an ORDER BY clause in the query for your result set if you want to use the refreshRow() method.

Let's examine the use of the `refreshRow()` method using an example. The following creates a `Statement` object and a `ResultSet` object (which is scrollable, insensitive, and updatable):

```
// create a Statement object from which an updatable scrollable
// insensitive ResultSet object will be created
Statement myStatement = myConnection.createStatement(
  ResultSet.TYPE_SCROLL_INSENSITIVE,
  ResultSet.CONCUR_UPDATABLE
);
```

```
// create a ResultSet object
ResultSet customerResultSet = myStatement.executeQuery(
  "SELECT id, first_name, last_name, dob, phone " +
  "FROM customers"
);
```

The next example navigates to row #2 and displays the id and last_name column values for that row:

```
customerResultSet.absolute(2);
System.out.println("id = " +
  customerResultSet.getInt("id"));
System.out.println("last_name = " +
  customerResultSet.getString("last_name"));
```

This will display the following:

```
id = 2
last_name = Green
```

These are the original values for row #2 in the customers table. Next, a new Statement object is created, which updates last_name to "Jones" (this update is also committed):

```
Statement updateStatement = myConnection.createStatement();
updateStatement.execute(
  "UPDATE customers " +
  "SET last_name = 'Jones' " +
  "WHERE id = 2"
);
myConnection.commit();
```

Normally, this change would not be visible to customerResultSet because it is insensitive (and insensitive result sets don't see external updates), but you can use the refreshRow() method to read the row from the database again:

```
customerResultSet.refreshRow();
```

This gets the new last_name column value from the database, which is set to "Jones".

The program `AdvResultSetExample3.java` illustrates the use of the `refreshRow()` method. That program is available in the `programs` directory where you unzipped the ZIP file for this book.

When Are Changes Visible?

The next question to ask is when are visible changes actually seen by these result sets? In other words, when do the get methods actually return a new value when one of the visible internal changes, or the one visible external change, has been made?

For internal changes, the get methods will immediately return the new value for a visible change after an update method has been used. In the example program `AdvResultSetExample2.java` shown earlier in this chapter, the row updates are immediately reflected, and the calls to the get methods return the updated values; also, the deleted row is immediately removed from the result set. Of course, the use of the `refreshRow()` method (described in the previous section) also gets any changes from database immediately; this is demonstrated in the program `AdvResultSetExample3.java`.

For the external update change that is visible to a scrollable sensitive result set, the answer as to when this update is visible is more complicated. The answer depends on the number of rows fetched by the scrollable sensitive result set. I'll now talk about these types of result sets.

Scrollable Sensitive Result Sets

By default, a scrollable sensitive result set will attempt to fetch up to 10 rows at a time from the database. By doing this, there are fewer calls to the database to fetch rows than if one row at a time were fetched, and this improves performance. Fetching multiple rows from the database in this manner is known as row *prefetching*, and I'll talk more about this performance tuning technique in Chapter 13. For now, I'll discuss how the number of rows fetched in one trip to the database affects visibility of an external update to a sensitive result set.

To aid your understanding, I'll use an example of a sensitive result set that prefetches 10 rows at a time from a table containing 20 rows. Let's assume the first 10 rows have been fetched from the table and stored in the result set. Next, a different transaction updates row #5 in the table and commits the change. The 10 rows originally fetched by the result set represent a snapshot of the rows as they were before the other transaction made the update, but the result set doesn't yet "see" this update. The only way the result set can see this change is if the entire group of 10 rows is fetched again. If you then move to a row after row 10 in the table using the result set, it causes the next 10 rows in the table to be prefetched by the result set. If you were to then return back to a row in the first 10 rows of the table, those first 10 rows would be prefetched again, and the change made to row #5 would be visible to the sensitive result set.

As you can see from this simple example, external updates are not immediately visible: they are only visible when the group of rows in which the update occurred is fetched again.

You can set the number of rows prefetched by a result set using the `setFetchSize()` method, which accepts an `int` value specifying the number of rows to prefetch. If you were to set the number of rows to prefetch to 1, every time you moved to a row, that row would be immediately fetched again, so any external updates would be visible straight away. However, this method is not recommended in practice, as it would significantly degrade performance.

The example program in the following section illustrates the use of a sensitive result set for which the number of rows to prefetch is set to 1. This is to illustrate the point of visibility of external updates, but as I said, don't set it to 1 in your own programs.

There are a number of limitations for the query used with a scrollable sensitive result set:

- You can only use a single table.

- You cannot use an `ORDER BY` clause.

- You cannot use `SELECT *`. You must either specify the columns individually, or use a table alias (`SELECT customers.* FROM customers`, for example).

Of course, if your scrollable sensitive result set is also updatable, the additional limitations on the query also apply. These limitations were defined in the earlier section on updatable result sets.

Example Program: AdvResultSetExample4.java

The program `AdvResultSetExample4.java`, shown in the following listing, illustrates the use of a scrollable sensitive result set and the visibility of an external update. The program performs the following tasks:

1. Creates a `Statement` object, specifying that any result sets created from it will be updatable and scrollable sensitive.

2. Sets the number of rows prefetch for the `Statement` object to 1 using the `setFetchSize()` method.

3. Creates and populates a `ResultSet` object with the five rows from the `customers` table.

4. Displays the `id` and `last_name` columns for row #2.

5. Performs an external update to change the `last_name` column for row #2.

6. Displays all the rows in the `customers` table using the `ResultSet` object. The update to row #2 is visible because every row is prefetched.

7. Sets the `last_name` column for row #2 back to the original.

```
/*
  AdvResultSetExample4.java shows the visibilty of changes
  to an updatable scrollable sensitive result set
*/

// import the JDBC packages
import java.sql.*;

public class AdvResultSetExample4 {

  public static void main (String args [])
  throws SQLException {

    // register the Oracle JDBC drivers
    DriverManager.registerDriver(
      new oracle.jdbc.OracleDriver()
    );

    // create a Connection object, and connect to the database
    // as store_user using the Oracle JDBC Thin driver
    Connection myConnection = DriverManager.getConnection(
      "jdbc:oracle:thin:@localhost:1521:ORCL",
      "store_user",
      "store_password"
    );

    // disable auto-commit mode
    myConnection.setAutoCommit(false);

    // create a Statement object from which a scrollable sensitive
    // ResultSet object will be created
    Statement myStatement = myConnection.createStatement(
      ResultSet.TYPE_SCROLL_SENSITIVE,
      ResultSet.CONCUR_UPDATABLE
    );

    // set the fetch size to 1
    myStatement.setFetchSize(1);

    // create a ResultSet object
    ResultSet customerResultSet = myStatement.executeQuery(
```

```
  "SELECT id, first_name, last_name, dob, phone " +
  "FROM customers"
);
System.out.println("Retrieved rows from customers table");

// display row #2's id and last name
customerResultSet.absolute(2);
System.out.println("id = " +
  customerResultSet.getInt("id"));
System.out.println("last_name = " +
  customerResultSet.getString("last_name"));

// update customer #2's last name to "Jones" using a separate
// Statement object - this is an external update
System.out.println("Updating customer #2's last name to 'Jones'");
Statement updateStatement = myConnection.createStatement();
updateStatement.execute(
  "UPDATE customers " +
  "SET last_name = 'Jones' " +
  "WHERE id = 2"
);
myConnection.commit();

// display all the customer ids and last names
System.out.println("Rows in customerResultSet");
customerResultSet.beforeFirst();
while (customerResultSet.next()) {
  System.out.println("id = " +
    customerResultSet.getInt("id"));
  System.out.println("last_name = " +
    customerResultSet.getString("last_name"));
} // end of while loop

// set customer #2's last name back to the original
updateStatement.execute(
  "UPDATE customers " +
  "SET last_name = 'Green' " +
  "WHERE id = 2"
);
myConnection.commit();

// close this ResultSet object using the close() method
customerResultSet.close();

// close the other JDBC objects
myStatement.close();
updateStatement.close();
```

```
        myConnection.close();

    } // end of main()
}
```

The output from this program is as follows:

```
Retrieved rows from customers table
id = 2
last_name = Green
Updating customer #2's last name to 'Jones'
Rows in customerResultSet
id = 1
last_name = Brown
id = 2
last_name = Jones
id = 3
last_name = White
id = 4
last_name = Black
id = 5
last_name = Blue
```

Meta Data

In this chapter's final section, I'll discuss meta data. You can use meta data to get information about the database and tables that your program accesses. There are two types of meta data:

- **Result set meta data**   This provides information about the table and columns accessed by a `ResultSet` object.

- **Database meta data**   This provides information about the database to which a `Connection` object is linked to.

You can use result set meta data to get things like the names of columns a `ResultSet` object accesses, the column types, whether the column is defined as `NULL` or `NOT NULL`, and the column precision and scale (useful for numeric columns). To get result set meta data, you first need a `ResultSetMetaData` object; the following example creates such an object named `myRSMetaData`, which gets the meta data for the `customerResultSet` created earlier (which selected the `id`, `first_name`, `last_name`, `dob`, and `phone` columns from the `customers` table):

```
ResultSetMetaData myRSMetaData = customerResultSet.getMetaData();
```

The getMetaData() method obtains the meta data for the ResultSet object. Once you have your ResultSetMetaData object, you can use the various methods that read the meta data for the ResultSet object. The following table shows some of the more useful methods for reading result set meta data:

Method	Return Type	Description
getColumnCount()	int	Returns the number of columns in the result set
getColumnName (int columnNumber)	String	Returns the name of the column at the position specified by columnNumber
getColumnType (int columnNumber)	int	Returns the column type number
getColumnTypeName (int columnNumber)	String	Returns the column type name
getColumnDisplaySize (int columnNumber)	int	Returns the maximum column width for displaying values
isNullable (int columnNumber)	int	Returns 0 if the column is defined as NOT NULL; otherwise, returns 1 (column is defined as NULL)
getPrecision (int columnNumber)	int	Returns the total number of digits for storage of a numeric column
getScale (int columnNumber)	int	Returns the number of digits to the right of the decimal point for storage of a numeric column

The following example gets the number of columns in customerResultSet:

```
int columnCount = myRSMetaData.getColumnCount();
```

This returns 5 because there are five columns in customerResultSet. You'll see examples of using the other methods in the following section, which shows a complete program.

To get database meta data, you first need a `DatabaseMetaData` object:

```
DatabaseMetaData myDBMetaData = myConnection.getMetaData();
```

The `getMetaData()` method is called using a `Connection` object, and reads the database meta data for that object. The following table shows some of the more useful methods for reading database meta data:

Method	Return Type	Description
getDatabaseProductName()	String	Returns the name of the database product
getDatabaseProductVersion()	String	Returns the database product version
getURL()	String	Returns the URL for the database
getUserName()	String	Returns the database user name

The following example displays the database product name:

```
System.out.println(myDBMetaData.getDatabaseProductName());
```

This will display "Oracle".

NOTE
You can also use `oracle.jdbc.`
`OracleResultSetMetaData` *and*
`oracle.jdbc.OracleResultSetMetaData`
objects to get result set and database meta
data. The methods of the `oracle.jdbc.`
`OracleResultSetMetaData` *class work*
with all of the Oracle database types.

The following section contains a complete program that illustrates how to obtain and display result set and database meta data.

Example Program: MetaDataExample.java

The program `MetaDataExample.java`, shown in the following listing, illustrates the use of some of the methods described in the previous section to obtain and display result set and database meta data:

```
/*
  MetaDataExample.java shows how to obtain and
  display result set and database meta data
*/

// import the JDBC packages
import java.sql.*;

public class MetaDataExample {

  public static void main (String args [])
  throws SQLException {

    // register the Oracle JDBC drivers
    DriverManager.registerDriver(
      new oracle.jdbc.OracleDriver()
    );

    // create a Connection object, and connect to the database
    // as store_user using the Oracle JDBC Thin driver
    Connection myConnection = DriverManager.getConnection(
      "jdbc:oracle:thin:@localhost:1521:ORCL",
      "store_user",
      "store_password"
    );

    // create a Statement object
    Statement myStatement = myConnection.createStatement();

    // create a ResultSet object
    ResultSet customerResultSet = myStatement.executeQuery(
      "SELECT id, first_name, last_name, dob, phone " +
      "FROM customers"
    );
    System.out.println("Retrieved rows from customers table");
```

```
      // get and display result set meta data
      ResultSetMetaData myRSMetaData = customerResultSet.getMetaData();
      System.out.println("Result set meta data follows");
      int columnCount = myRSMetaData.getColumnCount();
      System.out.println("Column count = " + columnCount);
      for (int counter = 1; counter <= columnCount; counter++) {
        System.out.println("Column name = " +
          myRSMetaData.getColumnName(counter));
        System.out.println("Column type = " +
          myRSMetaData.getColumnType(counter));
        System.out.println("Column type name = " +
          myRSMetaData.getColumnTypeName(counter));
        System.out.println("Column display size = " +
          myRSMetaData.getColumnDisplaySize(counter));
        System.out.println("Column is nullable = " +
          myRSMetaData.isNullable(counter));
        System.out.println("Column precision = " +
          myRSMetaData.getPrecision(counter));
        System.out.println("Column scale = " +
          myRSMetaData.getScale(counter));
      }

      // get and display database meta data
      DatabaseMetaData myDBMetaData = myConnection.getMetaData();
      System.out.println("Database meta data follows");
      System.out.println("Database product name = " +
        myDBMetaData.getDatabaseProductName());
      System.out.println("Database URL = " +
        myDBMetaData.getURL());
      System.out.println("Database user name = " +
        myDBMetaData.getUserName());

      // close the ResultSet object using the close() method
      customerResultSet.close();

      // close the other JDBC objects
      myStatement.close();
      myConnection.close();

    } // end of main()
}
```

The output from this program is as follows:

```
Retrieved rows from customers table
Result set meta data follows
Column count = 5
```

```
Column name = ID
Column type = 2
Column type name = NUMBER
Column display size = 21
Column is nullable = 0
Column precision = 38
Column scale = 0
Column name = FIRST_NAME
Column type = 12
Column type name = VARCHAR2
Column display size = 10
Column is nullable = 0
Column precision = 10
Column scale = 0
Column name = LAST_NAME
Column type = 12
Column type name = VARCHAR2
Column display size = 10
Column is nullable = 0
Column precision = 10
Column scale = 0
Column name = DOB
Column type = 93
Column type name = DATE
Column display size = 7
Column is nullable = 1
Column precision = 0
Column scale = 0
Column name = PHONE
Column type = 12
Column type name = VARCHAR2
Column display size = 12
Column is nullable = 1
Column precision = 12
Column scale = 0
Database meta data follows
Database product name = Oracle
Database URL = jdbc:oracle:thin:@localhost:1521:ORCL
Database user name = STORE_USER
```

CHAPTER
5

PL/SQL and JDBC

n Chapter 2, I introduced you to PL/SQL, Oracle's procedural programming language that extends SQL. PL/SQL enables you to write things like procedures that are stored in the database. In Chapter 2, I showed you how to create procedures, functions, and packages in PL/SQL that allow you to centralize your business logic in the database; this business logic may then be called by any program that can access the database—including a JDBC program.

Also, if you have a lot of database intensive code—code that performs a lot of database operations—then you might want to consider rewriting that code using PL/SQL, which may run more quickly than comparable JDBC statements. Of course, you should run your own benchmarking tests to ensure such code does indeed result in a performance increase before deploying the code to your production servers.

In this chapter, I'll show you how to call PL/SQL procedures and functions using JDBC. I'll also show you how to use PL/SQL packages and REF CURSORs in JDBC. REF CURSORs are similar to pointers in the C language and allow you to read the contents of PL/SQL cursors.

Calling PL/SQL Procedures

Chapter 2 showed the definition of a PL/SQL procedure named update_product_price(). This procedure may be used to update a price of product in the products table. The update_product_price() procedure accepts two parameters: the product id (defined as a PL/SQL INTEGER) and a factor that is used to multiply the original price (this factor is defined as a PL/SQL NUMBER).

The procedure update_product_price() is defined as follows:

```
CREATE PROCEDURE update_product_price(

  p_product_id IN products.id%TYPE,
  p_factor     IN NUMBER

) AS

  product_count INTEGER;

BEGIN

  -- count the number of products with the
  -- supplied id (should be 1 if the product exists)
  SELECT
    COUNT(*)
  INTO
    product_count
```

```
FROM
  products
WHERE
  id = p_product_id;

-- if the product exists (product_count = 1) then
-- update that product's price
IF product_count = 1 THEN
  UPDATE
    products
  SET
    price = price * p_factor;
  COMMIT;
END IF;

END update_product_price;
/
```

If you were to call `update_product_price(1, 1.1)`, then this procedure would increase the price of product #1 by 10 percent. Similarly, calling `update_product_price(1, 0.8)` would decrease the price of product #1 by 20 percent.

There are three steps involved in calling a PL/SQL procedure:

1. Create and prepare a JDBC `CallableStatement` object containing a call to your PL/SQL procedure.

2. Provide parameter values to your PL/SQL procedure, if required.

3. Call the `execute()` method for your `CallableStatement`, which performs the call to your PL/SQL procedure.

The following sections describe the details of these steps.

Step 1: Create and Prepare a CallableStatement Object

The first step in calling a PL/SQL procedure using JDBC is to create and prepare a JDBC `CallableStatement` object. A `CallableStatement` object is similar to the `PreparedStatement` object described in Chapter 3. The following example creates a `CallableStatement` object named `myCallableStatement`; this object is used to call the PL/SQL procedure `update_product_price()`:

```
CallableStatement myCallableStatement = myConnection.prepareCall(
  "{call update_product_price(?, ?)}"
);
```

The prepareCall() method accepts a Java String; this String has curly brackets at the beginning and end, followed by the call keyword and finally the name of the PL/SQL procedure to call. The question marks ("?") indicate placeholders where you must provide actual values for the procedure call. These placeholders are similar to the placeholders used in a PreparedStatement object.

The placeholders represent the parameters that are passed to the update_product_price() procedure. The first placeholder corresponds to the product id that is to be updated, and the second placeholder corresponds to the factor that this product's price is to be multiplied by.

Step 2: Provide Parameter Values

The second step is to provide values to your CallableStatement object's placeholders using the set methods—a process I referred to in Chapter 3 as *binding* the values. The following example binds the int value 1, which corresponds to the product id, to the first placeholder using the setInt() method:

```
myCallableStatement.setInt(1, 1);
```

The next example binds the double value 1.1 to the second placeholder using the setDouble() method; this value corresponds to the multiplication factor, and therefore product #1's price will be increased by 10 percent:

```
myCallableStatement.setDouble(2, 1.1);
```

Step 3: Call the execute() Method

The third step is to call the execute() method for your CallableStatement object; this method actually invokes the PL/SQL procedure. The following example calls the execute() method for myCallableStatement:

```
myCallableStatement.execute();
```

This causes the PL/SQL procedure update_product_price() to be called using the appropriate parameters that were set in the previous step. This example increases the price of product #1 by 10 percent.

When you're finished with your CallableStatement object, you should close it using the close() method; for example:

```
myCallableStatement.close();
```

You'll see a complete program that uses these example statements after the next section.

Calling PL/SQL Functions

Chapter 2 showed the definition of a PL/SQL function named update_product_ price_func(), which is similar to the procedure shown in the previous section. This function accepts two parameters: a product id and a factor that is used to multiply that product's price. However, because update_product_price_func() is a function, it also returns a result; if the product doesn't exist this function returns 0 (otherwise it returns 1). The definition for this function is as follows:

```
CREATE FUNCTION update_product_price_func(

  p_product_id IN products.id%TYPE,
  p_factor     IN NUMBER

) RETURN INTEGER AS

  product_count INTEGER;

BEGIN

  SELECT
    COUNT(*)
  INTO
    product_count
  FROM
    products
  WHERE
    id = p_product_id;

  -- if the product doesn't exist then return 0,
  -- otherwise perform the update and return 1
  IF product_count = 0 THEN
    RETURN 0;
  ELSE
    UPDATE
      products
    SET
      price = price * p_factor;
    COMMIT;
    RETURN 1;
  END IF;

END update_product_price_func;
/
```

If you were to call `update_product_price_func(1, 0.8)`, it would decrease the price of product #1 by 20 percent, and it would return 1 because that product exists in the `products` table. However, if you were to call `update_product_price_func(100, 0.8)`, it would return 0 because that product doesn't exist in the `products` table.

There are five steps involved in calling a PL/SQL function:

1. Create and prepare a JDBC `CallableStatement` object containing a call to your PL/SQL function.

2. Register the output parameter for your PL/SQL function.

3. Provide parameter values to your PL/SQL function, if required.

4. Call the `execute()` method for your `CallableStatement`, which performs the call to your PL/SQL function.

5. Read the returned value from your PL/SQL function.

The following sections describe the details of these steps.

Step 1: Create and Prepare a CallableStatement Object

The first step in calling a PL/SQL function using JDBC is to create and prepare a JDBC `CallableStatement` object:

```
CallableStatement
myCallableStatement = myConnection.prepareCall(
  "{? = call update_product_price_func(?, ?)}"
);
```

This example creates a `CallableStatement` object named `myCallableStatement`. The `prepareCall()` method accepts a Java `String` similar to that shown for a PL/SQL procedure in the previous section, except that an additional placeholder is added near the beginning to represent the value returned by the PL/SQL function.

The second placeholder in this example corresponds to the product id that is to be updated, and the third placeholder corresponds to the factor that this product's price is to be multiplied by.

Step 2: Register the Output Parameter

The second step is to register the output parameter from your PL/SQL function using the `registerOutParameter()` method. The following statement registers the integer parameter returned by the PL/SQL function `update_product_price_func()`:

```
myCallableStatement.registerOutParameter(1, java.sql.Types.INTEGER);
```

The `registerOutParameter()` method accepts two parameters: the numerical position of the placeholder from the string supplied to the `CallableStatement` object and the PL/SQL type for the output parameter. This PL/SQL type may come from the constants defined in the `java.sql.Types` class, which I discussed in Chapter 3. You can also use the constants defined in the `oracle.jdbc.OracleTypes` class, which may be used with all of the Oracle database and PL/SQL types. Tables C-3 and C-6 in Appendix C show the constants defined in the `java.sql.Types` and `oracle.jdbc.OracleTypes` classes.

> **NOTE**
> The `registerOutParameter()` method can also accept a third parameter that specifies the SQL type name, although this is only appropriate when using a REF, STRUCT, or ARRAY type. I'll discuss the use of these types later in this book.

For the previous example, a PL/SQL `INTEGER` is registered for the first placeholder; this placeholder corresponds to the result returned from the PL/SQL function `update_product_ price_func()` in the string supplied to the `prepareCall()` method in Step 1.

If you had a PL/SQL procedure or function with other output parameters, then you can also register those parameters using the `registerOutParameter()` method.

Step 3: Provide Parameter Values

The third step is to provide values to your `CallableStatement` object using the set methods. The following examples bind the `int` value 1 to the second placeholder (this value corresponds to the product id) using the `setInt()` method and bind the `double` value 0.8 to the third placeholder (this value corresponds to the multiplication factor) using the `setDouble()` method:

```
myCallableStatement.setInt(2, 1);
myCallableStatement.setDouble(3, 0.8);
```

Step 4: Run the CallableStatement

The fourth step is to call the execute() method for your CallableStatement object, which actually invokes your PL/SQL function. The following example calls the execute() method for myCallableStatement:

```
myCallableStatement.execute();
```

This causes the PL/SQL function update_product_price_func() to be called with the appropriate parameters set in Step 3. This example decreases the price of product #1 by 20 percent.

Step 5: Read the Returned Value

The fifth step is to read the result returned by your PL/SQL function. To do this, you use a get method. In the following example, the getInt() method is used to read the integer returned by update_product_price_func():

```
int result = myCallableStatement.getInt(1);
```

When you're finished with your CallableStatement, you must close it using the close() method.

Example Program: PLSQLExample1.java

The program PLSQLExample1.java, shown in the following listing, shows how to call the PL/SQL procedure update_product_price() and how to call the PL/SQL function update_product_price_func(). The program performs the following tasks:

1. Displays the id and original price for product #1.

2. Calls the PL/SQL procedure update_product_price() to increase the price of product #1 by 10 percent using a CallableStatement object.

3. Displays the id and new price for product #1.

4. Calls the PL/SQL function update_product_price_func() to decrease the price of product #1 by 20 percent using the same CallableStatement object. The returned result from update_product_price_func() is stored and displayed.

5. Displays the id and new price for product #1.

6. Resets the price of product #1 back the original value.

```
/*
  PLSQLExample1.java shows how to call a PL/SQL procedure
  and function
*/

// import the JDBC packages
import java.sql.*;

public class PLSQLExample1 {

  public static void main(String args [])
  throws SQLException {

    // register the Oracle JDBC drivers
    DriverManager.registerDriver(
      new oracle.jdbc.OracleDriver()
    );

    // create a Connection object, and connect to the database
    // as store_user using the Oracle JDBC Thin driver
    Connection myConnection = DriverManager.getConnection(
      "jdbc:oracle:thin:@localhost:1521:ORCL",
      "store_user",
      "store_password"
    );

    // disable auto-commit mode
    myConnection.setAutoCommit(false);

     // create a Statement object
    Statement myStatement = myConnection.createStatement();

    // display product #1's id and price
    System.out.println("Id and original price");
    displayProduct(myStatement, 1);

    // create a CallableStatement object to call the
    // PL/SQL procedure update_product_price()
    CallableStatement myCallableStatement =
     myConnection.prepareCall(
       "{call update_product_price(?, ?)}"
     );
```

```
// bind values to the CallableStatement object's parameters
myCallableStatement.setInt(1, 1);
myCallableStatement.setDouble(2, 1.1);

// execute the CallableStatement object - this increases the price
// for product #1 by 10%
myCallableStatement.execute();
System.out.println("Increased price by 10%");
displayProduct(myStatement, 1);

// call the PL/SQL function update_product_price_func()
myCallableStatement = myConnection.prepareCall(
  "{? = call update_product_price_func(?, ?)}"
);

// register the output parameter, and bind values to
// the CallableStatement object's parameters
myCallableStatement.registerOutParameter(1,
  java.sql.Types.INTEGER);
myCallableStatement.setInt(2, 1);
myCallableStatement.setDouble(3, 0.8);

// execute the CallableStatement object - this decreases the new
// price for product #1 by 20%
myCallableStatement.execute();
int result = myCallableStatement.getInt(1);
System.out.println("Result returned from function = " + result);
System.out.println("Decreased new price by 20%");
displayProduct(myStatement, 1);

// reset the price back to the original value
myStatement.execute(
  "UPDATE products " +
  "SET price = 19.95" +
  "WHERE id = 1"
);
myConnection.commit();
System.out.println("Reset price back to 19.95");

// close the JDBC objects
myCallableStatement.close();
myStatement.close();
```

```
    myConnection.close();

  } // end of main()


  public static void displayProduct(
    Statement myStatement,
    int id
  ) throws SQLException {

    // display the id and price columns
    ResultSet productResultSet = myStatement.executeQuery(
      "SELECT id, price " +
      "FROM products " +
      "WHERE id = " + id
    );
    productResultSet.next();
    System.out.println("id = " + productResultSet.getInt("id"));
    System.out.println("price = " +
      productResultSet.getDouble("price"));

    productResultSet.close();

  } // end of displayRow()

}
```

The output from this program is as follows:

```
Id and original price
id = 1
price = 19.95
Increased price by 10%
id = 1
price = 21.95
Result returned from function = 1
Decreased new price by 20%
id = 1
price = 17.56
Reset price back to 19.95
```

Using PL/SQL Packages and REF CURSORs

In Chapter 2, I showed you how PL/SQL procedures and functions could be grouped together into packages; packages are used to encapsulate functionality into one self-contained unit. I also introduced you to REF CURSORs, which are similar to pointers in the C programming language. You can use a REF CURSOR to point to the result set returned by a SELECT statement that you execute through a PL/SQL cursor.

Chapter 2 showed the definition of a package named ref_cursor_package. This package declares a function named get_products_ref_cursor(); this function retrieves the rows from the products table using a PL/SQL cursor and returns a REF CURSOR that points to the rows in that cursor. The package body for ref_cursor_package is declared as follows:

```
CREATE PACKAGE BODY ref_cursor_package AS

  -- function get_products_ref_cursor() returns a REF CURSOR
  FUNCTION get_products_ref_cursor
  RETURN t_ref_cursor IS

    products_ref_cursor t_ref_cursor;

  BEGIN

    -- get the REF CURSOR
    OPEN products_ref_cursor FOR
      SELECT
        id, name, price
      FROM
        products;

    -- return the REF CURSOR
    RETURN products_ref_cursor;

  END get_products_ref_cursor;

END ref_cursor_package;
/
```

To call the function get_products_ref_cursor() in the package ref_cursor_package, you may use the following statement:

```
OracleCallableStatement myCallableStatement =
    (OracleCallableStatement) myConnection.prepareCall(
     "{? = call ref_cursor_package.get_products_ref_cursor()}"
    );
```

Notice that I've created an `OracleCallableStatement` object, one of the Oracle JDBC extensions that I discussed in Chapter 3. The `OracleCallableStatement` class defines a method named `getCursor()` that enables you to read Oracle cursors. I'll use this method shortly.

Next, the following statements first register the output parameter from the function as an Oracle cursor (`oracle.jdbc.OracleTypes.CURSOR`) and then execute `myOracleCallableStatement`:

```
myCallableStatement.registerOutParameter(1, OracleTypes.CURSOR);
myCallableStatement.execute();
```

Calling the `execute()` method for `myCallableStatement` invokes the `get_customers_ref_cursor()` function. The following statement then retrieves the Oracle cursor returned by the call to `get_products_ref_cursor()` using the `getCursor()` method and stores it in an `OracleResultSet` object:

```
OracleResultSet productResultSet =
    (OracleResultSet) myCallableStatement.getCursor(1);
```

Finally the column values stored in `productResultSet` can then be read using the usual `next()` and get methods. For example, the following `while` loop displays the product ids stored in `productResultSet`:

```
while (productResultSet.next()) {
    System.out.println("id = " + productResultSet.getInt("id"));
} // end of while
```

You don't have to use `OracleCallableStatement` and `OracleResultSet` objects; you could use regular `CallableStatement` and `ResultSet` objects. If you were to use `CallableStatement` and `ResultSet` objects, however, you must use the `getObject()` method to read the Oracle cursor, as shown in the following example:

```
CallableStatement myCallableStatement = myConnection.prepareCall(
    "{? = call ref_cursor_package.get_products_ref_cursor()}"
    );

// register the output parameter as an Oracle CURSOR
myCallableStatement.registerOutParameter(1, OracleTypes.CURSOR);
```

```
// execute the call
myCallableStatement.execute();

// get the cursor using a call to the getObject() method,
// the returned object must be cast to a ResultSet
ResultSet productResultSet =
  (ResultSet) myCallableStatement.getObject(1);
```

There are two example programs available in the `program` directory where you unzipped the ZIP file for this book; these programs illustrate the use of PL/SQL packages and REF CURSORs to read the rows stored in the `products` table. These programs are `PLSQLExample2.java` and `PLSQLExample3.java`. The program `PLSQLExample2.java` uses `OracleCallableStatement` and `OracleResultSet` objects; `PLSQLExample3.java` uses `CallableStatement` and `ResultSet` objects. The listings for these programs are omitted from this book for brevity.

In Chapter 10, I'll show you how to create Java stored procedures, which are procedures that are written in Java and are stored in the database. Java stored procedures offer you an alternative way of providing procedures that are written in Java rather than Oracle's proprietary PL/SQL.

CHAPTER
6

Database Objects

bject-oriented programming languages such as Java and C++ allow you to define classes; these classes act as templates from which you can create objects. Classes define attributes and methods; attributes are used to store an object's state, and methods are used to model an object's behaviors. With the release of the Oracle8*i* database, objects became available within the database, and they contain even more features in Oracle9*i*. The availability of objects in the database was a major breakthrough because they enable you to define your own classes, known as *object types*, in the database. Like classes in Java, database object types can contain attributes and methods. Object types are also sometimes known as user-defined types.

A simple example of an object type would be a type that models a product. This object type could contain attributes for the product's name, description, price, and in the case of a product that is perishable, the number of days the product can sit on the shelves before it must be thrown away. This product object type could also contain a method that returns the sell-by date of the product, based on the shelf life of the product and the current date. Another example of an object type might be one that models a person; this object type could store attributes for the person's first name, last name, date of birth, and address. The address itself could be an object type, and it could store things like the street, city, state, and zip code. You'll see examples of object types that represent a product, person, and address in this chapter. You'll also see how to create tables from those object types, populate those tables with rows, and then access those tables using JDBC.

I provided a SQL*Plus script named `object_user.sql` in the `sql` directory where you unzipped the files for this book. This script may be run against an Oracle8*i* or Oracle9*i* database. This script contains the SQL DDL statements that create the object types and tables used in this chapter; this script also populates the tables with sample data. You should run this script (or have your DBA run it) before running the programs shown in this chapter. You'll also learn about some of the exciting new collection features introduced with the Oracle9*i* database in this chapter.

Creating Object Types

You create an object type using the SQL DDL `CREATE TYPE` statement. The following example uses the `CREATE TYPE` statement to create an object type named `address_typ`; this object type is used to represent an address and contains four attributes named `street`, `city`, `state`, and `zip`:

```
CREATE TYPE address_typ AS OBJECT (
   street VARCHAR2(15),
   city   VARCHAR2(15),
   state  CHAR(2),
   zip    VARCHAR2(5)
);
/
```

As you can see, each attribute is defined using a database type. For example, `street` is defined as `VARCHAR2(15)`. As you'll see shortly, the type of an attribute can itself be an object type.

NOTE
I add _typ to the end of my object types. You can follow this standard when creating your own object types, or you can use your own standard—just be sure to use your standard consistently.

As I mentioned at the start of this chapter, I'm going to represent a person using an object type. The following statement creates an object type named `person_typ`; notice that `person_typ` uses `address_typ` to define an attribute named `address`:

```
CREATE TYPE person_typ AS OBJECT (
    id          NUMBER,
    first_name  VARCHAR2(10),
    last_name   VARCHAR2(10),
    dob         DATE,
    phone       VARCHAR2(12),
    address     address_typ
);
/
```

The next example creates an object type named `product_typ` that will be used to represent products; notice that `product_typ` declares a function named `get_sell_by_date()`; this function will return the date by which the product must be sold based on the `days_valid` attribute and the current date:

```
CREATE TYPE product_typ AS OBJECT (
    id          NUMBER,
    name        VARCHAR2(15),
    description VARCHAR2(22),
    price       NUMBER(5, 2),
    days_valid  NUMBER,

    -- declare the get_sell_by_date() member function,
    -- get_sell_by_date() returns the date by which the
    -- product must be sold
    MEMBER FUNCTION get_sell_by_date RETURN DATE
);
/
```

The `MEMBER FUNCTION` clause is used to declare the `get_sell_by_date()` function. You can declare a procedure using the `MEMBER PROCEDURE` clause. A procedure is similar to a function, except that a procedure doesn't return a value.

Since `product_typ` contains a method declaration, a *body* for `product_typ` must also be created. The body defines the code for the method, and a body is created using the `CREATE TYPE BODY` statement. The following example creates the body for `product_typ`; notice that this body contains the code definition for the `get_sell_by_date()` method:

```
CREATE TYPE BODY product_typ AS

  -- define the get_sell_by_date() member function,
  -- get_sell_by_date() returns the date by which the
  -- product must be sold
  MEMBER FUNCTION get_sell_by_date RETURN DATE IS

    sell_by_date DATE;

  BEGIN

    -- calculate the sell by date by adding the days_valid attribute
    -- to the current date (sysdate)
    SELECT
      days_valid + sysdate
    INTO
      sell_by_date
    FROM
      dual;

    -- return the sell by date
    RETURN sell_by_date;

  END;

END;
/
```

As you can see, `get_sell_by_date()` calculates and returns the date by which the product must be sold by adding the `days_valid` attribute to the current date (obtained from the database using the `sysdate` variable).

Using Object Types to Define Column Objects and Object Tables

You can use an object type to define a column in table, and the column is known as a *column object*. Also, when an object type contains an embedded object type,

then that embedded object type is also a column object; an example of this is
person_typ, which contains an embedded address_typ column object.

The following example creates a table named products that contains a
column object of product_typ; notice that this table also contains a NUMBER
column named quantity_in_stock that is used to store the number of those
products currently in stock:

```
CREATE TABLE products (
  product            product_typ,
  quantity_in_stock NUMBER
);
```

You can also use an object type to define an entire table, and the table is
known as an *object table*. The following examples create two object tables, named
object_products and object_customers, which are defined using
product_typ and person_typ respectively; notice the use of the OF clause
to identify each table as an object table:

```
CREATE TABLE object_products OF product_typ;
CREATE TABLE object_customers OF person_typ;
```

One difference between a table containing a column object and an object
table is that the former can have more than one column. For example, I added
the additional quantity_in_stock column to the products table.

Object References and Object Identifiers

Another difference of object tables is that you use *object references* to model
relationships between object tables, rather than foreign keys. Object references
are defined using the REF type and are basically pointers to objects in an object
table. Each object in an object table has a unique *object identifier* (or OID) that
you can then store in a REF column. The following example creates a table
named purchases that contains two REF columns:

```
CREATE TABLE purchases (
  id         NUMBER PRIMARY KEY,
  customer REF person_typ  SCOPE IS object_customers,
  product  REF product_typ SCOPE IS object_products
);
```

The SCOPE IS clause restricts the object reference to point to objects in a
specific table. For example, the customer column is restricted to point to objects
in the object_customers table; similarly, the product column is restricted to
point to objects in the object_products table.

In the following sections, you'll learn how to perform SQL DML operations on the `products`, `object_products`, `object_customers`, and `purchases` tables. You might wonder why I cover so many DML examples. The answer is that I want you to see examples of the various DML statements when using column objects, object tables, and object references. This will make the Java code you'll see later much easier to follow.

Performing DML on the products Table

In this section, you'll see how to perform SQL DML statements to insert, select, update, and delete rows in the `products` table. The `products` table is defined as follows:

```
CREATE TABLE products (
  product             product_typ,
  quantity_in_stock NUMBER
);
```

Inserting Rows into the products Table

When inserting a row into a table containing a column object, you must supply the attribute values for that object using a *constructor*. The constructor for the object has the same name as the object type and accepts parameters for the attributes of the object. The following examples insert two rows into the `products` table; notice the use of the `product_typ` constructor to supply the attribute values for the `product` column object:

```
INSERT INTO products (
  product,
  quantity_in_stock
) VALUES (
  product_typ(1, 'Pasta', '20 oz bag of pasta', 3.95, 10),
  50
);

INSERT INTO products (
  product,
  quantity_in_stock
) VALUES (
  product_typ(2, 'Sardines', '12 oz box of sardines', 2.99, 5),
  25
);
```

The SQL*Plus script `object_user.sql` contains these two `INSERT` statements, along with the other `INSERT` statements featured in this chapter.

Selecting Rows from the products Table

The following example selects all the rows from the products table; notice that the product column object's attributes are displayed within a constructor for product_typ:

```
SQL> SELECT * FROM products;

PRODUCT(ID, NAME, DESCRIPTION, PRICE, DAYS_VALID)
----------------------------------------------------------
QUANTITY_IN_STOCK
-----------------
PRODUCT_TYP(1, 'Pasta', '20 oz bag of pasta', 3.95, 10)
             50

PRODUCT_TYP(2, 'Sardines', '12 oz box of sardines', 2.99, 5)
             25
```

You can go ahead and enter this SELECT statement in SQL*Plus if you want to. You can also select an individual column object from a table. To do this, you must supply a table alias through which you select the object (table aliases were introduced in Chapter 2). The following example selects a single product column object from the products table; notice the use of the table alias p through which the product object's id attribute is specified:

```
SQL> SELECT p.product FROM products p WHERE p.product.id = 1;

PRODUCT(ID, NAME, DESCRIPTION, PRICE, DAYS_VALID)
--------------------------------------------------------
PRODUCT_TYP(1, 'Pasta', '20 oz bag of pasta', 3.95, 10)
```

Earlier, you saw that the product_typ object type contains a function named get_sell_by_date() that calculates and returns the date by which the product must be sold; it does this by adding the days_valid attribute to the current date, which is obtained from the database using the sysdate variable. You can call the get_sell_by_date() function using a table alias, for example:

```
SQL> SELECT p.product.get_sell_by_date() FROM products p;

P.PRODUCT
---------
12-MAR-02
07-MAR-02
```

Of course, if you run this example your dates will be different because they are calculated using sysdate.

Updating a Row in the products Table

The following example updates a row in the products table; notice that a table alias is used to access the product column object:

```
UPDATE products p
SET p.product.description = '30 oz bag of pasta'
WHERE p.product.id = 1;
```

Deleting a Row from the products Table

The following example deletes a row from the products table; notice that a table alias is used to access the product column object:

```
DELETE FROM products p
WHERE p.product.id = 2;
```

> **NOTE**
> *If you're following along with these UPDATE and DELETE statements in SQL*Plus, don't bother committing your changes. You can either perform a rollback to undo any changes you make, or you can run the object_user.sql script again to recreate the schema and populate the tables. That way, the output from the programs you'll see later will be the same as the output shown in this chapter.*

Performing DML on the object_products Table

The object_products table is an object table consisting of product_typ objects; this table is defined as follows:

```
CREATE TABLE object_products OF product_typ;
```

In this section, you'll see how to perform SQL DML statements to insert, select, update, and delete rows in the object_products table.

Inserting Rows into the object_products Table

When inserting a row into an object table, you can choose whether to use a constructor to supply attribute values, or to supply the values in same way that you would supply column values in a relational table. The following example inserts a row into the `object_products` table using the constructor for `product_typ`:

```
INSERT INTO object_products VALUES (
   product_typ(1, 'Pasta', '20 oz bag of pasta', 3.95, 10)
);
```

The next example omits the constructor for `product_typ` when inserting a row into `object_products`; notice that the attribute values for `product_typ` are supplied in the same way that columns would be in a relational table:

```
INSERT INTO object_products (
   id, name, description, price, days_valid
) VALUES (
   2, 'Sardines', '12 oz box of sardines', 2.99, 5
);
```

Selecting Rows from the object_products Table

The following example selects all the rows from the `object_products` table:

```
SQL> SELECT * FROM object_products;

        ID NAME       DESCRIPTION               PRICE DAYS_VALID
---------- ---------- -------------------- ---------- ----------
         1 Pasta      20 oz bag of pasta         3.95         10
         2 Sardines   12 oz box of sardines      2.99          5
```

You can use the built-in Oracle database `VALUE()` function to select a row from an object table; this treats the row as an actual object and returns the attributes for the object within a constructor for the object type. The `VALUE()` function accepts a parameter containing a table alias, and the next example uses the `VALUE()` function when selecting the rows from `object_products`:

```
SQL> SELECT VALUE(op) FROM object_products op;

VALUE(OP)(ID, NAME, DESCRIPTION, PRICE, DAYS_VALID)
-----------------------------------------------------------
PRODUCT_TYP(1, 'Pasta', '20 oz bag of pasta', 3.95, 10)
PRODUCT_TYP(2, 'Sardines', '12 oz box of sardines', 2.99, 5)
```

You might be wondering why you'd use the `VALUE()` function. The answer is that you'd use it when selecting rows as objects using JDBC statements, and you'll see examples of this later.

Updating a Row in the object_products Table

The following example updates a row in the `object_products` table; notice that the attributes are treated like columns in a relational table:

```
UPDATE object_products
SET description = '25 oz bag of pasta'
WHERE id = 1;
```

Deleting a Row from the object_products Table

The following example deletes a row from the `object_products` table; notice that the `id` attribute is again treated like a relational column:

```
DELETE FROM object_products
WHERE id = 2;
```

Performing DML on the object_customers Table

The `object_customers` table is an object table of `person_typ`; `person_typ` contains an embedded `address_typ` column object named `address`. The `object_customers` table is defined as follows:

```
CREATE TABLE object_customers OF person_typ;
```

In this section, you'll see how to perform SQL DML statements to insert and select rows in the `object_customers` table. Since updates and deletes for `object_customers` are conceptually similar to the previous examples for `object_products`, I won't show examples of an update and delete for `object_products`.

Inserting Rows into the object_customers Table

The following examples insert two rows into `object_customers`; the first example uses constructors for `person_typ` and `address_typ`, while the second example omits the `person_typ` constructor:

```
INSERT INTO object_customers VALUES (
  person_typ(1, 'John', 'Brown', '01-FEB-1955', '800-555-1211',
    address_typ('2 State Street', 'Beantown', 'MA', '12345')
  )
);
```

```
INSERT INTO object_customers (
  id, first_name, last_name, dob, phone,
  address
) VALUES (
  2, 'Cynthia', 'Green', '05-FEB-1968', '800-555-1212',
  address_typ('3 Free Street', 'Middle Town', 'CA', '12345')
);
```

Selecting Rows from the object_customers Table

The object_customers table is an object table of person_typ; person_typ contains an embedded address_typ column object named address. The following example selects all the rows from the object_customers table; notice that the attributes for the embedded address column object are displayed within the address_typ constructor:

```
SQL> SELECT * FROM object_customers;

        ID FIRST_NAME LAST_NAME  DOB       PHONE
---------- ---------- ---------- --------- ------------
ADDRESS(STREET, CITY, STATE, ZIP)
----------------------------------------------------------
         1 John       Brown      01-FEB-55 800-555-1211
ADDRESS_TYP('2 State Street', 'Beantown', 'MA', '12345')

         2 Cynthia    Green      05-FEB-68 800-555-1212
ADDRESS_TYP('3 Free Street', 'Middle Town', 'CA', '12345')
```

The next example selects a single row from object_customers; notice the use of the table alias oc through which the id attribute is specified:

```
SQL> SELECT * FROM object_customers oc WHERE oc.id = 1;

        ID FIRST_NAME LAST_NAME  DOB       PHONE
---------- ---------- ---------- --------- ------------
ADDRESS(STREET, CITY, STATE, ZIP)
----------------------------------------------------------
         1 John       Brown      01-FEB-55 800-555-1211
ADDRESS_TYP('2 State Street', 'Beantown', 'MA', '12345')
```

In the following example, a row is selected based on the state attribute of the address column object:

```
SQL> SELECT * FROM object_customers oc WHERE oc.address.state = 'MA';

        ID FIRST_NAME LAST_NAME  DOB       PHONE
```

```
---------- ---------- ---------- --------- -----------
ADDRESS(STREET, CITY, STATE, ZIP)
------------------------------------------------------------------
         1 John       Brown       01-FEB-55 800-555-1211
ADDRESS_TYP('2 State Street', 'Beantown', 'MA', '12345')
```

Performing DML on the purchases Table

The purchases table contains a NUMBER column named id, along with two REF columns named customer and product. The purchases table is defined as follows:

```
CREATE TABLE purchases (
   id        NUMBER PRIMARY KEY,
   customer REF person_typ  SCOPE IS object_customers,
   product  REF product_typ SCOPE IS object_products
);
```

In this section, you'll see how to perform SQL DML statements to insert, select, and update a row in the purchases table.

Inserting a Row into the purchases Table

As I mentioned, each object in an object table has a unique object identifier that you can store in a REF column. You can access this object identifier using the REF() function and store the returned object identifier in a REF column. The following example inserts a row into the purchases table; notice the use of the REF() function to read the object identifiers for the rows from the object_customers and object_products tables:

```
INSERT INTO purchases (
   id,
   customer,
   product
) VALUES (
   1,
   (SELECT REF(oc) FROM object_customers oc WHERE oc.id = 1),
   (SELECT REF(op) FROM object_products  op WHERE op.id = 1)
);
```

This example records that customer #1 purchased product #1.

Selecting a Row from the purchases Table

The following example selects the row from the `purchases` table; notice that the `customer` and `product` columns contain long strings of numbers and letters; these are the object identifiers for the rows in the `object_customers` and `object_products` tables:

```
SQL> SELECT * FROM purchases;

        ID
----------
CUSTOMER
----------------------------------------------------------------------
PRODUCT
----------------------------------------------------------------------
         1
0000220208662E2AB6256711D6A1B50010A4E7AE8A662E2AB3256711D6A1B50010A4E
7AE8A
0000220208662E2AB4256711D6A1B50010A4E7AE8A662E2AB2256711D6A1B50010A4E
7AE8A
```

You can access the rows in the object tables that are pointed to by REF column values using the `DEREF()` function; this function accepts a REF column as a parameter. The following example uses the `DEREF()` function to access the rows pointed to by the `customer` and `product` columns of the `purchases` table:

```
SQL> SELECT DEREF(customer), DEREF(product) FROM purchases;

DEREF(CUSTOMER)(ID, FIRST_NAME, LAST_NAME, DOB, PHONE,
 ADDRESS(STREET, CITY, STATE, ZIP))
------------------------------------------------------
DEREF(PRODUCT)(ID, NAME, DESCRIPTION, PRICE, DAYS_VALID)
------------------------------------------------------
PERSON_TYP(1, 'John', 'Brown', '01-FEB-55', '800-555-1211',
 ADDRESS_TYP('2 State Street', 'Beantown', 'MA', '12345'))
PRODUCT_TYP(1, 'Pasta', '20 oz bag of pasta', 3.95, 10)
```

Updating a Row in the purchases Table

The following example updates the row in the `purchases` table; notice that the `product` column is changed to point to product #2 in the `object_products` table:

```
UPDATE purchases SET product = (
    SELECT REF(op) FROM object_products op WHERE op.id = 2
) WHERE id = 1;
```

Oracle9*i* Database Type Inheritance

With the release of the Oracle9*i* database, you can use object type *inheritance*. This is a major step forward because you can now define hierarchies of database types. For example, you might want to define a business person object type and have that type inherit existing attributes from `person_typ`. The business person type could extend `person_typ` with attributes to store the person's job title and the name of the company they work for. For `person_typ` to be inherited from, it must be defined using the `NOT FINAL` clause:

```
CREATE TYPE person_typ AS OBJECT (
    id          NUMBER,
    first_name VARCHAR2(10),
    last_name  VARCHAR2(10),
    dob         DATE,
    phone       VARCHAR2(12),
    address     address_typ
) NOT FINAL;
/
```

The `NOT FINAL` clause indicates that `person_typ` can be inherited from when defining another type. The default is `FINAL`, meaning that the object type cannot be inherited from.

NOTE
I've provided a SQL*Plus script named
`object_user_9i.sql` *in the* `sql` *directory.*
You can run this script if you are using an
Oracle9i database.

To have a new type inherit attributes and methods from an existing type, you use the `UNDER` clause when defining your new type. Our example business person type, which I'll name `business_person_typ`, uses the `UNDER` clause to inherit the attributes from `person_typ`:

```
CREATE TYPE business_person_typ UNDER person_typ (
    title   VARCHAR2(20),
    company VARCHAR2(20)
);
/
```

In this example, `person_typ` is known as the *supertype*, and `business_person_typ` is known as the *subtype*. You can then use `business_person_typ` when defining column objects or object tables. For example, the following statement creates an object table named `object_business_customers`:

```
CREATE TABLE object_business_customers OF business_person_typ;
```

The following example inserts a row into `object_business_customers`; notice that the two additional `title` and `company` attributes are supplied:

```
INSERT INTO object_business_customers VALUES (
    business_person_typ(1, 'John', 'Brown', '01-FEB-1955', '800-555-1211',
      address_typ('2 State Street', 'Beantown', 'MA', '12345'),
      'Manager', 'XYZ Corp'
    )
);
```

The final example selects this row:

```
SQL> SELECT * FROM object_business_customers;

       ID FIRST_NAME LAST_NAME  DOB       PHONE
---------- ---------- ---------- --------- ------------
ADDRESS(STREET, CITY, STATE, ZIP)
-------------------------------------------------------
TITLE                COMPANY
-------------------- --------------------
        1 John       Brown       01-FEB-55 800-555-1211
ADDRESS_TYP('2 State Street', 'Beantown', 'MA', '12345')
Manager              XYZ Corp
```

NOT INSTANTIABLE Object Types

You can mark an object type as NOT INSTANTIABLE, this prevents objects of that type from being added to tables. You might want to mark an object type as NOT INSTANTIABLE when you want to use that type only as part of another type or as a supertype. The following example marks `address_typ` as NOT INSTANTIABLE:

```
CREATE TYPE address_typ AS OBJECT (
    street VARCHAR2(15),
    city   VARCHAR2(15),
    state  CHAR(2),
    zip    VARCHAR2(5)
) NOT INSTANTIABLE;
/
```

Accessing Database Objects Using Weakly Typed Java Objects

In this section, you'll learn how to access object tables in a Java program using *weakly typed objects*. Weakly typed objects are objects of the `oracle.sql.STRUCT` class. `STRUCT` objects are referred to as weakly typed because their attributes are represented using the generic Java `Object` class and therefore don't have a specific type. When you use weakly typed objects, you must make sure you are casting the object attributes to the required type.

NOTE
The `Object` class is at the top of the Java class hierarchy; all other classes in Java are derived from `Object`.

As you'll see later, you can also use *strongly typed objects* that use a specific class to represent objects and their attributes. Why would you want to use weakly typed objects when you can use strongly typed objects? Weakly typed objects have two advantages:

- You can use weakly typed objects with any database object type. Strongly typed objects use a different class for each database object type.

- You save some memory and time since you don't incur the overhead associated with creating a strongly typed object.

For these reasons, you should typically use weakly typed objects if you are selecting and inserting data without doing a lot of manipulation of that data in memory. On the other hand, if you do need to do a lot of manipulation of data in memory, you should use strongly typed objects, since they store the data in a more convenient form for data manipulation using Java statements. You'll see how to use strongly typed objects later in this chapter.

Now, you could choose to treat object tables as relational tables in your code. If you do this, you treat the object attributes as relational columns, and you can use the standard techniques for accessing the columns shown in the earlier chapters. In this section, I'll treat object tables as consisting of objects so that you can learn how to handle such objects using JDBC. In the following sections, you'll see how to insert, select, update, and delete objects in the `object_products` table.

Inserting a Database Object Using a STRUCT

To insert a database object using a STRUCT, you follow these steps:

1. Create a StructDescriptor object for the database object type.

2. Create an Object array to store the attributes for your new database object.

3. Create a STRUCT object, passing your StructDescriptor, Connection, and Object array to the constructor of your STRUCT object.

4. Use a prepared statement to insert your STRUCT into the table.

In the following sections, I'll describe the details of these steps, along with example code that inserts a row into the object_products table.

Step 1: Create a StructDescriptor Object for the Database Object Type

The first step is to create a StructDescriptor object for the database object type. The StructDescriptor class is located in the oracle.sql package, and the examples in this section assume that oracle.sql.StructDescriptor has been imported.

The StructDescriptor object is used to represent the details of your database object type, and its contents are required later in Step 3 when creating the STRUCT object. The StructDescriptor class contains a method named createDescriptor() that accepts two parameters:

- The first parameter is the name of your database schema and object type, which is known as the *fully qualified* name of the database object type. For example: OBJECT_USER.PRODUCT_TYP.

- The second parameter is your Connection object.

The following example creates a StructDescriptor object named productDescriptor; notice that the parameters to createDescriptor() are "OBJECT_USER.PRODUCT_TYP" and myConnection:

```
StructDescriptor productDescriptor =
  StructDescriptor.createDescriptor(
    "OBJECT_USER.PRODUCT_TYP", myConnection
  );
```

The `productDescriptor` object contains the details for the `OBJECT_USER.PRODUCT_TYP` database object type. Some other methods in the `StructDescriptor` class are as follows:

- **getName()**   Returns the fully qualified name of the database object type.

- **getLength()**   Returns the number attributes in the database object type.

- **getMetaData()**   Returns the meta-data for the database object type. The meta-data is returned in a `ResultSetMetaData` object and contains the attribute name, type code, and precision for `NUMBER` attributes. I covered meta-data in Chapter 4.

Step 2: Create an Object Array to Store the Attributes for the New Database Object

The second step is to create an `Object` array to store the attributes for the database object. The five attributes for `PRODUCT_TYP` are as follows:

```
id           NUMBER
name         VARCHAR2(10)
description  VARCHAR2(22)
price        NUMBER(5, 2)
days_valid   NUMBER
```

Since your `Object` array must contain an element for each database object attribute, your array must contain five elements, one for each attribute in `PRODUCT_TYP`. The following example creates an `Object` array named `productAttributes` with five elements:

```
Object [] productAttributes = new Object[5];
```

Next, each element in `productAttributes` must be set to the values you want to set the attributes of the database object to. You must map the database attribute types to appropriate Java objects. For example, you map database `NUMBER` attributes to Java `BigDecimal` objects, you map `VARCHAR2` attributes to `String` objects, and you map `DATE` attributes to `Timestamp` objects (see Appendix A for more details). Using these mappings, `productAttributes[0]`, which corresponds to the `id NUMBER` attribute of `PRODUCT_TYP`, is mapped to a `BigDecimal`. The following examples set all the elements of `productAttributes` to appropriate values:

```
productAttributes[0] = new BigDecimal(3);  // id
productAttributes[1] = "Chips";  // name
productAttributes[2] = "10 oz bag of chips";  // description
```

```
productAttributes[3] = new BigDecimal(0.99);  // price
productAttributes[4] = new BigDecimal(20);    // days_valid
```

CAUTION
You cannot use primitive Java types like int for
NUMBER columns. This is because an Object array
can only store actual objects. You must either use
a BigDecimal object or one of the Java wrapper
classes shown in Table A-3 of Appendix A.

Step 3: Create a STRUCT Object

The third step is to create a STRUCT object, which will be used in Step 4 to insert a database object into the table. The STRUCT class is located in the oracle.sql package, and the examples in this section assume that oracle.sql.STRUCT has been imported.

When you create your STRUCT object, you pass your StructDescriptor, Connection, and Object array to the constructor of the STRUCT object. The following example creates a STRUCT object named product; notice that productDescriptor, myConnection, and productAttributes are passed to the constructor:

```
STRUCT product =
    new STRUCT(productDescriptor, myConnection, productAttributes);
```

The oracle.sql.STRUCT class implements the java.sql.Struct interface. The Struct interface declares the following methods:

- **getAttributes()** Returns the values of the attributes. You can pass a java.util.Map object to this method; if you do, the mappings specified in that Map object are used to create the attribute types. If you don't pass a Map object, the default JDBC mappings are used. You'll learn more about Map objects later in this chapter.

- **getSQLTypeName()** Returns the fully qualified name of the database object type.

In addition to implementing the standard methods contained in the Struct interface, the STRUCT class defines the following methods:

- **getOracleAttributes()** Returns the attribute values as oracle.sql.* objects

- **getDescriptor()** Returns the StructDescriptor object

- **getJavaSQLConnection()**   Returns the `Connection` object
- **toJdbc()**   Consults the default type map (or the `java.util.Map` object, if such an object is supplied as a parameter) for the connection to determine what class to map attributes to and then calls `toClass()` to convert the attributes to JDBC types

Step 4: Use a Prepared Statement to Insert the STRUCT into the Table

The fourth and final step is to use a prepared statement to insert your `STRUCT` into the table. Specifically, you create a `PreparedStatement` object and call its `setObject()` method to bind your `STRUCT` object to an `INSERT` statement for the object table.

The following example creates a `PreparedStatement` object named `myPrepStatement`, binds the `product` `STRUCT` to the placeholder using the `setObject()` method, and then calls the `execute()` method to perform the `INSERT`; at the end `myPrepStatement` is closed:

```
PreparedStatement myPrepStatement = myConnection.prepareStatement(
  "INSERT INTO object_products VALUES (?)"
);
myPrepStatement.setObject(1, product);
myPrepStatement.execute();
myPrepStatement.close();
```

Of course, to make the new row permanent you must perform a commit (or perform a rollback to undo the `INSERT`).

Selecting Database Objects into a STRUCT

To select objects from the database into a `STRUCT`, you follow these steps:

1. Create a result set and use it to select the objects.
2. While there are objects in your result set, perform the following:
   a. Retrieve each database object from your result set using the `getObject()` method, casting the returned `Object` to a `STRUCT`.
   b. Retrieve the attribute values from your `STRUCT` using the `getAttributes()` method, storing them in an `Object` array.
   c. Read the attribute values from your `Object` array, casting the `Object` elements to specific types if necessary.
3. Close your result set.

In the following sections, I'll describe the details of Steps 1 and 2, along with example code that selects the products from the object_products table.

NOTE
You've already seen examples of Step 3, which closes the result set, so I won't describe that step again. But do make sure you call the close() method for your result set in your own code.

Step 1: Create a Result Set to Select the Rows from the Object Table

The first step is to create a result set and use it to select the rows from the object table. The following example creates a ResultSet object named productResultSet using a Statement object named myStatement (which is assumed to already exist):

```
ResultSet productResultSet = myStatement.executeQuery(
    "SELECT VALUE(op) " +
    "FROM object_products op"
);
```

NOTE
I used the VALUE() function when retrieving rows from an object table into the ResultSet object. The VALUE() function treats the selected rows as database objects and is required when using the getObject() method in the next step.

Step 2: While There are Objects in the Result Set, Use the getObject() and getAttributes() Methods

The second step is to use the getObject() and getAttributes() methods within a while loop that calls productResultSet.next(). You use the getObject() method for your ResultSet to retrieve each database object, casting the returned Object to a STRUCT. The following example does this, storing the STRUCT in product:

```
STRUCT product = (STRUCT) productResultSet.getObject(1);
```

Once you have your STRUCT, you use the getAttributes() method of your STRUCT to retrieve the attribute values, storing them in an Object array:

```
Object [] productAttributes = product.getAttributes();
```

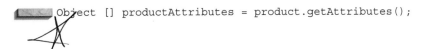

You can then read the attribute values stored in the elements of your Object array. The following example displays the attributes contained in productAttributes, and each element is implicitly cast to a String before being displayed by System.out.println():

```
System.out.println("id = " + productAttributes[0]);
System.out.println("name = " + productAttributes[1]);
System.out.println("description = " + productAttributes[2]);
System.out.println("price = " + productAttributes[3]);
System.out.println("days_valid = " + productAttributes[4]);
```

If you want to store an attribute, rather than simply displaying it, you must cast the attribute in your Object array to the appropriate class. For example, say you wanted to store productAttributes[0] (which contains the id attribute of the database object); you would cast productAttributes[0] to a BigDecimal before storing it:

```
BigDecimal id = (BigDecimal) productAttributes[0];
```

Calling Database Object Methods   You'll recall that the database object type product_typ defines a function named get_sell_by_date(); this function returns the date by which a particular product must be sold. You can call this function using a CallableStatement object (I covered CallableStatement objects in Chapter 5). The following example creates a CallableStatement to call the get_sell_by_date() function; notice the two placeholders:

```
CallableStatement myCallableStatement = myConnection.prepareCall(
  "{? = call product_typ.get_sell_by_date(?)}"
);
```

The first placeholder is used to retrieve the date returned by the get_sell_by_date() function. The second placeholder is used to specify a particular object for which to call the get_sell_by_date() function. The following examples register the output parameter for the first placeholder as a DATE, and bind the second placeholder to myProduct (the current product being processed by the while loop):

```
myCallableStatement.registerOutParameter(1, Types.DATE);
myCallableStatement.setObject(2, myProduct);
```

The only thing left to do is to run the CallableStatement using the execute() method and read the returned date using the getDate() method:

```
myCallableStatement.execute();
System.out.println("sell by date = " +
  myCallableStatement.getDate(1));
```

When you're finished with your `CallableStatement`, you should close it using the `close()` method:

```
myCallableStatement.close();
```

Updating a Database Object Using a STRUCT

To update an object in the database using a `STRUCT`, you follow these steps:

1. Create a result set and use it to select the objects.

2. Retrieve the original database object from your result set into a `STRUCT` using the `getObject()` method, casting the returned `Object` to a `STRUCT`.

3. Close your result set.

4. Retrieve the attributes from your `STRUCT` into an `Object` array using the `getAttributes()` method.

5. Change the attributes in your `Object` array to your new values.

6. Retrieve the `StructDescriptor` for your `STRUCT`.

7. Create a new `STRUCT`, passing your `StructDescriptor`, `Connection` object, and `Object` array to the constructor of your new `STRUCT`.

8. Use a prepared statement to perform the update using your new `STRUCT`.

You already saw an example of Steps 1 through 4 in the previous section, "Selecting Database Objects into a STRUCT," so I won't repeat those steps here.

In the example in this section, assume that you're going to modify product #2 from the `object_products` table. Assume also that you've already retrieved product #2 into a `STRUCT` named `product`, and the attributes for this product have been retrieved into an `Object` array named `productAttributes`. In the following sections, I'll describe the details of Steps 5 through 8, along with example code that updates the `description` and `price` attributes of product #2.

Step 5: Change the Attributes in the Object Array to the New Values

The fifth step is to change the attributes in your `Object` array to your new values. The assumption is that you've already retrieved the attributes for product #2 into an

Object array named `productAttributes`. The following example changes the `description` and `price` attributes in the `productAttributes` array; these attributes are stored in `productAttributes[2]` and `productAttributes[3]` respectively:

```
productAttributes[2] = "25 oz box of sardines";  // description
productAttributes[3] = new BigDecimal(3.49);  // price
```

Step 6: Retrieve the StructDescriptor for the STRUCT

The sixth step is to retrieve the `StructDescriptor` for your `STRUCT` using the `getDescriptor()` method; the following example calls this method using `product`:

```
StructDescriptor productDescriptor = product.getDescriptor();
```

Step 7: Create a New STRUCT

The seventh step is to create a new `STRUCT`, passing your `StructDescriptor`, `Connection`, and `Object` array to the constructor of this new `STRUCT`:

```
STRUCT updatedProduct =
   new STRUCT(productDescriptor, myConnection, productAttributes);
```

The `updatedProduct STRUCT` is now ready for use with a prepared statement to perform the update.

Step 8: Use a Prepared Statement to Perform the Update Using the New STRUCT

The eighth and final step is to use a prepared statement to perform the update using your new `STRUCT`. Specifically, you create a `PreparedStatement` object and call its `setObject()` method to bind your `STRUCT` to an `UPDATE` statement for the object table. Then you call the `execute()` method to perform the `UPDATE`. At the end, you close your `PreparedStatement` object.

The following example creates a `PreparedStatement` object named `myPrepStatement`, binds the `updatedProduct STRUCT` and `id` to the first and second placeholders, respectively, using the `setObject()` and `setInt()` methods, and then calls the `execute()` method to perform the `UPDATE`. At the end, `myPrepStatement` is closed:

```
int id = 2;
PreparedStatement myPrepStatement = myConnection.prepareStatement(
  "UPDATE object_products op " +
  "SET VALUE(op) = ? " +
```

```
  "WHERE op.id = ?"
);
myPrepStatement.setObject(1, updatedProduct);
myPrepStatement.setInt(2, id);
myPrepStatement.execute();
myPrepStatement.close();
```

You must perform a commit to make the update permanent.

Deleting an Object

To delete an object, you simply specify the object to be deleted using one or more attributes in the WHERE clause of a DELETE statement: you don't use a STRUCT in the DELETE. The following example deletes product #1 from the object_products table using a Statement object named myStatement (which is assumed to already exist):

```
int id = 1;
myStatement.execute(
  "DELETE FROM object_products op " +
  "WHERE op.id = " + id
);
```

You must perform a commit to make the delete permanent. Later in the sections on object references, you'll see how you can also delete an object using an object reference.

Example Program: ObjectExample1.java

The program ObjectExample1.java, shown in the following listing, illustrates the various steps shown in the previous sections to insert, select, update, and delete products from the object_products table. Products are represented using weakly typed STRUCT objects. This program contains four methods that are called in the main() method:

■ **insertProduct()** Follows the four steps described earlier in the section "Inserting a Database Object Using a STRUCT." Specifically, this method inserts a product into the object_products table.

■ **displayProducts()** Follows the three steps described earlier in the section "Selecting Database Objects into a STRUCT." Specifically, this method selects and displays the products from the object_products table and also calls the get_sell_by_date() object method for each product.

- **updateProduct()**   Follows the eight steps described earlier in the section "Updating a Database Object Using a STRUCT." Specifically, this method updates a product's `description` and `price` attributes.

- **deleteProduct()**   Follows the step described earlier in the section "Deleting an Object." Specifically, this method deletes a product from the `object_products` table.

```
/*
  ObjectExample1.java shows how to access database objects using
  weakly typed STRUCT objects
*/

// import the required packages
import java.sql.*;
import oracle.sql.STRUCT;
import oracle.sql.StructDescriptor;
import java.util.Map;
import java.math.BigDecimal;

public class ObjectExample1 {

  public static void insertProduct(
    Connection myConnection
  ) throws SQLException {

    System.out.println("Inserting a product");

    // step 1: create a StructDescriptor object for the database
    // object type (in this case, OBJECT_USER.PRODUCT_TYP)
    StructDescriptor productDescriptor =
      StructDescriptor.createDescriptor(
        "OBJECT_USER.PRODUCT_TYP", myConnection
      );

    // step 2: create an Object array to store the attributes for
    // the new database object (in this case, a new product)
    Object [] productAttributes = new Object[5];
    productAttributes[0] = new BigDecimal(3);  // id
    productAttributes[1] = "Chips";  // name
    productAttributes[2] = "10 oz bag of chips";  // description
    productAttributes[3] = new BigDecimal(0.99);  // price
    productAttributes[4] = new BigDecimal(20);  // days_valid

    // step 3: create a STRUCT object
    STRUCT product =
      new STRUCT(productDescriptor, myConnection, productAttributes);
```

```
  // step 4: use a prepared statement to insert the STRUCT
  // into the table
  PreparedStatement myPrepStatement =
    myConnection.prepareStatement(
      "INSERT INTO object_products VALUES (?)"
    );
  myPrepStatement.setObject(1, product);
  myPrepStatement.execute();
  myPrepStatement.close();

} // end of insertProduct()


public static void displayProducts(
  Connection myConnection,
  Statement myStatement
) throws SQLException {

  System.out.println("Products from the object_products table:");

  // step 1: create a result set and use it to select
  // the objects
  ResultSet productResultSet = myStatement.executeQuery(
    "SELECT VALUE(op) " +
    "FROM object_products op"
  );

  // step 2: while there are objects in the result set ...
  while (productResultSet.next()) {

    // a: retrieve each database object from the result set
    // using the getObject() method, casting the returned Object
    // to a STRUCT
    STRUCT product = (STRUCT) productResultSet.getObject(1);

    // b: retrieve the attribute values from the STRUCT using
    // the getAttributes() method, storing them in an Object array
    Object [] productAttributes = product.getAttributes();

    // c: read the attribute values from the Object array
    System.out.println("id = " + productAttributes[0]);
    System.out.println("name = " + productAttributes[1]);
    System.out.println("description = " + productAttributes[2]);
    System.out.println("price = " + productAttributes[3]);
    System.out.println("days_valid = " + productAttributes[4]);

    // create a CallableStatement object and use it to call the
    // get_sell_by_date() function
```

```
        CallableStatement myCallableStatement =
          myConnection.prepareCall(
            "{? = call product_typ.get_sell_by_date(?)}"
          );
        myCallableStatement.registerOutParameter(1, Types.DATE);
        myCallableStatement.setObject(2, product);
        myCallableStatement.execute();
        System.out.println("sell by date = " +
          myCallableStatement.getDate(1));
        myCallableStatement.close();

      } // end of while loop

      // step 3: close the result set
      productResultSet.close();

    } // end of displayProducts()


    public static void updateProduct(
      Connection myConnection,
      Statement myStatement,
      int id
    ) throws SQLException {

      System.out.println("Updating product #" + id +
        "'s description and price");

      // step 1: create a result set and use it to select
      // the object (in this case, the product with the specified id)
      ResultSet productResultSet = myStatement.executeQuery(
        "SELECT VALUE(op) " +
        "FROM object_products op " +
        "WHERE op.id = " + id
      );
      productResultSet.next();

      // step 2: retrieve the original database object from the
      // result set into a STRUCT using the getObject() method,
      // casting the returned Object to a STRUCT
      STRUCT product = (STRUCT) productResultSet.getObject(1);

      // step 3: close the result set
      productResultSet.close();

      // step 4: retrieve the attributes from the STRUCT into an
      // Object array using the getAttributes() method
      Object [] productAttributes = product.getAttributes();
```

```java
    // step 5: change the attributes in the Object array
    productAttributes[2] = "25 oz box of sardines";  // description
    productAttributes[3] = new BigDecimal(3.49);  // price

    // step 6: retrieve the StructDescriptor using the
    // getDescriptor() method
    StructDescriptor productDescriptor = product.getDescriptor();

    // step 7: create a new STRUCT object
    STRUCT updatedProduct =
      new STRUCT(productDescriptor, myConnection, productAttributes);

    // step 8: use a prepared statement to perform the update
    PreparedStatement myPrepStatement =
      myConnection.prepareStatement(
        "UPDATE object_products op " +
        "SET VALUE(op) = ? " +
        "WHERE op.id = ?"
      );
    myPrepStatement.setObject(1, updatedProduct);
    myPrepStatement.setInt(2, id);
    myPrepStatement.execute();
    myPrepStatement.close();

} // end of updateProduct()


public static void deleteProduct(
  Connection myConnection,
  Statement myStatement,
  int id
) throws SQLException {

  System.out.println("Deleting product #" + id +
    " from the object_products table");

  // delete a product from the object_products table
  myStatement.execute(
    "DELETE FROM object_products op " +
    "WHERE op.id = " + id
  );

} // end of deleteProduct()


public static void main(String args [])
throws SQLException {
```

```
    // register the Oracle JDBC drivers
    DriverManager.registerDriver(
      new oracle.jdbc.OracleDriver()
    );

    // create a Connection object, and connect to the database
    // as object_user using the Oracle JDBC Thin driver
    Connection myConnection = DriverManager.getConnection(
      "jdbc:oracle:thin:@localhost:1521:ORCL",
      "object_user",
      "object_password"
    );

    // disable auto-commit mode
    myConnection.setAutoCommit(false);

    // create a Statement object
    Statement myStatement = myConnection.createStatement();

    // display the products in the object_products table
    displayProducts(myConnection, myStatement);

    // insert a product
    insertProduct(myConnection);

    // update product #2's description and price attributes
    updateProduct(myConnection, myStatement, 2);

    // delete product #1
    deleteProduct(myConnection, myStatement, 1);

    // display the products
    displayProducts(myConnection, myStatement);

    // rollback the changes made to the database
    myConnection.rollback();

    // close the Statement and Connection objects
    myStatement.close();
    myConnection.close();

  } // end of main()

}
```

NOTE
The Oracle JDBC `classes12.zip` file only provides support for the US7ASCII, WE8DEC, ISO-LATIN-1, and UTF-8 character sets for VARCHAR2 and CHAR attributes of database object types. If you are using other character sets, you'll need to add `nls_charset12.zip` to your CLASSPATH environment variable. The `nls_charset12.zip` file contains classes that support all character sets, and this file is located in the ORACLE_HOME\jdbc\lib directory where your Oracle software is installed. If you only need a specific character set from this zip file, you can unzip the file, extract the character set you need, and add it to your CLASSPATH.

The output from this program is as follows:

```
Products from the object_products table:
id = 1
name = Pasta
description = 20 oz bag of pasta
price = 3.95
days_valid = 10
sell by date = 2002-03-12
id = 2
name = Sardines
description = 12 oz box of sardines
price = 2.99
days_valid = 5
sell by date = 2002-03-07
Inserting a product
Updating product #2's description and price
Deleting product #1 from the object_products table
Products from the object_products table:
id = 2
name = Sardines
description = 25 oz box of sardines
price = 3.49
days_valid = 5
sell by date = 2002-03-07
id = 3
name = Chips
```

```
description = 10 oz bag of chips
price = 0.99
days_valid = 20
sell by date = 2002-03-22
```

Weakly Typed Object References

As I mentioned earlier, an object reference is a pointer to an object. You can store an object reference in a table using the `REF` database type, and the `purchases` table created earlier contains two `REF` columns named `customer` and `product`. These columns point to objects in the `object_customers` and `object_products` tables, respectively. You can store an object reference in your Java program using the `oracle.sql.REF` class; this class implements the `java.sql.Ref` interface.

Selecting an Object Reference into a REF Object

In this section, I'll show you how to select an object reference stored in a `REF` column and subsequently read the actual object pointed to by that object reference. To do this, you follow these steps:

1. Create a result set and select the object reference from the `REF` column.

2. Retrieve the object reference from your result set using the `getRef()` method; this method returns a `java.sql.Ref` object that you cast to an `oracle.sql.REF` object, which you then store.

3. Close your result set.

4. Retrieve the actual object from your `REF` object using the `getValue()` method; this method returns an `Object` that you cast to a `STRUCT`, which you then store.

NOTE
You could also use the `DEREF()` database function to get the object pointed to by the object reference stored in a `REF` column directly, but I want to show you how to handle an object reference using a `REF` object.

Rather than go through each of the previous steps in detail, I'll show you the code that retrieves the `customer` and `product` object references stored in the `purchases` table and then retrieves the actual objects pointed to by those object references:

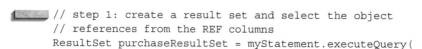

```
// step 1: create a result set and select the object
// references from the REF columns
ResultSet purchaseResultSet = myStatement.executeQuery(
```

```
  "SELECT customer, product " +
  "FROM purchases"
);
purchaseResultSet.next();

// step 2: retrieve the object references from the result set
// using the getRef() method; this method returns a java.sql.Ref
// object that is cast to an oracle.sql.REF object, which is
// then stored
REF customerRef = (REF) purchaseResultSet.getRef("customer");
REF productRef = (REF) purchaseResultSet.getRef("product");

// step 3: close the result set
purchaseResultSet.close();

// step 4: retrieve the actual objects from the REF objects using
// the getValue() method; this method returns an Object that
// is cast to a STRUCT, which is then stored
STRUCT customer = (STRUCT) customerRef.getValue();
STRUCT product = (STRUCT) productRef.getValue();
```

Once you have a STRUCT, you can call the getAttributes() method to get
the object attributes, as you saw earlier.

Updating an Object Reference Using a REF Object

You can update an existing object reference with a new object reference. For example,
you might want to replace the object reference that points to product #1 in the
purchases table with a pointer to product #2. To do this, you follow these steps:

1. Create a result set and use it to select the new object reference that you
   want to use in the update.

2. Retrieve the object reference from your result set using the getRef()
   method, storing it in a REF object.

3. Close your result set.

4. Use a prepared statement to perform the update of the existing object
   reference stored in the REF column with your new object reference, using
   the setRef() method to bind your new object reference to the REF column.

The following example uses these steps to replace the object reference that
points to product #1 in the purchases table with a pointer to product #2:

```
// step 1: create a result set and use it to
// select the new object reference
```

```
ResultSet productResultSet = myStatement.executeQuery(
  "SELECT REF(op) " +
  "FROM object_products op " +
  "WHERE op.id = 2"
);
productResultSet.next();

// step 2: retrieve the object reference from the result set
// using the getRef() method, storing it in a REF object
REF productRef = (REF) productResultSet.getRef(1);

// step 3: close the result set
productResultSet.close();

// step 4: use a prepared statement to perform the update of
// the existing object reference stored in the REF column with the
// new object reference
PreparedStatement myPrepStatement = myConnection.prepareStatement(
  "UPDATE purchases " +
  "SET product = ? " +
  "WHERE id = 1"
);
myPrepStatement.setRef(1, productRef);  // the new object reference
myPrepStatement.execute();
myPrepStatement.close();
```

Using an Object Reference to Update an Object

You can use an object reference to update an object in the database. To do this, you follow these steps:

1. Create a result set and use it to select the object reference.

2. Retrieve the object reference from your result set using the getRef() method, storing it in a REF object.

3. Close your result set.

4. Retrieve the object from your REF using the getValue() method, storing it in a STRUCT object.

5. Retrieve the object attributes from your STRUCT using the getAttributes() method, storing them in an Object array.

6. Change the object attributes in your Object array.

7. Retrieve the StructDescriptor from your object using the getDescriptor() method.

8. Create a new STRUCT object, passing your StructDescriptor, Connection, and Object array to the STRUCT constructor.

9. Update the object in the database using the setValue() method for your REF, passing your new STRUCT to the setValue() method.

Most of these steps should be familiar to you. The only new step is Step 9, which uses the setValue() method.

NOTE
You could also update an object using the steps I described earlier in the section "Updating a Database Object Using a STRUCT," but I want to show you how you can also use object references to update an object. Although the steps seem very complicated to update a couple of object attributes, using the setValue() method to do the update can be very useful if you already have the object reference in your program.

Rather than go through the details of each step, I'll show you some code that illustrates the use of all the steps; this code updates the description and price attributes for product #2 in the object_products table:

```
// step 1: create a result set and use it to select
// the object reference
ResultSet productResultSet = myStatement.executeQuery(
  "SELECT REF(op) " +
  "FROM object_products op " +
  "WHERE op.id = 2"
);
productResultSet.next();

// step 2: retrieve the object reference from the result set
// using the getRef() method, storing it in a REF object
REF productRef = (REF) productResultSet.getRef(1);

// step 3: close the result set
productResultSet.close();

// step 4: retrieve the object from the REF using
// the getValue()method, storing it in a STRUCT object
STRUCT product = (STRUCT) productRef.getValue();
```

```
// step 5: retrieve the object attributes from the STRUCT
// using the getAttributes() method, storing them in an Object array
Object [] productAttributes = product.getAttributes();

// step 6: change the object attributes in the Object array
productAttributes[2] = "25 oz box of sardines";  // description
productAttributes[3] = new BigDecimal(3.49);   // price

// step 7: retrieve the StructDescriptor from your object
// using the getDescriptor() method
StructDescriptor productDescriptor = product.getDescriptor();

// step 8: create a new STRUCT object
STRUCT updatedProduct =
  new STRUCT(productDescriptor, myConnection, productAttributes);

// step 9: update the object in the database using the setValue()
// method for the REF
productRef.setValue(updatedProduct);
```

Notice that no UPDATE statement was used anywhere in this section—that's because the setValue() method used in Step 9 performs an implicit UPDATE for you.

Example Program: ObjectExample2.java

The program ObjectExample2.java, shown in the following listing, illustrates the various steps shown in the previous sections to access the object references. Specifically, this program accesses the object references stored in the customer and product REF columns of the purchases table. This program subsequently uses those object references to access the actual objects stored in the object_customers and object_products tables. This program contains four methods that are called in the main() method:

- **displayPurchase()**   Follows the four steps described earlier in the section "Selecting an Object Reference into a REF Object." Specifically, this method selects the customer and product REF columns contained in the purchases table—these are the object references. It also retrieves and displays the actual customer and product objects pointed to by these object references.

- **updateProductPurchased()**   Follows the four steps described earlier in the section "Updating an Object Reference using a REF Object." Specifically, this method updates a product pointed to by the product column in the purchases table.

■ **updateProduct()** Follows the nine steps described earlier in the section "Using an Object Reference to Update an Object." Specifically, this method updates a product's description and price attributes through a product object reference.

```
/*
  ObjectExample2.java shows how to access object references using
  weakly typed REF objects
*/

// import the required packages
import java.sql.*;
import oracle.sql.STRUCT;
import oracle.sql.REF;
import oracle.sql.StructDescriptor;
import java.util.Map;
import java.math.BigDecimal;

public class ObjectExample2 {

  public static void displayPurchase(
    Connection myConnection,
    Statement myStatement
  ) throws SQLException {

    System.out.println("Purchase from the purchases table:");

    // step 1: create a result set and select the object
    // references from the REF columns
    ResultSet purchaseResultSet = myStatement.executeQuery(
      "SELECT customer, product " +
      "FROM purchases"
    );
    purchaseResultSet.next();

    // step 2: retrieve the object references from the result set
    // using the getRef() method; this method returns a java.sql.Ref
    // object that is cast to an oracle.sql.REF object
    REF customerRef = (REF) purchaseResultSet.getRef("customer");
    REF productRef = (REF) purchaseResultSet.getRef("product");

    // step 3: close the result set
    purchaseResultSet.close();

    // step 4: retrieve the actual objects from the REFs using
    // the getValue() method; this method returns an Object that
```

```
// is cast to a STRUCT, which is then stored
STRUCT customer = (STRUCT) customerRef.getValue();
STRUCT product = (STRUCT) productRef.getValue();

// retrieve the attribute values from the STRUCTs using
// the getAttributes() method, storing them in an Object array
Object [] productAttributes = product.getAttributes();
Object [] customerAttributes = customer.getAttributes();

// read the attribute values from the Object array for
// the product
System.out.println("Product:");
System.out.println("id = " + productAttributes[0]);
System.out.println("name = " + productAttributes[1]);
System.out.println("description = " + productAttributes[2]);
System.out.println("price = " + productAttributes[3]);
System.out.println("days_valid = " + productAttributes[4]);

// read the attribute values from the Object array for
// the customer
System.out.println("Customer:");
System.out.println("id = " + customerAttributes[0]);
System.out.println("first_name = " + customerAttributes[1]);
System.out.println("last_name = " + customerAttributes[2]);
System.out.println("dob = " + customerAttributes[3]);
System.out.println("phone = " + customerAttributes[4]);

// get the customer address
STRUCT address = (STRUCT) customerAttributes[5];
Object [] addressAttributes = address.getAttributes();
System.out.println("street = " + addressAttributes[0]);
System.out.println("city = " + addressAttributes[1]);
System.out.println("state = " + addressAttributes[2]);
System.out.println("zip = " + addressAttributes[3]);

} // end of displayPurchase()


public static void updateProductPurchased(
  Connection myConnection,
  Statement myStatement,
  int purchaseId,
  int productId
) throws SQLException {

  System.out.println("Updating purchase #" + purchaseId +
    " with product #" + productId);
```

```java
    // step 1: create a result set and use it to
    // select the new object reference
    ResultSet productResultSet = myStatement.executeQuery(
      "SELECT REF(op) " +
      "FROM object_products op " +
      "WHERE op.id = " + productId
    );
    productResultSet.next();

    // step 2: retrieve the object reference from the result set
    // using the getRef() method, storing it in a REF object
    REF productRef = (REF) productResultSet.getRef(1);

    // step 3: close the result set
    productResultSet.close();

    // step 4: use a prepared statement to perform the update of
    // the existing object reference stored in the REF column
    // with the new object reference
    PreparedStatement myPrepStatement =
      myConnection.prepareStatement(
        "UPDATE purchases " +
        "SET product = ? " +
        "WHERE id = ?"
      );
    myPrepStatement.setRef(1, productRef);   // new object reference
    myPrepStatement.setInt(2, purchaseId);
    myPrepStatement.execute();
    myPrepStatement.close();

  } // end of updateProductPurchased()


  public static void updateProduct(
    Connection myConnection,
    Statement myStatement,
    int productId
  ) throws SQLException {

    System.out.println("Updating product #" + productId +
      "'s description and price");

    // step 1: create a result set and use it to select
    // the object reference
    ResultSet productResultSet = myStatement.executeQuery(
      "SELECT REF(op) " +
      "FROM object_products op " +
      "WHERE op.id = " + productId
```

```
  );
  productResultSet.next();

  // step 2: retrieve the object reference from the result set
  // using the getRef() method, storing it in a REF object
  REF productRef = (REF) productResultSet.getRef(1);

  // step 3: close the result set
  productResultSet.close();

  // step 4: retrieve the object from the REF using
  // the getValue()method, storing it in a STRUCT object
  STRUCT product = (STRUCT) productRef.getValue();

  // step 5: retrieve the object attributes from the STRUCT
  // using the getAttributes() method, storing them in an
  // Object array
  Object [] productAttributes = product.getAttributes();

  // step 6: change the object attributes in the Object array
  productAttributes[2] = "25 oz box of sardines";  // description
  productAttributes[3] = new BigDecimal(3.49);   // price

  // step 7: retrieve the StructDescriptor from your object
  // using the getDescriptor() method
  StructDescriptor productDescriptor = product.getDescriptor();

  // step 8: create a new STRUCT object
  STRUCT updatedProduct =
    new STRUCT(productDescriptor, myConnection, productAttributes);

  // step 9: update the object in the database using the setValue()
  // method for the REF
  productRef.setValue(updatedProduct);

} // end of updateProduct()


public static void main(String args [])
throws SQLException {

  // register the Oracle JDBC drivers
  DriverManager.registerDriver(
    new oracle.jdbc.OracleDriver()
  );

  // create a Connection object, and connect to the database
  // as object_user using the Oracle JDBC Thin driver
```

```
Connection myConnection = DriverManager.getConnection(
  "jdbc:oracle:thin:@localhost:1521:ORCL",
  "object_user",
  "object_password"
);

// disable auto-commit mode
myConnection.setAutoCommit(false);

// create a Statement object
Statement myStatement = myConnection.createStatement();

// display the purchases
displayPurchase(myConnection, myStatement);

// update product #2's description and price attributes
updateProduct(myConnection, myStatement, 2);

// update purchase #1 to reference product #2
updateProductPurchased(myConnection, myStatement, 1, 2);

// display the purchases
displayPurchase(myConnection, myStatement);

// rollback the changes made to the database
myConnection.rollback();

// close the Statement and Connection objects
myStatement.close();
myConnection.close();

  } // end of main()

}
```

The output from this program is as follows:

```
Purchase from the purchases table:
Product:
id = 1
name = Pasta
description = 20 oz bag of pasta
price = 3.95
days_valid = 10
Customer:
id = 1
first_name = John
```

```
last_name = Brown
dob = 1955-02-01 00:00:00.0
phone = 800-555-1211
street = 2 State Street
city = Beantown
state = MA
zip = 12345
Updating product #2's description and price
Updating purchase #1 with product #2
Purchase from the purchases table:
Product:
id = 2
name = Sardines
description = 25 oz box of sardines
price = 3.49
days_valid = 5
Customer:
id = 1
first_name = John
last_name = Brown
dob = 1955-02-01 00:00:00.0
phone = 800-555-1211
street = 2 State Street
city = Beantown
state = MA
zip = 12345
```

Strongly Typed Interfaces and Custom Classes

Strongly typed objects represent the attributes of a database object using a specific type. This makes them superior to the weakly typed objects when you need the database object attributes in a convenient form for manipulation in Java.

Strongly typed objects are of a custom class that implements one of the following interfaces:

- **java.sql.SQLData**   Part of the JDBC standard.

- **oracle.sql.ORAData**   Part of the Oracle extensions to the JDBC standard. ORAData is a replacement for the older `oracle.sql.CustomDatum` interface.

You'll learn about the `SQLData` and `ORAData` interfaces in this section. In the first part of this section, I'll describe the main differences between `SQLData` and

ORAData and when you should use each one. Then you'll learn how to use Oracle's JPublisher tool to generate custom classes. After that, you'll learn how to use custom classes in your Java programs.

Main Differences Between SQLData and ORAData

In this section, I'll highlight the main differences between SQLData and ORAData, and tell you when you should pick one over the other. The following points summarize the advantages and disadvantages of SQLData and ORAData:

- SQLData is part of the JDBC standard, so if you want your code to be portable, you should pick SQLData. However, SQLData doesn't support all the Oracle-specific database types, like BFILE, for example. ORAData supports all of the Oracle-specific database types that extend the standard SQL types.

- SQLData may only be used with database objects: SQLData doesn't support object references or collections (you'll learn about collections in the next chapter). ORAData may be used with objects, object references, and collections.

- ORAData offers higher performance than SQLData because it works directly with oracle.sql.Datum objects, which is the format used for internal representation of objects.

TIP
I recommend you use ORAData rather than SQLData, unless your code must be portable.

Let's look at how you generate custom classes using JPublisher.

Generating Custom Classes Using JPublisher

Oracle's JPublisher tool allows you to generate the custom classes that are required to access database objects in your Java programs. You could choose to write your own custom classes if you wanted, but I don't recommend that; you're better off letting JPublisher do the hard work for you. If you really want to write your own classes, study the classes generated by JPublisher and use them to create your classes. You can extend generated custom classes, and I'll describe how you do that in this section.

In a nutshell, JPublisher connects to the database, reads the definitions for your database object types that you want custom classes for, and generates the classes that you can use to create objects in your Java programs. You can then use those Java objects to store objects retrieved from the database, and you can use those Java objects when binding to placeholders in prepared statements. You can run JPublisher from the command line and through Oracle JDeveloper. I'll describe how to do both in this section.

Running JPublisher from the Command Line

You run JPublisher from the command line by running the `jpub` program. The following example runs `jpub` with the `-help` option (this option displays usage information):

```
jpub -help
```

> **NOTE**
> *The `jpub` program is stored in the ORACLE_HOME\BIN directory where your Oracle software is installed. Make sure this directory is in the PATH environment variable for your system.*

The `jpub` program has many options, which are documented in Table B-1 of Appendix B. I'll illustrate the use of the options you'll use most often in this section. I've provided two subdirectories in the programs directory: `ObjectExample3` and `ObjectExample4And5`. The `ObjectExample3` directory contains an example program named `ObjectExample3.java` that uses custom classes that implement the `SQLData` interface. The `ObjectExample4And5` directory contains two example programs named `ObjectExample4.java` and `ObjectExample5.java` that use custom classes that implement the `ORAData` interface. I'll describe the details of these programs later in this chapter.

In this section, you'll be running `jpub` from the `ObjectExample3` directory to generate the required custom classes that the `ObjectExample3.java` program later requires. Later in the section on `ORAData`, you'll run `jpub` again to generate custom classes that implement `ORAData`.

Generating Custom Classes that Implement SQLData

First, from the command line for your operating system, you should change directories to the `ObjectExample3` directory. Next, run the following command:

```
jpub -user=object_user/object_password
  -url=jdbc:oracle:thin:@localhost:1521:ORCL
  -usertypes=jdbc -methods=none
```

You enter this command on the same line and press ENTER to run the command. The options used in this command and their meanings are as follows:

- **-user**   Specifies the username and password to connect to the database.

- **-url**   Specifies the location of the database to connect to.

- **-usertypes**   Specifies the type mappings that JPublisher will use for your database object types. This controls whether JPublisher generates custom classes that implement the SQLData or ORAData interfaces. If set to jdbc, the custom classes implement SQLData; if set to oracle (the default), the custom classes implement ORAData.

- **-methods**   Specifies whether JPublisher generates wrapper methods for your database object types. For now, you won't generate methods, so this option is set to none. Later, you'll set this to all (the default) when generating the custom classes that implement ORAData.

When you run the previous command, JPublisher will connect to the database as object_user and generate custom class files for all of the object types it finds in the object_user schema. There are three object types in the object_user schema: address_typ, person_typ, and product_typ. Once this command has completed, JPublisher will have generated the following three custom class files for the corresponding database object type:

- AddressTyp.java
- PersonTyp.java
- ProductTyp.java

Notice that the name of a custom class is generated by taking the name of the database object type, removing the underscores, and making the first letter of each word uppercase; for example, address_typ becomes AddressTyp.

NOTE
You'll see how you can set your own names for the custom class files later in the section on the -sql option.

Each of the three custom classes implements the SQLData interface. Let's take a look at the ProductTyp.java file.

The ProductTyp.java File   The `ProductTyp.java` file is as follows:

```java
import java.sql.SQLException;
import oracle.jdbc.OracleConnection;
import oracle.jdbc.OracleTypes;
import java.sql.SQLData;
import java.sql.SQLInput;
import java.sql.SQLOutput;
import oracle.sql.STRUCT;
import oracle.jpub.runtime.MutableStruct;

public class ProductTyp implements SQLData
{
  public static final String _SQL_NAME = "OBJECT_USER.PRODUCT_TYP";
  public static final int _SQL_TYPECODE = OracleTypes.STRUCT;

  private java.math.BigDecimal m_id;
  private String m_name;
  private String m_description;
  private java.math.BigDecimal m_price;
  private java.math.BigDecimal m_daysValid;

  /* constructor */
  public ProductTyp()
  {
  }

  public void readSQL(SQLInput stream, String type)
  throws SQLException
  {
      setId(stream.readBigDecimal());
      setName(stream.readString());
      setDescription(stream.readString());
      setPrice(stream.readBigDecimal());
      setDaysValid(stream.readBigDecimal());
  }

  public void writeSQL(SQLOutput stream)
  throws SQLException
  {
      stream.writeBigDecimal(getId());
      stream.writeString(getName());
      stream.writeString(getDescription());
      stream.writeBigDecimal(getPrice());
      stream.writeBigDecimal(getDaysValid());
  }

  public String getSQLTypeName() throws SQLException
  {
```

```java
    return _SQL_NAME;
}

/* accessor methods */
public java.math.BigDecimal getId()
{ return m_id; }

public void setId(java.math.BigDecimal id)
{ m_id = id; }


public String getName()
{ return m_name; }

public void setName(String name)
{ m_name = name; }


public String getDescription()
{ return m_description; }

public void setDescription(String description)
{ m_description = description; }


public java.math.BigDecimal getPrice()
{ return m_price; }

public void setPrice(java.math.BigDecimal price)
{ m_price = price; }


public java.math.BigDecimal getDaysValid()
{ return m_daysValid; }

public void setDaysValid(java.math.BigDecimal daysValid)
{ m_daysValid = daysValid; }

}
```

There are three things you should notice about this Java source file:

- It defines a class named `ProductTyp` that implements the `SQLData` interface.
- It contains a number of private attributes whose values are read from using various *get* methods and whose values are written to using various *set* methods. You'll see how to use these methods shortly.

■ It contains two methods named `readSQL()` and `writeSQL()`. The
`readSQL()` method is used to read a stream of data values from the database
and populate an object of the custom class; this method is called by the
JDBC driver when you call the `getObject()` method to read an object
from a result set. The `writeSQL()` method is used to write a stream of
data values from an object of the custom class to the database; this method
is called by the JDBC driver when you call the `setObject()` method to
bind an object of the custom class using a prepared statement.

As you'll see later, you can retrieve database objects from the `object_products`
table and store them in Java objects of the `ProductTyp` class shown in the previous
listing. You'll also see how you can bind `ProductTyp` objects to prepared statements.

The JPublisher -sql Option

In this section, I'll show you examples that use the `-sql` option with JPublisher. By
default, JPublisher will generate custom classes for all of the database object types
in a particular schema. If you want to generate custom classes for a particular database
object type, you do so using the `-sql` option. The following example uses `-sql` to
generate a custom class for the `product_typ` database object type only:

```
jpub -user=object_user/object_password
  -url=jdbc:oracle:thin:@localhost:1521:ORCL
  -usertypes=jdbc -methods=none -sql=product_typ
```

The custom class for `product_typ` generated by JPublisher is also
named `product_typ`, and the source file for this class is therefore named
`product_typ.java`. If you want to use a different name for the custom class,
you can use the `-sql` option to specify the name. You do this by adding the
name for the class after a colon (`:`), which you place after the name of your
database object type. The following example names the custom class `MyProduct`,
and the name of the generated source file is therefore `MyProduct.java`:

```
jpub -user=object_user/object_password
  -url=jdbc:oracle:thin:@localhost:1521:ORCL
  -usertypes=jdbc -methods=none -sql=product_typ:MyProduct
```

Extending Generated Custom Classes   You might want to extend a class
generated by JPublisher; for example, you might want to add additional attributes
and methods to a class. You can use the `-sql` option to specify a class that you
have written. For example, let's say you wanted to write your own class named
`MyAddressTyp`; your `-sql` option would be as follows:

```
-sql=address_typ:AddressTyp:MyAddressTyp
```

JPublisher would generate two files: `AddressTyp.java` and `MyAddressTypRef.java`. `MyAddressTyp` is the class that you have written. JPublisher will then map the `address_typ` objects to your `MyAddressTyp` class. Your `MyAddressTyp` class must satisfy the following requirements:

- It must have a constructor that accepts no arguments.

- It must implement the `ORAData` or `SQLData` interface. If your class extends the `ORAData` interface, it must also implement the `ORADataFactory` interface (you'll learn more about this interface later). You can achieve this requirement by having your `MyAddressTyp` class extend the `AddressTyp` class generated by JPublisher.

Supplying a Properties File to JPublisher

Instead of supplying all your options to JPublisher using the command line, you can supply a file containing the settings for your command-line options instead. Such a file is known as a *properties file*. You might want to use a properties file when you have a lot of options to send to JPublisher. Let's take a look at an example. Assume you have a file named `MyJpubProperties.txt` that contains the following text:

```
jpub.user=object_user/object_password
jpub.url=jdbc:oracle:thin:@localhost:1521:ORCL
jpub.usertypes=jdbc
jpub.methods=none
jpub.sql=product_typ:MyProduct
```

Notice that each option begins with `jpub` followed by a period (`.`). You can then tell JPublisher to read the `MyJpubProperties.txt` file using the `-props` option. JPublisher will then use the options defined in your file, for example:

```
jpub -props=MyJpubProperties.txt
```

Supplying an Input File to JPublisher

You can also supply a file that specifies the object types that you want JPublisher to generate custom classes for. Such a file is known as an *input file*. You might want to use an input file when you have many object types that you want to generate custom classes for. You can also use an input file to specify the names of the Java wrappers for your object type methods. The following example shows the structure of an input file:

```
SQL person_typ AS PersonTyp
SQL address_typ GENERATE AddessTyp AS MyAddressTyp
SQL product_typ AS MyProductTyp
  TRANSLATE get_sell_by_date AS getSellByDate
```

Note that each object type is preceded by SQL. The AS clause specifies the name for your custom class; for example, SQL person_typ AS PersonTyp specifies that the class name to be generated for the person_typ object type is PersonTyp.

The GENERATE clause is used to specify a class and class that you've written; for example, SQL address_typ GENERATE AddessTyp AS MyAddressTyp specifies that the custom class is AddressTyp and that the class you've written is MyAddressTyp (see the section "Extending Custom Classes" for further details).

The TRANSLATE clause specifies the name of the object method and the name of the generated Java wrapper method; for example, TRANSLATE get_sell_by_date AS getSellByDate specifies that the wrapper method for the get_sell_by_date object method is getSellByDate.

You specify the name of an input file using the -input option. Assuming the previous input file is contained in a file named MyJpubInputFile.txt, the following example shows the use of the -input option with JPublisher:

```
jpub -user=object_user/object_password
 -url=jdbc:oracle:thin:@localhost:1521:ORCL
 -input=MyJpubInputFile.txt
```

You can supply both a properties file and an input file to JPublisher.

Running JPublisher from JDeveloper

You can also run JPublisher from within JDeveloper. You do this by first creating a new database connection by selecting New from the File menu and selecting Database Connection from the Connections category. Once you create a database connection, you expand that database connection and display the object types. Next, select the object type for which you want to generate custom classes for and right-click that object type. Then use the JPublisher wizard to enter the options for JPublisher.

Using Custom Classes that Implement SQLData

In this section, you'll learn how to use custom classes that implement SQLData. Specifically, you'll see how to use the custom classes you generated earlier in the ObjectExample3 directory to insert, select, and update products in the object_products table. Deleting a product is done in the same way as I showed you earlier in the section on weakly typed objects, so I won't show you how to do that again here.

Type Maps for SQLData Implementations

Before you can use objects of custom classes that implement SQLData with database objects, you must provide the mapping between your database object type and your custom class. This mapping tells JDBC which custom class to use for the database object type. To provide the mapping, you perform the following steps:

1. Retrieve the current map from your Connection object.

2. Add your mapping for the custom class and object type to the map.

3. Replace the current map in your Connection object.

In the following sections, you'll learn the details of these steps.

Step 1: Retrieve the Current Map from the Connection Object

The first step is to retrieve the current map from your Connection object using the getTypeMap() method. The getTypeMap() method returns a java.util.Map object. The following example calls the getTypeMap() method for a Connection object named myConnection:

```
Map myMap = myConnection.getTypeMap();
```

This example assumes that the java.util.Map class has been imported.

Step 2: Add your Mapping for the Custom Class and Object Type to the Map

The second step is to add your mapping for the custom class and object type to the map. You do this using the put() method for your Map object. The first parameter to put() is the name of your database object type, and the second parameter is the custom class (you provide this parameter using the Class.forName() method, passing the name of your custom class to this method).

The following example uses the put() method for myMap, creating a mapping for OBJECT_USER.PRODUCT_TYP and the ProductTyp custom class you generated earlier using JPublisher; notice that the Class.forName() method is used to create a copy of the ProductTyp class:

```
myMap.put("OBJECT_USER.PRODUCT_TYP", Class.forName("ProductTyp"));
```

Step 3: Replace the Current Map in the Connection Object

The third step is to replace the current map in your Connection object. You do this using the setTypeMap() method for your Connection object, passing your Map object to this method:

```
myConnection.setTypeMap(myMap);
```

Once you set the type map, you can use objects of your custom class to represent database objects; you'll learn about that next.

Inserting a Database Object Using a Custom Java Object

To insert a database object using an object of your custom class, you follow these steps:

1. Create a Java object of your custom class.

2. Set the attributes of your Java object using the various set methods defined in your custom class.

3. Use a prepared statement to insert your Java object into the table, binding your object to the placeholder for your database object to your Java object.

In the following sections, I'll describe the details of these steps along with example code that inserts a product into the `object_products` table.

Step 1: Create a Java Object of the Custom Class

The first step is to create a Java object of your custom class. The following example creates an object named `product` of the `ProductTyp` custom class (you generated this class earlier using JPublisher):

```
ProductTyp product = new ProductTyp();
```

You may then use `product` to represent an object from the `object_products` table.

Step 2: Set the Attributes of the Java Object Using the Various Set Methods

The second step is to set the attributes of your Java object using the various set methods defined in your custom class. The `ProductTyp` class you generated earlier contains set methods for each of the attributes, and the following examples show the use of these methods to set the attributes of the `product` object; notice that the numeric attributes require a `BigDecimal` object:

```
product.setId(new BigDecimal(3));
product.setName("Chips");
product.setDescription("10 oz bag of chips");
product.setPrice(new BigDecimal(0.99));
product.setDaysValid(new BigDecimal(20));
```

In the next step, you'll use the `product` object to insert a database object into the `object_products` table.

Step 3: Use a Prepared Statement to Insert the Java Object into the Table

The third step is to use a prepared statement to insert your Java object into the table, binding your object to the placeholder for your database object to your Java object. You bind your Java object to the placeholder of an appropriate `INSERT` statement using the `setObject()` method.

The following example creates a `PreparedStatement` object named `myPrepStatement`, binds the `product` object to the placeholder using the `setObject()` method, and then calls the `execute()` method to perform the `INSERT`; at the end, `myPrepStatement` is closed:

```
PreparedStatement myPrepStatement = myConnection.prepareStatement(
    "INSERT INTO object_products VALUES (?)"
);
myPrepStatement.setObject(1, product);
myPrepStatement.execute();
myPrepStatement.close();
```

Of course, to make the new row permanent, you must perform a commit (or perform a rollback to undo the `INSERT`).

Selecting Database Objects into a Custom Java Object

To select objects from the database into a Java object of a custom class, you follow these steps:

1. Create a result set and use it to select the database objects.

2. While there are objects in your result set, perform the following:

    a. Retrieve each database object from your result set.

    b. Retrieve the attribute values from your Java object using the various get methods defined in your custom class.

3. Close your result set.

In the following sections, I'll describe the details of these steps along with example code that selects the products from the `object_products` table.

Step 1: Create a Result Set to Select the Database Objects

The first step is to create a result set and use it to select the database objects. The following example creates a ResultSet object named productResultSet that selects the products from the object_products table:

```
ResultSet productResultSet = myStatement.executeQuery(
  "SELECT VALUE(op) " +
  "FROM object_products op"
);
```

Step 2: While There Are Objects in the Result Set, Retrieve the Objects and Their Attributes

The second step is to use the getObject() method and the other get methods within a while loop that calls productResultSet.next(). You use the getObject() method for your result set to retrieve each database object, casting the returned Object to an object of your custom class. For example, when retrieving a product from productResultSet, you cast the Object returned by getObject() to the ProductTyp class:

```
ProductTyp product = (ProductTyp) productResultSet.getObject(1);
```

You then use the various get methods for the product object to retrieve the attribute values, for example:

```
System.out.println("id = " + product.getId());
System.out.println("name = " + product.getName());
System.out.println("description = " + product.getDescription());
System.out.println("price = " + product.getPrice());
System.out.println("days valid = " + product.getDaysValid());
```

You can store each attribute in an appropriate object, and the following example stores the BigDecimal returned by the getId() method:

```
BigDecimal id = product.getId();
```

You can also call a database object method using a prepared statement as described earlier in the section "Calling Database Object Methods," so I won't repeat that here.

Updating a Database Object Using a Custom Java Object

To update an object in the database using a Java object of a custom class, you follow these steps:

1. Create a result set and use it to select the object.

2. Retrieve the original database object from your result set into a Java object of your custom class using the getObject() method, casting the returned Object to your custom class.

3. Close your result set.

4. Change any attributes in your Java object using the appropriate set methods.

5. Use a prepared statement object to perform the update.

You've already seen an example of Steps 1 through 3 in the previous section "Selecting Database Objects into a Custom Java Object," so I won't repeat those steps here.

In the example in this section, assume that you want to modify product #2 from the object_products table and that you've already retrieved product #2 into an object named product. In the following sections, you'll see example code that updates the description and price attributes of product #2.

Step 4: Change Any Attributes in the Java Object Using the Appropriate Set Methods

The following example changes the description and price attributes for the product object using the setDescription() and setPrice() methods:

```
product.setDescription("25 oz box of sardines");
product.setPrice(new BigDecimal(3.49));
```

Step 5: Use a Prepared Statement to Perform the Update Using the Java Object

The following example creates a PreparedStatement object named myPrepStatement, binds the product object and id to the first and second placeholders, respectively, using the setObject() and setInt() methods, and then calls the execute() method to perform the UPDATE; at the end myPrepStatement is closed:

```
int id = 2;
PreparedStatement myPrepStatement = myConnection.prepareStatement(
  "UPDATE object_products op " +
  "SET VALUE(op) = ? " +
  "WHERE op.id = ?"
);
myPrepStatement.setObject(1, product);
myPrepStatement.setInt(2, id);
myPrepStatement.execute();
myPrepStatement.close();
```

You must perform a commit to make the UPDATE permanent.

Example Program: ObjectExample3.java

The program `ObjectExample3.java`, shown in the following listing, illustrates the various steps shown in the previous sections to insert, select, and update products in the `object_products` table. The program contains four methods that are called in the `main()` method:

- **insertProduct()**   Follows the three steps described earlier in the section "Inserting a Database Object Using a Custom Java Object." Specifically, this method inserts a product into the `object_products` table using an object of the `ProductTyp` class.

- **displayProducts()**   Follows the three steps described earlier in the section "Selecting Database Objects into a Custom Java Object." Specifically, this method selects and displays the products from the `object_products` table using objects of the `ProductTyp` class.

- **updateProduct()**   Follows the five steps described earlier in the section "Updating a Database Object Using a Custom Java Object." Specifically, this method updates the `description` and `price` attributes of a product in the `object_products` table using an object of the `ProductTyp` class.

The `main()` method also sets the type map.

```
/*
    ObjectExample3.java shows how to access database objects
    using strongly typed objects of the ProductTyp custom class
    generated by JPublisher (the version of ProductTyp used
    implements SQLData)
*/

// import the required packages
import java.sql.*;
import oracle.jdbc.OracleResultSet;
import java.math.BigDecimal;
import java.util.Map;

public class ObjectExample3 {

  public static void insertProduct(
    Connection myConnection
  ) throws SQLException {

    System.out.println("Inserting a product");
```

```
    // step 1: create an object of the ProductTyp custom class
    ProductTyp product = new ProductTyp();

    // step 2: set the attributes of the product object using the
    // various set methods
    product.setId(new BigDecimal(3));
    product.setName("Chips");
    product.setDescription("10 oz bag of chips");
    product.setPrice(new BigDecimal(0.99));
    product.setDaysValid(new BigDecimal(20));

    // step 3: use a prepared statement to insert the
    // product object into the table
    PreparedStatement myPrepStatement =
      myConnection.prepareStatement(
        "INSERT INTO object_products VALUES (?)"
      );
    myPrepStatement.setObject(1, product);
    myPrepStatement.execute();
    myPrepStatement.close();

} // end of insertProduct()


public static void displayProducts(
  Connection myConnection,
  Statement myStatement
) throws SQLException {

  System.out.println("Products from the object_products table:");

  // step 1: create a result set and use it to select
  // the objects
  ResultSet productResultSet = myStatement.executeQuery(
    "SELECT VALUE(op) " +
    "FROM object_products op"
  );

  // step 2: while there are objects in the result set ...
  while (productResultSet.next()) {

    // a: retrieve each database object from the result set
    // using the getObject() method, casting the returned Object
    // to the ProductTyp custom class
    ProductTyp product =
      (ProductTyp) productResultSet.getObject(1);

    // b: read the attribute values from the product object
```

```
      // using the various get methods
      System.out.println("id = " + product.getId());
      System.out.println("name = " + product.getName());
      System.out.println("description = " + product.getDescription());
      System.out.println("price = " + product.getPrice());
      System.out.println("days valid = " + product.getDaysValid());

      // use a callable statement to call the
      // get_sell_by_date() function
      CallableStatement myCallableStatement =
        myConnection.prepareCall(
          "{? = call product_typ.get_sell_by_date(?)}"
        );
      myCallableStatement.registerOutParameter(1, Types.DATE);
      myCallableStatement.setObject(2, product);
      myCallableStatement.execute();
      System.out.println("sell by date = " +
        myCallableStatement.getDate(1));
      myCallableStatement.close();

    } // end of while loop

    // step 3: close the result set
    productResultSet.close();

  } // end of displayProducts()


  public static void updateProduct(
    Connection myConnection,
    Statement myStatement,
    int id
  ) throws SQLException {

    System.out.println("Updating product #" + id +
      "'s description and price");

    // step 1: create a result set and use it to select
    // the object (in this case, the product with the specified id)
    ResultSet productResultSet = myStatement.executeQuery(
      "SELECT VALUE(op) " +
      "FROM object_products op " +
      "WHERE op.id = " + id
    );
    productResultSet.next();

    // step 2: retrieve the original database object from the result set
    // using the getObject() method, casting the returned Object
```

```
  // to the ProductTyp custom class
  ProductTyp product = (ProductTyp) productResultSet.getObject(1);

  // step 3: close the result set
  productResultSet.close();

  // step 4: change the attributes in the ProductTyp object using
  // the appropriate set methods (in this case, the description and
  // price attributes are changed using setDescription()
  // and setPrice())
  product.setDescription("25 oz box of sardines");
  product.setPrice(new BigDecimal(3.49));

  // step 5: use a prepared statement to perform the update
  PreparedStatement myPrepStatement =
    myConnection.prepareStatement(
      "UPDATE object_products op " +
      "SET VALUE(op) = ? " +
      "WHERE op.id = ?"
    );
  myPrepStatement.setObject(1, product);
  myPrepStatement.setInt(2, id);
  myPrepStatement.execute();
  myPrepStatement.close();

} // end of updateProduct()


public static void main(String args [])
throws SQLException, ClassNotFoundException {

  // register the Oracle JDBC drivers
  DriverManager.registerDriver(
    new oracle.jdbc.OracleDriver()
  );

  // create a Connection object, and connect to the database
  // as object_user using the Oracle JDBC Thin driver
  Connection myConnection = DriverManager.getConnection(
    "jdbc:oracle:thin:@localhost:1521:ORCL",
    "object_user",
    "object_password"
  );

  // disable auto-commit mode
  myConnection.setAutoCommit(false);

  // set the type map
```

```
Map myMap = myConnection.getTypeMap();
myMap.put("OBJECT_USER.PRODUCT_TYP",
  Class.forName("ProductTyp"));
myConnection.setTypeMap(myMap);

// create a Statement object
Statement myStatement = myConnection.createStatement();

// display the products in the object_products table
displayProducts(myConnection, myStatement);

// insert a product
insertProduct(myConnection);

// update product #2's description and price attributes
updateProduct(myConnection, myStatement, 2);

// display the products
displayProducts(myConnection, myStatement);

// rollback the changes made to the database
myConnection.rollback();

// close the Statement and Connection objects
myStatement.close();
myConnection.close();

} // end of main()

}
```

The output from this program is as follows:

```
Products from the object_products table:
id = 1
name = Pasta
description = 20 oz bag of pasta
price = 3.95
days valid = 10
sell by date = 2002-03-12
id = 2
name = Sardines
description = 12 oz box of sardines
price = 2.99
days valid = 5
sell by date = 2002-03-07
```

```
Inserting a product
Updating product #2's description and price
Products from the object_products table:
id = 1
name = Pasta
description = 20 oz bag of pasta
price = 3.95
days valid = 10
sell by date = 2002-03-12
id = 2
name = Sardines
description = 25 oz box of sardines
price = 3.49
days valid = 5
sell by date = 2002-03-07
id = 3
name = Chips
description = 10 oz bag of chips
price = 0.99
days valid = 20
sell by date = 2002-03-22
```

Using Custom Classes that Implement ORAData

In this section, you'll learn how to use custom classes that implement ORAData. Specifically, you'll see how to use JPublisher to generate the custom classes that implement ORAData, and then you'll learn how to insert, select, and update products in the object_products table. Deleting a product is done in the same way I showed you earlier in the section "Deleting an Object," so I won't show you how to do that again here. You'll also learn how to use custom classes with object references in this section.

Generating Custom Classes That Implement ORAData Using JPublisher

In this section, you'll generate the required custom classes that implement the ORAData interface. To have JPublisher generate custom classes that implement ORAData, you can either omit the -usertypes option, or use -usertypes=oracle. When you omit -usertypes, the default is to generate custom classes that implement ORAData. Also, you use the -method option to specify whether you want JPublisher to generate method wrappers for your database object type methods; by using -methods=all, wrappers will be generated for all your object type methods (this is also the default).

Go ahead and change directories to the `ObjectExample4And5` directory using your command line. Next, run the following command to generate the required custom classes:

```
jpub -user=object_user/object_password
  -url=jdbc:oracle:thin:@localhost:1521:ORCL
  -usertypes=oracle
  -methods=all
```

Once this command has completed, JPublisher will have generated the following files:

- **AddressTyp.java**   Custom class file for the `address_typ` database object type

- **AddressTypRef.java**   Custom class file for an `address_typ` object reference

- **PersonTyp.java**   Custom class file for the `person_typ` database object type

- **PersonTypRef.java**   Custom class file for a `person_typ` object reference

- **ProductTypRef.java**   Custom class file for a `product_typ` object reference

- **ProductTyp.sqlj**   SQLJ source file for the `product_typ` database object type

Notice that for each database object type, there are custom classes not only for the object type but also for object references. You only get custom classes for object references when using JPublisher to generate classes that implement `ORAData` (you don't get them when generating classes that implement `SQLData`, because `SQLData` doesn't support object references). You'll see programs that use these custom classes for objects and object references later in this section.

You'll notice that the last file in the previous list, `ProductTyp.sqlj`, has the file extension `.sqlj`. This file is a *SQLJ file*.

NOTE
SQLJ is another standard for embedding SQL statements within Java programs. SQLJ operates at higher level of abstraction than JDBC, and I advise that you learn SQLJ as well as JDBC. You can learn about SQLJ in my book Java Programming with Oracle SQLJ *(O'Reilly, 2001).*

You get a SQLJ file because the `product_typ` database object type contains a method, named `get_sell_by_date()`, and SQLJ is used to call that method.

Let's take a look at the `ProductTyp.sqlj` file.

The ProductTyp.sqlj File

The `ProductTyp.sqlj` file is shown in the following listing; notice that it contains a number of get and set methods that are used to set an object's attributes and that it contains a method named `getSellByDate()` that calls the `get_sell_by_date()` database object method:

```
import java.sql.SQLException;
import java.sql.Connection;
import oracle.jdbc.OracleTypes;
import oracle.sql.ORAData;
import oracle.sql.ORADataFactory;
import oracle.sql.Datum;
import oracle.sql.STRUCT;
import oracle.jpub.runtime.MutableStruct;
import sqlj.runtime.ref.DefaultContext;
import sqlj.runtime.ConnectionContext;
import java.sql.Connection;

public class ProductTyp implements ORAData, ORADataFactory
{
  public static final String _SQL_NAME = "OBJECT_USER.PRODUCT_TYP";
  public static final int _SQL_TYPECODE = OracleTypes.STRUCT;

  /* connection management */
  protected DefaultContext __tx = null;
  protected Connection __onn = null;
  public void setConnectionContext(DefaultContext ctx)
    throws SQLException
  { release(); __tx = ctx; }
  public DefaultContext getConnectionContext() throws SQLException
  { if (__tx==null)
    { __tx = (__onn==null) ? DefaultContext.getDefaultContext() :
    new DefaultContext(__onn); }
    return __tx;
  };
  public Connection getConnection() throws SQLException
  { return (__onn==null) ? ((__tx==null) ? null :
    __tx.getConnection()) :
    __onn; }
  public void release() throws SQLException
  { if (__tx!=null && __onn!=null)
    __tx.close(ConnectionContext.KEEP_CONNECTION);
    __onn = null; __tx = null;
  }
```

```
   protected MutableStruct _struct;

   private static int[] _sqlType =  { 2,12,12,2,2 };
   private static ORADataFactory[] _factory = new ORADataFactory[5];
   private static final ProductTyp _ProductTypFactory =
     new ProductTyp(false);

   public static ORADataFactory getORADataFactory()
   { return _ProductTypFactory; }
   /* constructors */
   protected ProductTyp(boolean init)
   { if (init) _struct = new MutableStruct(new Object[5], _sqlType,
       _factory); }
   public ProductTyp()
   { this(true); __tx = DefaultContext.getDefaultContext(); }
   public ProductTyp(DefaultContext c) throws SQLException
   { this(true); __tx = c; }
   public ProductTyp(Connection c) throws SQLException
   { this(true); __onn = c; }

   /* ORAData interface */
   public Datum toDatum(Connection c) throws SQLException
   {
     if (__tx!=null && __onn!=c) release();
     __onn = c;
     return _struct.toDatum(c, _SQL_NAME);
   }

   /* ORADataFactory interface */
   public ORAData create(Datum d, int sqlType) throws SQLException
   { return create(null, d, sqlType); }
   public void setFrom(ProductTyp o) throws SQLException
   { release(); _struct = o._struct; __tx = o.__tx; __onn = o.__onn; }
   protected void setValueFrom(ProductTyp o) { _struct = o._struct; }
   protected ORAData create(ProductTyp o, Datum d, int sqlType)
     throws SQLException
   {
     if (d == null) { if (o!=null) { o.release(); }; return null; }
     if (o == null) o = new ProductTyp(false);
     o._struct = new MutableStruct((STRUCT) d, _sqlType, _factory);
     o.__onn = ((STRUCT) d).getJavaSqlConnection();
     return o;
   }
   /* accessor methods */
   public java.math.BigDecimal getId() throws SQLException
   { return (java.math.BigDecimal) _struct.getAttribute(0); }

   public void setId(java.math.BigDecimal id) throws SQLException
```

```java
  { _struct.setAttribute(0, id); }


  public String getName() throws SQLException
  { return (String) _struct.getAttribute(1); }

  public void setName(String name) throws SQLException
  { _struct.setAttribute(1, name); }


  public String getDescription() throws SQLException
  { return (String) _struct.getAttribute(2); }

  public void setDescription(String description) throws SQLException
  { _struct.setAttribute(2, description); }


  public java.math.BigDecimal getPrice() throws SQLException
  { return (java.math.BigDecimal) _struct.getAttribute(3); }

  public void setPrice(java.math.BigDecimal price)
    throws SQLException
  { _struct.setAttribute(3, price); }


  public java.math.BigDecimal getDaysValid() throws SQLException
  { return (java.math.BigDecimal) _struct.getAttribute(4); }

  public void setDaysValid(java.math.BigDecimal daysValid)
    throws SQLException
  { _struct.setAttribute(4, daysValid); }


  public java.sql.Timestamp getSellByDate ()
  throws SQLException
  {
    ProductTyp __jPt_temp = this;
    java.sql.Timestamp __jPt_result;
    #sql [getConnectionContext()] {
      BEGIN
      :OUT __jPt_result := :__jPt_temp.GET_SELL_BY_DATE();
      END;
    };
    return __jPt_result;
  }
}
```

As you can see, this class implements ORAData and ORADataFactory; you'll learn more about ORADataFactory later. To use this file in the example programs, you'll need to use the SQLJ translator tool to translate the SQLJ file to a Java source file. The SQLJ translator will also compile the Java source file into a class file.

Using the SQLJ Translator

You run the SQLJ translator using the sqlj program, which is located in the ORACLE_HOME\BIN directory where your Oracle software is installed; make sure you have this directory in the PATH environment variable for your operating system.

To translate and compile ProductTyp.sqlj, enter the following command:

```
sqlj ProductTyp.sqlj
```

NOTE

As I mentioned in Chapter 1, you'll need to add translator.zip *and* runtime.zip *to your* CLASSPATH *in order to use SQLJ. Both of these files are located in the* ORACLE_HOME\sqlj\lib *directory.*

Once the previous command has completed, you'll find a Java source file named ProductTyp.java and a class file named ProductTyp.class in the ObjectExample4And5 directory. The ObjectExample4.java and ObjectExample5.java programs that I'll show you later use this class file.

Inserting, Selecting, and Updating Database Objects Using Custom Java Objects

To insert, select, and update database objects using objects of your custom class, you follow the same basic steps that were shown earlier when using a custom class that implements SQLData. You could, in fact, use exactly the same code shown in the earlier section "Example Program: ObjectExample3.java". You could, therefore, copy ObjectExample3.java into the ObjectExample4And5 directory, compile it and then run it, and the results would be exactly the same.

One disadvantage of using ObjectExample3.java is that it first creates a type map before inserting, selecting, and updating an object. Creating a type map takes a certain amount of time to perform, but you can forego this step by using the getORAData() and setORAData() methods when retrieving and binding objects. This saves you some time and makes your program run faster. The following sections describe these methods.

The getORAData() Method

You can use the getORAData() method to retrieve an object from an OracleResultSet. The getORAData() method accepts two parameters: the first parameter is the numeric position or name of the column to retrieve, and the second parameter is an oracle.sql.ORADataFactory object. The ORADataFactory object is used to return objects of your custom class. You can use the getORADataFactory() method for your custom class to get an ORADataFactory object. The getORAData() method returns an ORAData object, and you must cast it to an object of your custom class.

Let's take a look at an example that uses getORAData() to retrieve products from the object_products table. First, you need a ResultSet object; the following example creates a ResultSet object named productResultSet to select the products:

```
ResultSet productResultSet = myStatement.executeQuery(
    "SELECT VALUE(op) " +
    "FROM object_products op"
);
```

Also assume that a call to the productResultSet.next() method is made within a while loop to retrieve each product. The following example uses the getORAData() method to retrieve the product; notice that productResultSet is cast to an OracleResultSet in order to call the getORAData() method, and that the ORAData object returned by getORAData() is cast to ProductTyp:

```
ProductTyp product =
    (ProductTyp) ((OracleResultSet) productResultSet).getORAData(
      1, ProductTyp.getORADataFactory()
    );
```

You can then use the various get methods to read the attributes from product:

```
System.out.println("id = " + product.getId());
System.out.println("name = " + product.getName());
System.out.println("description = " + product.getDescription());
System.out.println("price = " + product.getPrice());
System.out.println("days valid = " + product.getDaysValid());
```

Also, you can call the getSellByDate() wrapper method defined in ProductTyp to get the sell-by date of the product:

```
System.out.println("sell by date = " + product.getSellByDate());
```

The `getSellByDate()` wrapper method calls the `get_sell_by_date()` database object method for you.

The setORAData() Method

You can use the `setORAData()` method to bind an object to an `OraclePreparedStatement`. The `setORAData()` method accepts two parameters: the first is the numeric position of the placeholder in the prepared statement, and the second is the object to bind to the placeholder.

Let's take a look at an example that uses `setORAData()` to bind a `ProductTyp` object to an `UPDATE` statement that modifies a product in the `object_products` table. First, I'll create a `PreparedStatement` object named `myPrepStatement`:

```
PreparedStatement myPrepStatement = myConnection.prepareStatement(
    "UPDATE object_products op " +
    "SET VALUE(op) = ? " +
    "WHERE op.id = 1"
);
```

Next, the `setORAData()` method is used to bind a `ProductTyp` object named `product` to the placeholder; notice that `myPrepStatement` is cast to an `OraclePreparedStatement` in order to call the `setORAData()` method:

```
((OraclePreparedStatement) myPrepStatement).setORAData(
    1, product
);
```

You then call the `execute()` method for `myPrepStatement` to run the `UPDATE` statement.

Example Program: ObjectExample4.java

The program `ObjectExample4.java`, shown in the following listing, illustrates the use of the `getORAData()` and `setORAData()` methods. This program inserts, selects, and updates products in the `object_products` table using objects of the custom classes that implement `ORAData`. The program contains four methods that are called in the `main()` method:

- **insertProduct()**   Follows the three steps described earlier in the section "Inserting a Database Object Using a Custom Java Object," where I described the `SQLData` custom classes. The `insertProduct()` method uses the `setORAData()` method instead of `setObject()` in Step 3 to bind a `ProductTyp` object to a prepared statement. The `insertProduct()` method inserts a product into the `object_products` table using an object of the `ProductTyp` class (this class implements the `ORAData` interface).

■ **displayProducts()**   Follows the three steps described earlier in the section "Selecting Database Objects into a Custom Java Object," except it uses the `getORAData()` method instead of `getObject()` in Step 2 when retrieving the product from the result set. The `displayProducts()` method selects and displays the products from the `object_products` table using objects of the `ProductTyp` class.

■ **updateProduct()**   Follows the five steps described earlier in the section "Updating a Database Object Using a Custom Java Object," except that it uses the `getORAData()` in Step 2 and `setORAData()` in Step 5. The `updateProduct()` method updates the `description` and `price` attributes of a product in the `object_products` table using an object of the `ProductTyp` class.

```
/*
  ObjectExample4.java shows how to access database objects
  using strongly typed objects of the ProductTyp class
  generated by JPublisher (the version of ProductTyp used
  implements ORAData and ORADataFactory)
*/

// import the required packages
import java.sql.*;
import oracle.jdbc.OracleResultSet;
import oracle.jdbc.OraclePreparedStatement;
import java.math.BigDecimal;

public class ObjectExample4 {

  public static void insertProduct(
    Connection myConnection
  ) throws SQLException {

    System.out.println("Inserting a product");

    // step 1: create an object of the ProductTyp custom class
    ProductTyp product = new ProductTyp();

    // step 2: set the attributes of the product object using the
    // various set methods
    product.setId(new BigDecimal(3));
    product.setName("Chips");
    product.setDescription("10 oz bag of chips");
    product.setPrice(new BigDecimal(0.99));
    product.setDaysValid(new BigDecimal(20));

    // step 3: use a prepared statement to insert the
```

```
    // product object into the table
    PreparedStatement myPrepStatement =
      myConnection.prepareStatement(
        "INSERT INTO object_products VALUES (?)"
      );
    ((OraclePreparedStatement) myPrepStatement).setORAData(
      1, product
    );
    myPrepStatement.execute();
    myPrepStatement.close();

  } // end of insertProduct()


  public static void displayProducts(
    Connection myConnection,
    Statement myStatement
  ) throws SQLException {

    System.out.println("Products from the object_products table:");

    // step 1: create a result set and use it to select
    // the object(s)
    ResultSet productResultSet = myStatement.executeQuery(
      "SELECT VALUE(op) " +
      "FROM object_products op"
    );

    // step 2: while there are objects in the result set ...
    while (productResultSet.next()) {

      // a: retrieve each database object from the result set
      // using the getORAData() method, casting the returned ORAData
      // object to the ProductTyp custom class
      ProductTyp product =
        (ProductTyp) ((OracleResultSet) productResultSet).getORAData(
          1, ProductTyp.getORADataFactory()
        );

      // b: read the attribute values from the product object
      // using the various get methods
      System.out.println("id = " + product.getId());
      System.out.println("name = " + product.getName());
      System.out.println("description = " +
        product.getDescription());
      System.out.println("price = " + product.getPrice());
      System.out.println("days valid = " + product.getDaysValid());
```

```
    // call the getSellByDate() method to get the sell by date
    System.out.println("sell by date = " +
      product.getSellByDate());

  } // end of while loop

  // step 3: close the result set
  productResultSet.close();

} // end of displayProducts()


public static void updateProduct(
  Connection myConnection,
  Statement myStatement,
  int id
) throws SQLException {

  System.out.println("Updating product #" + id +
    "'s description and price");

  // step 1: create a result set and use it to select
  // the object (in this case, the product with the specified id)
  ResultSet productResultSet = myStatement.executeQuery(
    "SELECT VALUE(op) " +
    "FROM object_products op " +
    "WHERE op.id = " + id
  );
  productResultSet.next();

  // step 2: retrieve the original database object from the
  // result set using the getObject() method, casting the
  // returned Object to the ProductTyp custom class
  ProductTyp product =
    (ProductTyp) ((OracleResultSet) productResultSet).getORAData(
      1, ProductTyp.getORADataFactory()
    );

  // step 3: close the result set
  productResultSet.close();

  // step 4: change the attributes in the ProductTyp object using
  // the appropriate set methods (in this case, the description and
  // price attributes are changed using setDescription()
  // and setPrice()
  product.setDescription("25 oz box of sardines");
  product.setPrice(new BigDecimal(3.49));
```

```
  // step 5: use a prepared statement to perform the update
  PreparedStatement myPrepStatement =
    myConnection.prepareStatement(
      "UPDATE object_products op " +
      "SET VALUE(op) = ? " +
      "WHERE op.id = ?"
    );
  ((OraclePreparedStatement) myPrepStatement).setORAData(
    1, product
  );
  myPrepStatement.setInt(2, id);
  myPrepStatement.execute();
  myPrepStatement.close();

} // end of updateProduct()


public static void main (String args [])
throws SQLException {

  // register the Oracle JDBC drivers
  DriverManager.registerDriver(
    new oracle.jdbc.OracleDriver()
  );

  // create a Connection object, and connect to the database
  // as object_user using the Oracle JDBC Thin driver
  Connection myConnection = DriverManager.getConnection(
    "jdbc:oracle:thin:@localhost:1521:ORCL",
    "object_user",
    "object_password"
  );

  // disable auto-commit mode
  myConnection.setAutoCommit(false);

  // create a Statement object
  Statement myStatement = myConnection.createStatement();

  // display the products in the object_products table
  displayProducts(myConnection, myStatement);

  // insert a product
  insertProduct(myConnection);

  // update product #2's description and price attributes
  updateProduct(myConnection, myStatement, 2);
```

```
    // display the products
    displayProducts(myConnection, myStatement);

    // rollback the changes made to the database
    myConnection.rollback();

    // close the other JDBC objects
    myStatement.close();
    myConnection.close();

  } // end of main()

}
```

NOTE

Because ObjectExample4.java uses the ProductTyp class, you'll need to compile the ProductTyp.java file before you compile ObjectExample4.java.

The output from this program is as follows:

```
Products from the object_products table:
id = 1
name = Pasta
description = 20 oz bag of pasta
price = 3.95
days valid = 10
sell by date = 2002-03-12 11:41:04.0
id = 2
name = Sardines
description = 12 oz box of sardines
price = 2.99
days valid = 5
sell by date = 2002-03-07 11:41:04.0
Inserting a product
Updating product #2's description and price
Products from the object_products table:
id = 1
name = Pasta
description = 20 oz bag of pasta
price = 3.95
days valid = 10
sell by date = 2002-03-12 11:41:05.0
id = 2
name = Sardines
```

```
description = 25 oz box of sardines
price = 3.49
days valid = 5
sell by date = 2002-03-07 11:41:05.0
id = 3
name = Chips
description = 10 oz bag of chips
price = 0.99
days valid = 20
sell by date = 2002-03-22 11:41:05.0
```

Strongly Typed Object References

As you know, an object reference is a pointer to an object. Earlier in the section "Weakly Typed Object References," you saw how `oracle.sql.REF` objects are used to represent database object references, which are stored in `REF` columns. You also saw examples that insert, select, and update rows in the `purchases` table, which contains two `REF` columns named `customer` and `product`. These columns point to objects in the `object_customers` and `object_products` tables, respectively. In the section on weakly typed object references, you saw the various steps required to insert, select, and update rows in the `purchases` table, and you saw a complete program (`ObjectExample2.java`) that featured these various steps.

When you generated the custom classes that implement `ORAData` earlier in this section, you saw that JPublisher generated custom classes that are used to represent object references. For example, the `ProductTypRef.java` file contains the definition for the `ProductTypRef` class; this class is used to represent references to `product_typ` database objects. Similarly, the `PersonTypRef.java` file contains the definition for the `PersonTypRef` class; this class is used to represent references to `person_typ` database objects. You can use objects of these custom classes when accessing object references in the database.

Since the steps required to insert, select, and update rows using the custom classes are similar to those shown earlier in the section "Weakly Typed Object References," I'll just show you a complete program that illustrates the steps.

Example Program: ObjectExample5.java

The program `ObjectExample5.java`, shown in the following listing, illustrates the use of objects of the `ProductTypRef` and `PersonTypRef` custom classes. You can compare this program with `ObjectExample2.java`, which I described earlier. The main thing you should notice about `ObjectExample5.java` is that it uses the `getORAData()` and `setORAData()` methods.

```
/*
    ObjectExample5.java shows how to access object references using
    strongly typed objects of the ProductTypRef and PersonTypRef
```

```
  classes generated by JPublisher (these classes implement ORAData
  and ORADataFactory)
*/

// import the required packages
import java.sql.*;
import oracle.jdbc.OracleResultSet;
import oracle.jdbc.OraclePreparedStatement;
import java.math.BigDecimal;

public class ObjectExample5 {

  public static void displayPurchase(
    Connection myConnection,
    Statement myStatement
  ) throws SQLException {

    System.out.println("Purchase from the purchases table:");

    // step 1: create a result set and select the object
    // references from the REF columns
    ResultSet purchaseResultSet = myStatement.executeQuery(
      "SELECT customer, product " +
      "FROM purchases"
    );
    purchaseResultSet.next();

    // step 2: retrieve the object references from the result set
    // using the getORAData() method
    PersonTypRef customerRef =
      (PersonTypRef)
        ((OracleResultSet) purchaseResultSet).getORAData(
          1, PersonTypRef.getORADataFactory()
        );
    ProductTypRef productRef =
      (ProductTypRef)
        ((OracleResultSet) purchaseResultSet).getORAData(
          2, ProductTypRef.getORADataFactory()
        );

    // step 3: close the result set
    purchaseResultSet.close();

    // step 4: retrieve the actual objects from the references using
    // the getValue() method
    PersonTyp customer = customerRef.getValue();
    ProductTyp product = productRef.getValue();
```

```
    // read the attribute values from the product object using the
    // get methods
    System.out.println("Product:");
    System.out.println("id = " + product.getId());
    System.out.println("price = " + product.getPrice());
    System.out.println("name = " + product.getName());
    System.out.println("description = " + product.getDescription());
    System.out.println("days_valid = " + product.getDaysValid());

    // read the attribute values from the customer object using the
    // get methods
    System.out.println("Customer:");
    System.out.println("id = " + customer.getId());
    System.out.println("first_name = " + customer.getFirstName());
    System.out.println("last_name = " + customer.getLastName());
    System.out.println("dob = " + customer.getDob());
    System.out.println("phone = " + customer.getPhone());

    // get the customer address
    AddressTyp address = (AddressTyp) customer.getAddress();
    System.out.println("street = " + address.getStreet());
    System.out.println("city = " + address.getCity());
    System.out.println("state = " + address.getState());
    System.out.println("zip = " + address.getZip());

  } // end of displayPurchase()


  public static void updateProduct(
    Connection myConnection,
    Statement myStatement,
    int productId
  ) throws SQLException {

    System.out.println("Updating product #" + productId +
      "'s description and price");

    // step 1: create a result set and use it to select
    // the object reference
    ResultSet productResultSet = myStatement.executeQuery(
      "SELECT REF(op) " +
      "FROM object_products op " +
      "WHERE op.id = " + productId
    );
    productResultSet.next();

    // step 2: retrieve the object reference from the result set
    // using the getORAData() method, storing it in a
```

```
// ProductTypRef object
ProductTypRef productRef =
  (ProductTypRef)
    ((OracleResultSet) productResultSet).getORAData(
      1, ProductTypRef.getORADataFactory()
    );

// step 3: close the result set
productResultSet.close();

// step 4: retrieve the object from the object reference using
// the getValue() method
ProductTyp product = (ProductTyp) productRef.getValue();

// step 5: change the object attributes using the set methods
product.setDescription("25 oz box of sardines");
product.setPrice(new BigDecimal(3.49));

// step 6: update the object in the database using the setValue()
// method
productRef.setValue(product);

} // end of updateProduct()


public static void updateProductPurchased(
  Connection myConnection,
  Statement myStatement,
  int purchaseId,
  int productId
) throws SQLException {

  System.out.println("Updating purchase #" + purchaseId +
    " with product #" + productId);

  // step 1: create a result set and use it to
  // select the new object reference
  ResultSet productResultSet = myStatement.executeQuery(
    "SELECT REF(op) " +
    "FROM object_products op " +
    "WHERE op.id = " + productId
  );
  productResultSet.next();

  // step 2: retrieve the object reference from the result set
  // using the getORAData() method, storing it in a
  // ProductTypRef object
  ProductTypRef productRef =
```

```
        (ProductTypRef)
          ((OracleResultSet) productResultSet).getORAData(
            1, ProductTypRef.getORADataFactory()
          );

    // step 3: close the result set
    productResultSet.close();

    // step 4: use a prepared statement to perform the update of
    // the existing object reference stored in the REF column with
    // the new object reference
    PreparedStatement myPrepStatement =
      myConnection.prepareStatement(
        "UPDATE purchases " +
        "SET product = ? " +
        "WHERE id = ?"
      );
    ((OraclePreparedStatement) myPrepStatement).setORAData(
      1, productRef
    );
    myPrepStatement.setInt(2, purchaseId);
    myPrepStatement.execute();
    myPrepStatement.close();

  } // end of updateProductPurchased()


  public static void main(String args [])
  throws SQLException {

    // register the Oracle JDBC drivers
    DriverManager.registerDriver(
      new oracle.jdbc.OracleDriver()
    );

    // create a Connection object, and connect to the database
    // as object_user using the Oracle JDBC Thin driver
    Connection myConnection = DriverManager.getConnection(
      "jdbc:oracle:thin:@localhost:1521:ORCL",
      "object_user",
      "object_password"
    );

    // disable auto-commit mode
    myConnection.setAutoCommit(false);

    // create a Statement object
    Statement myStatement = myConnection.createStatement();
```

```
    // display the purchases
    displayPurchase(myConnection, myStatement);

    // update product #2's description and price attributes
    updateProduct(myConnection, myStatement, 2);

    // update purchase #1 to reference product #2
    updateProductPurchased(myConnection, myStatement, 1, 2);

    // display the purchases
    displayPurchase(myConnection, myStatement);

    // rollback the changes made to the database
    myConnection.rollback();

    // close the Statement and Connection objects
    myStatement.close();
    myConnection.close();

  } // end of main()

}
```

NOTE

*Because ObjectExample5.java uses the
PersonTyp, PersonTypRef, ProductTyp,
ProductTypRef, and AddressTyp classes,
you'll need to compile the source files for
each of these classes before you compile
ObjectExample5.java.*

The output from this program is as follows:

```
Purchase from the purchases table:
Product:
id = 1
price = 3.95
name = Pasta
description = 20 oz bag of pasta
days_valid = 10
Customer:
id = 1
first_name = John
last_name = Brown
dob = 1955-02-01 00:00:00.0
phone = 800-555-1211
street = 2 State Street
```

```
city = Beantown
state = MA
zip = 12345
Updating product #2's description and price
Updating purchase #1 with product #2
Purchase from the purchases table:
Product:
id = 2
price = 3.49
name = Sardines
description = 25 oz box of sardines
days_valid = 5
Customer:
id = 1
first_name = John
last_name = Brown
dob = 1955-02-01 00:00:00.0
phone = 800-555-1211
street = 2 State Street
city = Beantown
state = MA
zip = 12345
```

CHAPTER
7

Collections

he Oracle8i database introduced two new database types known as *collections*. As you'll see later, the Oracle9i database extends these features to include multilevel collections, which allow you to create a collection that is itself a collection. There are two types of collections: *varrays* and *nested tables*.

A varray is similar to an array in Java; you can use a varray to store an ordered set of elements with each element having an index associated with it. The elements in a varray are of the same type, and a varray has one dimension. A varray has a maximum size that you set when creating it, but you can change the size later.

A nested table is a table that is embedded within another table, and you can insert, update, and delete individual elements in a nested table. Because you can modify individual elements in a nested table, this makes them more flexible than a varray because elements in a varray can only be modified as a whole, not individually. A nested table doesn't have a maximum size, and you can store an arbitrary number of elements in a nested table.

TIP

If you only need to store a fixed set of elements, you should use a varray. If you need to store an arbitrary number of elements, or if you need more flexible access to your elements, you should use a nested table.

You create varray and nested table types using the SQL DDL CREATE TYPE statement, and you then use these types to define columns in a table. The elements stored in a varray are stored with the table; the elements for a nested table are stored in a separate table with a link to the table that references it. Because a varray is stored with the table, accessing its elements is faster than accessing elements in a nested table.

You might be asking yourself why would you want to use collections in the first place. After all, using two tables with a foreign key already allows you to model relationships between data. The answer is that the data stored in the collection may be accessed more rapidly by the database than if you were to use two tables instead. Typically, you'll want to use a collection if you have data that is only used by one table. For example, this chapter uses collections to store addresses for customer, and those addresses are used only within the tables they are stored in. You'll learn how to create collection types, create tables containing collections, populate those tables with rows, and access those tables using JDBC. You'll also learn about the multilevel collections introduced with the Oracle9i database.

I've provided a SQL*Plus script named collection_user.sql in the sql directory where you unzipped the files for this book. This script may be run against an Oracle8*i* or Oracle9*i* database. This script contains the SQL DDL statements that create the collection types and tables used in this chapter; this script also populates the tables with sample data. You should run this script (or have your DBA run it) before running the programs shown in this chapter.

Varrays

You use a varray to store an ordered set of elements, with each element having an index associated with it that corresponds to its position in the array. A varray has a maximum size that you can change dynamically.

Creating a Varray Type

You create a varray type using the SQL DDL CREATE TYPE statement, and you specify the maximum size and the type of elements stored in the varray when creating the type. You can change the maximum size of a varray using the ALTER TYPE statement. The following CREATE TYPE statement creates a varray type named varray_address_typ that can store up to two VARCHAR2 strings:

```
CREATE TYPE varray_address_typ AS VARRAY(2) OF VARCHAR2(50);
/
```

Each VARCHAR2 can be used to represent a different address for a customer of our imaginary store. One address could be the customer's shipping address where they receive products, and the other their billing address where they receive the bill for the product (both addresses could, of course, be the same). You can also store object types in a collection, and you'll see an example of that when I show you how to create a nested table type later.

Using a Varray Type to Define a Column in a Table

Once you define your varray type, you can use it to define a column in a table. For example, the following table named customers_with_varray uses varray_address_typ to define a column named addresses:

```
CREATE TABLE customers_with_varray (
   id          INTEGER PRIMARY KEY,
   first_name VARCHAR2(10),
   last_name  VARCHAR2(10),
   addresses  varray_address_typ
);
```

Notice that `customers_with_varray` also contains columns named `id`, `first_name`, and `last_name` in addition to the `addresses` column.

Populating a Varray with Elements

You initially populate the elements in a varray using an `INSERT` statement. The following `INSERT` statement adds a row to the `customers_with_varray` table; notice the use of the `varray_address_typ` constructor to specify two strings for the `addresses` varray column:

```
INSERT INTO customers_with_varray VALUES (
    1, 'Steve', 'Brown',
    varray_address_typ(
      '2 State Street, Beantown, MA, 12345',
      '4 Hill Street, Lost Town, CA, 54321'
    )
);
```

Selecting Varray Elements

You select the elements in a varray using a `SELECT` statement. The following `SELECT` statement selects the row from the `customers_with_varray` table:

```
SQL> SELECT * FROM customers_with_varray;

        ID FIRST_NAME LAST_NAME
---------- ---------- ----------
ADDRESSES
----------------------------------------------------------
         1 Steve      Brown
VARRAY_ADDRESS_TYP('2 State Street, Beantown, MA, 12345',
 '4 Hill Street, Lost Town, CA, 54321')
```

Modifying Varray Elements

As I mentioned earlier, the elements in a varray can only be modified as a whole. This means that even if you only want to modify one element, you must supply all the elements for the varray. The following `UPDATE` statement modifies the first address of customer #1 in the `customers_with_varray` table; notice that the second address is also supplied even though it hasn't changed:

```
UPDATE customers_with_varray
    SET addresses = varray_address_typ(
      '3 New Street, Middle Town, CA, 123435',
      '4 Hiil Street, Lost Town, CA, 54321'
    )
WHERE id = 1;
```

Nested Tables

A *nested table* is an unordered set of any number of *elements*, all of the same data type. A nested table has a single column, and the type of that column may be a built-in Oracle database type or an object type that you previously created (object types were covered in the previous chapter). If the column in a nested table is an object type, the table can also be viewed as a multicolumn table, with a column for each attribute of the object type. You can insert, update, and delete individual elements in a nested table.

Creating a Nested Table Type

In this section, I'll show you how to create a nested table type that stores address_typ object types. You saw the use of address_typ in the previous chapter; it is used to represent an address and is defined as follows:

```
CREATE TYPE address_typ AS OBJECT (
   street VARCHAR2(15),
   city   VARCHAR2(15),
   state  CHAR(2),
   zip    VARCHAR2(5)
);
/
```

You create a nested table type using the CREATE TYPE statement, and the following example creates a nested table type named nested_table_address_typ that stores address_typ object types:

```
CREATE TYPE nested_table_address_typ AS TABLE OF address_typ;
/
```

Notice that you don't specify the maximum size of a nested table—that's because you can insert any number of elements in a nested table.

Using a Nested Table Type to Define a Column in a Table

Once you have defined your nested table type, you can use it to define a column in a table. For example, the following table named customers_with_nested_table uses nested_table_address_typ to define a column named addresses:

```
CREATE TABLE customers_with_nested_table (
   id       INTEGER PRIMARY KEY,
```

```
    first_name VARCHAR2(10),
    last_name  VARCHAR2(10),
    addresses  nested_table_address_typ
)
NESTED TABLE
  addresses
STORE AS
  nested_addresses;
```

The NESTED TABLE clause identifies the name of the nested table column (addresses), and the STORE AS clause specifies the name of the actual nested table (nested_addresses). You cannot access the nested table independently of the table in which it is embedded.

Populating a Nested Table with Elements

You initially populate the elements in a nested table using an INSERT statement. The following INSERT statement adds a row to customers_with_nested_table; notice the use of the nested_table_address_typ and address_typ constructors to specify the addresses:

```
INSERT INTO customers_with_nested_table VALUES (
    1, 'Steve', 'Brown',
    nested_table_address_typ(
      address_typ('2 State Street', 'Beantown', 'MA', '12345'),
      address_typ('4 Hill Street', 'Lost Town', 'CA', '54321')
    )
);
```

As you can see, this row has two addresses, but any number of addresses can be stored in a nested table.

Selecting Nested Table Elements

You select the elements in a nested table using a SELECT statement. The following SELECT statement selects the row from customers_with_nested_table:

```
SQL> SELECT * FROM customers_with_nested_table;

        ID FIRST_NAME LAST_NAME
---------- ---------- ----------
ADDRESSES(STREET, CITY, STATE, ZIP)
----------------------------------------------------------
         1 Steve      Brown
```

```
NESTED_TABLE_ADDRESS_TYP(
 ADDRESS_TYP('2 State Street', 'Beantown', 'MA', '12345'),
 ADDRESS_TYP('4 Hill Street', 'Lost Town', 'CA', '54321'))
```

Modifying Nested Table Elements

Unlike a varray, elements in a nested table can be modified individually: you can insert, update, and delete elements in a nested table. You do this using the TABLE clause in conjunction with a subquery that selects the nested table. The following example inserts an address at the end of the addresses nested table column for customer #1 in customer_with_nested_table:

```
INSERT INTO TABLE (
   SELECT addresses FROM customers_with_nested_table WHERE id = 1
) VALUES (
   address_typ('5 Main Street', 'Uptown', 'NY', '55512')
);
```

The next example updates the first address of customer #1 in customers_with_nested_table; notice the use of the alias addr to identify the first address and subsequently set it:

```
UPDATE TABLE (
   SELECT addresses FROM customers_with_nested_table WHERE id = 1
) addr
SET
   VALUE(addr) = address_typ(
     '1 Market Street', 'Main Town', 'MA', '54321'
   )
WHERE
   VALUE(addr) = address_typ(
     '2 State Street', 'Beantown', 'MA', '12345'
   );
```

The final example deletes the second address for customer #1 in customers_with_nested_table:

```
DELETE FROM TABLE (
   SELECT addresses FROM customers_with_nested_table WHERE id = 1
) addr
WHERE
   VALUE(addr) = address_typ(
     '4 Hill Street', 'Lost Town', 'CA', '54321'
   );
```

Oracle9*i* Multilevel Collection Types

With the release of the Oracle9*i* database, you can create a collection type in the database whose elements are also a collection type; this is known as a *multilevel collection type*. The following list shows the valid multilevel collection types:

- A nested table containing a nested table type

- A nested table containing a varray type

- A varray containing a varray type

- A varray containing a nested table type

- A varray or nested table of an object type that has an attribute that is a varray or nested table type

NOTE
I've provided a SQL*Plus script named
`collection_user_9i.sql` *in the* `sql` *directory
that creates the types and the table described in this
section. You can run this script if you are using an
Oracle9i database.*

To consider an example of a multilevel collection type, let's say you wanted to store a set of phone numbers with associated with each address of a customer. The following example creates a varray type of three `VARCHAR2` strings named `varray_phone_typ` to represent phone numbers:

```
CREATE TYPE varray_phone_typ AS VARRAY(3) OF VARCHAR2(14);
/
```

Next, the following example creates an object type named `address_typ` that contains an attribute named `phone_numbers`; this attribute is defined using `varray_phone_typ`:

```
CREATE TYPE address_typ AS OBJECT (
    street         VARCHAR2(15),
    city           VARCHAR2(15),
    state          CHAR(2),
    zip            VARCHAR2(5),
    phone_numbers varray_phone_typ
);
/
```

The next example creates a nested table type of `address_typ` objects:

```
CREATE TYPE nested_table_address_typ AS TABLE OF address_typ;
/
```

The following example creates a table named
`customers_with_nested_table` that contains a column named `addresses`
of `nested_table_address_typ`:

```
CREATE TABLE customers_with_nested_table (
    id          INTEGER PRIMARY KEY,
    first_name  VARCHAR2(10),
    last_name   VARCHAR2(10),
    addresses   nested_table_address_typ
)
NESTED TABLE
    addresses
STORE AS
    nested_addresses;
```

Finally, the next example inserts a row into `customers_with_`
`nested_table`; notice the use of the constructors for the three types in the
INSERT statement:

```
INSERT INTO customers_with_nested_table VALUES (
    1, 'Steve', 'Brown',
    nested_table_address_typ(
      address_typ('2 State Street', 'Beantown', 'MA', '12345',
        varray_phone_typ(
          '(800)-555-1211',
          '(800)-555-1212',
          '(800)-555-1213'
        )
      ),
      address_typ('4 Hill Street', 'Lost Town', 'CA', '54321',
        varray_phone_typ(
          '(800)-555-1211',
          '(800)-555-1212'
        )
      )
    )
);
```

You can see that the first address has three phone numbers, while the second
address only has two. Multilevel collection types are a very powerful extension to
the Oracle9*i* database, and you might want to consider using them in any database
designs you contribute to.

Accessing Collections Using Weakly Typed Objects

In the previous chapter, you saw how database objects can be accessed using both weakly typed objects of the `oracle.sql.STRUCT` class and strongly typed objects of classes generated by JPublisher. Collections can also be accessed using weakly and strongly typed objects. In this section, you'll learn how to access collections using weakly typed objects of the `oracle.sql.ARRAY` class, which implements the `java.sql.Array` interface. The `ARRAY` class is known as weakly typed because it stores its elements as an array of generic Java `Objects`.

Strongly typed objects are of custom classes that you can generate using JPublisher. Custom classes represent the elements of a collection using a specific class based on the type of elements in the actual collection type in the database, rather than the generic `Object` class.

You may still want to use weakly typed `ARRAY` objects to represent collections if you are selecting data and then inserting data without doing a lot of manipulation of that data in memory. On the other hand, if you need to do a lot of manipulation of data in memory, you should use strongly typed objects, since they store the data in a more convenient form for data manipulation using Java statements. You'll see how to use strongly typed objects with collections later in this chapter.

Inserting a Collection Using an ARRAY

You'll learn how to insert a row into a table containing a collection in this section. To insert a row containing a collection using an `ARRAY` object you follow these steps:

1. Create an `ArrayDescriptor` for the collection type.

2. Create an `Object` array to store the elements for your collection.

3. Create an `ARRAY` object, passing your `ArrayDescriptor`, `Connection`, and `Object` array to the constructor of your `ARRAY`.

4. Use a prepared statement to insert your `ARRAY` into the table, along with any other columns required for the new row.

In the following sections, I'll describe the details of these steps along with example code that inserts a row into the `customers_with_varray` table; this table contains a varray of `VARCHAR2` strings in the `addresses` column.

Step 1: Create an ArrayDescriptor Object
for the Collection Type

The first step is to create an `ArrayDescriptor` object for the collection type.
The `ArrayDescriptor` class is located in the `oracle.sql` package, and the
examples in this section assume that `oracle.sql.ArrayDescriptor` has been
imported.

The `ArrayDescriptor` object is used to represent the details of the collection
type, and its contents are required later in Step 3 when creating the ARRAY object.
The `ArrayDescriptor` class contains a method named `createDescriptor()`
that accepts two parameters:

- The name of your database schema and collection type, which is
  known as the *fully qualified* name of the collection type; for example:
  `COLLECTION_USER.VARRAY_ADDRESS_TYP`

- Your `Connection` object

The following example creates an `ArrayDescriptor` object named
`addressDescriptor`; notice that the parameters to `createDescriptor()`
are `"COLLECTION_USER.VARRAY_ADDRESS_TYP"` (the fully qualified name
of the varray type used in the examples in this section) and `myConnection`
(a `Connection` object that is assumed to already exist):

```
ArrayDescriptor addressDescriptor =
  ArrayDescriptor.createDescriptor(
    "COLLECTION_USER.VARRAY_ADDRESS_TYP", myConnection
  );
```

The `addressDescriptor` object contains the details for the COLLECTION_
USER.VARRAY_ADDRESS_TYP collection type. Some other methods in the
`ArrayDescriptor` class are as follows:

- **getBaseType()**   Returns the integer typecode for the `ArrayDescriptor`.
  (You can see the integer typecode constants for the
  `oracle.jdbc.OracleTypes` class in Table C-8 of Appendix C.)

- **getBaseName()**   Returns a string containing the type name.

- **getArrayType()**   Returns an integer that indicates whether the array
  is a varray (in which case the returned integer is set to the
  `ArrayDescriptor.TYPE_VARRAY` constant) or a nested table (in which
  case the returned integer is set to the `ArrayDescriptor.TYPE_
  NESTED_TABLE` constant).

- **getMaxLength()**   Returns an integer containing the maximum number of
  elements for the array.

Step 2: Create an Object Array to Store the Elements for the Collection

The second step is to create an `Object` array to store the elements for the collection. The following example creates an array of two `Object` elements named `addressElements`:

```
Object [] addressElements = {
    "1 Main Street, Uptown, NY, 55512",
    "2 Side Street, Beantown, MA, 12345"
};
```

Notice that this example initializes `addressElements` with two addresses.

Step 3: Create an ARRAY Object

The third step is to create an `ARRAY` object. The `ARRAY` class is located in the `oracle.sql` package, and the examples in this section assume that `oracle.sql.ARRAY` has been imported.

When you create your `ARRAY` object, you pass your `ArrayDescriptor`, `Connection`, and `Object` array to the constructor of your `ARRAY` object. The following example creates an `ARRAY` object named `addressARRAY`; notice that the `addressDescriptor`, `myConnection`, and `addressElements` objects are passed to the constructor:

```
ARRAY addressARRAY =
    new ARRAY(addressDescriptor, myConnection, addressElements);
```

The `oracle.sql.ARRAY` class implements the `java.sql.Array` interface. The `Array` interface declares the following methods:

- **getArray()**   Returns the elements of the array as an `Object`. You can pass a `java.util.Map` object to this method; if you do this, the mappings specified in that `Map` object are used to create the attribute types. If you don't pass a `Map` object, the default JDBC mappings are used. `Map` objects were covered in the previous chapter.

- **getBaseType()**   Returns the integer typecode for the elements of the array.

- **getBaseTypeName()**   Returns the SQL type name for the elements of the array.

- **getResultSet()**   Returns the elements of the array in a result set. You can then use standard result set methods like `next()` to retrieve the elements. You can use this method when reading elements from a nested table. You can also pass a `Map` object to this method.

In addition to implementing the standard methods contained in the `Array` interface, the `ARRAY` class defines additional methods, some of which are as follows:

- **getDescriptor()**   Returns the `ArrayDescriptor` object

- **getOracleArray()**   The same as `getArray()`, except that it returns the elements in `oracle.sql.*` format

- **getSQLTypeName()**   Returns the fully qualified collection type name

- **getJavaSQLConnection()**   Returns the `Connection` object

- **toJdbc()**   Consults the default type map (or the `java.util.Map` object, if such an object is supplied as a parameter) for the connection to determine what class to map elements to and then calls `toClass()` to convert the elements to JDBC types

- **length()**   Returns the number of elements in the array

Step 4: Use a Prepared Statement to Insert the ARRAY into the Table

The fourth and final step is to use a prepared statement to insert your `ARRAY` into the table, along with any other columns required for the new row. Specifically, you create an `OraclePreparedStatement` object (or cast an existing `PreparedStatement` to an `OraclePreparedStatement`) and call its `setARRAY()` method to bind your `ARRAY` object to an `INSERT` statement for the table.

The following example inserts a new row into the `customers_with_varray` table; notice the use of the `setARRAY()` method to bind `addressARRAY` to the fourth placeholder that is for the `addresses` column:

```
PreparedStatement myPrepStatement =
  myConnection.prepareStatement(
    "INSERT INTO customers_with_varray VALUES (?, ?, ?, ?)"
  );
myPrepStatement.setInt(1, 2); // id
myPrepStatement.setString(2, "Cynthia"); //first_name
myPrepStatement.setString(3, "Green"); // last_name
((OraclePreparedStatement) myPrepStatement).setARRAY(
  4, addressARRAY
); // addresses
myPrepStatement.execute();
myPrepStatement.close();
```

Of course, to make the new row permanent you must perform a commit.

Selecting Collections into an ARRAY

You'll learn how to select collections from a table in this section. To select collections from a table into an ARRAY you follow these steps:

1. Create a result set and use it to select the rows from the table containing the collection column, along with any other columns you want to retrieve from the table.

2. While there are rows in your result set, perform the following:

   a. Retrieve the collection from your result set into an ARRAY using the getARRAY() method.

   b. Retrieve the element values from your ARRAY using the getArray() method, storing the element values in an Object array.

   c. Read the element values from your Object array, casting the Object elements to specific types if necessary.

3. Close your result set.

In the following sections, I'll describe the details of Steps 1 and 2, along with example code that selects the rows from the customers_with_varray table.

NOTE
You've already seen examples of Step 3 that closes a result set, so I won't describe that step again. Make sure you call the close() method for the result set in your own code.

Step 1: Create a Result Set to Select the Rows

The first step is to create a result set and use it to select the rows from the table containing the collection column, along with any other columns you want to retrieve from the table. The following example creates a ResultSet object named customerResultSet that selects the id, first_name, last_name, and addresses columns from the customers_with_varray table:

```
ResultSet customerResultSet = myStatement.executeQuery(
  "SELECT id, first_name, last_name, addresses " +
  "FROM customers_with_varray"
);
```

In the next step, you'll see how to retrieve the strings stored in the addresses column.

Step 2: While There Are Rows in the Result Set, Retrieve the Collection and Element Values

The second step is to retrieve the collection and its element values from the collection in your result set (along with the other column values that you've selected into your result set). To retrieve the collection and its element values, you use the getARRAY() and getArray() methods within a while loop that calls customerResultSet.next(). You use the getARRAY() method for an OracleResultSet (or cast an existing ResultSet to an OracleResultSet) to retrieve the collection as an ARRAY object.

The following example casts customerResultSet to an OracleResultSet and then calls the getARRAY() method to retrieve the addresses column, storing the returned ARRAY in addressARRAY:

```
ARRAY addressARRAY =
  ((OracleResultSet) customerResultSet).getARRAY("addresses");
```

Once you have your ARRAY, you call the getArray() method of your ARRAY to retrieve the element values, storing them in an Object array:

```
Object [] addresses = (Object []) addressARRAY.getArray();
```

You can then read the element values stored in your Object array. The following for loop displays the element values contained in addresses, and each element is implicitly cast to a String before being displayed by System.out.println():

```
for (int count = 0; count < addresses.length; count++) {
  System.out.println("addresses[" + count + "] = " +
    addresses[count]);
}
```

Updating a Collection Using an ARRAY

You'll learn how to update a row containing a collection in this section. To update a collection using an ARRAY you follow these steps:

1. Create a result set and use it to select the collection.

2. Retrieve the original collection from your result set into an ARRAY using the getARRAY() method.

3. Close your result set.

4. Retrieve the elements from your ARRAY into an Object array using the getArray() method.

5. Change the elements in your Object array to your new values.

6. Retrieve the ArrayDescriptor from your ARRAY using the getDescriptor() method.

7. Create a new ARRAY, passing your ArrayDescriptor, Connection object, and Object array to the constructor of your new ARRAY.

8. Use a prepared statement to perform the update using your new ARRAY.

You've already seen an example of Steps 1 through 4 in the previous section entitled "Selecting Collections into an ARRAY," so I won't repeat those steps here. In the following sections, I'll describe the details of Steps 5 through 8, along with example code that updates the first address of customer #1 in the customers_with_varray table.

In the case of updating a nested table, you can update a single element in a nested table, and you can omit Steps 6 and 7 from the previous list. I'll show you the appropriate UPDATE statements when updating a varray or nested table in the details for Step 8.

Step 5: Change the Elements in the Object Array to the New Values

The fifth step is to change the elements in your Object array. Assume you've already retrieved customer #1's addresses into an ARRAY named addressARRAY, and these address elements have been stored in an Object array named addresses. The following example changes the first element, which is stored in addresses[0], to a new address:

```
addresses[0] = "3 New Street, Middle Town, CA, 12345";
```

Step 6: Retrieve the ArrayDescriptor for the ARRAY

The sixth step is to retrieve the ArrayDescriptor for your ARRAY, which you do using the getDescriptor() method. The assumption is that you've already retrieved the addresses for customer #1 into an ARRAY named addressARRAY, and the following example calls getDescriptor() using addressARRAY:

```
ArrayDescriptor addressDescriptor = addressARRAY.getDescriptor();
```

Step 7: Create a New ARRAY

The seventh step is to create a new ARRAY, passing your ArrayDescriptor, Connection, and Object array to the constructor of this new ARRAY:

```
ARRAY newAddressARRAY =
  new ARRAY(addressDescriptor, myConnection, addresses);
```

Step 8: Use a Prepared Statement to Perform the Update Using the New ARRAY

The eighth and final step is to use a prepared statement to perform the update using your new ARRAY. If you're updating a varray, you must replace all the elements in the varray. If you're updating a nested table, you can choose to either replace all the elements, or you can just replace the element that has changed. In the following sections, I'll show you how to replace all elements in collection (varray and nested table), and how to replace just one element in a nested table.

Replacing All the Elements in a Collection   To replace all the elements in a collection, you create an OraclePreparedStatement object (or cast a PreparedStatement to an OraclePreparedStatement) and call its setARRAY() method to bind your ARRAY to a placeholder in an UPDATE statement. Then you call the execute() method to perform the UPDATE. At the end, you close your prepared statement using the close() method.

The following example creates a PreparedStatement object named myPrepStatement, binds newAddressARRAY and an int containing the customer's id to the first and second placeholders using the setARRAY() and setInt() methods, and then calls the execute() method to perform the UPDATE; at the end myPrepStatement is closed:

```
int id = 1;
PreparedStatement myPrepStatement =
  myConnection.prepareStatement(
    "UPDATE customers_with_varray " +
    "SET addresses = ? " +
    "WHERE id = ?"
  );
((OraclePreparedStatement) myPrepStatement).setARRAY(
  1, newAddressARRAY
);  // addresses
myPrepStatement.setInt(2, id);  // id
myPrepStatement.execute();
myPrepStatement.close();
```

The program `CollectionExample1.java`, which I'll cover in detail in the next section uses the previous code example.

Replacing One Element in a Nested Table   To replace just one element in a collection, you create a `PreparedStatement` object that contains an `UPDATE` statement with a `TABLE` clause and subquery.

NOTE
Earlier, in the section entitled "Modifying Nested Table Elements," I showed you how to update individual elements in a nested table using the `TABLE` clause with a subquery. You should refer back to that section if necessary.

Let's consider an example. The `customers_with_nested_table` contains a column named `addresses`, and let's say you want to update only the first address in this nested table for customer #1. The `addresses` column is a nested table of `address_typ` elements, and `address_typ` is an object type that contains four attributes that store the street, city, state, and zip code for the address. As you saw in the previous chapter, you can use a `STRUCT` to represent an `address_typ` database object. Let's assume you have two `STRUCT`s named `oldAddressSTRUCT` and `newAddressSTRUCT`; assume `oldAddressSTRUCT` contains the old address that you want to update, and `newAddressSTRUCT` contains the new address. You can use the following code to perform the update of the customer #1's first address; notice the use of the `setObject()` method to bind `oldAddressSTRUCT` and `newAddressSTRUCT` to the prepared statement:

```
int id = 1;
PreparedStatement myPrepStatement =
  myConnection.prepareStatement(
    "UPDATE TABLE (" +
    "  SELECT addresses FROM customers_with_nested_table " +
    "  WHERE id = ? " +
    ") a " +
    "SET VALUE(a) = ? " +
    "WHERE VALUE(a) = ?"
  );
myPrepStatement.setInt(1, id);
myPrepStatement.setObject(2, newAddressSTRUCT);
myPrepStatement.setObject(3, oldAddressSTRUCT);
myPrepStatement.execute();
myPrepStatement.close();
```

The program `CollectionExample2.java`, which I'll cover at the end of the next section, uses the previous code example.

Example Program: CollectionExample1.java

The program `CollectionExample1.java`, shown in the following listing, illustrates the various steps shown in the previous sections to insert, select, and update customers in the `customers_with_varray` table; this table contains a varray in the `addresses` column. This program contains three methods that are called in the `main()` method:

- **insertCustomer()**   Follows the four steps described earlier in the section entitled "Inserting a Collection Using an ARRAY." Specifically, this method inserts a new customer into the `customers_with_varray` table.

- **displayCustomers()**   Follows the three steps described earlier in the section entitled "Selecting Collections into an ARRAY." Specifically, this method selects and displays the customers in the `customers_with_varray` table.

- **updateCustomerAddress()**   Follows the eight steps described earlier in the section entitled "Updating a Collection Using an ARRAY." Specifically, this method updates a customer's first address in the `addresses` column. Since the `addresses` column contains a varray, all the address elements are replaced, even though only the first address is actually changed.

```
/*
   CollectionExample1.java shows how to access varrays
   using using weakly typed ARRAY objects
*/

// import the required packages
import java.sql.*;
import oracle.sql.ARRAY;
import oracle.sql.ArrayDescriptor;
import oracle.jdbc.OraclePreparedStatement;
import oracle.jdbc.OracleResultSet;

public class CollectionExample1 {

  public static void insertCustomer(
    Connection myConnection
  ) throws SQLException {

    System.out.println(
```

```
      "Inserting a customer into customers_with_varray"
    );

    // step 1: create an ArrayDescriptor object for the collection
    // object type (in this case, COLLECTION_USER.VARRAY_ADDRESS_TYP)
    ArrayDescriptor addressDescriptor =
      ArrayDescriptor.createDescriptor(
        "COLLECTION_USER.VARRAY_ADDRESS_TYP", myConnection
      );

    // step 2: create an Object array to store the elements for the
    // collection
    Object [] addressElements = {
      "1 Main Street, Uptown, NY, 55512",
      "2 Side Street, Beantown, MA, 12345"
    };

    // step 3: create an ARRAY object
    ARRAY addressARRAY =
      new ARRAY(addressDescriptor, myConnection, addressElements);

    // step 4: use a prepared statement to insert the ARRAY
    // into the table, along with the other columns required
    // for the new row
    PreparedStatement myPrepStatement =
      myConnection.prepareStatement(
        "INSERT INTO customers_with_varray VALUES (?, ?, ?, ?)"
      );
    myPrepStatement.setInt(1, 2);
    myPrepStatement.setString(2, "Cynthia");
    myPrepStatement.setString(3, "Green");
    ((OraclePreparedStatement) myPrepStatement).setARRAY(
      4, addressARRAY
    );
    myPrepStatement.execute();
    myPrepStatement.close();

} // end of insertCustomer()


public static void displayCustomers(
  Connection myConnection,
  Statement myStatement
) throws SQLException {

  System.out.println("Customers from customers_with_varray:");

  // step 1: create a result set and use it to select
```

```
  // the rows from customers_with_varray
  ResultSet customerResultSet = myStatement.executeQuery(
    "SELECT id, first_name, last_name, addresses " +
    "FROM customers_with_varray"
  );

  // step 2: while there are rows in the result set ...
  while (customerResultSet.next()) {

    System.out.println("id = " +
      customerResultSet.getInt("id"));
    System.out.println("first_name = " +
      customerResultSet.getString("first_name"));
    System.out.println("last_name = " +
      customerResultSet.getString("last_name"));

    // a: retrieve the collection from the result set into an
    // ARRAY using the getARRAY() method
    ARRAY addressARRAY =
      ((OracleResultSet) customerResultSet).getARRAY("addresses");

    // b: retrieve the element values from the ARRAY using the
    // getArray() method, storing the element values in an Object
    // array
    Object [] addresses = (Object []) addressARRAY.getArray();

    // c: read the element values from the Object array
    for (int count = 0; count < addresses.length; count++) {
      System.out.println("addresses[" + count + "] = " +
        addresses[count]);
    }

  } // end of while loop

  // step 3: close the result set
  customerResultSet.close();

} // end of displayCustomers()


public static void updateCustomerAddress(
  Connection myConnection,
  Statement myStatement,
  int id
) throws SQLException {

  System.out.println("Updating customer #" + id +
    "'s first address");
```

```
// step 1: create a result set and use it to select
// the collection (in this case, the addresses for a customer
// with the specified id)
ResultSet customerResultSet = myStatement.executeQuery(
  "SELECT addresses " +
  "FROM customers_with_varray " +
  "WHERE id = " + id
);
customerResultSet.next();

// step 2: retrieve the original collection from the
// result set into an ARRAY using the getARRAY() method
ARRAY addressARRAY =
  ((OracleResultSet) customerResultSet).getARRAY("addresses");

// step 3: close the result set
customerResultSet.close();

// step 4: retrieve the elements from the ARRAY into an
// Object array using the getArray() method
Object [] addresses = (Object []) addressARRAY.getArray();

// step 5: change the first element in the Object array
addresses[0] = "3 New Street, Middle Town, CA, 12345";

// step 6: retrieve the ArrayDescriptor from the ARRAY using the
// getDescriptor() method
ArrayDescriptor addressDescriptor = addressARRAY.getDescriptor();

// step 7: create a new ARRAY object
ARRAY newAddressARRAY =
  new ARRAY(addressDescriptor, myConnection, addresses);

// step 8: use a prepared statement to perform the update
PreparedStatement myPrepStatement =
  myConnection.prepareStatement(
    "UPDATE customers_with_varray " +
    "SET addresses = ? " +
    "WHERE id = ?"
  );
((OraclePreparedStatement) myPrepStatement).setARRAY(
  1, newAddressARRAY
);
myPrepStatement.setInt(2, id);
myPrepStatement.execute();
myPrepStatement.close();
```

```java
} // end of updateCustomerAddress()


public static void main(String args [])
throws SQLException {

  // register the Oracle JDBC drivers
  DriverManager.registerDriver(
    new oracle.jdbc.OracleDriver()
  );

  // create a Connection object, and connect to the database
  // as collection_user using the Oracle JDBC Thin driver
  Connection myConnection = DriverManager.getConnection(
    "jdbc:oracle:thin:@localhost:1521:ORCL",
    "collection_user",
    "collection_password"
  );

  // disable auto-commit mode
  myConnection.setAutoCommit(false);

  // create a Statement object
  Statement myStatement = myConnection.createStatement();

  // display the customers in the customers_with_varray table
  displayCustomers(myConnection, myStatement);

  // insert a customer
  insertCustomer(myConnection);

  // update customer #1's address
  updateCustomerAddress(myConnection, myStatement, 1);

  // display the customers
  displayCustomers(myConnection, myStatement);

  // rollback the changes made to the database
  myConnection.rollback();

  // close the Statement and Connection objects
  myStatement.close();
  myConnection.close();

} // end of main()

}
```

The output from this program is as follows:

```
Customers from customers_with_varray:
id = 1
first_name = Steve
last_name = Brown
addresses[0] = 2 State Street, Beantown, MA, 12345
addresses[1] = 4 Hill Street, Lost Town, CA, 54321
Inserting a customer into customers_with_varray
Updating customer #1's first address
Customers from customers_with_varray:
id = 1
first_name = Steve
last_name = Brown
addresses[0] = 3 New Street, Middle Town, CA, 12345
addresses[1] = 4 Hill Street, Lost Town, CA, 54321
id = 2
first_name = Cynthia
last_name = Green
addresses[0] = 1 Main Street, Uptown, NY, 55512
addresses[1] = 2 Side Street, Beantown, MA, 12345
```

I've also supplied another program in the `programs` directory, `CollectionExample2.java`, which contains similar methods to `CollectionExample1.java` except that it accesses `customers_with_nested_table` and updates only one address instead of all addresses for customer #1. `CollectionExample2.java` is omitted from this book for brevity, but I encourage you to examine and run it. That program also shows you how to use STRUCTs in combination with ARRAYs.

Accessing Collections Using Strongly Typed Objects

Strongly typed objects represent the elements of a collection using a specific type. This makes them superior to the weakly typed objects when you need the collection elements in a convenient form for manipulation in Java.

In the previous chapter, you saw how to use strongly typed objects of a custom class to represent a database object. You also saw that custom classes for database objects may implement either the SQLData or ORAData interfaces, and you saw how to use JPublisher to generate custom classes. In this section, you'll learn how to use custom classes generated by JPublisher to represent collections.

NOTE
*SQLData doesn't support collections; therefore,
you have to use custom classes that implement
ORAData.*

Later in this section, I'll discuss two example programs named
`CollectionExample3.java` and `CollectionExample4.java`. These
programs are stored in the `CollectionExample3And4` subdirectory of the
`programs` directory, and they require the use of custom classes that you'll
generate using JPublisher in the next section.

Generating the Custom Classes Using JPublisher

To generate the required custom classes using JPublisher, you change directories to
the `CollectionExample3And4` directory and run JPublisher using the following
command:

```
jpub -user=collection_user/collection_password
  -url=jdbc:oracle:thin:@localhost:1521:ORCL -usertypes=oracle
```

When you run this command, JPublisher will connect to the database as
`collection_user` and generate custom classes for all of the collection types
it finds in the `collection_user` schema. There is one object type in the
`collection_user` schema (`address_typ`), along with two collection types
(`nested_table_address_typ` and `varray_address_typ`).

Once the previous command has completed, JPublisher will have generated
the following four custom class files:

- **AddressTyp.java**   For the `address_typ` database object type.

- **AddressTypRef.java**   For a reference to the `address_typ` database object
  type. This file won't be used in the examples in this chapter. For details on
  object references, refer to the previous chapter.

- **NestedTableAddressTyp.java**   For the `nested_table_address_typ`
  collection type.

- **VarrayAddressTyp.java**   For the `varray_address_typ` collection type.

Each of these custom classes implements the `ORAData` interface. Let's take a
look at the `VarrayAddressTyp.java` file.

The VarrayAddressTyp.java File

The VarrayAddressTyp.java file contains the definition for the custom class that I'll use to represent varray_address_typ collections shortly. The VarrayAddressTyp.java file is as follows:

```java
import java.sql.SQLException;
import java.sql.Connection;
import oracle.jdbc.OracleTypes;
import oracle.sql.ORAData;
import oracle.sql.ORADataFactory;
import oracle.sql.Datum;
import oracle.sql.ARRAY;
import oracle.sql.ArrayDescriptor;
import oracle.jpub.runtime.MutableArray;

public class VarrayAddressTyp implements ORAData, ORADataFactory
{
  public static final String _SQL_NAME =
    "COLLECTION_USER.VARRAY_ADDRESS_TYP";
  public static final int _SQL_TYPECODE = OracleTypes.ARRAY;

  MutableArray _array;

  private static final VarrayAddressTyp _VarrayAddressTypFactory =
    new VarrayAddressTyp();

  public static ORADataFactory getORADataFactory()
  { return _VarrayAddressTypFactory; }
  /* constructors */
  public VarrayAddressTyp()
  {
    this((String[])null);
  }

  public VarrayAddressTyp(String[] a)
  {
    _array = new MutableArray(12, a, null);
  }

  /* ORAData interface */
  public Datum toDatum(Connection c) throws SQLException
  {
    return _array.toDatum(c, _SQL_NAME);
  }

  /* ORADataFactory interface */
  public ORAData create(Datum d, int sqlType) throws SQLException
```

```
{
  if (d == null) return null;
  VarrayAddressTyp a = new VarrayAddressTyp();
  a._array = new MutableArray(12, (ARRAY) d, null);
  return a;
}

public int length() throws SQLException
{
  return _array.length();
}

public int getBaseType() throws SQLException
{
  return _array.getBaseType();
}

public String getBaseTypeName() throws SQLException
{
  return _array.getBaseTypeName();
}

public ArrayDescriptor getDescriptor() throws SQLException
{
  return _array.getDescriptor();
}

/* array accessor methods */
public String[] getArray() throws SQLException
{
  return (String[]) _array.getObjectArray();
}

public void setArray(String[] a) throws SQLException
{
  _array.setObjectArray(a);
}

public String[] getArray(long index, int count) throws SQLException
{
  return (String[]) _array.getObjectArray(index, count);
}

public void setArray(String[] a, long index) throws SQLException
{
  _array.setObjectArray(a, index);
}
```

```
public String getElement(long index) throws SQLException
{
  return (String) _array.getObjectElement(index);
}

public void setElement(String a, long index) throws SQLException
{
  _array.setObjectElement(a, index);
}

}
```

There are several things you should notice about this file:

- It defines a class named `VarrayAddressTyp` that implements the `ORAData` and `ORADataFactory` interfaces. These interfaces were described in the previous chapter.

- It has two constructors, one that accepts no parameters and another that accepts an array of strings. An array of strings is used because the `varray_address_typ` collection type uses `VARCHAR2` elements.

- It has two `getArray()` methods. The first accepts no parameters and returns the entire array of strings. The second accepts an index and length parameter; this method returns the subset of the strings in the array, starting at the index and ending at the index plus the length. Arrays in Java start at index 0.

- It has two `setArray()` methods. The first accepts an array of strings and sets the entire array to the contents of the array parameter. The second accepts an array of strings in addition to an index parameter; this method sets a subset of the strings in the array, starting at the supplied index and ending at the index plus the size of the supplied array.

- It has a `getElement()` method, which accepts an index parameter. This method returns the string element at the supplied index.

- It has a `setElement()` method, which accepts a string and an index parameter. This method sets the element at the index to the supplied string.

If you open the `NestedTableAddressTyp.java` file, you'll see that it has similar methods, except that instead of dealing with strings, its methods deal with `AddressTyp` objects; this is because the `nested_table_address_typ` collection type uses `addess_typ` database object types.

Once you have your custom class, you can use objects of that custom class to represent collections, and you'll learn about that next.

Inserting a Collection Using a Custom Java Object

In this section, you'll learn how to insert a row containing a collection into a table using an object of your custom class. To do this you follow these steps:

1. Create an array to store the elements for your collection.

2. Create an object of your custom class, passing your array created in the previous step to the constructor.

3. Use a prepared statement to insert a row into the table, binding your object to the placeholder for the collection to your object, along with any other columns for the row.

In the following sections, I'll describe the details of these steps along with example code that inserts a row into the `customers_with_varray` table.

Step 1: Create an Array to Store the Elements for the Collection

The first step is to create an array to store the elements for your collection. The following example creates an array of two strings named `addresses`:

```
String [] addresses = {
  "1 Main Street, Uptown, NY, 55512",
  "2 Side Street, Beantown, MA, 12345"
};
```

Notice that the `addresses` array contains strings, as required by the constructor for the `VarrayAddressTyp` custom class.

Step 2: Create an Object of the Custom Class

The second step is to create an object of your custom class, passing your array created in the previous step to the constructor of your custom class. The following example creates a `VarrayAddressTyp` object named `varrayAddress`, passing the `addresses` array to the constructor:

```
VarrayAddressTyp varrayAddress = new VarrayAddressTyp(addresses);
```

Step 3: Use a Prepared Statement
to Insert the Object into the Table

The third step is to use a prepared statement to insert your object created in the previous step into the table; you bind your object to the placeholder for the collection, along with any other columns required for the new row. You use the setORAData() method of an OraclePreparedStatement to bind your object to the placeholder for the collection.

The following example inserts a row into the customers_with_varray table. Notice that the PreparedStatement is cast to an OraclePreparedStatement to call the setORAData() method. This method is used to bind varrayAddress to the fourth placeholder for the addresses column; also, values are bound to the id, first_name, and last_name columns to complete the values for the new row:

```
PreparedStatement myPrepStatement =
  myConnection.prepareStatement(
    "INSERT INTO customers_with_varray VALUES (?, ?, ?, ?)"
  );
myPrepStatement.setInt(1, 2);  // id
myPrepStatement.setString(2, "Cynthia");  // first_name
myPrepStatement.setString(3, "Green");  // last_name
((OraclePreparedStatement) myPrepStatement).setORAData(
  4, varrayAddress
);  // addresses
myPrepStatement.execute();
myPrepStatement.close();
```

Selecting Collections into a Custom Java Object

To select collections from the database into a Java object of a custom class you follow these steps:

1. Create a result set and use it to select the rows from the table containing the collection column, along with any other columns you want to retrieve from the table.

2. While there are rows in your result set, perform the following:

   a. Retrieve the collection from your result set using the getORAData() method, casting the returned ORAData object to your custom class and storing it in an object of that custom class.

   b. Retrieve the element values from your object using the getArray() method, storing the element values in an array.

    c. Read the element values from your array.

  3. Close your result set.

In the following sections, I'll describe the details of Steps 1 and 2, along with example code that selects the rows from the `customers_with_varray` table. You already know how to close a result set in Step 3.

Step 1: Create a Result Set to Select the Rows

The first step is to create a result set and use it to select the rows from the table containing the collection column, along with any other columns you want to retrieve from the table. The following example creates a `ResultSet` object named `customerResultSet` that selects the `id`, `first_name`, `last_name`, and `addresses` columns from the `customers_with_varray` table:

```
ResultSet customerResultSet = myStatement.executeQuery(
  "SELECT id, first_name, last_name, addresses " +
  "FROM customers_with_varray"
);
```

Step 2: While There Are Rows in the Result Set, Retrieve the Collection and Element Values

The second step is to retrieve the collection and its element values from the rows in your result set, along with the other column values that you've selected into your result set. To retrieve the collection and its element values, you use the `getORAData()` and `getArray()` methods within a `while` loop that calls `customerResultSet.next()`. You use the `getORAData()` method for an `OracleResultSet` (or cast an existing `ResultSet` to an `OracleResultSet`) to retrieve the collection as an `ORAData` object. You then cast the returned `ORAData` object to your custom class and then store that object.

The following example retrieves the addresses from `customerResultSet`, storing them in a `VarrayAddressTyp` object named `varrayAddress`:

```
VarrayAddressTyp varrayAddress =
  (VarrayAddressTyp)
    ((OracleResultSet) customerResultSet).getORAData(
      "addresses", VarrayAddressTyp.getORADataFactory()
    );
```

Nest, you retrieve the element values from `varrayAddress` using the `getArray()` method, storing the element values in an array of strings:

```
String [] addresses = (String []) varrayAddress.getArray();
```

Finally, you read the element values from `addresses`. For example, the following `for` loop displays the string elements in the `addresses` array:

```
for (int count = 0; count < addresses.length; count++) {
  System.out.println("addresses[" + count + "] = " +
    addresses[count]);
}
```

Updating a Collection Using a Custom Java Object

To update a collection in a database table using an object of your custom class, you follow these steps:

1. Create a result set and use it to select the collection from the table.

2. Retrieve the original collection from your result set using the `getORAData()` method, casting the returned `ORAData` object to your custom class and storing it.

3. Close your result set.

4. Retrieve and modify the element you want to change in your custom object using the `getElement()` and `setElement()` methods, respectively. You may repeat this step to modify as many elements as you want.

5. Use a prepared statement to perform the update using your modified object.

You've already seen an example of Steps 1 and 2 in the previous section entitled "Selecting Collections into a Custom Java Object," so I won't repeat those steps here. You also know how to close a result set, so I'll omit the description of Step 3. In the following sections, I'll describe the details of Steps 4 and 5, along with example code to modify customer #1's first address in the `customers_with_varray` table.

Step 4: Retrieve and Modify the Element in the Custom Object

The fourth step is to retrieve and modify the element you want to change in your custom object using the `getElement()` and `setElement()` methods respectively. You could also simply create a whole new custom object and use that instead of modifying each individual element, but if you only want to modify one or two elements, this wouldn't necessarily be the most efficient way.

Assume you've already retrieved customer #1's addresses into a `VarrayAddressTyp` object named `varrayAddress`. The following example

retrieves the first element from `varrayAddress` using the `getElement()`
method and modifies that element using the `setElement()` method:

```
varrayAddress.getElement(0);
varrayAddress.setElement("3 New Street, Middle Town, CA, 12345", 0);
```

NOTE
*You must remember to retrieve the element you
want to modify using the `getElement()` method
first. Otherwise, `setElement()` will not change
the element.*

Step 5: Use a Prepared Statement to Perform the Update Using the Modified Object

The fifth and final step is to use a prepared statement to perform the update using
your modified custom Java object. If you're updating a varray, you must replace
all the elements in the varray at once. If you're updating a nested table, you can
choose to either replace all the elements, or you can just replace the element that
has changed. I'll show you how to replace all the elements in a collection (varray
and nested table), and how to replace just one element in a nested table in the
following sections.

Replacing All the Elements in a Collection   To replace all the elements in
a collection, you create an `OraclePreparedStatement` object (or cast a
`PreparedStatement` to an `OraclePreparedStatement`) and call its
`setORAData()` method to bind your custom Java object to the collection column
in `UPDATE` statement. The following example creates a `PreparedStatement`
object named `myPrepStatement`, binds `varrayAddress` and an int containing
the customer `id` to the first and second placeholders using the `setORAData()`
and `setInt()` methods, and then calls the `execute()` method to perform the
`UPDATE`; at the end `myPrepStatement` is closed using the `close()` method:

```
int id = 1;
PreparedStatement myPrepStatement =
  myConnection.prepareStatement(
    "UPDATE customers_with_varray " +
    "SET addresses = ? " +
    "WHERE id = ?"
  );
((OraclePreparedStatement) myPrepStatement).setORAData(
  1, varrayAddress
); // addresses
myPrepStatement.setInt(2, id);  // id
```

```
myPrepStatement.execute();
myPrepStatement.close();
```

The program `CollectionExample3.java`, which I'll cover in the next section, uses the previous code example.

Replacing One Element in a Nested Table   To replace just one element in a collection, you create a `PreparedStatement` object that contains an `UPDATE` statement that uses a `TABLE` clause and subquery. Let's consider an example. The `customers_with_nested_table` contains a column named `addresses`, and let's say you want to only update the first address in this nested table for customer #1. The `addresses` column is a nested table of `address_typ` elements; `address_typ` is an object type that contains four attributes that store the street, city, state, and zip code for the address. You can use an object of the strongly typed `AddressTyp` custom class to represent an address. Let's assume you have two `AddressTyp` objects named `oldAddress` and `newAddress`; assume `oldAddress` contains the old address that you want to update, and `newAddress` contains the new address. You can use the following code to perform the update; notice the use of the `setORAData()` method to bind `oldAddress` and `newAddress` to the prepared statement:

```
int id = 1;
PreparedStatement myPrepStatement =
  myConnection.prepareStatement(
    "UPDATE TABLE (" +
    "  SELECT addresses FROM customers_with_nested_table " +
    "  WHERE id = ? " +
    ") a " +
    "SET VALUE(a) = ? " +
    "WHERE VALUE(a) = ?"
  );
myPrepStatement.setInt(1, id);
((OraclePreparedStatement) myPrepStatement).setORAData(
  2, newAddress
);
((OraclePreparedStatement) myPrepStatement).setORAData(
  3, oldAddress
);
myPrepStatement.execute();
myPrepStatement.close();
```

The program `CollectionExample4.java`, which I'll cover at the end of the next section, uses the previous code example.

Example Program: CollectionExample3.java

The program `CollectionExample3.java`, shown in the following listing, illustrates the various steps shown in the previous sections to insert, select, and update customers in the `customers_with_varray` table; this table contains a varray in the `addresses` column. This program contains three methods that are called in the `main()` method:

- **insertCustomer()**   Follows the three steps described earlier in the section entitled "Inserting a Collection Using a Custom Java Object." Specifically, this method inserts a new customer into the `customers_with_varray` table using a `VarrayAddressTyp` object to set the `addresses` column.

- **displayCustomers()**   Follows the three steps described earlier in the section entitled "Selecting Collections into a Custom Java Object." Specifically, this method selects and displays the customers in the `customers_with_varray` table.

- **updateCustomerAddress()**   Follows the five steps described earlier in the section entitled "Updating a Collection Using a Custom Java Object." Specifically, this method updates a customer's first address in the addresses column. Since `addresses` contains a varray, all the address elements are replaced, even though only the first address is actually changed.

```
/*
  CollectionExample3.java shows how to access varrays
  using strongly typed objects of the VarrayAddressTyp
  custom class generated by JPublisher
*/

// import the required packages
import java.sql.*;
import oracle.jdbc.OraclePreparedStatement;
import oracle.jdbc.OracleResultSet;

public class CollectionExample3 {

  public static void insertCustomer(
    Connection myConnection
  ) throws SQLException {

    System.out.println(
      "Inserting a customer into customers_with_varray"
    );
```

```
  // step 1: create an array to store the elements for the
  // collection
  String [] addresses = {
    "1 Main Street, Uptown, NY, 55512",
    "2 Side Street, Beantown, MA, 12345"
  };

  // step 2: create an object of the VarrayAddressTyp custom class
  VarrayAddressTyp varrayAddress =
    new VarrayAddressTyp(addresses);

  // step 3: use a prepared statement to insert the object
  // into the table, along with the other columns required
  // for the new row
  PreparedStatement myPrepStatement =
    myConnection.prepareStatement(
      "INSERT INTO customers_with_varray VALUES (?, ?, ?, ?)"
    );
  myPrepStatement.setInt(1, 2);
  myPrepStatement.setString(2, "Cynthia");
  myPrepStatement.setString(3, "Green");
  ((OraclePreparedStatement) myPrepStatement).setORAData(
    4, varrayAddress
  );
  myPrepStatement.execute();
  myPrepStatement.close();

} // end of insertCustomer()


public static void displayCustomers(
  Connection myConnection,
  Statement myStatement
) throws SQLException {

  System.out.println("Customers from customers_with_varray:");

  // step 1: create a result set and use it to select
  // the rows from customers_with_varray
  ResultSet customerResultSet = myStatement.executeQuery(
    "SELECT id, first_name, last_name, addresses " +
    "FROM customers_with_varray"
  );

  // step 2: while there are rows in the result set ...
  while (customerResultSet.next()) {

    System.out.println("id = " +
```

```
        customerResultSet.getInt("id"));
      System.out.println("first_name = " +
        customerResultSet.getString("first_name"));
      System.out.println("last_name = " +
        customerResultSet.getString("last_name"));

      // a: retrieve the collection from the result set using the
      // getORAData() method, casting the returned ORAData object
      // to the VarrayAddressTyp custom class
      VarrayAddressTyp varrayAddress =
        (VarrayAddressTyp)
          ((OracleResultSet) customerResultSet).getORAData(
            "addresses", VarrayAddressTyp.getORADataFactory()
          );

      // b: retrieve the element values from the object using the
      // getArray() method, storing the element values in a
      // string array
      String [] addresses = (String []) varrayAddress.getArray();

      // c: read the element values from the string array
      for (int count = 0; count < addresses.length; count++) {
        System.out.println("addresses[" + count + "] = " +
          addresses[count]);
      }

    } // end of while loop

    // step 3: close the result set
    customerResultSet.close();

  } // end of displayCustomers()


  public static void updateCustomerAddress(
    Connection myConnection,
    Statement myStatement,
    int id
  ) throws SQLException {

    System.out.println("Updating customer #" + id +
      "'s first address");

    // step 1: create a result set and use it to select
    // the collection (in this case, the addresses for a customer
    // with the specified id)
    ResultSet customerResultSet = myStatement.executeQuery(
      "SELECT addresses " +
```

```
      "FROM customers_with_varray " +
      "WHERE id = " + id
    );
    customerResultSet.next();

    // step 2: retrieve the original collection from the
    // result set using the getORAData() method, casting the
    // returned ORAData object to VarrayAddressTyp and storing it
    VarrayAddressTyp varrayAddress =
      (VarrayAddressTyp)
        ((OracleResultSet) customerResultSet).getORAData(
          "addresses", VarrayAddressTyp.getORADataFactory()
        );

    // step 3: close the result set
    customerResultSet.close();

    // step 4: retrieve the first element from varrayAddress using
    // the getElement() method and then modify it using the
    // setElement() method
    varrayAddress.getElement(0);
    varrayAddress.setElement(
      "3 New Street, Middle Town, CA, 12345", 0
    );

    // step 5: use a prepared statement to perform the update
    PreparedStatement myPrepStatement =
      myConnection.prepareStatement(
        "UPDATE customers_with_varray " +
        "SET addresses = ? " +
        "WHERE id = ?"
      );
    ((OraclePreparedStatement) myPrepStatement).setORAData(
      1, varrayAddress
    );
    myPrepStatement.setInt(2, id);
    myPrepStatement.execute();
    myPrepStatement.close();

  } // end of updateCustomerAddress()


  public static void main(String args [])
  throws SQLException {

    // register the Oracle JDBC drivers
```

```
DriverManager.registerDriver(
  new oracle.jdbc.OracleDriver()
);

// create a Connection object, and connect to the database
// as collection_user using the Oracle JDBC Thin driver
Connection myConnection = DriverManager.getConnection(
  "jdbc:oracle:thin:@localhost:1521:ORCL",
  "collection_user",
  "collection_password"
);

// disable auto-commit mode
myConnection.setAutoCommit(false);

// create a Statement object
Statement myStatement = myConnection.createStatement();

// display the customers in the customers_with_varray table
displayCustomers(myConnection, myStatement);

// insert a customer
insertCustomer(myConnection);

// update customer #1's address
updateCustomerAddress(myConnection, myStatement, 1);

// display the customers
displayCustomers(myConnection, myStatement);

// rollback the changes made to the database
myConnection.rollback();

// close the Statement and Connection objects
myStatement.close();
myConnection.close();

} // end of main()

}
```

NOTE
Make sure you've compiled
VarrayAddressTyp.java before compiling
CollectionExample3.java.

The output from this program is as follows:

```
Customers from customers_with_varray:
id = 1
first_name = Steve
last_name = Brown
addresses[0] = 2 State Street, Beantown, MA, 12345
addresses[1] = 4 Hill Street, Lost Town, CA, 54321
Inserting a customer into customers_with_varray
Updating customer #1's first address
Customers from customers_with_varray:
id = 1
first_name = Steve
last_name = Brown
addresses[0] = 3 New Street, Middle Town, CA, 12345
addresses[1] = 4 Hill Street, Lost Town, CA, 54321
id = 2
first_name = Cynthia
last_name = Green
addresses[0] = 1 Main Street, Uptown, NY, 55512
addresses[1] = 2 Side Street, Beantown, MA, 12345
```

I've also supplied another program in the `CollectionExample3And4` subdirectory of the `programs` directory, `CollectionExample4.java`. This program contains similar methods to `CollectionExample3.java` except that the methods access `customers_with_nested_table`, and the `updateCustomerAddress()` method only updates one address instead of all addresses for customer #1. `CollectionExample4.java` is omitted from this book for brevity, but I encourage you to examine and run it. That program also shows you how to use strongly typed `AddressTyp` objects in combination with `NestedTableAddressTyp` objects.

NOTE
Make sure you've compiled `AddressTyp.java` *and* `NestedTableAddressTyp.java` *before compiling* `CollectionExample4.java`.

CHAPTER
8

Large Objects

oday's applications and websites demand more than just the storage and retrieval of text and numbers: they may also require multimedia to make the user experience friendlier. Because of this, databases are now being called upon to store things like images, sounds, and video. Prior to the release of Oracle8, you had to store large blocks of character data using the LONG database type, and large blocks of binary data had to be stored using either the LONG RAW type or the shorter RAW type. The LONG type can store up to 2 gigabytes of character data, the LONG RAW type can store up to 2 gigabytes of binary data, and the RAW type can store up to 4 kilobytes of binary data.

After the release of Oracle8 (and all subsequent releases of the database), a new class of types known as *large object*s (LOBs) was introduced. LOBs may be used to store binary data, character data, and references to external files. LOBs can store up to 4 gigabytes of data and enable you to meet the demands of today's multimedia intensive applications and websites.

In this chapter, I'll show you examples that illustrate how to use LOBs with JDBC. The SQL*Plus script `lob_user.sql`, which you can download from this book's website, contains the SQL DDL statements to create the database tables and other items required by the examples. You should run this script if you wish to run the example programs.

Now, although the Oracle8, 8*i*, and 9*i* databases still support the older LONG, LONG RAW, and RAW types, you should use LOBs for your new applications. As you will see, LOBs have several advantages over those older types, although I will still discuss the older types in the final section of this chapter.

The Example Files

Some of the example programs read files and store their contents in the database, but the contents of a LOB doesn't have to come from a file—the content can come from any valid source that your Java program can read as a string of characters or bytes. Files are used in the examples because they are an easy and common way of handling large blocks of data.

I will use two files in the examples:

- **textContent.txt**   A text file

- **binaryContent.doc**   A Word 2000 file

The file `textContent.txt` contains an extract from Shakespeare's play *Macbeth*. The following text shows the speech made by Macbeth shortly before he is killed:

```
To-morrow, and to-morrow, and to-morrow,
Creeps in this petty pace from day to day,
To the last syllable of recorded time;
And all our yesterdays have lighted fools
The way to a dusty death. Out, out, brief candle!
Life's but a walking shadow; a poor player,
That struts and frets his hour upon the stage,
And then is heard no more: it is a tale
Told by an idiot, full of sound and fury,
Signifying nothing.
```

The file `binaryContent.doc` is a Word 2000 document containing the same text as the `textContent.txt` file; `binaryContent.doc`, being a Word 2000 document, is a binary file. The two files are contained in the directory `sample_files`, available in the program directory where you unzipped the ZIP file for this book.

NOTE
Within the `sample_files` directory, you must create a subdirectory named `retrieved`.

The `retrieved` directory will be used by the example programs to store content retrieved from the database. The example programs expect the path to the `sample_files` directory to be `C:\sample_files`. If you plan to run these example programs, you should either copy the `sample_files` directory to that location and create a subdirectory named `retrieved`, or modify the path in the programs to point to your own directory.

Large Objects (LOBs)

JDBC supports three large object types:

- **CLOB** The Character LOB type, which is used to store character data.

- **BLOB** The Binary LOB type, which is used to store binary data.

- **BFILE** The Binary FILE type, which is used to store pointers to files located in the file system. As you'll see later, you can read the contents of the actual file via a `BFILE` pointer in a Java program. These external files can be on a hard disk, a CD, a DVD, or through any other device that is accessible through the computer's file system.

As I mentioned earlier, prior to Oracle8 your only choice for storing large amounts of character or binary data was to use the LONG and LONG RAW types (for smaller binary files, you could also use the RAW type). Columns created using CLOB and BLOB types have three advantages over those created using the older LONG and LONG RAW types:

1. LOB columns can store up to four gigabytes of data, double the amount of data that you can store in a LONG and LONG RAW column.

2. A table can have multiple LOB columns, but a table can only have one LONG or LONG RAW column.

3. LOB data can be accessed in random order; LONG and LONG RAW data can only be accessed in sequential order.

LOBs consist of two parts:

■ **The LOB *locator***   A pointer that specifies the location of the LOB content

■ **The LOB *content***   The actual character or byte data stored in the LOB

Depending on the size of your LOB content, the actual data will either be stored in the table or out of the table. If your LOB content is less than four kilobytes in size, the content is stored in the table containing the LOB column. If it's bigger than 4 kilobytes, the content is stored outside the table. With BFILE columns, only the locator is stored in the database—the locator points to the external file.

The Example Tables

I'll use three tables for the examples in this section:

1. The clob_content table, which contains a CLOB column named clob_column. This column is used to store the character data contained in the textContent.txt file.

2. The blob_content table, which contains a BLOB column named blob_column. This column is used to store the binary data stored in the binaryContent.doc file.

3. The bfile_content table, which contains a BFILE column named bfile_column. This column is used to store pointers to the two external files.

These tables also contain a column to store the name of the file that was used to populate the LOB column. The three tables are defined as follows:

```
CREATE TABLE clob_content (
  file_name    VARCHAR2(40) NOT NULL,
  clob_column CLOB NOT NULL
);

CREATE TABLE blob_content (
  file_name    VARCHAR2(40) NOT NULL,
  blob_column BLOB NOT NULL
);

CREATE TABLE bfile_content (
  file_name    VARCHAR2(40) NOT NULL,
  bfile_column BFILE NOT NULL
);
```

Notice that all the columns are NOT NULL, meaning that values must be supplied for the columns.

The Put, Get, and Stream Methods

There are two ways you can use to write content to CLOB and BLOB columns using JDBC: you can use the put methods, or you can use streams. The *put* methods allow you to directly write content to a CLOB or BLOB column (similarly, the get methods allow you to directly read content from a CLOB or BLOB column). *Streams* are long strings of bytes that allow you to move information around in a Java program; streams are at the heart of all file input and output in Java. You can also use streams to read content from a CLOB or BLOB column.

TIP
I've found that using the put (and get) methods is slightly faster than using streams when you are dealing with content of less than about 10 kilobytes in size. When dealing with more content than this, streams are faster.

Java provides two classes in the java.io package that allow you to manipulate data in the form of streams: InputStream and OutputStream. You use an object of the InputStream class to read a stream of bytes from a source; you use an object of the OutputStream class to write a stream of bytes to a destination. The source or destination for a stream may include an array of bytes, a file, a CLOB, or a BLOB, among others.

When working with LOBs using JDBC, you generally need to create a LOB object. It is through this LOB object that you access a LOB column. The `oracle.sql` package contains the following classes:

- `oracle.sql.CLOB`
- `oracle.sql.BLOB`
- `oracle.sql.BFILE`

[handwritten:) — Map Periscope to there!]

As you'll see shortly, you may use these classes to declare the required LOB objects in your JDBC programs.

NOTE
Standard JDBC has two interfaces: `java.sql.Clob` *and* `java.sql.Blob`. *These interfaces are implemented by the* `oracle.sql.CLOB` *and* `oracle.sql.BLOB` *classes. While you can use* `java.sql.Clob` *and* `java.sql.Blob` *objects to handle* `CLOB` *and* `BLOB` *columns, the Oracle JDBC extended classes offer higher performance and more functionality, so I will illustrate only the use of the Oracle classes in this chapter.*

In the following sections, I'll show you how to:

- Use the put methods to write to `CLOB` and `BLOB` columns
- Use streams to write to `CLOB` and `BLOB` columns
- Store pointers to external files using `BFILE` columns
- Use the get methods to read from `CLOB` and `BLOB` columns
- Use streams to read from `CLOB` and `BLOB` columns
- Read external files using `BFILE` pointers

First off, I'll show you how to use the put methods to write to `CLOB` and `BLOB` columns.

Using the Put Methods to Write to CLOB and BLOB Columns

In this section, I'll show you how to read the contents of the `textContent.txt` and `binaryContent.doc` files, and then write that content to a CLOB or BLOB column using the put methods. Now, the content of a LOB is accessed in discrete blocks, which are known as *chunks*. Chunks break up the content into manageable amounts of data.

To write character content to a CLOB column, you use the `putChars()` method; to write binary content to a BLOB column, you use the `putBytes()` method. If you use the put methods to store content in a CLOB or BLOB column and that content is read from a file—which is what you're going to see in the examples—you may use the following ten steps to read content from that file and write it to a CLOB or BLOB column:

1. Initialize the LOB column to set the LOB locator.

2. Retrieve the row containing the LOB locator into a result set.

3. Create a LOB object in the Java program and read the LOB locator from the result set.

4. Get the chunk size of the LOB from the LOB object.

5. Create a buffer to hold a block of data from the file.

6. Create a file object.

7. Create input stream objects to read the file contents.

8. Read the contents of the file and write it to the LOB using the following loop. While the end of the file has not been reached:

    a. Read a block of data from the file into the buffer created in Step 5.

    b. Write the buffer contents to the LOB host object.

9. Perform a commit to permanently save the changes.

10. Close the objects used to read the file.

I'll flesh out each of these ten steps and show you example code that reads the characters from the `textContent.txt` file and writes them to the `clob_content` table. In addition, since the code for reading binary content from a file and writing that content to a BLOB column is similar, I'll show you how to read the bytes from the `binaryContent.doc` file and write them to the `blob_content` table.

Step 1: Initialize the LOB Column to Set the LOB Locator

As I mentioned earlier, LOB columns store a locator that points to the LOB contents. Before you can actually write content to a LOB, you must first initialize the LOB column. You do this by calling an Oracle database function that generates and returns a value for the locator. To initialize a CLOB column, you use the EMPTY_CLOB() function; a BLOB column must be initialized using the EMPTY_BLOB() function.

Before I show you examples that use these functions, the following example creates two strings to hold the name of the directory and the name of the directory and file that is going to be read:

```
String sourceDirectory = "C:\\sample_files\\";
String fileName = sourceDirectory + "textContent.txt";
```

You'll notice that two backslashes (\\) are used in the sourceDirectory string. The first backslash is used to escape the second one, so the final string is set to "C:\sample_files\". The fileName string is subsequently set to "C:\sample_files\textContent.txt".

Next, the EMPTY_CLOB() function is used to initialize clob_column. This function is used inside an INSERT statement that adds a row to the clob_content table:

```
myStatement.executeUpdate(
  "INSERT INTO clob_content(file_name, clob_column) " +
  "VALUES ('" + fileName + "', EMPTY_CLOB())"
);
```

instead of NULL

Similarly, the following example sets the fileName string to "C:\sample_files\binaryContent.doc" and uses the EMPTY_BLOB() function to initialize blob_column:

```
fileName = sourceDirectory + "binaryContent.doc";
myStatement.executeUpdate(
  "INSERT INTO blob_content(file_name, blob_column) " +
  "VALUES ('" + fileName + "', EMPTY_BLOB())"
);
```

Step 2: Retrieve the Row Containing the LOB Locator into a Result Set

Once you've set the LOB locator, the second step is to retrieve the row containing the LOB locator into a result set. The following example creates a ResultSet object named clobResultSet. This result set is used to retrieve the locator set for clob_column in the row previously added to the clob_content table (also, the next() method is called to navigate to that row):

```
ResultSet clobResultSet = myStatement.executeQuery(
    "SELECT clob_column " +
    "FROM clob_content " +
    "WHERE file_name = '" + fileName + "' " +
    "FOR UPDATE"
);
clobResultSet.next();
```

Similarly, the next example creates a `ResultSet` object named `blobResultSet` and retrieves the locator set for `blob_column`:

```
ResultSet blobResultSet = myStatement.executeQuery(
    "SELECT blob_column " +
    "FROM blob_content " +
    "WHERE file_name = '" + fileName + "' " +
    "FOR UPDATE"
);
blobResultSet.next();
```

Notice the use of the FOR UPDATE clause in the SELECT statement in each of these examples. I'll be updating each of these rows later in Step 8.

Step 3: Create a LOB Object in the Java Program and Read the LOB Locator from the Result Set

As I mentioned earlier, to access a LOB column using JDBC statements, you must declare a LOB object in your Java program and then read the LOB locator from the result set into that LOB object. It is through this LOB object that your program accesses the LOB column. Your LOB object must be of the same type as the LOB column.

The following example creates a CLOB object named `myClob`, and the CLOB column `clob_column` is read from the result set `clobResultSet` using the `getCLOB()` method:

```
CLOB myClob =
    ((OracleResultSet) clobResultSet).getCLOB("clob_column");
```

NOTE
Prior to this statement, you should have imported
`oracle.sql.CLOB` *(or simply imported*
`oracle.sql.*) to use this class.*

Similarly, the next example creates a BLOB object named myBlob, and blob_column is read from blobResultSet using the getBLOB() method:

```
BLOB myBlob =
    ((OracleResultSet) blobResultSet).getBLOB("blob_column");
```

Step 4: Get the LOB Chunk Size from the LOB Object

As I mentioned earlier, you access LOB content in manageable blocks known as chunks. To get the size of the chunk, you call the getChunkSize() function using the LOB object you previously created. This function returns the optimal size of a LOB chunk in bytes. The optimal size of a chunk is determined by the Oracle database, and the getChunkSize() function returns 8,132 bytes for both CLOB and BLOB objects.

The following example gets the chunk size for myClob and stores it in an int variable named chunkSize:

```
int chunkSize = myClob.getChunkSize();
```

You can use a similar statement to get the chunk size for myBlob.

Step 5: Create a Buffer to Hold a Block of Data from the File

For the example in this section, the content for the LOB columns is read from one of the sample files. The text from the file textContent.txt is going to be stored in clob_column, and the binary data from binaryContent.doc is going to be stored in blob_column.

Since the content is going to be sent to the LOB columns in chunks, you may read the content into a Java array, also known as a *buffer*, of the same size as the chunk. To read the characters from the textContent.txt file, you need to declare an array of characters:

```
char [] textBuffer = new char[chunkSize];
```

Similarly, you need an array of bytes to buffer the binary data read from the binaryContent.doc file:

```
byte [] byteBuffer = new byte[chunkSize];
```

Step 6: Create a File Object

In order to access a file using Java, you need a File object. The File object acts as a "handle" to your file. Using this handle, you can read that file using a Java input stream object (you'll see how to do that in Steps 7 and 8).

The following example creates a File object named myFile:

```
File myFile = new File(fileName);
```

Step 7: Create Input Stream Objects to Read the File Contents

To read the contents of a file, you need to create a number of additional objects through which you can then read the file. To read the contents of the textContent.txt file as ASCII text using a buffer, you need a FileInputStream, an InputStreamReader, and a BufferedReader object.

The following example creates these three objects. Notice that each object is used in the constructor of the subsequent object (starting with the File object created in the previous step):

```
FileInputStream myFileInputStream = new FileInputStream(myFile);
InputStreamReader myReader = new InputStreamReader(myFileInputStream);
BufferedReader myBufferedReader = new BufferedReader(myReader);
```

The myFileInputStream object provides the low-level functionality to read the contents of a file as a stream of bytes. The myReader object is a wrapper around myFileInputStream and allows you to interpret the bytes as a stream of ASCII characters. Finally, myBufferedReader allows you to read the stream of characters as blocks of multiple characters. Each block of characters will subsequently be stored in the textBuffer char array created earlier—and you'll see how to do that in the next step.

To read the contents of the binaryContent.doc file, you need only a FileInputStream object. This is because binaryContent.doc is a binary file, and the bytes will be read without the need for conversion to ASCII text. Each block of bytes read from the file will be stored in byteBuffer, which you'll see in the next step.

Step 8: Read the File Contents and Write It to the LOB

This step of reading the file contents and writing it to the LOB may be further broken down into the following loop:

While the end of the file has not been reached:

1. Read a block of data from the file into the buffer created in Step 5.

2. Copy the buffer contents to the LOB object.

I mentioned earlier that a CLOB object may be populated using the putChars() method, which writes characters to a specified position in the CLOB object. You specify the position by passing a long value as a parameter, and the first character of the CLOB is considered to be at position 1. Similarly, a BLOB object may be populated using the putBytes() method; this method works in a similar way to putChars(), except that it writes bytes rather than characters.

NOTE
Both the putChars() *and* putBytes() *methods provide random access to a LOB object, and therefore allow you to jump to any position in the LOB object and start writing.*

The following example uses a while loop to read characters from the textContent.txt file and write them to myClob. Each block of characters is read using the myBufferedReader object's read() method, which returns −1 when the end of the file has been reached. Each block is temporarily stored in textBuffer, the contents of which are then written to the end of myClob using the putChars() method.

```
long position = 1;
int charsRead;

while ((charsRead = myBufferedReader.read(textBuffer)) != -1) {

  // write the buffer contents to myClob using the putChars() method
  myClob.putChars(position, textBuffer);

  // increment the end position
  position += charsRead;

} // end of while
```

Similarly, the following while loop does the same thing for the BLOB: it reads each block of bytes from the binaryContent.doc file, stores those bytes in byteBuffer, and writes the contents of that buffer to the end of myBlob using the putBytes() method:

```
long position = 1;
int bytesRead;

while ((bytesRead = myFileInputStream.read(byteBuffer)) != -1) {

  // write the buffer contents to myBlob using the putBytes() method
  myBlob.putBytes(position, byteBuffer);

  // increment the end position
  position += bytesRead;

} // end of while
```

Step 9: Perform a Commit to Permanently Save the Changes

If auto-commit is disabled, you must perform a commit to permanently record the contents of the LOB objects in the database:

```
myStatement.execute("COMMIT");
```

Step 10: Close the Objects Used to Read the File

In this final step, you close the objects that were used to read the file. For example, the following statements close the various objects that were used to read the `textContent.txt` file in the previous steps:

```
myBufferedReader.close();
myReader.close();
myFileInputStream.close();
```

In the case of the BLOB, the only object to close is `myFileInputStream`, since that was the only object created.

Using Streams to Write to CLOB and BLOB Columns

I mentioned earlier that streams might be slightly faster when dealing with larger files. In this section, I'll show you how to read content from a file and write it to CLOB and BLOB columns using Java streams. There are ten steps to follow to read content from a file and write it to a CLOB or BLOB column; these steps are similar to those described in the previous section:

1. Initialize the LOB column to set the LOB locator.

2. Retrieve the row containing the LOB locator into a result set.

3. Create a LOB object in the Java program and read the LOB locator from the result set.

4. Get the buffer size of the LOB from the LOB object.

5. Create a byte buffer to hold a block of data from the file.

6. Create a file object.

7. Create a file input stream object to read the file contents.

8. Create an output stream object.

9. Read the contents of the file and write it to the LOB using the following steps: While the end of the file has not been reached:

a. Read a block of data from the file into the buffer created in Step 5.

b. Write the buffer contents to the output stream object, which sends the buffer contents to the LOB.

10. Close the file object.

NOTE
If you are using the OCI driver, you can stream content directly into a CLOB *or* BLOB *column without first initializing the LOB locator using the* EMPTY_CLOB() *or* EMPTY_BLOB() *methods. This should also be supported by the Thin driver in Oracle9i Release 2.*

Steps 1–3, 6, and 7 are the same in this process as those shown in the previous section using the put methods. One big difference is that there is no commit step because content streamed to the LOB column is sent directly to the database and immediately made permanent: you cannot commit or rollback the change. In the rest of this section, I'll go through the remaining steps.

NOTE
Since the example code for streaming content to a BLOB *is so similar to that for a* CLOB, *I'll show you example code using only a* CLOB.

Step 4: Get the Buffer Size of the LOB from the LOB Object

In the previous section, you saw how to use the put methods to write content to a LOB one chunk at a time. In this section, you'll see how to stream a buffer containing multiple chunks to a LOB. But before you can do that, you need to obtain the default buffer size used by a LOB; you do this by calling the getBufferSize() function, which returns the buffer size in bytes. The value returned by this function is three times the LOB default chunk size, which equals 24,396 bytes.

The following example calls getBufferSize() using the CLOB object myClob:

```
int bufferSize = myClob.getBufferSize();
```

Step 5: Create a Byte Buffer to Hold a Block of Data from the File

As you'll see in Step 8, you stream content to a CLOB or BLOB column as bytes using an OutputStream object, and because of this, a byte array is required to temporarily store the content that will be sent to the LOB.

The following example creates an array of bytes using the buffer size obtained in the previous step:

```
byte [] byteBuffer = new byte[bufferSize];
```

NOTE
You can use byte arrays even when reading content from an ASCII text file that will be sent to a CLOB.

Step 8: Create an Output Stream Object to Read the File Contents

Now, you can use a Java OutputStream object to send content to a CLOB or BLOB object as a stream of bytes. To do this for a CLOB object, you first open an output stream to the CLOB object using the getAsciiOutputStream() method. This causes the CLOB to interpret the stream of bytes sent to it as ASCII text. You can also use the getCharacterOutputStream() method, which causes the CLOB to interpret the stream of bytes as Unicode text. (Unicode uses a two-byte character set and can represent over 65,000 characters; it may also be used to represent non-English characters.)

In the case of a BLOB, you must use the getBinaryOutputStream() method to tell the BLOB to interpret the stream as bytes.

CAUTION
Once you've opened a stream to a LOB using one of these methods, you must not perform any other database operation until that stream has been closed. Data from the stream might be lost if you don't follow this rule.

The following example creates an OutputStream object named myOutputStream by calling the getAsciiOutputStream() method for myClob:

```
OutputStream myOutputStream = myClob.getAsciiOutputStream();
```

The `myClob` object is now ready to receive a stream of bytes, and because the `getAsciiOutputStream()` method is used, `myClob` will interpret those bytes as ASCII characters.

Step 9: Read the File Contents and Write It to the LOB

The next step is to read the file contents and write it to the LOB. This step may be further broken down into the following loop:

While the end of the file has not been reached:

1. Read a block of data from the file into the buffer created in Step 5.

2. Write the buffer contents to the output stream object, which sends the buffer contents to the LOB.

The following loop reads blocks from `myFileInputStream` into `byteBuffer`. It then writes the contents of `byteBuffer` to `myOutputStream` using the `write()` method, which sends the bytes to `myClob`:

```
int bytesRead;

while ((bytesRead = myFileInputStream.read(byteBuffer)) != -1) {

  // write the buffer contents to the output stream
  // using the write() method
  myOutputStream.write(byteBuffer);

} // end of while
```

Now, because the `getAsciiOutputStream()` method was used to open the output stream in Step 8, the bytes sent to `myClob` are interpreted as ASCII characters. A similar loop may be constructed when using a `BLOB`.

Step 10: Close the Stream Objects

In this final step, you close your stream objects. The following statements close `myFileInputStream` and `myOutputStream` using the `close()` methods:

```
myFileInputStream.close();
myOutputStream.close();
```

I'll show you a complete program using the code examples shown in these steps later in this chapter.

Storing Pointers to External Files Using BFILE Columns

The BFILE LOB type enables you to store a *pointer* to a file that is accessible through the computer's file system. The important point to note is that these files are located outside of the database. BFILE columns can point to files located on any media: a hard disk, CD, DVD, and so on.

NOTE

A BFILE contains a pointer to an external file. The actual file itself is not stored in the database, only a pointer to that file is stored. The file must be accessible through the file system.

Creating a Directory Object

Before you can store a pointer to a file in a BFILE column, you must first create a *directory object* in the database that represents the directory in the file system where your files are stored. You create a directory object using the CREATE DIRECTORY statement. To perform such a statement, you must have the CREATE ANY DIRECTORY database privilege.

The following example creates a directory object named SAMPLE_FILES_DIR for the file system directory C:\sample_files:

```
CREATE DIRECTORY SAMPLE_FILES_DIR AS 'C:\sample_files';
```

NOTE

Windows uses the backslash character (\) in directories, while Linux and UNIX use the forward slash character (/).

When you create a directory object you must ensure that:

■ The actual directory exists in the file system.

■ The user account in the operating system that was used to install the Oracle software has read permission on the directory and on any files that are to be pointed to.

If you are using Windows, you shouldn't need to worry about the second point. The Oracle database software should have been installed using a user account that has administrator privileges, and such a user account has read permission on everything in the Windows file system. If you are using Linux or UNIX, you may have to grant read access to the physical directory and to the files, using the chmod command, for example.

Populating a BFILE Column with a Pointer to a File

Because a BFILE is just a pointer to an external file, populating a BFILE column is very simple. All you have to do is to use the Oracle database's BFILENAME() function to populate the BFILE column with a pointer to your external file. The BFILENAME() function accepts two parameters: the database directory object's name (which must already be created) and the name of your file.

The following example creates two strings. The first contains the directory object's name ("SAMPLE_FILES_DIR"), and the second contains the name of the file to point to ("textContent.txt"):

```
String directory = "SAMPLE_FILES_DIR";
String fileName = "textContent.txt";
```

The next example adds a row to the bfile_content table using the BFILENAME() function; this populates the bfile_column with a pointer to the textContent.txt file:

```
myStatement.executeUpdate(
    "INSERT INTO bfile_content(file_name, bfile_column) " +
    "VALUES ('" + fileName + "', " +
    "BFILENAME('" + directory + "', '" + fileName + "'))"
);
```

This example stores a pointer to a text file. A similar statement can be used to add a row containing a pointer to a binary file. To store a pointer to the binaryContent.doc file, just change the fileName string to "binaryContent.doc" and perform another INSERT statement.

Example Program: LobExample1.java

So far, you've seen a lot of small pieces of code. It's time to show you a complete example program that puts these pieces together. This section shows a program named LobExample1.java, which illustrates how to use the put methods to write content to CLOB and BLOB columns. It also shows how to store pointers to external files using BFILE columns.

This program contains the following methods:

- **writeCLOB()** Reads the characters from an ASCII text file and writes those characters to `clob_column` in the `clob_content` table using the `putChars()` method. This method is invoked by the program once to write the contents of the `textContent.txt` file to `clob_column`.

- **writeBLOB()** Reads the bytes from a binary file and writes those bytes to `blob_column` in the `blob_content` table using the `putBytes()` method. This method is invoked by the program once to write the contents of the `binaryContent.doc` file to `blob_column`.

- **addBFILE()** Adds a pointer, which is stored in `bfile_column` of the `bfile_content` table, to a specified file. This method is invoked twice by the program to add pointers to the `textContent.txt` and `binaryContent.doc` files.

```
/*
  LobExample1.java illustrates how to
  use the put methods to write content to
  CLOB and BLOB columns in the database.
  It also shows how to add pointers to
  external files using BFILE columns.
*/

// import the JDBC packages
import java.sql.*;
import java.io.*;

// import the Oracle JDBC extension packages
import oracle.sql.*;
import oracle.jdbc.*;

public class LobExample1 {

  public static void main(String [] args)
  throws SQLException, IOException {

    // register the Oracle JDBC drivers
    DriverManager.registerDriver(
      new oracle.jdbc.OracleDriver()
    );

    // create a Connection object, and connect to the database
```

```
  // as lob_user using the Oracle JDBC Thin driver
  Connection myConnection = DriverManager.getConnection(
    "jdbc:oracle:thin:@localhost:1521:ORCL",
    "lob_user",
    "lob_password"
  );

  // disable auto-commit mode
  myConnection.setAutoCommit(false);

  // create a statement object
  Statement myStatement = myConnection.createStatement();

  String sourceDirectory = "C:\\sample_files\\";
  writeCLOB(myStatement, sourceDirectory + "textContent.txt");
  writeBLOB(myStatement, sourceDirectory + "binaryContent.doc");
  addBFILE(myStatement, "SAMPLE_FILES_DIR", "textContent.txt");
  addBFILE(myStatement, "SAMPLE_FILES_DIR", "binaryContent.doc");

  // close the JDBC objects
  myStatement.close();
  myConnection.close();

} // end of main()


private static void writeCLOB(
  Statement myStatement,
  String fileName
) throws SQLException, IOException {

  // step 1: initialize the LOB column to set the LOB locator
  myStatement.executeUpdate(
    "INSERT INTO clob_content(file_name, clob_column) " +
    "VALUES ('" + fileName + "', EMPTY_CLOB())"
  );

  // step 2: retrieve the row containing the LOB locator
  ResultSet clobResultSet = myStatement.executeQuery(
    "SELECT clob_column " +
    "FROM clob_content " +
    "WHERE file_name = '" + fileName + "' " +
    "FOR UPDATE"
  );
  clobResultSet.next();

  // step 3: create a LOB object and read the LOB locator
  CLOB myClob =
```

```
  ((OracleResultSet) clobResultSet).getCLOB("clob_column");

// step 4: get the chunk size of the LOB from the LOB object
int chunkSize = myClob.getChunkSize();

// step 5: create a buffer to hold a block of data from the file
char [] textBuffer = new char[chunkSize];

// step 6: create a file object
File myFile = new File(fileName);

// step 7: create input stream objects to read the file contents
FileInputStream myFileInputStream = new FileInputStream(myFile);
InputStreamReader myReader =
  new InputStreamReader(myFileInputStream);
BufferedReader myBufferedReader = new BufferedReader(myReader);

// step 8: read the file contents and write it to the LOB
long position = 1;
int charsRead;

while ((charsRead = myBufferedReader.read(textBuffer)) != -1) {

  // write the buffer contents to myClob using the putChars()
  //method
  myClob.putChars(position, textBuffer);

  // increment the end position
  position += charsRead;

} // end of while

// step 9: perform a commit
myStatement.execute("COMMIT");

// step 10: close the objects used to read the file
myBufferedReader.close();
myReader.close();
myFileInputStream.close();

System.out.println("Wrote content from file " +
  fileName + " to CLOB");

} // end of writeCLOB()


private static void writeBLOB(
  Statement myStatement,
```

```
    String fileName
) throws SQLException, IOException {

    // step 1: initialize the LOB column to set the LOB locator
    myStatement.executeUpdate(
      "INSERT INTO blob_content(file_name, blob_column) " +
      "VALUES ('" + fileName + "', EMPTY_BLOB())"
    );

    // step 2: retrieve the row containing the LOB locator
    ResultSet blobResultSet = myStatement.executeQuery(
      "SELECT blob_column " +
      "FROM blob_content " +
      "WHERE file_name = '" + fileName + "' " +
      "FOR UPDATE"
    );
    blobResultSet.next();

    // step 3: create a LOB object and read the LOB locator
    BLOB myBlob =
      ((OracleResultSet) blobResultSet).getBLOB("blob_column");

    // step 4: get the chunk size of the LOB from the LOB object
    int chunkSize = myBlob.getChunkSize();

    // step 5: create a buffer to hold a block of data from the file
    byte [] byteBuffer = new byte[chunkSize];

    // step 6: create a file object to open the file
    File myFile = new File(fileName);

    // step 7: create an input stream object to read the file contents
    FileInputStream myFileInputStream = new FileInputStream(myFile);

    // step 8: read the file contents and write it to the LOB
    long position = 1;
    int bytesRead;

    while ((bytesRead = myFileInputStream.read(byteBuffer)) != -1) {

      // write the buffer contents to myBlob using the
      // putBytes() method
      myBlob.putBytes(position, byteBuffer);

      // increment the end position
      position += bytesRead;
```

```
    } // end of while

    // step 9: perform a COMMIT
    myStatement.execute("COMMIT");

    // step 10: close the objects used to read the file
    myFileInputStream.close();

    System.out.println("Wrote content from file " +
      fileName + " to BLOB");

  } // end of writeBLOB()


  private static void addBFILE(
    Statement myStatement,
    String directory,
    String fileName
  ) throws SQLException {

    myStatement.executeUpdate(
      "INSERT INTO bfile_content(file_name, bfile_column) " +
      "VALUES ('" + fileName + "', " +
      "BFILENAME('" + directory + "', '" + fileName + "'))"
    );
    myStatement.execute("COMMIT");

    System.out.println("Added pointer to file " +
      fileName + " to BFILE in database directory " + directory);

  } // end of addBFILE()

}
```

The output from this program is as follows:

```
Wrote content from file C:\sample_files\textContent.txt to CLOB
Wrote content from file C:\sample_files\binaryContent.doc to BLOB
Added pointer to file textContent.txt to BFILE in database directory
 SAMPLE_FILES_DIR
Added pointer to file binaryContent.doc to BFILE in database directory
 SAMPLE_FILES_DIR
```

The program LobExample3.java, which is not printed in this book for brevity but is available for download, uses Java streams to write the same file content in the clob_content and blob_content tables. Feel free to examine and run that program.

Using the Get Methods to Read from CLOB and BLOB Columns

In this section, I'll show you how to read content from CLOB and BLOB columns using the get methods. Specifically, I'll show you how to read the data previously stored in clob_column and blob_column and how to write that data out to a new file. Just as before when we wrote content from a file to a CLOB or BLOB using the put methods, there are a series of steps to follow to read content from a CLOB or BLOB and write it to a file. These nine steps are as follows:

1. Retrieve the row containing the LOB locator into a result set.

2. Create a LOB object in your Java program and read the LOB locator from the result set into that LOB object.

3. Get the chunk size of the LOB from the LOB object.

4. Create a buffer to hold a chunk of data retrieved from the LOB object.

5. Create a file object.

6. Create output stream objects to write the LOB contents to the new file.

7. Get the length of the LOB contents from the LOB object.

8. Read the contents of the LOB and write it to the file using the following steps (while the end of the LOB contents has not been reached):

   a. Read a chunk of data from the LOB object into the buffer created in Step 4.

   b. Write the buffer contents to the new file.

9. Close the stream objects.

Only Steps 6, 7, and 8 in this list are new—you've already seen code for the other steps earlier in this chapter. For each of these steps, I'll use example code to show you how read the text content previously stored in clob_column and write it to a new file. Where the code differs, I'll also you show how to read the binary content previously stored in blob_column.

You can assume that Steps 1 through 5 have already been done and the LOB locator for clob_column has been read into a LOB object named myClob. The content will be read from the database using this object. You can also assume that the new file, to which the content will be written, is accessed using a File object named myFile.

Step 6: Create Output Stream Objects to Write the LOB Contents to the New File

To write the text content contained in clob_column to a file, you need a FileOutputStream, an OutputStreamWriter, and a BufferedWriter object:

```
FileOutputStream myFileOutputStream = new FileOutputStream(myFile);
OutputStreamWriter myWriter =
  new OutputStreamWriter(myFileOutputStream);
BufferedWriter myBufferedWriter = new BufferedWriter(myWriter);
```

The myFileOutputStream object provides the low-level functionality to write the contents of a file as a stream of bytes. The myWriter object is a wrapper around myFileOutputStream, and allows those bytes to be interpreted as a stream of ASCII characters. Finally, myBufferedWriter allows you to write the stream of characters as blocks of multiple characters.

To write binary content, you only need a FileOuputStream object because the bytes can be written to the file without the need for conversion.

Step 7: Get the LOB Content Length from the LOB Object

The total length of the content stored in the LOB is required in Step 8. To get the total, you call the length() function using your LOB object, which returns the length of content in bytes. The following example gets the length of the text content from the CLOB object myClob, and stores it in a long variable named clobLength:

```
long clobLength = myClob.length();
```

Step 8: Read the LOB Contents and Write It to the File

This step involves reading the contents of the LOB and writing it to the file. This can be done using the following loop:

While the end of the LOB contents has not been reached:

1. Read a chunk of data from the LOB into the buffer created in Step 4.

2. Write the buffer contents to the new file.

The content stored in a CLOB object is read using the getChars() method, which gets the characters starting from a position that you pass as a parameter to this method. This position is a long value, and the content starts at position 1. Similarly, the content stored in a BLOB object is read using the getBytes() method.

NOTE
*Both the getChars () and getBytes () methods
provide random access to a LOB object, and therefore
allow you jump to any position in the LOB object
and start reading.*

The following example uses a `for` loop to read a chunk of characters from
`myClob` using the `getChars()` method. This chunk is temporarily stored in the
character array `textBuffer`, whose contents are then appended to the file using
the `myBufferedWriter.write()` method. This method accepts an array of
characters. The loop repeats until all of the content in `myClob` has been read. The
end is determined by checking the current position value against the value stored
in `clobLength` (which was set in Step 8).

```
for (
   long position = 1;
   position <= clobLength;
   position += chunkSize
) {

   // read a chunk of data from myClob using the getChars() method
   // and store it in the buffer
   int charsRead =
     myClob.getChars(position, chunkSize, textBuffer);

   // write the buffer contents to the file
   myBufferedWriter.write(textBuffer);

} // end of for
```

Similarly, the following example reads the binary data contained in `myBlob`.
The `for` loop reads a chunk of bytes from `myBlob` using the `getBytes()` method.
The chunk is temporarily stored in the byte array `byteBuffer`, whose contents are
then appended to the file using the `myFileOutputStream.write()` method.

```
for (
   long position = 1;
   position <= blobLength;
   position += chunkSize
) {

   // read a chunk of data from myBlob using the getBytes() method
   // and store it in the buffer
   int bytesRead =
     myBlob.getBytes(position, chunkSize, byteBuffer);
```

```
    // write the buffer contents to the file
    myFileOutputStream.write(byteBuffer);

} // end of for
```

Later in this chapter, you'll see a program named `LobExample2.java` that uses the examples shown in this section.

Using Streams to Read from CLOB and BLOB Columns

In this section, you'll see how to read content from `CLOB` and `BLOB` columns using streams and then store that content in new files. To do this, there are five steps:

1. Retrieve the row containing the LOB locator into a result set.

2. Create a LOB object in your Java program and read the LOB locator from the result set.

3. Create an input stream object and call the appropriate LOB object input stream function.

4. Read the LOB contents using the input stream object and write it to a file.

5. Close the input stream object.

You've already seen how to perform Steps 1 and 2. For Steps 3 through 5, I'll use example code to show how to read the text previously stored in `clob_column`.

Step 3: Create an Input Stream Object

In this step, you create an input stream object and call the appropriate LOB object input stream function. In order to open an input stream to a `CLOB` object, interpreting the content as ASCII text, you call the `getAsciiStream()` method for the `CLOB`. You can also read the content from a `CLOB` as Unicode using the `getUnicodeStream()` method. (As I mentioned earlier, Unicode uses a two-byte character set.) For a `BLOB` object, you use the `getBinaryStream()` method to interpret the content as binary data.

CAUTION
Once a stream has been opened, you must not perform any other database operation until that stream has been closed. Data from the stream might be lost if you don't follow this rule.

The following example calls the getAsciiStream() method for myClob:

```
InputStream myInputStream = myClob.getAsciiStream();
```

You can use a Java InputStream object to read content from a CLOB or a BLOB object. The InputStream object shown in the example is now ready for reading ASCII characters from myClob.

Step 4: Read the LOB Contents Using
the Input Stream Object and Write It to a File

The next step is to read the LOB contents from the InputStream object, which was created in the Step 3, and save the contents to a new file.

To save the LOB contents, you can use a new method named saveFile(), which is shown in the following example. The method accepts two parameters: an InputStream object and a file name. This method creates a new file using the file name parameter and writes the contents read from the specified InputStream object to the new file. Here's the listing for the saveFile() method:

```
private static void saveFile(
    InputStream myInputStream,
    String fileName
) throws IOException {

    // create a file object
    File myFile = new File(fileName);

    // create a file output stream
    FileOutputStream myFileOutputStream =
      new FileOutputStream(myFile);

    // read the contents from the input stream until
    // the end has been reached (the read() method
    // returns -1 at the end)
    byte [] byteBuffer = new byte[8132];
    int bytesRead;
    while ((bytesRead = myInputStream.read(byteBuffer)) != -1) {

      // write the buffer contents to the file
      myFileOutputStream.write(byteBuffer);

    } // end of while

    // close the file output stream
```

```
    myFileOutputStream.close();

} // end of saveFile()
```

Notice the use of an array of 8,132 bytes named `byteBuffer`—this buffer has the same size as the default chunk size for a `CLOB` or `BLOB`. You can pick your own array size for your programs based on the total length of the LOB contents. You might want to use a bigger buffer if your LOBs contain a large amount of data.

The next example creates a string named `saveFileName`, which is set to the file name for the new file, and calls the `saveFile()` method to read the LOB contents from `myInputStream`. It then saves the contents into a new file (using the name specified by `saveFileName`):

```
String saveFileName = "C:\\sample_files\\retrieved\\" + fileName;
saveFile(myInputStream, saveFileName);
```

Because `myInputStream` reads the content from `myClob`, the new file created by the `saveFile()` method contains a copy of the text currently stored in `myClob`. Earlier in this chapter, the text from `textFile.txt` was stored in `myClob`; therefore, this same text is read from `myClob` and stored in the new file.

Step 5: Close the Input Stream Object

The final step, once the LOB contents have been read and written to the destination file, is to close the `InputStream` object using the `close()` method:

```
myInputStream.close();
```

Reading External Files Using BFILE Pointers

As I mentioned earlier, although a `BFILE` column only stores a pointer to the external file, you can actually read the file via that pointer. The following nine steps may be used to read a file through a `BFILE` pointer and save it to a new file:

1. Retrieve the row containing the `BFILE` column into a result set.

2. Create a `BFILE` object and read the `BFILE` locator from the result set.

3. Get the external file name from the `BFILE` object.

4. Check that the external file pointed to by the `BFILE` object exists.

5. Open the external file via the `BFILE` object.

6. Create an input stream object to read the external file contents via the BFILE object.

7. Save the file contents read from the input stream to a new file.

8. Close the input stream object.

9. Close the external file via the BFILE object.

For each step, I'll use example code to show you how to retrieve the bfile_column value that points to the external file textContent.txt. Then I'll show you how to read the contents of the file through this pointer and how to write the file contents to a new file. This code basically shows how to do a file copy via a BFILE pointer.

Step 1: Retrieve the Row Containing the BFILE Column into a Result Set

The first step is to retrieve the row containing the BFILE column into a result set. The following example creates a ResultSet object, named bfileResultSet, which retrieves the bfile_column from the bfile_content table for the row where the file_name column is equal to "textContent.txt". The next() method is also called to navigate to that row stored in bfileResultSet:

```
String fileName = "textContent.txt";
ResultSet bfileResultSet = myStatement.executeQuery(
  "SELECT bfile_column " +
  "FROM bfile_content " +
  "WHERE file_name = '" + fileName + "'"
);
bfileResultSet.next();
```

Step 2: Create a BFILE Object and Read the BFILE Locator from the Result Set

Next, a BFILE object must be created and set to the BFILE locator read from the result set created in the previous step. The following example creates a BFILE object named myBfile, and the bfile_column is read from bfileResultSet using the getBFILE() method:

```
BFILE myBfile =
    ((OracleResultSet) bfileResultSet).getBFILE("bfile_column");
```

Step 3: Get the External File Name from the BFILE Object

The next step is to get the name of the external file from the BFILE object. You use the getName() method to do this.

```
String bfileName = myBfile.getName();
```

Step 4: Check That the External File
Pointed to by the BFILE Object Exists

Once you have the file name, you should check that the file actually exists before you attempt to open it. To do this, you use the fileExists() method:

```
myBfile.fileExists();
```

Step 5: Open the External File via the BFILE Object

Once you're sure the file actually exists, you can open it using the openFile() method:

```
myBfile.openFile();
```

Step 6: Create an Input Stream Object to Read
the External File Contents via the BFILE Object

Next, you need a Java InputStream object to read the external file contents via the BFILE object. The external file will be interpreted as a stream of bytes:

```
InputStream myInputStream = myBfile.getBinaryStream();
```

The external file pointed to by myBfile is now ready to be read as a stream of bytes via the InputStream object myInputStream.

Step 7: Save the File Contents Read
from the Input Stream to a New File

You then save the file contents read from the input stream to a new file. The following example uses the saveFile() method shown earlier to save the file contents read using myInputStream to a new file:

```
String saveFileName = "C:\\sample_files\\retrieved\\" + bfileName;
saveFile(myInputStream, saveFileName);
```

Step 8: Close the Input Stream Object

The last step, once the file contents have been read and written to the destination file, is to close myInputStream using the close() method:

```
myInputStream.close();
```

Step 9: Close the External File via the BFILE Object

You should also close the external file once you are finished with it using the closeFile() method for the BFILE object:

```
myBfile.closeFile();
```

Example Program: LobExample2.java

This section shows a program named LobExample2.java, which illustrates how to read from CLOB and BLOB columns using the get methods and how to read external files pointed to by BFILE columns.

NOTE
Prior to running this program, the clob_content, blob_content and bfile_content tables should already contain rows. You can add rows to these tables by running the LobExample1 program shown earlier.

This program contains the following methods that do the work:

- **readCLOB()**   Reads the text previously stored in clob_column using the getChars() method and writes that text to a new file. This method is invoked once by the program and writes the text from clob_column to a new file named readCLOBtextContent.txt in the directory C:\sample_files\retrieved.

- **readBLOB()**   Reads the bytes previously stored in blob_column using the getBytes() method and writes those bytes to a new file. This method is invoked once by the program and writes the bytes from clob_column to a new file named readBLOBbinaryContent.doc in the directory C:\sample_files\retrieved.

- **retrieveBFILE()**   Retrieves a pointer to a file previously stored in bfile_column. This method then reads the content from that file and writes it to two new files. This method is invoked twice by the program to retrieve the pointers to the textContent.txt and binaryContent.doc files and to copy the contents of those files to two new files named retrievedBFILEtextContent.txt and retrievedBFILEbinaryContent.doc in the directory C:\sample_files\retrieved.

```
/*
  LobExample2.java illustrates how to
  use the get methods to read from CLOB and BLOB columns.
  It also shows how to retrieve pointers to
  external files using BFILE columns, and copy
  the contents of those files to new files.
*/

// import the JDBC packages
import java.sql.*;
import java.io.*;

// import the Oracle JDBC extension packages
import oracle.sql.*;
import oracle.jdbc.*;

public class LobExample2 {

  public static void main(String [] args)
  throws SQLException, IOException {

    // register the Oracle JDBC drivers
    DriverManager.registerDriver(
      new oracle.jdbc.OracleDriver()
    );

    // create a Connection object, and connect to the database
    // as lob_user using the Oracle JDBC Thin driver
    Connection myConnection = DriverManager.getConnection(
      "jdbc:oracle:thin:@localhost:1521:ORCL",
      "lob_user",
      "lob_password"
    );

    // disable auto-commit mode
    myConnection.setAutoCommit(false);

    // create a Statement object
    Statement myStatement = myConnection.createStatement();
```

```
    String sourceDirectory = "C:\\sample_files\\";
    String targetDirectory = "C:\\sample_files\\retrieved\\";
    readCLOB(
      myStatement, "textContent.txt", sourceDirectory,
      targetDirectory
    );
    readBLOB(
      myStatement, "binaryContent.doc", sourceDirectory,
      targetDirectory
    );
    retrieveBFILE(myStatement, "textContent.txt", targetDirectory);
    retrieveBFILE(myStatement, "binaryContent.doc", targetDirectory);

    // close the JDBC objects
    myStatement.close();
    myConnection.close();

  } // end of main()


  private static void readCLOB(
    Statement myStatement,
    String fileName,
    String sourceDirectory,
    String targetDirectory
  ) throws SQLException, IOException {

    // step 1: retrieve the row containing the LOB locator
    ResultSet clobResultSet = myStatement.executeQuery(
      "SELECT clob_column " +
      "FROM clob_content " +
      "WHERE file_name = '" + sourceDirectory + fileName + "'"
    );
    clobResultSet.next();

    // step 2: create a LOB object and read the LOB locator
    CLOB myClob =
      ((OracleResultSet) clobResultSet).getCLOB("clob_column");

    // step 3: get the chunk size of the LOB from the LOB object
    int chunkSize = myClob.getChunkSize();

    // step 4: create a buffer to hold a chunk of data retrieved from
    // the LOB object
    char [] textBuffer = new char[chunkSize];

    // step 5: create a file object
    String saveFile = targetDirectory + "retrievedCLOB" + fileName;
```

```
    File myFile = new File(saveFile);

    // step 6: create output stream objects to write the LOB contents
    // to the new file
    FileOutputStream myFileOutputStream =
      new FileOutputStream(myFile);
    OutputStreamWriter myWriter =
      new OutputStreamWriter(myFileOutputStream);
    BufferedWriter myBufferedWriter = new BufferedWriter(myWriter);

    // step 7: get the length of the LOB contents from the LOB object
    long clobLength = myClob.length();

    // step 8: while the end of the LOB contents has not been reached,
    // read a chunk of data from the LOB into the buffer,
    // and write the buffer contents to the file
    for (
      long position = 1;
      position <= clobLength;
      position += chunkSize
    ) {

      // read a chunk of data from myClob using the getChars() method
      // and store it in the buffer
      int charsRead =
        myClob.getChars(position, chunkSize, textBuffer);

      // write the buffer contents to the file
      myBufferedWriter.write(textBuffer);

    } // end of for

    // step 9: close the stream objects
    myBufferedWriter.close();
    myWriter.close();
    myFileOutputStream.close();

    System.out.println(
      "Read CLOB and saved file " + saveFile
    );

} // end of readCLOB()


private static void readBLOB(
  Statement myStatement,
  String fileName,
  String sourceDirectory,
```

```
    String targetDirectory
) throws SQLException, IOException {

    // step 1: retrieve the row containing the LOB locator
    ResultSet blobResultSet = myStatement.executeQuery(
      "SELECT blob_column " +
      "FROM blob_content " +
      "WHERE file_name = '" + sourceDirectory + fileName + "'"
    );
    blobResultSet.next();

    // step 2: create a LOB object and read the LOB locator
    BLOB myBlob =
      ((OracleResultSet) blobResultSet).getBLOB("blob_column");

    // step 3: get the chunk size of the LOB from the LOB object
    int chunkSize = myBlob.getChunkSize();

    // step 4: create a buffer to hold a chunk of data retrieved from
    // the LOB object
    byte [] byteBuffer = new byte[chunkSize];

    // step 5: create a file object
    String saveFile = targetDirectory + "retrievedBLOB" + fileName;
    File myFile = new File(saveFile);

    // step 6: create output stream objects to write the LOB contents
    // to the new file
    FileOutputStream myFileOutputStream =
      new FileOutputStream(myFile);

    // step 7: get the length of the LOB contents from the LOB object
    long blobLength = myBlob.length();

    // step 8: while the end of the LOB contents has not been reached,
    // read a chunk of data from the LOB into the buffer,
    // and write the buffer contents to the file
    for (
      long position = 1;
      position <= blobLength;
      position += chunkSize
    ) {

      // read a chunk of data from myBlob using the getBytes() method
      // and store it in the buffer
      int bytesRead =
        myBlob.getBytes(position, chunkSize, byteBuffer);

      // write the buffer contents to the file
```

```
      myFileOutputStream.write(byteBuffer);

  } // end of for

  // step 9: close the stream objects
  myFileOutputStream.close();

  System.out.println(
    "Read BLOB and saved file " + saveFile
  );

} // end of readBLOB()


private static void retrieveBFILE(
  Statement myStatement,
  String fileName,
  String targetDirectory
) throws SQLException, IOException {

  // step 1: retrieve the row containing the BFILE locator
  ResultSet bfileResultSet = myStatement.executeQuery(
    "SELECT bfile_column " +
    "FROM bfile_content " +
    "WHERE file_name = '" + fileName + "'"
  );
  bfileResultSet.next();

  // step 2: create a BFILE object and read the locator
  BFILE myBfile =
    ((OracleResultSet) bfileResultSet).getBFILE("bfile_column");

  // step 3: get the file name from the BFILE object
  String bfileName = myBfile.getName();

  // step 4: check that the external file pointed to
  // by the BFILE object exists
  myBfile.fileExists();

  // step 5: open the external file via the BFILE object
  myBfile.openFile();

  // step 6: create an input stream object to read the external
  // file contents via the BFILE object
  InputStream myInputStream = myBfile.getBinaryStream();

  // step 7: save the file contents read from the
  // input stream to a new file
  String saveFileName = targetDirectory + "retrievedBFILE" +
```

```
      bfileName;
    saveFile(myInputStream, saveFileName);

    // step 8: close the input stream
    myInputStream.close();

    // step 9: close the external file via the BFILE object
    myBfile.closeFile();

    System.out.println(
      "Retrieved pointer from BFILE and saved file " + saveFileName
    );

  } // end of retrieveBFILE()


  private static void saveFile(
    InputStream myInputStream,
    String fileName
  ) throws IOException {

    // create a file object
    File myFile = new File(fileName);

    // create a file output stream
    FileOutputStream myFileOutputStream =
      new FileOutputStream(myFile);

    // read the contents from the input stream until
    // the end has been reached (the read() method
    // returns -1 at the end)
    byte [] byteBuffer = new byte[8132];
    int bytesRead;
    while ((bytesRead = myInputStream.read(byteBuffer)) != -1) {

      // write the input to the file
      myFileOutputStream.write(byteBuffer);

    } // end of while

    // close the file output stream
    myFileOutputStream.close();

  } // end of saveFile()

}
```

The output from this program is as follows:

```
Read CLOB and saved file
  C:\sample_files\retrieved\retrievedCLOBtextContent.txt
Read BLOB and saved file
  C:\sample_files\retrieved\retrievedBLOBbinaryContent.doc
Retrieved pointer from BFILE and saved file
  C:\sample_files\retrieved\retrievedBFILEtextContent.txt
Retrieved pointer from BFILE and saved file
  C:\sample_files\retrieved\retrievedBFILEbinaryContent.doc
```

The program LobExample4.java, omitted from this book for brevity, contains an example that uses streams to read the content from CLOB and BLOB columns. That program is available in the program directory where you unzipped the ZIP file for this book.

LONG and LONG RAW Columns

I mentioned at the start of this chapter that LOBs are now the preferred storage type for large blocks of data, but you may encounter older databases that still use LONG and LONG RAW types. In this section, I'll show you how to handle these older types using JDBC.

In this section, I'll use two new tables in the examples (created by the lob_user.sql script):

- **long_content**   Contains a LONG column named long_column.

- **long_raw_content**   Contains a LONG RAW column named long_raw_column.

In addition, both of these tables also contain a column to store the name of the file from which the content was originally read. These two tables are defined as follows:

```
CREATE TABLE long_content (
  file_name   VARCHAR2(40) NOT NULL,
  long_column LONG NOT NULL
);

CREATE TABLE long_raw_content (
  file_name       VARCHAR2(40) NOT NULL,
  long_raw_column LONG RAW NOT NULL
);
```

To write to LONG and LONG RAW columns, you can use streams. In the following sections, I'll show you how to write to LONG and LONG RAW columns and how to read from those columns.

Writing to LONG and LONG RAW Columns

You can use the following eight steps to use a stream to write to a LONG or LONG RAW column, assuming that the content is read from a file:

1. Create a file object.

2. Get the file length in bytes.

3. Create an input stream object to read the file contents.

4. Create a prepared statement object containing a SQL INSERT statement to add a row to the table.

5. Bind the file name and input stream object to the prepared statement object.

6. Run the SQL statement contained in the prepared statement object.

7. Perform a commit to permanently save the changes.

8. Close the input stream and prepared statement objects.

For each of these steps, I'll show you example code to illustrate how to store the contents of the textContent.txt file in the long_content table. Where the code differs substantially, I'll also show you how to store the contents of the binaryContent.doc file in the long_raw_content table.

Step 1: Create a File Object

The first step is to create a File object, which acts as a "handle" to the file. You use it to access a file:

```
String sourceDirectory = "C:\\sample_files\\";
String fileName = "textContent.txt";
File myFile = new File(sourceDirectory + fileName);
```

As you can see, this File object is used to read the textContent.txt file. To read the binaryContent.doc file, all you have to is to change the fileName string to "binaryContent.doc".

Step 2: Get the File Length in Bytes

The length of the file in bytes is required later in Step 5. You can get the file length using the length() method, which returns a long value. Because an int value is needed later, it should be cast to an int:

```
int fileLength = (int) myFile.length();
```

Step 3: Create an Input Stream Object to Read the File Contents

To read the file contents, you need an InputStream object:

```
InputStream myInputStream = new FileInputStream(myFile);
```

You can use an InputStream object to read from a text or binary file.

Step 4: Create a Prepared Statement Object
Containing a SQL INSERT Statement

In order to add a row to the long_content table, you need a prepared statement object containing a SQL INSERT statement to add a row to the table. The following example creates a PreparedStatement object named myPrepStatement:

```
PreparedStatement myPrepStatement = myConnection.prepareStatement(
    "INSERT INTO long_content(file_name, long_column) " +
    "VALUES (?, ?)"
);
```

This statement will add a row to the long_content table, with the values for the file_name and long_column columns being supplied via the two placeholders. The placeholders are indicated by the question marks.

A similar PreparedStatement object may be used to add a row to the long_raw_content table—you just need to replace the table and column names.

Step 5: Bind the File Name and Input Stream
to the Prepared Statement Object

The next step is to bind the fileName string and myInputStream object to the placeholders in myPrepStatement. To do this, you use the set methods. Specifically, to bind the fileName string, you use the setString() method, and to bind the myInputStream object, you may use the setAsciiStream() method, which causes the characters in myInputStream to be interpreted as ASCII text. The following examples show the use of these set methods to bind the fileName string and the myInputStream object to the two placeholders in myPrepStatement:

```
myPrepStatement.setString(1, fileName);
myPrepStatement.setAsciiStream(2, myInputStream, fileLength);
```

Notice that the call to setAsciiStream() also uses the fileLength variable that was previously set in Step 2.

To add a row to the long_raw_content table, you use the setBinaryStream() method to bind myInputStream to the second placeholder:

```
myPrepStatement.setBinaryStream(2, myInputStream, fileLength);
```

The setBinaryStream() method causes myInputStream to be interpreted as bytes.

> **NOTE**
> *If you are using a Unicode file, you use the setUnicodeStream() method to bind the InputStream object to the PreparedStatement object.*

Step 6: Run the SQL Statement Contained in the Prepared Statement Object

To run the SQL statement contained in the prepared statement object, you use the execute() method. The following example does this for the myPrepStatement object:

```
myPrepStatement.execute();
```

This runs the INSERT statement, which adds a row to the long_content table.

Step 7: Perform a Commit to Permanently Save the Changes

To permanently record the results of the INSERT statement, you call the commit() method for the Connection object used to make the connection to the database. Assuming that the name of the Connection object in use is myConnection, the following example performs the required commit:

```
myConnection.commit();
```

The row added in the previous step is now made permanent in the database.

Step 8: Close the Input Stream and Prepared Statement Objects

The final step is to close the input stream and prepared statement objects used in the previous steps:

```
myInputStream.close();
myPrepStatement.close();
```

Example Program: LongExample1.java

This section shows a complete program named LongExample1.java that illustrates how to write content to LONG and LONG RAW columns.

This program contains the following methods that do the work:

- **writeLONG()**   Reads the characters from an ASCII text file and writes those characters to `long_column` in the `long_content` table. This method is invoked by the program to write the contents of the `textContent.txt` file to `long_column`.

- **writeLONGRAW()**   Reads the bytes from a binary file and writes those bytes to `long_raw_column` in the `long_raw_content` table. This method is invoked by the program to write the contents of the `binaryContent.doc` file to `long_raw_column`.

```
/*
  LongExample1.java illustrates how to
  write content to LONG and LONG RAW columns.
*/

// import the JDBC packages
import java.sql.*;
import java.io.*;

// import the Oracle JDBC extension packages
import oracle.sql.*;
import oracle.jdbc.*;

public class LongExample1 {

  public static void main(String [] args)
  throws SQLException, IOException {

    // register the Oracle JDBC drivers
    DriverManager.registerDriver(
      new oracle.jdbc.OracleDriver()
    );

    // create a Connection object, and connect to the database
    // as lob_user using the Oracle JDBC Thin driver
    Connection myConnection = DriverManager.getConnection(
      "jdbc:oracle:thin:@localhost:1521:ORCL",
      "lob_user",
      "lob_password"
    );

    // disable auto-commit mode
```

```
    myConnection.setAutoCommit(false);

    String sourceDirectory = "C:\\sample_files\\";
    writeLONG(myConnection, sourceDirectory, "textContent.txt");
    writeLONGRAW(myConnection, sourceDirectory, "binaryContent.doc");

    // close the JDBC connection object
    myConnection.close();

} // end of main()


private static void writeLONG(
  Connection myConnection,
  String sourceDirectory,
  String fileName
) throws SQLException, IOException {

  // step 1: create a file object
  File myFile = new File(sourceDirectory + fileName);

  // step 2: get the file length
  int fileLength = (int) myFile.length();

  // step 3: create an input stream object to read
  // the file contents
  InputStream myInputStream = new FileInputStream(myFile);

  // step 4: create a prepared statetment object
  // to add a row to the long_content table
  PreparedStatement myPrepStatement = myConnection.prepareStatement(
    "INSERT INTO long_content(file_name, long_column) " +
    "VALUES (?, ?)"
  );

  // step 5: bind the file name and input stream to the
  // prepared statement object
  myPrepStatement.setString(1, fileName);
  myPrepStatement.setAsciiStream(2, myInputStream, fileLength);

  // step 6: run the SQL statement contained in the
  // prepared statement object
  myPrepStatement.execute();

  // step 7: perform a commit
  myConnection.commit();

  // step 8: close the input stream and prepared statement objects
```

```
      myInputStream.close();
      myPrepStatement.close();

      System.out.println("Wrote content from file " +
        fileName + " to LONG");

} // end of writeLONG()


private static void writeLONGRAW(
    Connection myConnection,
    String sourceDirectory,
    String fileName
) throws SQLException, IOException {

    // step 1: create a file object
    File myFile = new File(sourceDirectory + fileName);

    // step 2: get the file length
    int fileLength = (int) myFile.length();

    // step 3: create an input stream object to read
    // the file contents
    InputStream myInputStream = new FileInputStream(myFile);

    // step 4: create a prepared statetment object
    // to add a row to the long_raw_content table
    PreparedStatement myPrepStatement = myConnection.prepareStatement(
      "INSERT INTO long_raw_content(file_name, long_raw_column) " +
      "VALUES (?, ?)"
    );

    // step 5: bind the file name and input stream to the
    // prepared statement object
    myPrepStatement.setString(1, fileName);
    myPrepStatement.setBinaryStream(2, myInputStream, fileLength);

    // step 6: run the SQL statement contained in the
    // prepared statement object
    myPrepStatement.execute();

    // step 7: perform a commit
    myConnection.commit();

    // step 8: close the input stream and prepared statement objects
    myInputStream.close();
    myPrepStatement.close();
```

```
    System.out.println("Wrote content from file " +
      fileName + " to LONG RAW");

  } // end of writeLONGRAW()

}
```

The output from this program is as follows:

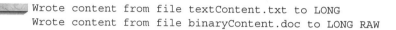

```
Wrote content from file textContent.txt to LONG
Wrote content from file binaryContent.doc to LONG RAW
```

Reading from LONG and LONG RAW Columns

To read content previously stored in a LONG or LONG RAW column, you can
use streams. Since the code for reading from LONG and LONG RAW columns
isn't dramatically different from that for reading from CLOB and BLOB columns
using streams, I'll just show you a complete example program that includes the
steps required to read from such columns and save the content to a new file.

In the earlier section, "Using Streams to Read from CLOB and BLOB
Columns," I discussed the getAsciiStream(), getBinaryStream(), and
getUnicodeStream() methods. These ResultSet object methods allow
you to get at the content in the database as a stream of ASCII characters, a
stream of bytes, or a stream of Unicode characters, respectively. For example,
to get at the text previously stored in long_column of the long_content
table, you can use the getAsciiStream() method; to get at the bytes previously
stored in long_raw_column of the long_raw_content table, you use the
getBinaryStream() method.

The following listing shows a program named LongExample2.java that
illustrates how to read content from LONG and LONG RAW columns using streams.

NOTE
*Prior to running this program, the long_content
and long_raw_content tables should already
contain a row. You can add a row to these tables by
running the LongExample1 program shown earlier.*

This program contains the following methods that do the work:

- **readLONG()**   Reads the text previously stored in long_column
  and writes that text to a new file. This method is invoked once
  by the program and writes the text from long_column to a
  new file named readLONGtextContent.txt in the directory
  C:\sample_files\retrieved.

■ **readLONGRAW()**   Reads the bytes previously stored in
`long_raw_column` and writes those bytes to a new file.
This method is invoked once by the program and writes
the bytes from `long_raw_column` to a new file named
`readLONGRAWbinaryContent.doc` in the directory
`C:\sample_files\retrieved`.

```
/*
  LongExample2.java illustrates how to
  read content from LONG and LONG RAW
  columns using streams.
*/

// import the JDBC packages
import java.sql.*;
import java.io.*;

// import the Oracle JDBC extension packages
import oracle.sql.*;
import oracle.jdbc.*;

public class LongExample2 {

  public static void main(String [] args)
  throws SQLException, IOException {

    // register the Oracle JDBC drivers
    DriverManager.registerDriver(
      new oracle.jdbc.OracleDriver()
    );

    // create a Connection object, and connect to the database
    // as lob_user using the Oracle JDBC Thin driver
    Connection myConnection = DriverManager.getConnection(
      "jdbc:oracle:thin:@localhost:1521:ORCL",
      "lob_user",
      "lob_password"
    );

    // disable auto-commit mode
    myConnection.setAutoCommit(false);

    // create a Statement object
    Statement myStatement = myConnection.createStatement();

    String sourceDirectory = "C:\\sample_files\\";
```

```
  String targetDirectory = "C:\\sample_files\\retrieved\\";
  readLONG(myStatement, targetDirectory);
  readLONGRAW(myStatement, targetDirectory);

  // close the JDBC objects
  myStatement.close();
  myConnection.close();

} // end of main()


private static void readLONG(
  Statement myStatement,
  String targetDirectory
) throws SQLException, IOException {

  // step 1: retrieve the rows into a result set object
  ResultSet longResultSet = myStatement.executeQuery(
    "SELECT file_name, long_column " +
    "FROM long_content"
  );

  // step 2: create an input stream object
  InputStream myInputStream = null;

  // step 3: read the rows from the result set object
  while (longResultSet.next()) {

    String fileName = longResultSet.getString("file_name");
    String saveFileName =
      targetDirectory + "readLONG" + fileName;

    // step 3a: get the ASCII stream from the
    // the result set, and store it in the
    // input stream object
    myInputStream = longResultSet.getAsciiStream("long_column");

    // step 3b: save the input stream object to a new file
    saveFile(myInputStream, saveFileName);

    System.out.println("Read LONG and saved file " +
      saveFileName);

  } // end of while

  // step 4: close the input stream object
  myInputStream.close();
```

```
} // end of readLONG()


private static void readLONGRAW(
  Statement myStatement,
  String targetDirectory
) throws SQLException, IOException {

  // step 1: retrieve the rows into a result set object
  ResultSet longRawResultSet = myStatement.executeQuery(
    "SELECT file_name, long_raw_column " +
    "FROM long_raw_content"
  );

  // step 2: create an input stream object
  InputStream myInputStream = null;

  // step 3: read the rows from the result set object
  while (longRawResultSet.next()) {

    String fileName = longRawResultSet.getString("file_name");
    String saveFileName =
      targetDirectory + "readLONGRAW" + fileName;

    // step 3a: get the binary stream from the
    // the result set, and store it in the
    // input stream object
    myInputStream =
      longRawResultSet.getBinaryStream("long_raw_column");

    // step 3b: save the input stream object to a new file
    saveFile(myInputStream, saveFileName);

    System.out.println(
      "Read LONG RAW and saved file " +
      saveFileName
    );

  } // end of while

  // step 4: close the input stream object
  myInputStream.close();

} // end of readLONGRAW()


private static void saveFile(
  InputStream myInputStream,
```

```
        String fileName
    ) throws IOException {

        // create a file object
        File myFile = new File(fileName);

        // create a file output stream
        FileOutputStream myFileOutputStream =
          new FileOutputStream(myFile);

        // read the contents from the input stream until
        // the end has been reached (the read() method
        // returns -1 at the end)
        byte [] byteBuffer = new byte[8132];
        int bytesRead;
        while ((bytesRead = myInputStream.read(byteBuffer)) != -1) {

            // write the input to the file
            myFileOutputStream.write(byteBuffer);

        } // end of while

        // close the file output stream
        myFileOutputStream.close();

    } // end of saveFile()

}
```

The output from this program is as follows:

```
Read LONG and saved file
  C:\sample_files\retrieved\readLONGtextContent.txt
Read LONG RAW and saved file
  C:\sample_files\retrieved\readLONGRAWbinaryContent.doc
```

CHAPTER
9

Advanced
Transaction Control

oday's databases can handle many users and programs accessing the database at the same time, each potentially running their own transactions in the database. The database software must be able to satisfy the needs of all these concurrent transactions, as well as maintain the integrity of rows stored in the database tables. You can control the level of isolation that exists between your transactions and other transactions that may be running in the database using JDBC.

In this chapter, I'll go deeper into the details of database transactions, which were introduced in Chapter 2. I'll also show you a worked example that shows how to set the level of isolation for your transactions using JDBC and the subsequent effect on a transaction. In the final section of this chapter, I'll briefly discuss distributed transactions, which allow you to use transactions that span multiple databases.

ACID Transaction Properties

In Chapter 2, I defined a transaction as being a *logical unit of work*, that is, a grouping of related SQL statements that are either committed or rolled back as one unit. One example of this is a transfer of money from one bank account to another using two UPDATE statements, one that takes money out of one account, and another that puts that money into a different account. Both UPDATE statements may be considered to be a single transaction because both statements must be either committed or rolled back together; otherwise, money might be lost.

Database theory has a more rigorous definition of a transaction and states that a transaction has four fundamental properties, known as *ACID* properties:

- **Atomicity** Transactions are committed or rolled back as a group, and are *atomic*, meaning that all SQL statements contained in a transaction are considered to be a single indivisible unit.

- **Consistency** Transactions ensure that the database state remains *consistent*, meaning that the database starts at one consistent state and ends in another consistent state when the transaction finishes.

- **Isolation** Separate transactions should appear to run without interfering with each other.

- **Durability** Once a transaction has been committed, the database changes are preserved, even if the machine on which the database software runs later crashes.

The Oracle database software ensures that each transaction possesses these ACID properties and has extensive recovery facilities for restoring databases that may have crashed for one reason or another. The SQL standard defines several levels of transaction isolation, as described in the next section.

Transaction Isolation

The *transaction isolation level* is the degree to which the changes made by one transaction are separated from other transactions running concurrently. Before I get into the details of the various transaction isolation levels, I'll describe the types of problems that may occur when current transactions attempt to access the same rows in a table. In the following bullets, I'll use examples of two concurrent transactions that are accessing the same rows to illustrate the three types of potential transaction processing problems:

- **Phantom reads**   Transaction 1 reads a set of rows returned by a specified WHERE clause. Transaction 2 then inserts a new row, which also happens to satisfy the WHERE clause of the query previously used by Transaction 1. Transaction 1 then reads the rows again using the same query but now sees the additional row just inserted by Transaction 2. This new row is known as a *phantom*, because to Transaction 1 this row seems to have magically appeared.

- **Nonrepeatable reads**   Transaction 1 reads a row, and Transaction 2 updates the same row just read by Transaction 1. Transaction 1 then reads the same row again and discovers that the row it read earlier is now different. This is known as a *nonrepeatable* read, because the row originally read by Transaction 1 has been changed.

- **Dirty reads**   Transaction 1 updates a row but doesn't commit the update. Transaction 2 reads the updated row. Transaction 1 then performs a rollback, undoing the previous update. Now the row just read by Transaction 2 is no longer valid (or it's *dirty*) because the update made by Transaction 1 wasn't committed when the row was read by Transaction 2.

To deal with these potential problems, databases implement various levels of transaction isolation to prevent concurrent transactions from interfering with each other. The SQL standard defines the following transaction isolation levels, shown in order of increasing isolation:

- **READ UNCOMMITTED**   Phantom reads, nonrepeatable reads, and dirty reads are permitted.

- **READ COMMITTED**   Phantom reads and nonrepeatable reads are permitted, but dirty reads are not.

- **REPEATABLE READ**   Phantom reads are permitted, but nonrepeatable and dirty reads are not.

- **SERIALIZABLE**   Phantom reads, nonrepeatable reads, and dirty reads are not permitted.

The Oracle database supports the READ COMMITTED and SERIALIZABLE transaction isolation levels; it doesn't support READ UNCOMMITTED or REPEATABLE READ levels.

The default transaction isolation level defined by the SQL standard is SERIALIZABLE, but the default used by the Oracle database is READ COMMITTED, which is acceptable for nearly all applications.

TIP
Although you can use SERIALIZABLE with the Oracle database, it may increase the time your SQL statements take to complete, so you should only use SERILIZABLE if you absolutely have to.

A Worked Example Using JDBC

In this section, I'll show you a worked example that the uses two JDBC `Connection` objects, each of which will run a concurrent transaction. One `Connection` object will use the default transaction isolation level of READ COMMITTED, and the other `Connection` object will use the SERIALIZABLE level. Both transactions will then read the rows in the `products` table, and the READ COMMITTED transaction will add a new row and update an existing row. I'll then show that the SERIALIZABLE transaction doesn't "see" either of these changes.

The following example creates the first `Connection` object, named `rcConnection`, and disables auto-commit:

```
Connection rcConnection = DriverManager.getConnection(
  "jdbc:oracle:thin:@localhost:1521:ORCL",
  "store_user",
  "store_password"
);
rcConnection.setAutoCommit(false);
```

NOTE
When you create a `Connection` or `OracleConnection` object in JDBC, that object will use the default Oracle database transaction isolation level of READ COMMITTED.

A transaction performed using `rcConnection` will have the default transaction isolation level of READ COMMITTED. The following example creates the second `Connection` object, named `serConnection` and disables auto-commit.

```
Connection serConnection = DriverManager.getConnection(
    "jdbc:oracle:thin:@localhost:1521:ORCL",
    "store_user",
    "store_password"
);
serConnection.setAutoCommit(false);
```

You can change the transaction isolation level for a `Connection` or `OracleConnection` object from the default using the `setTransactionIsolation()` method. The following statement sets the transaction isolation level to SERIALIZABLE for `serConnection` using the `setTransactionIsolation()` method:

```
serConnection.setTransactionIsolation(
    oracle.jdbc.OracleConnection.TRANSACTION_SERIALIZABLE
);
```

A transaction performed using `serConnection` will now have a transaction isolation level of SERIALIZABLE. The constants that may be passed to the `setTransactionIsolation()` method are defined in the `oracle.jdbc.OracleConnection` class. As I mentioned earlier, the Oracle database supports two transaction isolation levels: READ COMMITTED and SERIALIZABLE, and the corresponding constants in the `oracle.jdbc.OracleConnection` class for these isolation levels are `TRANSACTION_READ_COMMITTED` and `TRANSACTION_SERIALIZABLE`.

You can get the transaction isolation level setting for a `Connection` or `OracleConnection` object using the `getTransactionIsolation()` method, which returns an `int` value. For example, the following statements display the `int` values for the transaction isolation level setting for `rcConnection` and `serConnection` using the `getTransactionIsolation()` method:

```
System.out.println(rcConnection.getTransactionIsolation());
System.out.println(serConnection.getTransactionIsolation());
```

The next step is to create `Statement` objects from the `Connection` objects (remember, a `Statement` object is used to perform SQL statements). The following example creates two `Statement` objects, named `rcStatement` and `serStatement`, from `rcConnection` and `serConnection` respectively:

```
Statement rcStatement = rcConnection.createStatement();
Statement serStatement = serConnection.createStatement();
```

To display the rows in the `products` table, I'll define a new method named `displayProducts()` that accepts a `Statement` object and then retrieves and

displays the id and name columns from the products table. The
displayProducts() method is defined as follows:

```
private static void displayProducts(
    Statement myStatement
) throws SQLException {

    ResultSet productResultSet = myStatement.executeQuery(
        "SELECT id, name " +
        "FROM products"
    );

    while (productResultSet.next()) {
        System.out.println(
            productResultSet.getInt("id") + "    " +
            productResultSet.getString("name")
        );
    }

    productResultSet.close();

} // end of displayProducts()
```

The following example displays the rows from the products table using the
displayProducts() method, passing the rcStatement and serStatement
objects to this method:

```
displayProducts(rcStatement);
displayProducts(serStatement);
```

At this point, since no changes have yet been made to the products table,
both of these statements will display the same results:

```
1   Modern Science
2   Chemistry
3   Supernova
4   Tank War
5   Z Files
6   2412: The Return
7   Space Force 9
8   From Another Planet
9   Classical Music
10  Pop 3
11  Creative Yell
12  My Front Line
```

Next, I'll add a new row to the `products` table, update product #1's name using `rcStatement`, and commit the two changes:

```
rcStatement.executeUpdate(
  "INSERT INTO products " +
  "(id, type_id, name, description, price) VALUES " +
  "(13, 1, 'JDBC Programming', 'Java programming', 49.99)"
);

rcStatement.executeUpdate(
  "UPDATE products " +
  "SET name = 'New Science' " +
  "WHERE id = 1"
);

rcConnection.commit();
```

Next, I'll call the `displayProducts()` method again using `rcStatement`:

```
displayProducts(rcStatement);
```

This time, the following results will be displayed; notice that the updated name and the new row are displayed:

```
1   New Science
2   Chemistry
3   Supernova
4   Tank War
5   Z Files
6   2412: The Return
7   Space Force 9
8   From Another Planet
9   Classical Music
10  Pop 3
11  Creative Yell
12  My Front Line
13  JDBC Programming
```

If `displayProducts()` is called again using `serStatement`, the original unchanged rows will be displayed: the new row and the updated name won't show up. This is because `serConnection`'s transaction isolation level is set to SERIALIZABLE, and such transactions don't see phantom rows or nonrepeatable reads (nor dirty reads). The new row added by `rcStatement` is considered a phantom row because it was added *after* the rows were read by `serStatement` in the first call to the `displayProducts()` method. The update is considered nonrepeatable because it also occurred *after* the row was read; therefore, neither of the changes is seen by `serStatement`.

Example Program: AdvTransExample1.java

This section shows a complete program containing the statements shown in the previous section.

```
/*
   AdvTransExample1.java illustrates transaction isolation
   and how to set the transaction isolation level to
   TRANSACTION_SERIALIZABLE for a Connection object,
   along with the subsequent effect on a transaction
*/

// import the JDBC packages
import java.sql.*;
import java.io.*;

public class AdvTransExample1 {

  public static void main(String [] args)
  throws SQLException, IOException {

    // register the Oracle JDBC drivers
    DriverManager.registerDriver(
      new oracle.jdbc.OracleDriver()
    );

    // create a Connection object named rcConnection
    Connection rcConnection = DriverManager.getConnection(
      "jdbc:oracle:thin:@localhost:1521:ORCL",
      "store_user",
      "store_password"
    );
    rcConnection.setAutoCommit(false);

    // create a Connection object named serConnection
    Connection serConnection = DriverManager.getConnection(
      "jdbc:oracle:thin:@localhost:1521:ORCL",
      "store_user",
      "store_password"
    );
    serConnection.setAutoCommit(false);

    // set transaction isolation level to TRANSACTION_SERIALIZABLE
    // for serConnection - serConnection will no longer see
```

```java
// phantom rows, non-repeatable reads or dirty reads
System.out.println("Setting transaction isolation level to " +
  "TRANSACTION_SERIALIZABLE for serConnection");
serConnection.setTransactionIsolation(
  oracle.jdbc.OracleConnection.TRANSACTION_SERIALIZABLE
);

// create two Statement objects, named rcStatement and
// serStatement
Statement rcStatement = rcConnection.createStatement();
Statement serStatement = serConnection.createStatement();

// display all products using rcStatement
System.out.println("List of products using rcStatement");
displayProducts(rcStatement);

// display all products using serStatement
System.out.println("List of products using serStatement");
displayProducts(serStatement);

// add product #6 using rcStatement
System.out.println("Adding product #13 " +
  "using rcStatement");
rcStatement.executeUpdate(
  "INSERT INTO products " +
  "(id, type_id, name, description, price) VALUES " +
  "(13, 1, 'JDBC Programming', 'Java programming', 49.99)"
);

// update product #1 using rcStatement
System.out.println("Updating product #1's name to New Science " +
  "using rcStatement");
rcStatement.executeUpdate(
  "UPDATE products " +
  "SET name = 'New Science' " +
  "WHERE id = 1"
);

// commit the changes using rcConnection
System.out.println("Committing changes using rcConnection");
rcConnection.commit();

// display all products using rcStatement
System.out.println("List of products using rcStatement");
displayProducts(rcStatement);

// display all products using serStatement -
// the new product (a phantom row) and the
```

```
      // modified product name (a non-repeatable read)
      // are not visible to serStatement because it has a transaction
      // isolation level of TRANSACTION_SERIALIZABLE
      System.out.println("List of products using serStatement");
      displayProducts(serStatement);

      // delete the new product, change the first product name
      // back to Modern Science, and commit the changes using
      // rcStatement
      rcStatement.executeUpdate(
        "DELETE FROM products " +
        "WHERE id = 13"
      );
      rcStatement.executeUpdate(
        "UPDATE products " +
        "SET name = 'Modern Science' " +
        "WHERE id = 1"
      );
      rcConnection.commit();

      // close the JDBC objects
      rcStatement.close();
      rcConnection.close();
      serStatement.close();
      serConnection.close();

  } // end of main()


  private static void displayProducts(
    Statement myStatement
  ) throws SQLException {

    ResultSet productResultSet = myStatement.executeQuery(
      "SELECT id, name " +
      "FROM products"
    );

    while (productResultSet.next()) {
      System.out.println(
        productResultSet.getInt("id") + "   " +
        productResultSet.getString("name") + " "
      );
    }

    productResultSet.close();

  } // end of displayProducts()

}
```

The output from this program is as follows:

```
Setting transaction isolation level to TRANSACTION_SERIALIZABLE
  for serConnection
List of products using rcStatement
1   Modern Science
2   Chemistry
3   Supernova
4   Tank War
5   Z Files
6   2412: The Return
7   Space Force 9
8   From Another Planet
9   Classical Music
10   Pop 3
11   Creative Yell
12   My Front Line
List of products using serStatement
1   Modern Science
2   Chemistry
3   Supernova
4   Tank War
5   Z Files
6   2412: The Return
7   Space Force 9
8   From Another Planet
9   Classical Music
10   Pop 3
11   Creative Yell
12   My Front Line
Adding product #13 using rcStatement
Updating product #1's name to New Science using rcStatement
Committing changes using rcConnection
List of products using rcStatement
1   New Science
2   Chemistry
3   Supernova
4   Tank War
5   Z Files
6   2412: The Return
7   Space Force 9
8   From Another Planet
9   Classical Music
10   Pop 3
11   Creative Yell
12   My Front Line
13   JDBC Programming
```

```
List of products using serStatement
1   Modern Science
2   Chemistry
3   Supernova
4   Tank War
5   Z Files
6   2412: The Return
7   Space Force 9
8   From Another Planet
9   Classical Music
10  Pop 3
11  Creative Yell
12  My Front Line
```

Distributed Transactions

So far, you've only seen transactions that involve one database. In some cases, however, you may need to write a transaction that involves multiple databases, and you use *distributed transactions* for that purpose. For example, you might be developing a financial system that writes some information to one database and other information to a different database, and both sets of information must be committed or rolled back together.

A distributed transaction allows transactions to be managed across different databases, and you can perform separate SQL statements and then commit or roll back those statements as one unit. The different parts of the distributed transaction are known as *branches*.

The act of committing the distributed transaction requires two phases and is therefore known as a *two-phase commit*. The first phase requires you to prepare each branch of the transaction. Depending on whether the transaction branches report that they are able to commit, the second phase is to commit (or roll back) the transaction.

The JDBC optional package provides a set of interfaces that the Oracle JDBC extensions implement to provide support for distributed transactions, and these are contained in the `javax.transaction.xa` and `oracle.jdbc.xa` packages, respectively.

TIP
Enterprise JavaBeans also supports distributed transactions. For further details, refer to the book Enterprise JavaBeans *by Richard Monson-Haefel (O'Reilly, 2000).*

If you need to write your own program that uses distributed transactions, you may examine the program shown in the next section to see the various steps you need to follow.

Example Program: AdvTransExample2.java

The program `AdvTransExample2.java` illustrates a simple distributed transaction that uses one transaction branch to insert a row into the `products` table in the `store_user` schema and then uses another transaction branch to insert a row into the `purchases` table in the same schema and database. In a real distributed transaction, the transaction branches would typically access different databases, but this example program gives you some basic information on how to use distributed transactions.

NOTE

For further information on the classes used in this program, you can examine the Java documentation for standard JDBC and the Oracle JDBC extensions. Chapter 1 contains information on where you can find this documentation. You can also find additional information on distributed transactions at Sun's Java website at `http://java.sun.com` *and at the Oracle Technology Network website at* `http://otn.oracle.com.`

```
/*
  AdvTransExample2.java shows how to use a
  distributed transaction
*/

// import the required packages
import java.sql.*;
import javax.sql.*;
import javax.transaction.xa.*;
import oracle.jdbc.xa.OracleXid;
import oracle.jdbc.xa.client.*;

public class AdvTransExample2 {

  public static void main(String args [])
  throws SQLException, XAException {

    // register the Oracle JDBC drivers
    DriverManager.registerDriver(
      new oracle.jdbc.OracleDriver()
    );

    // step 1: create two OracleXADataSource objects and set their
    // attributes
    // (one represents the local data source, the other the remote
```

```
// data source, these data sources would typically access
// different databases, but in this example they access the same
// database and schema)
OracleXADataSource myOXADSLocal = new OracleXADataSource();
myOXADSLocal.setURL("jdbc:oracle:thin:@localhost:1521:orcl");
myOXADSLocal.setUser("store_user");
myOXADSLocal.setPassword("store_password");
OracleXADataSource myOXADSRemote = new OracleXADataSource();
myOXADSRemote.setURL("jdbc:oracle:thin:@localhost:1521:orcl");
myOXADSRemote.setUser("store_user");
myOXADSRemote.setPassword("store_password");

// step 2: create two XAConnection objects, these represent
// physical connections to the database
XAConnection myXACLocal = myOXADSLocal.getXAConnection();
XAConnection myXACRemote = myOXADSRemote.getXAConnection();

// step 3: create two Connection objects
Connection myConnLocal = myXACLocal.getConnection();
Connection myConnRemote = myXACRemote.getConnection();

// step 4: create two XAResource objects, these manage
// the two transaction branches
XAResource myXARLocal = myXACLocal.getXAResource();
XAResource myXARRemote = myXACRemote.getXAResource();

// step 5: create the global transaction id to identify
// the distributed transaction
byte [] gid = new byte[64];
gid[0] = (byte) 1;

// step 6: create two branch qualifier ids, these identify
// the different transaction branches
byte [] bqidLocal = new byte[64];
bqidLocal[0] = (byte) 1;
byte[] bqidRemote = new byte[64];
bqidRemote[0] = (byte) 2;

// step 7: create two Xids, these are the transaction
// branch ids
Xid myXidLocal = new OracleXid(0x1234, gid, bqidLocal);
Xid myXidRemote = new OracleXid(0x1234, gid, bqidRemote);

// step 8: start the two transaction branches that make up the
// distributed transaction by calling the XARResource object's
// start() method
myXARLocal.start(myXidLocal, XAResource.TMNOFLAGS);
myXARRemote.start(myXidRemote, XAResource.TMNOFLAGS);
```

```java
// step 9: perform the SQL statements for each transaction branch
Statement myStatement = myConnLocal.createStatement();
myStatement.executeUpdate(
  "INSERT INTO products " +
  "(id, type_id, name, description, price) VALUES " +
  "(13, 1, 'JDBC Programming', 'Java programming', 49.99)");
myStatement = myConnRemote.createStatement();
myStatement.executeUpdate(
  "INSERT INTO purchases " +
  "(product_id, purchased_by, quantity) VALUES " +
  "(13, 1, 1)");

// step 10: end the two transaction branches that make up the
// distributed transaction by calling the XARResource object's
// end() method
myXARRemote.end(myXidRemote, XAResource.TMSUCCESS);
myXARLocal.end(myXidLocal, XAResource.TMSUCCESS);

// step 11: prepare the two transaction branches (phase 1 of the
// two-phase commit) by calling the XARResouce object's
/// prepare() method
int resultLocal = myXARLocal.prepare(myXidLocal);
int resultRemote = myXARRemote.prepare(myXidRemote);

// step 12: check the results of the prepare phase
boolean doCommit = true;
if (!((resultLocal == XAResource.XA_OK) ||
      (resultLocal == XAResource.XA_RDONLY))) {
  doCommit = false;
}
if (!((resultRemote == XAResource.XA_OK) ||
      (resultRemote == XAResource.XA_RDONLY))) {
  doCommit = false;
}

// step 13: either do the commit or rollback (phase 2 of
// the two-phase commit)
if (resultLocal == XAResource.XA_OK) {
  if (doCommit) {
    System.out.println("Performing local commit");
    myXARLocal.commit(myXidLocal, false);
  } else {
    System.out.println("Performing local rollback");
    myXARLocal.rollback(myXidLocal);
  }
}
if (resultRemote == XAResource.XA_OK) {
  if (doCommit) {
```

```
        System.out.println("Performing remote commit");
        myXARRemote.commit(myXidRemote, false);
      } else {
        System.out.println("Performing remote rollback");
        myXARRemote.rollback(myXidRemote);
      }
    }

    // step 14: close the JDBC objects
    myConnLocal.close();
    myConnRemote.close();
    myXACLocal.close();
    myXACRemote.close();
    myStatement.close();

  } // end of main()

}
```

PART
III

Deploying Java

CHAPTER
10

Java Stored
Procedures and
Triggers

he Oracle9*i* and 8*i* databases come with an integrated Java Virtual Machine known as the *Oracle JVM*. The Oracle JVM allows you to deploy and run Java programs from within the database, with such programs being known in official Oracle parlance as *Java stored procedures.*

You can also deploy and run Java stored functions, which are similar to procedures, except that functions must return a value. I will refer to Java stored procedures and functions in the rest of this chapter collectively as *Java stored programs*, so as not to confuse between procedures and functions.

Java stored programs provide an alternative to writing your business logic in PL/SQL. PL/SQL is an Oracle proprietary language, whereas Java is a language adopted by many software vendors and follows an open standard. The advent of Java stored programs means you can use Java as your primary coding language, even within the database. Although, as you will see shortly, you still have to use a small amount of PL/SQL to make your Java stored programs available within the database.

In this chapter, I'll outline the architecture of the Oracle JVM and show you how to write, deploy, and run Java stored programs in the database. These programs will access the database using JDBC. I'll show you how to use both the command-line tools and JDeveloper to deploy Java stored programs.

I'll also introduce you to database triggers, which enable you to write code that is run automatically by the database when a certain event occurs, for example, before a SQL UPDATE on a specific column is performed.

For this chapter, I've written another SQL*Plus script, jvm_examples.sql, which you or your DBA will need to run if you want to follow along with the examples and programs examples in this chapter. This script adds a number of database items to the store_user schema that will be used to illustrate the use of the Oracle JVM.

The Oracle JVM Architecture

The Oracle JVM is a complete Java Virtual Machine that conforms to the Java 2 Standard Edition (J2SE). The Oracle JVM is intended to run Java stored programs and runs in the same process and memory space as the database. This gives the Oracle JVM a great performance boost when running your Java stored programs because the Oracle JVM shares the same memory heaps and data structures as those used in the database.

The executable code of a Java stored program is also automatically cached in memory and may be shared among multiple database users. This reduces the overall memory requirements for a given application.

As an additional performance boost, Oracle delivers the standard Java class libraries and the JDBC drivers precompiled as native binary code. Native code runs up to ten times faster than Java bytecodes (bytecodes are the usual format for Java classes and are produced when you compile a Java source file).

NOTE
You can also precompile your own classes using the ncomp command-line tool, described in Appendix B; ncomp was introduced in Oracle8i (8.1.7).

One thing to keep in mind is that the Oracle JVM is designed to run back-end programs. It cannot be used to run graphical programs like applets directly because it doesn't come with any graphical Java components.

NOTE
You can run Java 2 Enterprise Edition (J2EE) components using Oracle9iAS Containers for J2EE (OC4J). OC4J allows you to run components like Enterprise JavaBeans (EJB), servlets, and JavaServer Pages (JSP). You can then use JDBC within these components to access the database. Generally, J2EE components are deployed in the middle tier of your system. I'll talk more about OC4J in the next chapter.

The Oracle JVM consists of the following major software subsystems that make up its high-level architecture:

- **RDBMS library manager**   Loads Java source, class, and resource files into the database as a result of running the `loadjava` command-line tool. As you'll see shortly, the `loadjava` tool is used to load Java files into the database.

- **RDBMS memory manager**   Allocates memory as Java programs are run.

- **Compiler**   Compiles the Java source files into Java classes (these classes contain bytecodes that the Oracle JVM is able to run).

- **Bytecode interpreter and runtime system**   The bytecode interpreter reads the bytecodes from the Java classes, which are then run by the runtime system.

- **Class loader**   As Java stored programs are run, the runtime system makes requests to the class loader to load the required Java classes. The class loader then finds and loads the Java classes into the Oracle JVM.

- **Verifier**   Checks the Java classes to ensure that they don't attempt to alter program flow or violate Java's access restrictions. This protects the Oracle JVM from "spoofed" Java classes and ensures the security of the system.

- **Garbage collector**   Removes Java objects from memory when they are no longer needed. This memory cleanup is performed on a regular basis, which means that your Java objects may not be removed as soon as they are closed: they will stay in memory until the garbage collector runs.

This information is provided as background information for your understanding; you don't need to know the details of the Oracle JVM to use it.

Features of Java Stored Programs

So far in this book, I've only showed you standalone Java applications that have used the JDBC Thin driver to access the database. Java stored programs use either the JDBC server-side internal driver or the server-side Thin driver to communicate with a database. The server-side internal driver is used to communicate with the local database, this is the same database that the Java stored program is deployed to. The server-side Thin driver may be used to communicate with a remote database.

As you might expect, there are a number of features that are unique to Java stored programs, and I've summarized these features in the following bullets:

- The JDBC server-side internal driver uses a built-in default connection to the local database. This means that a Java stored program doesn't create a new connection to the local database because a connection is already provided through the server-side internal driver. I'll discuss this point in more detail in the following section, "Using the Default Database Connection."

- The database connection through the server-side internal driver is permanent, and you cannot close the connection from a Java stored program. If you close the `Connection` object used by a Java stored program using the `close()` method, you don't actually close the default database connection, but you will need to call `getConnection()` again prior to accessing the database.

- The server-side internal driver doesn't allow auto-commit functionality. This means you have to perform a commit or rollback in your Java stored program; you should perform this commit (or rollback) outside of your Java stored program. By not having the Java stored program do the commit, you are free to perform the commit (or rollback) as part of the transaction to which a call to the Java stored program forms a part. You'll see an example of this later.

- The Java class for your Java stored program doesn't need a `main()` method.

- The output from calls to the Java `System.out.println()` method that would normally display output on the screen is sent to a database trace file by default. This is because the Oracle JVM doesn't have direct access to the screen. Fortunately, you can route such output to the screen of the client computer.

The first and last points require some additional explanation.

Using the Default Database Connection

Even though a default connection to the local database is provided through the server-side internal driver, your Java methods must still call the `getConnection()` method, but you don't specify a database user name and password. As I'll discuss later, the Java method will use either the database privileges of the user who invokes the Java stored program, or the privileges of the user who creates the Java stored program.

To use the default database connection, your Java method must call the `getConnection()` method and store the returned `Connection` object, as shown in the following example:

```
Connection myConnection = DriverManager.getConnection(
  "jdbc:default:connection"
);
```

Subsequent JDBC statements in your Java method can then use this `Connection` object to access the database.

Output

The database *trace files* contain log messages produced by the Oracle database software as it runs. These messages include things like the date and time the database was started and stopped. These trace files are located in a directory specified in the database's `init.ora` file, which sets various parameters used by the Oracle database software. This file is normally only read and normally only modified by the DBA.

You can usually find the `init.ora` file for your database in a subdirectory of the `admin` directory where the Oracle database software is installed—on my development machine, the `init.ora` file for the database with the SID of `ORCL` is located in the directory `E:\Oracle\admin\ORCL\pfile`.

The parameter that sets the directory for the trace files is called `user_dump_dest`, and on my machine, the setting for `user_dump_dest` in my `init.ora` file is as follows:

```
user_dump_dest = E:\Oracle\admin\ORCL\udump
```

This means that the trace files for the database are contained in the directory E:\Oracle\admin\ORCL\udump. The init.ora file also specifies the maximum length of a trace file in bytes using the parameter max_dump_file_size; in my init.ora file it is set to:

```
max_dump_file_size = 10240
```

This means that the maximum size for each trace file is 10,240 bytes. When the file reaches this length, it is closed and a new one is opened. Generally, if your database has been running for a long period of time, the user_dump_dest directory will contain quite a few trace files. To view the latest messages produced by the database software, you should look at the trace file with the newest data and time stamp—this trace file is known as the *current* trace file.

You can also get the settings for user_dump_dest and max_dump_file_size using the SQL*Plus command SHOW PARAMETER, followed by the parameter name. You must connect to the database as the system user (which has a default password of "manager") to do this. The following example shows the use of the SHOW PARAMETER command:

```
SQL> SHOW PARAMETER user_dump_dest

NAME                                 TYPE    VALUE
------------------------------------ ------- ------------------------------
user_dump_dest                       string  E:\Oracle\admin\ORCL\udump

SQL> SHOW PARAMETER max_dump_file_size

NAME                                 TYPE    VALUE
------------------------------------ ------- ------------------------------
max_dump_file_size                   string  10240
```

Getting back to the issue of where output is sent, if a Java stored program calls the System.out.println() method, by default its output will be sent to the current database trace file. You'll see this shortly in an example.

If you are running your Java stored program through SQL*Plus, you can set up a buffer using the PL/SQL procedure dbms_java.set_output(). This buffer can accept output from your Java stored program's calls to System.out.println(), and you can display the contents of the buffer using SQL*Plus.

NOTE
You can also use the PL/SQL dbms_output.enable() procedure, which creates a buffer that accepts output from calls to the PL/SQL dbms_output.put_line() procedure, which may also be used to display output.

The `dbms_java.set_output()` procedure (and the `dbms_output.enable()` procedure) accepts an integer parameter that specifies the size of the buffer in bytes. For example, let's say you wanted a buffer that is 2,000 bytes in size, then you would use the following PL/SQL call to set it up:

```
call dbms_java.set_ouput(2000);
```

The following JDBC statement does the same thing:

cool way :-) + turn on

```
CallableStatement myCallableStatement = myConnection.prepareCall(
    "{call dbms_java.set_ouput(2000)}"
);
```

CAUTION
It is important that you make your buffer large enough to accept all the output you think you'll need for your Java stored program because once your buffer is full, any further output will be lost.

Once you've set up your buffer, all output from calls to `System.out.println()` will be sent to the buffer instead of the trace file. To view the contents of the buffer in SQL*Plus, you must first enter the command SET SERVEROUTPUT ON. When your Java stored program has finished running, the output that has been buffered is displayed on the screen.

Now that I've described the issues associated with Java stored programs, I'll take you through a worked example.

A Worked Example

In this section, I'll show you an example Java source file, `JvmExample1.java`, which illustrates how to use the default database connection, set up output buffers, and perform other database operations. The file `JvmExample1.java` defines a class named `JvmExample1` that contains five methods (four procedures and one function). You will later load this class into the database and run the methods using the Oracle JVM. These five methods are as follows:

- **displayMessageInTraceFile()** Calls `System.out.println()` to show that, by default, output goes to the current database trace file.

- **displayMessageOnScreen()** Calls `dbms_java.set_output()` to set up a buffer and then calls `System.out.println()` to show that output has been routed to the buffer. It also calls `dbms_output.enable()` and `dbms_output.put_line()` to show that output from PL/SQL can also be routed to the buffer. The buffer contents are subsequently displayed on the screen.

■ **displayProduct()** Displays the column values for a row in the `products` table. The `id` column for that row is specified by a parameter. It then sets up a buffer using `dbms_java.set_ouput()`, retrieves the column values for the specified row, and finally, writes the column values to the buffer.

■ **addProduct()** Adds a row to the `products` table, with the values for the `type_id`, `name`, `description`, and `price` columns being passed as parameters. The value for the new row's `id` column is generated by first retrieving the highest `id` value from the `products` table using the SQL `MAX()` function, and then adding 1 to that number. The procedure then adds the new row using an `INSERT` statement. This procedure intentionally does not perform a commit; this way, you are free to perform the commit (or rollback) as part of a transaction of which a call to the Java stored program forms a part.

■ **countProducts()** Counts the number of rows in the `products` table using the SQL `COUNT()` function and then returns the result.

The following listing shows `JvmExample1.java`:

```
/*
    JvmExample1.java contains methods that are designed
    to run in the Oracle JVM.
*/

// import the JDBC packages
import java.sql.*;

public class JvmExample1 {

  public static void displayMessageInTraceFile()
  throws SQLException {

    // the following line writes output to the database trace file
    System.out.println("Output from displayMessageInTraceFile() " +
      "appears in the current database trace file");

  }


  public static void displayMessageOnScreen()
  throws SQLException {
```

```java
  // create a Connection object, and use the default
  // database connection provided by the JDBC server-side
  // internal driver
  Connection myConnection = DriverManager.getConnection(
    "jdbc:default:connection"
  );

  // create a Statement object
  Statement myStatement = myConnection.createStatement();

  // call dbms_java.set_output(2000) to
  // set up an output buffer of 2000 bytes, this causes
  // output from System.out.println() calls to be routed
  // to this buffer
  myStatement.execute(
    "{call dbms_java.set_output(2000)}"
  );

  // the following output is displayed on the screen
  System.out.println("Output from displayMessageOnScreen() " +
    "appears on the screen");

  // call dbms_output.enable(2000) to
  // set up an output buffer of 2000 bytes
  myStatement.execute(
    "{call dbms_output.enable(2000)}"
  );

  // call dbms_output.put_line()
  // to write the output to this buffer
  myStatement.execute(
    "{call dbms_output.put_line(" +
    "'Displayed on the screen from dbms_output.put_line()'" +
    ")}"
  );

  // close the Statement and Connection objects
  myStatement.close();
  myConnection.close();

}


public static void displayProduct(
  int id
) throws SQLException {

  // create a Connection object
```

```
    Connection myConnection = DriverManager.getConnection(
      "jdbc:default:connection"
    );

    // create a Statement object
    Statement myStatement = myConnection.createStatement();

    // set up an output buffer
    myStatement.execute(
      "{call dbms_java.set_output(2000)}"
    );

    // retrieve the column values for the specified product
    ResultSet productResultSet = myStatement.executeQuery(
      "SELECT type_id, name, description, price " +
      "FROM products " +
      "WHERE id = " + id
    );

    // display the column values
    productResultSet.next();
    System.out.println("type_id = " +
      productResultSet.getString("type_id"));
    System.out.println("name = " +
      productResultSet.getString("name"));
    System.out.println("description = " +
      productResultSet.getString("description"));
    System.out.println("price = " +
      productResultSet.getString("price"));
    productResultSet.close();

    // close the Statement and Connection objects
    myStatement.close();
    myConnection.close();

  }


  public static void addProduct(
    int type_id,
    String name,
    String description,
    double price
  )
  throws SQLException {

    // create a Connection object
    Connection myConnection = DriverManager.getConnection(
      "jdbc:default:connection"
```

```java
  );

  // create a Statement object
  Statement myStatement = myConnection.createStatement();

  // set up an output buffer
  myStatement.execute(
    "{call dbms_java.set_output(2000)}"
  );

  // retrieve the maximum product id using the SQL MAX() function
  ResultSet productResultSet = myStatement.executeQuery(
    "SELECT MAX(id) " +
    "FROM products"
  );
  productResultSet.next();
  int maxId = productResultSet.getInt(1);
  productResultSet.close();

  // add 1 to the maximum id to generate the id for the new row
  int id = maxId + 1;

  // perform SQL INSERT statement to add a new row to the
  // products table
  myStatement.executeUpdate(
    "INSERT INTO products " +
    "(id, type_id, name, description, price) VALUES (" +
    id + ", " + type_id + ", '" + name +
    "', '" + description + "', " + price + ")"
  );
  System.out.println("Added new product with an id of " + id);

  // close the Statement and Connection objects
  myStatement.close();
  myConnection.close();

}


public static int countProducts()
throws SQLException {

  int numberOfProducts = 0;

  // create a Connection object
  Connection myConnection = DriverManager.getConnection(
    "jdbc:default:connection"
  );
```

```
  // create a Statement object
  Statement myStatement = myConnection.createStatement();

  // set up an output buffer
  myStatement.execute(
    "{call dbms_java.set_output(2000)}"
  );

  // retrieve the number of products using the SQL COUNT() function
  ResultSet productResultSet = myStatement.executeQuery(
    "SELECT COUNT(*) " +
    "FROM products"
  );
  productResultSet.next();
  numberOfProducts = productResultSet.getInt(1);
  productResultSet.close();

  System.out.println("There are " + numberOfProducts + " products");

  // close the Statement and Connection objects
  myStatement.close();
  myConnection.close();

  return numberOfProducts;

  }

}
```

You can develop and compile your own Java classes using JDeveloper, or you can use a text editor and compile the Java source file using the `javac` command-line tool. Before you can run these methods using the Oracle JVM, you must first perform the following three steps:

1. Compile the Java source file to produce a class file using either the `javac` command-line tool or JDeveloper.

2. Load the class file into the database using either the `loadjava` command-line tool or JDeveloper.

3. Publish the Java methods using PL/SQL, which involves creating a PL/SQL procedure or function (known as a *call specification* or simply a *call spec*) for each method in your Java class that you want to make available to the database (you can also create a PL/SQL package to group these PL/SQL procedures and functions together in one unit). You can create a SQL*Plus script to create your PL/SQL procedures and functions (and packages), or you can use JDeveloper.

NOTE
The call spec is also sometimes referred to as a wrapper because it "wraps around" your Java method.

After you've published your Java methods, you can then invoke the call specs for those methods using SQL*Plus, PL/SQL, or Java. When you invoke a call spec, it causes the underlying Java method referenced by that call spec to be run by the Oracle JVM.

In the following sections, I'll go through each of the previous steps in detail using the command-line tools to compile, load, and publish the five Java methods defined in the JvmExample1.java source file. Later in this chapter, I'll show you how to use JDeveloper to accomplish the same tasks for just one of these Java methods.

Step 1: Compile the Java Source File
The first step is to compile your Java source file. The following command compiles the JvmExample1.java source file using the javac command-line tool:

```
javac JvmExample1.java
```

This compiles JvmExample1.java and produces a class file named JvmExample1.class.

Step 2: Load the Class File into the Database
The second step is to load the class file produced in Step 1 into the database. You can do this using the loadjava command-line tool. The loadjava tool has many options, which are documented in Appendix B, of which I'll demonstrate the most used ones here.

The following example loads JvmExample1.class into the store_user schema:

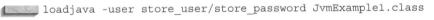
```
loadjava -user store_user/store_password JvmExample1.class
```

As you can see, the database user name and password are specified using the -user option. This creates a Java class object for the JvmExample1 class in the store_user schema.

NOTE
A Java class object is a structure used by the database to represent the Java class and is not to be confused with a Java object, which is an instance of the Java class.

By default, loadjava uses the JDBC OCI driver to communicate with the database when loading Java classes.

Checking That the Java Class was Loaded Successfully into the Database
You can check that the Java class was successfully loaded into the database schema by performing the following query using SQL*Plus (after connecting to the database as the same user you used to load the Java class):

```
SELECT object_name, object_type
FROM user_objects
WHERE object_type = 'JAVA CLASS';
```

The user_objects view contains a list of the objects owned by that user, and using the clause WHERE object_type = 'JAVA CLASS' will show the Java class objects owned by that user. If you run this query while connected as store_user using SQL*Plus, the output should be as follows:

```
OBJECT_NAME
------------------
OBJECT_TYPE
------------------
JvmExample1
JAVA CLASS
```

This shows that the JvmExample1 class was loaded successfully into the database schema.

Loading Packaged Java Classes   Java classes can also be part of a Java *package*, which allows you to group your classes together, much like you can group PL/SQL procedures and functions together into packages. For example, say you had a class named MyClass that is part of a Java package named MyPackage—this gives a fully qualified name of MyPackage.MyClass for that class. If you load that class into the database, the dots (.) that separate the package and class name are replaced by forward slashes (/) in the resulting database Java class name. For example, MyPackage.MyClass would become MyPackage/MyClass when loaded into the database.

If the package and class name in your Java source file exceeds 30 characters or contains characters that can't be converted to a character in the character set used by the database, then a short name for the class is automatically produced by the database to identify the Java class in the schema.

Loading Multiple Java Classes   If you have more than one class to load, you can load those classes together using loadjava. For example, if you had two class files named `MyClass1.class` and `MyClass2.class`, the following command would identify those two class files using a wildcard asterisk character (*) in place of the number:

```
loadjava -user store_user/store_password MyClass*.class
```

You could also create a Java Archive (JAR) file and then load that JAR file using `loadjava`. A JAR file may contain many class files, and you can create a JAR file using the `jar` command-line tool. The following example shows the use of the `jar` tool to create a JAR file that contains the `MyClass1.class` and `MyClass2.class` files:

```
jar -cf MyJarFile.jar MyClass*.class
```

The `-c` option specifies that the class files are to be compressed, and the `-f` option allows you to specify the file name for the JAR file. In this example, the JAR file is named `MyJarFile.jar`.

CAUTION
If you are using a version of the database older than 8.1.6, you cannot use compressed JAR files: you can only use noncompressed JAR files, which you can create using the -0 (dash-zero) option to prevent file compression of the files by the `jar` tool.

You can then load the JAR file into the database using `loadjava`, for example:

```
loadjava -user store_user/store_password MyJarFile.jar
```

Loading Java Classes into a Remote Database   The previous examples assumed you were loading class files into a database running on the same machine that `loadjava` is running on. If your database is running on a remote machine accessible through Oracle Net, you have to specify the location of that database when running `loadjava`. The database location may be specified using a database URL (I covered database URLs in Chapter 3). The following is an example of a database URL: `remotehost:1521:ORCL`. The machine is identified as `remotehost`, with an Oracle Net listener assumed to be waiting for connection requests on port 1521 for the database with a System Identifier (SID) of `ORCL`.

You can also specify that JDBC driver is used by `loadjava` when communicating with the database: `-thin` for the Thin driver, `-oci` for the OCI driver (the OCI driver is the default one used). The following example uses

loadjava to load JvmExample1.class into the database located at the URL
remotehost:1521:ORCL, using the JDBC Thin driver:

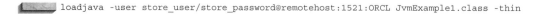

```
loadjava -user store_user/store_password@remotehost:1521:ORCL JvmExample1.class -thin
```

NOTE
*You can use the machine name localhost in
a database URL to identify your local machine.*

If you need to replace a Java class, you can just load the class again using
loadjava.

Dropping Java Classes from the Database   Should you need to, you can
remove Java classes from the database using the dropjava command-line tool. The
dropjava tool has a similar set of options as the loadjava tool, and those options are
documented in Appendix B. The following example uses dropjava to drop the Java
class JvmExample1 that was previously loaded from the JvmExample1.class file:

```
dropjava -user store_user/store_password JvmExample1.class
```

You can also drop Java classes from a remote database, for example:

```
dropjava -user store_user/store_password@remotehost:1521:ORCL JvmExample1.class -thin
```

You can verify that the Java class has indeed been dropped from the database by
repeating the query previously used to verify that the class was loaded.

If you loaded a JAR file, you should specify that JAR file when using dropjava.
For example, say you had loaded classes from a JAR file named MyJarFile.jar—
you would use the following command to drop those classes:

```
dropjava -user store_user/store_password MyJarFile.jar
```

Step 3: Publish the Java Methods Using PL/SQL

Once you've loaded your Java class, the next step is to publish the methods contained
in that class that you want to make available for execution. You'll generally want to
write call specs for all the public static Java methods in your class, these are the
methods that are available to the users of your class.

You publish your Java methods by creating procedures and functions using
PL/SQL. As I mentioned earlier, these PL/SQL procedures and functions are referred
to as *call specifications* or *call specs,* and you use these call specs to invoke your Java
methods. They are also sometimes referred to as *wrappers.*

You can also group your call specs into PL/SQL packages. This allows you to group the call specs for your Java class methods together in one place, and it can make maintenance easier. I'll show you how to group call specs into PL/SQL packages later in this chapter.

Way back in Chapter 2, I showed you how to create PL/SQL procedures and functions; the syntax for creating call specs is similar. You use the PL/SQL `CREATE PROCEDURE` statement to create a call spec for a Java procedure in your class, and you use the PL/SQL `CREATE FUNCTION` statement to create a call spec for a Java function. The syntax for creating a call spec using a `CREATE PROCEDURE` or `CREATE FUNCTION` statement is as follows:

```
CREATE [OR REPLACE] {
    PROCEDURE procedure_name [(parameter[, parameter ...])]
  | FUNCTION function_name [(parameter[, parameter ...])] RETURN plsql_type
}
[AUTHID {DEFINER |CURRENT_USER}]
[PARALLEL_ENABLE]
[DETERMINISTIC]
{IS | AS} LANGUAGE JAVA
NAME
  'java_class_object.java_method(java_type[, java_type ...])
    [return java_type ]';
```

Where `parameter` has the following syntax:

```
parameter_name [IN |OUT | IN OUT] plsql_type2
```

The syntax elements and options are as follows:

- **procedure_name/function_name**   The name that you want to assign to the call spec.

- **plsql_type**   The PL/SQL type of the value returned by the call spec. Only a Java function returns a value, therefore this is only used when the call spec is for a Java function. This PL/SQL type must be compatible with the Java type returned by the Java function. I'll talk more about this shortly.

- **AUTHID {DEFINER | CURRENT_USER}**   Indicates whether you want the Java procedure or function to run with the database privileges of the user in whose schema the Java class object is located (the `DEFINER`), or the database privileges of the user who invokes the call spec (the `CURRENT_USER`); `CURRENT_USER` is the default. You cannot override the `loadjava` option `-definer` by using `CURRENT_USER`.

- **PARALLEL_ENABLE**   Parallel DML can improve performance of DML statements by creating multiple processes to handle the operation; the

PARALLEL_ENABLE option indicates that the Java function can be used in the slave sessions of parallel DML evaluations.

- **DETERMINISTIC** A deterministic function is one whose returned result is only dependent on the values that are passed to it—the *sin(x)* function is one such example, because the value returned is only dependent on the input value *x*. The DETERMINISTIC option instructs the database to avoid calling the Java function twice if the same input value (or values) is used. If the input values are the same, the same result is returned again but without calling the function again. This can improve performance.

- **LANGUAGE JAVA** Indicates that the method is written in Java.

- **NAME clause** This string contains the name of the Java class object stored in the database schema (java_class_object), the name of the Java method (java_method), and the Java types of the parameters used by the method (java_type).

- **parameter_name** Specifies the name of a parameter for the call spec. The parameters are routed to the Java method when the call spec is invoked.

- **IN | OUT | IN OUT** Specifies the mode for the parameter. There are three parameter modes:

  - **IN** The default mode for a parameter. This mode is specified for parameters that already have a value when the call spec is invoked, and that value may not be changed. This is the default.

  - **OUT** Specified for parameters whose values are only set.

  - **IN OUT** Specified for parameters that may already have a value when the call spec is invoked, but their value may also be changed.

- **plsql_type2** The PL/SQL type of the parameter for a call spec. The PL/SQL type must be compatible with the Java type used by the Java method.

The best way to learn how to write call specs is to take a look at some examples, and in the following sections I'll show you how to write call specs for the Java methods in the JvmExample1 class. These methods consist of the four procedures displayMessageInTraceFile(), displayMessageOnScreen(), addProduct(), and displayProduct(), along with the function countProducts(). At the end of this section, I'll show you how to write a call spec for a Java method that modifies a parameter value.

Publishing and Calling the displayMessageInTraceFile() Procedure   The displayMessageInTraceFile() procedure calls System.out.println() to show that, by default, output goes to the current database trace file. When writing a call spec, you need to examine the Java method's header, which shows the name of the method and the parameters. The header for `displayMessageInTraceFile()` is as follows:

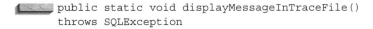

```
public static void displayMessageInTraceFile()
throws SQLException
```

Because `displayMessageInTraceFile()` doesn't use any parameters, the call spec for it is fairly simple, and since it is a Java procedure, the PL/SQL CREATE PROCEDURE statement is used to create the call spec:

```
CREATE OR REPLACE PROCEDURE display_message_in_trace_file
AS
LANGUAGE JAVA
NAME 'JvmExample1.displayMessageInTraceFile()';
/
```

NOTE
You don't have to type in this statement (or any of the other statements that create the call specs in this chapter). They are contained in the `jvm_examples.sql` *script, which you should have already run.*

There are three things to notice about this statement:

- **I've used CREATE OR REPLACE PROCEDURE**   This will replace the current procedure definition if it already exists.

- **I've named the PL/SQL procedure display_message_in_trace_file, rather than displayMessageInTraceFile**   This is because PL/SQL, like SQL, is not case sensitive. In PL/SQL and SQL, the accepted standard for splitting up multiple words is to use underscore characters (_) between the words.

- **The Java class name and the method name are used in the NAME clause of the CREATE PROCEDURE statement**   In this example, the class name is `JvmExample1` and the method name is `displayMessageInTraceFile()`, so `'JvmExample1. displayMessageInTraceFile()'` is used in the NAME clause.

Once the call spec is created, you can call the resulting PL/SQL procedure using SQL*Plus, as shown in the following example (assuming you are connected to the database as `store_user`):

```
SQL> call display_message_in_trace_file();

Call completed.
```

That's it! You have successfully deployed and run a Java stored procedure.

CAUTION
If you reload a method in a Java class using `loadjava` and then attempt to invoke the PL/SQL call spec for that method again, you may get the database error `ORA-29549`, stating that the class has changed and the Java session state is cleared. This error sounds a lot worse than it really is—all you have to do is invoke the call spec again and it will run properly.

When you call the PL/SQL procedure `display_message_in_trace_file()`, it causes the Java procedure `displayMessageInTraceFile()` to be run. As I mentioned earlier, the output from this procedure is sent to the current database trace file, so you should locate that file using the instructions I gave earlier and open that file. Your database trace file should contain a line near the end similar to the following:

```
Output from displayMessageInTraceFile() appears in the
 current database trace file
```

This is the output from the procedure.

Publishing and Calling the displayMessageOnScreen() Procedure The `displayMessageOnScreen()` procedure calls `dbms_java.set_output()` to set up a buffer and then calls `System.out.println()` to show that output has been routed to the buffer. It also calls `dbms_output.enable()` and `dbms_output.put_line()` to show that output from PL/SQL can also be routed to the buffer.

The header for the `displayMessageOnScreen()` procedure is as follows:

```
public static void displayMessageOnScreen()
throws SQLException
```

So the call spec is:

```
CREATE OR REPLACE PROCEDURE display_message_on_screen
AS
LANGUAGE JAVA
NAME 'JvmExample1.displayMessageOnScreen()';
/
```

To view the output that is sent to the buffers by displayMessageOnScreen(), you must first run the SQL*Plus command SET SERVEROUTPUT ON, as shown in the following example, which also calls the PL/SQL procedure display_message_on_screen():

```
SQL> SET SERVEROUTPUT ON
SQL> call display_message_on_screen();
Output from displayMessageOnScreen() appears on the screen
Displayed on the screen from dbms_output.put_line()

Call completed.
```

As you can see, this example displays the contents of the output buffer on the screen.

Publishing and Calling the displayProduct() Procedure   The displayProduct() procedure displays the column values for a row in the products table whose id is specified by a parameter. It then sets up a buffer using dbms_java.set_ouput(), retrieves the column values for that row, and finally writes the column values to the buffer.

The header for displayProduct() is as follows:

```
public static void displayProduct(
    int id
) throws SQLException
```

Notice that it uses a single int parameter named id. This is the id for the row in the products table that is to be displayed. The call spec must provide a PL/SQL parameter that is compatible with a Java int, and this is the PL/SQL NUMBER type.

CAUTION
You cannot use a subtype for a PL/SQL parameter.
So, in this example, you cannot use INTEGER (a
subtype of NUMBER): you have to use NUMBER.

The call spec for `displayProduct()` is:

```
CREATE OR REPLACE PROCEDURE display_product(
    id NUMBER
) AS
LANGUAGE JAVA
NAME 'JvmExample1.displayProduct(int)';
/
```

The following example uses SQL*Plus to call `display_product()`:

```
SQL> call display_product(12);
type_id = null
name = My Front Line
description = Their greatest hits
price = 13.49

Call completed.
```

As you can see, the column values for product #12 are displayed.

Publishing and Calling the addProduct() Procedure   The `addProduct()` procedure adds a row to the `products` table, with the values for the `type_id`, `name`, `description`, and `price` columns being passed as parameters. The value for the new row's id column is generated by first retrieving the highest `id` value from the `products` table using the SQL `MAX()` function, and then adding 1 to that number. The procedure then adds the new row using an `INSERT` statement.

The header for `addProduct()` is as follows:

```
public static void addProduct(
    int type_id,
    String name,
    String description,
    double price
)
throws SQLException
```

Therefore, two PL/SQL `NUMBER` parameters are required for the `int type_id` and `double price` Java parameters, and two PL/SQL `VARCHAR2` parameters are required for the `name` and `description` Java `String` parameters. These are shown in the following call spec:

```
CREATE OR REPLACE PROCEDURE add_product(
    type_id    NUMBER,
    name       VARCHAR2,
```

```
  description VARCHAR2,
  price       NUMBER
) AS
LANGUAGE JAVA
NAME 'JvmExample1.addProduct(int, java.lang.String, java.lang.String, double)';
/
```

The following example uses SQL*Plus to call add_product() to add a row to the products table:

```
SQL> call add_product(1, 'Classic Cars', 'Cars from the 1970s', 19.95);
Added new product with an id of 13

Call completed.
```

Notice that the id for the product was not supplied: it is generated automatically by the Java addProduct() procedure, which also displays that id.

NOTE
*The underlying Java method addProduct ()
doesn't perform a commit—this is intentional. By
not having the Java method do a commit, you are
free to perform the commit (or rollback) as part of
a transaction of which the call to the Java stored
program forms a part.*

To commit the row added by the previous statement, you perform a COMMIT in SQL*Plus:

```
SQL> COMMIT;

Commit complete.
```

Publishing and Calling the countProducts() Function   The countProducts() function counts the number of rows in the products table using the SQL COUNT() function and then returns the result.
    The header for countProducts() is as follows:

```
public static int countProducts()
throws SQLException
```

Because countProducts() is a Java function, the call spec is created using the PL/SQL CREATE FUNCTION statement. Also, since countProducts() returns a Java int value, the call spec must specify that a PL/SQL NUMBER value is returned:

```
CREATE OR REPLACE FUNCTION count_products
RETURN NUMBER AS
LANGUAGE JAVA
NAME 'JvmExample1.countProducts() return int';
/
```

To call a function in SQL, you may use a SELECT statement that uses the dual table (the dual table contains a single dummy row), as shown in the following example:

```
SQL> SELECT count_products() FROM dual;

COUNT_PRODUCTS()
----------------
              13
```

Since the products table now contains 13 rows, the function returns the expected value of 13.

A Java Method that Modifies a Parameter Value   If your Java method modifies a parameter's value, you must use the parameter mode OUT or IN OUT in your call spec's parameter definitions. Also, the Java parameter must be an array.

For example, say you had a Java procedure named swapProc() that swaps two integers. Those integers must be int arrays, as shown in the following example:

```
public class MySwap {
  public static void swapProc(
    int [] numberArray1,
    int [] numberArray2
  ) {
    int temp = numberArray1[0];
    numberArray1[0] = numberArray2[0];
    numberArray2[0] = temp;
  }
}
```

Notice that only the first element of the int arrays numberArray1 and numberArray2 are used, and Java array elements start at zero. The call spec for swapProc() has to use two PL/SQL NUMBER parameters that use the IN OUT mode; they use NUMBER because that PL/SQL type is compatible with Java int, and they use the IN OUT mode because the Java method modifies the parameter values:

```
CREATE PROCEDURE swap_proc(
   number1 IN OUT NUMBER,
   number2 IN OUT NUMBER
) AS
LANGUAGE JAVA
NAME 'MySwap.swapProc(int [], int [])';
/
```

Notice the use of the `IN OUT` mode for the PL/SQL `NUMBER` parameters
`number1` and `number2` in this call spec and the use of the Java `int` arrays in the
`NAME` clause.

Publishing and Calling Java Methods Using PL/SQL Packages

I mentioned earlier that you could also publish Java methods using PL/SQL
packages (I covered PL/SQL packages in Chapter2). Packages allow you to group
PL/SQL procedures and functions together into one self-contained unit, and a
logical use for them is to group call specs for a Java class together.

Normally, a package should consist of a specification and a body, each created
with separate statements, but if you only want to group call specs together, you
can use just one `CREATE PACKAGE` statement. The following statement creates a
package containing the call specs previously shown for the Java methods in the
`JvmExample1` class:

```
CREATE OR REPLACE PACKAGE jvm_example1 AS

   PROCEDURE display_message_in_trace_file
   AS
   LANGUAGE JAVA
   NAME 'JvmExample1.displayMessageInTraceFile()';

   PROCEDURE display_message_on_screen
   AS
   LANGUAGE JAVA
   NAME 'JvmExample1.displayMessageOnScreen()';

   PROCEDURE display_product(
     id NUMBER
   ) AS
   LANGUAGE JAVA
   NAME 'JvmExample1.displayProduct(int)';

   PROCEDURE add_product(
     type_id      NUMBER,
     name         VARCHAR2,
     description VARCHAR2,
```

```
    price        NUMBER
) AS
LANGUAGE JAVA
NAME 'JvmExample1.addProduct(int, java.lang.String, java.lang.String, double)';

    FUNCTION count_products
    RETURN NUMBER AS
    LANGUAGE JAVA
    NAME 'JvmExample1.countProducts() return int';

END jvm_example1;
/
```

As you can see, the actual call specs contained in this package are the same as those shown in the previous sections.

Calling these procedures and functions in SQL is also similar to the previous examples, except that you must use the *dot notation*, in which you must include the package name along with the procedure or function name, separated by a dot. To call the add_product() procedure in the jvm_example1 package, you use jvm_example1.add_product(), as shown in the following example:

```
SQL> SET SERVEROUTPUT ON
SQL> call jvm_example1.add_product(1, 'JDBC Progamming', 'A good book', 39.99);
Added new product with an id of 14

Call completed.
```

Similarly, the following example displays the new product details using the display_product() procedure:

```
SQL> call jvm_example1.display_product(14);
type_id = 1
name = JDBC Progamming
description = A good book
price = 39.99

Call completed.
```

Calling Java Stored Programs from PL/SQL Procedures

Because the call spec for a Java stored program is just a PL/SQL procedure or function, you can call them from anywhere that a call to a regular PL/SQL procedure or function is allowed. For example, you could call a Java stored program's call spec from within a PL/SQL procedure or function. In this section, I'll show you a PL/SQL procedure that calls the `add_product()`, `display_product()`, and `count_products()` call specs contained in the `jvm_example1` package shown in the previous section.

The following statement creates a PL/SQL procedure named `add_display_and_count_products()`. This procedure adds a new product using a call to `jvm_example1.add_product()`, displays that product using `jvm_example1.display_product()`, and finally counts the number of products using `jvm_example1.count_products()`:

```
CREATE OR REPLACE PROCEDURE add_display_and_count_products AS

  number_of_products INTEGER;

BEGIN

  jvm_example1.add_product(1, 'Java', 'Learning Java', 19.95);
  jvm_example1.display_product(15);
  number_of_products := jvm_example1.count_products;
  dbms_output.put_line('Total number of products = ' || number_of_products);

END add_display_and_count_products;
/
```

As you can see, the calls are made to the packaged call specs within this PL/SQL procedure. The following example calls `add_display_and_count_products()` using SQL*Plus:

```
SQL> call add_display_and_count_products();
Added new product with an id of 15
type_id = 1
name = Java
description = Learning Java
price = 19.95
There are 15 products
Total number of products = 15

Call completed.
```

Calling Java Stored Programs from Java

You can also invoke call specs from within Java itself; this completes the full circle of Java and PL/SQL. Invoking a call spec from JDBC is just like calling any other PL/SQL procedure or function.

The program `JvmExample2.java` is a standalone Java program (not deployed to the Oracle JVM) that uses a `CallableStatement` object to invoke the `add_product()` and `count_products()` call specs contained in the `jvm_example1` package. The `main()` method in `JvmExample2.java` adds a new product using a call to `jvm_example1.add_product()`, displays that product using `displayProduct()` (a Java procedure defined in `JvmExample2.java`), and finally counts the number of products using `jvm_example1.count_products()`:

```
/*
   JvmExample2.java shows how to call
   Java stored programs.
*/

// import the JDBC packages
import java.sql.*;

public class JvmExample2 {

  public static void main(String args [])
  throws SQLException {

    // register the Oracle JDBC drivers
    DriverManager.registerDriver(
      new oracle.jdbc.OracleDriver()
    );

    // create a Connection object, and connect to the database
    // as store_user using the Oracle JDBC Thin driver
    Connection myConnection = DriverManager.getConnection(
      "jdbc:oracle:thin:@localhost:1521:ORCL",
      "store_user",
      "store_password"
    );

    // disable auto-commit mode
    myConnection.setAutoCommit(false);

    // create a Statement object
    Statement myStatement = myConnection.createStatement();

    // create a CallableStatement object to call the
    // Java stored procedure jvm_example1.add_product()
    CallableStatement myCallableStatement = myConnection.prepareCall(
      "{call jvm_example1.add_product(?, ?, ?, ?)}"
    );
```

```java
  // bind values to the CallableStatement object's parameters
  myCallableStatement.setInt(1, 1);
  myCallableStatement.setString(2, "Enterprise JavaBeans");
  myCallableStatement.setString(3, "A book on programming EJBs");
  myCallableStatement.setDouble(4, 35.95);

  // execute the CallableStatement object
  myCallableStatement.execute();
  System.out.println("Added a new product");

  // display the product
  displayProduct(myStatement, 16);

  // call the Java stored function jvm_example1.count_products()
  myCallableStatement = myConnection.prepareCall(
    "{? = call jvm_example1.count_products()}"
  );

  // register the output parameter, and bind values to
  // the CallableStatement object's parameters
  myCallableStatement.registerOutParameter(
    1, java.sql.Types.INTEGER
  );

  // execute the CallableStatement object
  myCallableStatement.execute();
  int result = myCallableStatement.getInt(1);
  System.out.println("Total number of products = " + result);

  // close the JDBC objects
  myStatement.close();
  myCallableStatement.close();
  myConnection.close();

} // end of main()

public static void displayProduct(
  Statement myStatement,
  int id
) throws SQLException {

  // display the id and price columns
  ResultSet productResultSet = myStatement.executeQuery(
    "SELECT id, type_id, name, description, price " +
    "FROM products " +
    "WHERE id = " + id
  );
  productResultSet.next();
```

```
System.out.println("id = " + productResultSet.getString("id"));
System.out.println("type_id = " +
    productResultSet.getString("type_id"));
System.out.println("name = " +
    productResultSet.getString("name"));
System.out.println("description = " +
    productResultSet.getString("description"));
System.out.println("price = " +
    productResultSet.getString("price"));
productResultSet.close();

  } // end of displayProduct()

}
```

You can, of course, compile and run this program using `javac` or JDeveloper. The output from this program is as follows:

```
Added a new product
id = 16
type_id = 1
name = Enterprise JavaBeans
description = A book on programming EJBs
price = 35.95
Total number of products = 16
```

Loading and Publishing Java Stored Programs Using JDeveloper

You can also use JDeveloper to load a Java class, and then subsequently publish one or more of the methods in that class as Java stored procedures. In this section, I'll show you how to load the `JvmExample1` class and publish the `countProducts()` method of that class.

I've already created an example JDeveloper workspace file for you named `jdbc_workspace2.jws`. This file is located in the `programs` subdirectory of the `jdbc_book` directory. If you want to follow along with the examples, you should start JDeveloper and open the `jdbc_workspace2.jws` workspace file. This workspace also has a new project associated with it, and the `JvmExample1.java` class has been added to this project.

Once you've opened the workspace file, expand the workspace elements all the way down to the `JvmExample1.java` file and expand the Connections elements. Your JDeveloper screen should look similar to that shown in Figure 10-1.

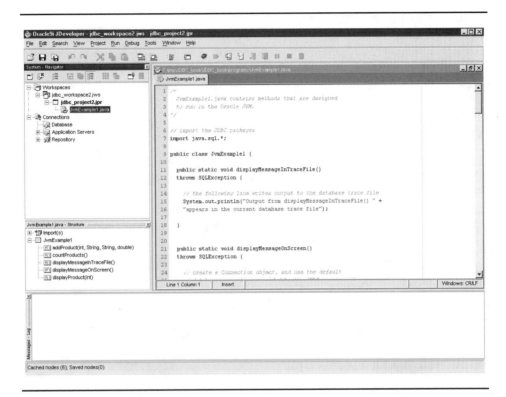

FIGURE 10-1. *JDeveloper after opening the jdbc_workspace2.jws file*

To load and publish a Java stored program, perform the following four steps:

1. Create a connection to the database; this tells JDeveloper which database and schema to use.

2. Create a *deployment profile*; this tells JDeveloper which Java class you want to load and which methods of that class to publish. It is called a deployment profile because the steps of loading and publishing are referred to as *deployment*.

3. Add the Java methods to the deployment profile.

4. Load the Java class and publish the methods using the deployment profile. JDeveloper will invoke the `loadjava` tool to load the Java class and publish the Java methods by creating the PL/SQL call specs.

I'll describe these steps in the following sections.

Step 1: Create a Database Connection

To create a database connection, right-click the Database element under the Connections element and select New Connection from the context-sensitive menu. This will start the Connection Wizard, as shown in Figure 10-2.

Click the Next button, which takes you to Step 1 of the Connection Wizard. Enter `store_user` as the Connection name in the Step 1 dialog, as shown in Figure 10-3.

Click the Next button, which takes you to Step 2. Enter `store_user` as the Username and `store_password` as the password, as shown in Figure 10-4.

Click the Next button, which takes you to Step 3, as shown in Figure 10-5.

If your database is running on your local machine, you shouldn't need to change these settings. If your database is on another machine, you may need to contact your DBA to get the correct values for these settings.

Once you're satisfied with these settings, click the Next button, which takes you to Step 4 of the Connection Wizard. Click the Test Connection button, to ensure that the connection to the database can be made, as shown in Figure 10-6.

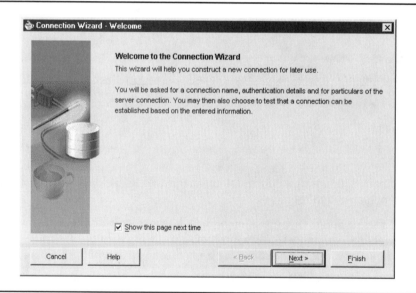

FIGURE 10-2. *The Connection Wizard Welcome dialog*

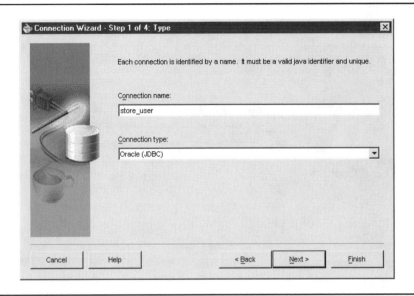

FIGURE 10-3. *Step 1 of the Connection Wizard*

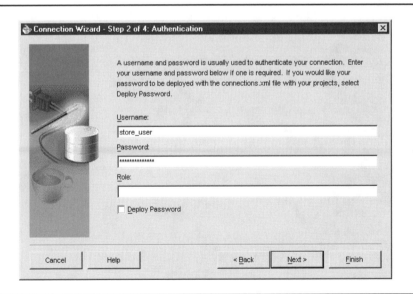

FIGURE 10-4. *Step 2 of the Connection Wizard*

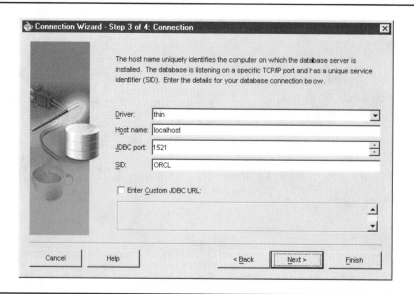

FIGURE 10-5. *Step 3 of the Connection Wizard*

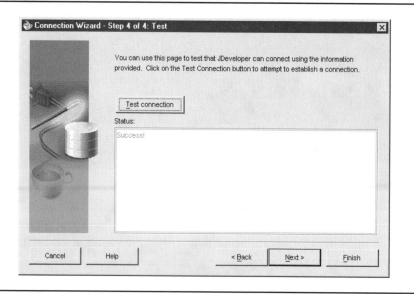

FIGURE 10-6. *Step 4 of the Connection Wizard*

If the test failed, contact your DBA to resolve the problem. Once the test succeeds, click the Next button, which takes you to the Connection Wizard Summary dialog, as shown in Figure 10-7.

Click the Finish button.

You should now have a new database connection named `store_user`. Go ahead and expand the `store_user` connection if you want to. You can use it to examine database structures (table definitions, for example) in the `store_user` schema.

The next step is to create a deployment profile.

Step 2: Create a Deployment Profile

To create a deployment profile, you should right-click `jdbc_project2` and select New from the menu. This opens the New dialog, from which you can create many different kinds of JDeveloper and Java items, including projects, workspaces, classes, and deployment profiles.

Since you're going to create a deployment profile for a Java stored procedure, go ahead and select Deployment Profiles from the left under Categories and Stored Procedures on the right under Items, as shown in Figure 10-8.

Click the OK button, which this takes you to the Save Deployment Profile dialog. Enter `jvm_example1.deploy` as the file name, as shown in Figure 10-9.

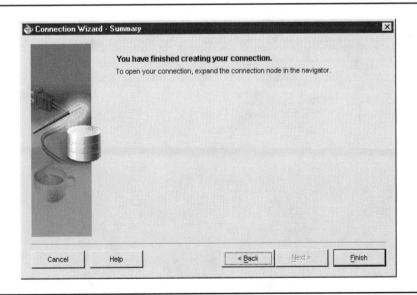

FIGURE 10-7.   *The Connection Wizard Summary dialog*

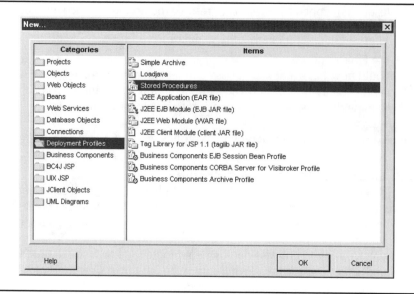

FIGURE 10-8. *The New dialog, creating a deployment profile for a stored procedure*

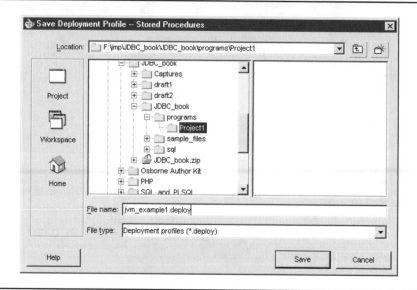

FIGURE 10-9. *The Save Deployment Profile dialog*

Click the Save button to save the file using the file name
`jvm_example1.deploy`. After the file has been saved, the Java Stored Procedures
Deployment Profile Settings dialog is displayed, which allows you to specify the
classes that will be loaded along with any other settings you want to specify for the
`loadjava` tool (`loadjava` is invoked by JDeveloper to actually load the Java
class). Make sure the box to the left of `JvmExample1.java` is checked to specify
that the `JvmExample1` class is to be loaded, as shown in Figure 10-10.

Click the OK button to finish the creation of the deployment profile. The new
deployment profile, named `jvm_example1`, is shown in Figure 10-11.

Step 3: Add the Java Method to the Deployment Profile

Figure 10-11 showed the `jvm_example1` deployment profile. To add a Java
method to the `jvm_example1` deployment profile, right-click it and select Add
Stored Procedure from the menu. This opens the Add Java Stored Procedure dialog,
from which you can select the Java method from the `JvmExample1` class you want
to deploy. In this example, you're going to deploy the `countProducts()` method,
as shown in Figure 10-12.

Click the Settings button to display the Method Settings dialog, as shown in
Figure 10-13.

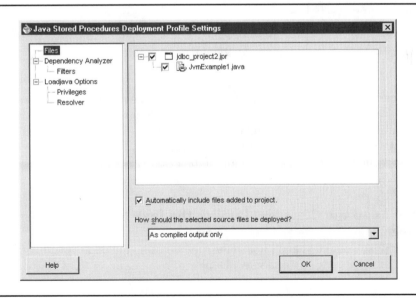

FIGURE 10-10.   *The Java Stored Procedures Deployment Profile Settings dialog*

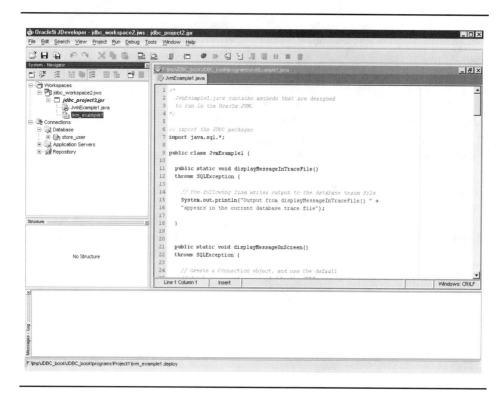

FIGURE 10-11. *The jvm_example1 deployment profile*

You can use this dialog to change the settings for the method, including the name of the PL/SQL method that will be used when JDeveloper create the call spec; you can also change the PL/SQL return type of the function. Leave these settings as they are and click the OK button to return to the Add Java Stored Procedure dialog. Click OK again to complete the addition of the `countProducts()` method to the `jvm_example1` deployment profile, as shown in Figure 10-14.

Step 4: Load the Class and Publish the Java Method Using the Deployment Descriptor

Finally, to load your class and publish the method using the deployment descriptor, right-click `jvm_example1` and select Deploy to `store_user` from the menu.

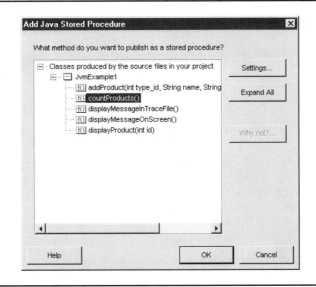

FIGURE 10-12. *The Add Java Stored Procedure dialog*

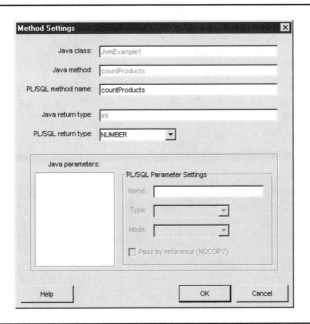

FIGURE 10-13. *The Method Settings dialog*

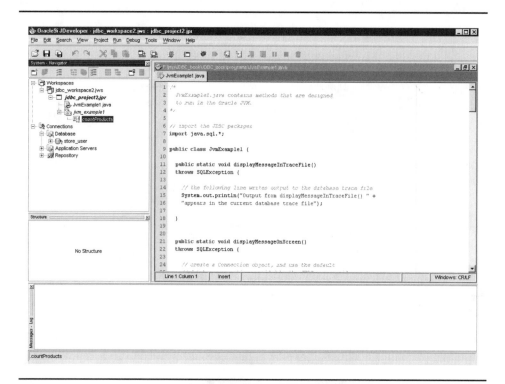

FIGURE 10-14. *The countProducts() method is added to the jvm_example1 deployment profile*

JDeveloper will invoke the `loadjava` tool to load the `JvmExample1` class into the `store_user` schema and create the PL/SQL call spec for the `countCustomers()` method of that class. JDeveloper will report its progress in the Deployment tab at the bottom of the screen:

```
Invoking loadjava with arguments (suppressing connect string):
-order -resolve -thin
Loadjava finished.
Executing SQL Statement:
CREATE OR REPLACE FUNCTION countProducts RETURN NUMBER
AUTHID CURRENT_USER AS LANGUAGE JAVA NAME 'JvmExample1.countProducts()
return int';
Success.
Publishing finished.
----  Stored procedure deployment finished.   ----
```

You can then run the Java stored program through the PL/SQL call spec, as shown in the following example:

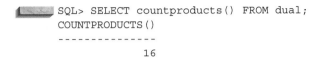

```
SQL> SELECT countproducts() FROM dual;
COUNTPRODUCTS()
--------------
            16
```

Now that I've covered Java stored programs, I'll introduce you to database triggers.

Database Triggers

A database *trigger* is a PL/SQL procedure or Java stored procedure that is run automatically by the database—or in trigger terms, *fired*—when a specified SQL DML INSERT, UPDATE, or DELETE statement is run against a specified database table. Triggers are very useful for doing things like advanced auditing of changes made to column values in a table.

Triggers can fire before or after the SQL statement runs. Also, since a DML statement can affect more than one row at the same time, the procedure code for the trigger may be run once for every row affected (such a trigger is known as a *row-level trigger*), or just once for all the rows (known as a *statement-level trigger*). For example, if you had an UPDATE statement that modified ten rows and you had also created a row trigger that would fire for this UPDATE statement, then that trigger would run ten times—once for each row. If, however, your trigger was a statement-level trigger, the trigger would only fire once for the whole UPDATE statement.

NOTE
A statement-level trigger has access to the old and new column values when the trigger fires as a result of an UPDATE statement on that column.

The firing of a trigger may also be limited using a trigger *condition*, for example, when a column value is less than a specified value.

As I mentioned earlier, triggers are very useful for doing advanced auditing of changes made to column values. In this section, I'll show you an example of a trigger that will audit the change made to the price column of a row in the products table, if the price column value is lowered by more than 25 percent. After such a change is made, the trigger will add a row to the product_price_ audit table (this table is created by the jvm_examples.sql script, which you should have already run). The product_price_audit table is created using the following CREATE TABLE statement:

```
CREATE TABLE product_price_audit (
   product_id INTEGER
```

```
    CONSTRAINT price_audit_fk_products
    REFERENCES products(id),
  old_price  NUMBER(5, 2),
  new_price  NUMBER(5, 2)
);
```

As you can see, the `product_id` column of the `product_price_audit` table is a foreign key to the `id` column of the `products` table. The `old_price` column will be used to store the old price of a product prior to the change, and the `new_price` column will be used to store the new price after the change.

Because the trigger will fire before an update of the `price` column from the `products` table, I'll call this trigger `before_product_price_update`. Also, because I want to use the `price` column values before and after any UPDATE statement modifies that column value, I must use a statement-level trigger. Finally, since I only want to audit a price change when the new price is lowered by more than 25 percent of the old value, I'll need to specify a trigger condition.

You create a trigger using the CREATE TRIGGER statement, and the following example creates the `before_product_price_update` trigger with the required attributes:

```
CREATE OR REPLACE TRIGGER
  before_product_price_update
BEFORE UPDATE OF
  price
ON
  products
FOR EACH ROW
WHEN
  (new.price < old.price * 0.75)
BEGIN

  dbms_output.put_line('For product id ' || :old.id);
  dbms_output.put_line('Old price = ' || :old.price);
  dbms_output.put_line('New price = ' || :new.price);
  dbms_output.put_line('The price reduction is more than 25%');

  -- insert row into the product_price_audit table
  INSERT INTO
    product_price_audit
  VALUES (
    :old.id, :old.price, :new.price
  );

END before_product_price_update;
/
```

There are four things to notice about this statement:

- The BEFORE UPDATE OF clause specifies that the trigger is to fire before the update of the column. In this case, before the price column is updated.

- The FOR EACH ROW clause identifies this as a statement-level trigger. This states that the trigger code (contained within the BEGIN and END keywords) is to be run for each row.

- The WHEN clause specifies the trigger limit condition. Only when this condition is true will the trigger actually run its code. In this case, the WHEN clause is (new.price < old.price * 0.75), meaning that the trigger code will only be run when the new price is less than 75 percent of the old price (when the price reduction is more than 25 percent). The new and old column values are accessed using the :old and :new aliases in the trigger.

- The trigger code displays the product id, the old and new prices, and a message stating that the price reduction is more than 25 percent. The code then adds a row to the product_price_audit table containing the product id, and the old and new prices.

To see the before_product_price_update trigger in action, you must reduce a product's price by more than 25 percent, but before you do that, go ahead and retrieve the id and price columns from the products table:

```
SQL> SELECT id, price
  2  FROM products
  3  ORDER BY id;
        ID      PRICE
---------- ----------
         1      19.95
         2         30
         3      25.99
         4      13.95
         5      49.99
         6      14.95
         7      13.49
         8      12.99
         9      10.99
        10      15.99
        11      14.99

        ID      PRICE
---------- ----------
        12      13.49
        13      19.95
```

```
        14        39.99
        15        19.95
        16        35.95

16 rows selected.
```

Also, to see any output from the trigger, you need to run the SET SERVEROUTPUT ON command:

SQL> SET SERVEROUTPUT ON

Go ahead and perform the following UPDATE statement to reduce the price of product #5 and #10 by 30 percent—do this by multiplying the price column by .7 for those rows. This will cause the trigger to fire and run its code:

```
SQL> UPDATE products
  2    SET price = price * .7
  3    WHERE id IN (5, 10);
For product id 10
Old price = 15.99
New price = 11.19
The price reduction is more than 25%
For product id 5
Old price = 49.99
New price = 34.99
The price reduction is more than 25%

2 rows updated.
```

As you can see, the trigger fired and ran its code as a result of the update made to the price of product #5 and product #10. You can see that the trigger did indeed add the two required rows containing the product ids, along with the old and new prices, to the product_price_audit table using the following query:

SQL> SELECT * FROM product_price_audit;

```
PRODUCT_ID   OLD_PRICE   NEW_PRICE
----------   ---------   ---------
        10       15.99       11.19
         5       49.99       34.99
```

This trigger's code was written in PL/SQL, but you can also write trigger code using Java, replacing the PL/SQL code in the trigger body with a Java stored procedure. To replace the PL/SQL code in a trigger with a Java stored procedure you follow these four steps:

1. Create and compile a Java source file containing a class and method. The method should perform the same basic steps as the PL/SQL trigger code it is intended to replace.

2. Load the Java class into the database.

3. Publish the Java method using a PL/SQL call spec.

4. Recreate the trigger with the PL/SQL trigger code replaced with an invocation of the call spec.

Of course, you can also create a brand new trigger using these four basic steps. I will now go through these steps in detail, replacing the PL/SQL code of the previous before_product_price_update trigger with Java.

Step 1: Create and Compile a Java Source File

You can create and compile a Java source file containing a class and method using either a text editor and javac, or JDeveloper. The file JvmExample3.java defines the class JvmExample3 that contains the method triggerCode(), which performs the same functionality as the PL/SQL trigger code of the before_product_price_update trigger:

```
/*
    JvmExample3.java illustrates how to
    replace the PL/SQL code of the trigger
    before_product_price_update with Java.
*/

// import the JDBC packages
import java.sql.*;

public class JvmExample3 {

  public static void triggerCode(

    int     product_id,
    double old_price,
    double new_price

  ) throws SQLException {

    // create a Connection object, and use the default
    // database connection provided by the JDBC server-side
    // internal driver
    Connection myConnection = DriverManager.getConnection(
      "jdbc:default:connection"
```

```
    );

    // create a Statement object
    Statement myStatement = myConnection.createStatement();

    // call dbms_java.set_output(2000) to
    // set up an output buffer of 2000 bytes, this causes
    // output from System.out.println() calls to be routed
    // to this buffer
    myStatement.execute(
      "{call dbms_java.set_output(2000)}"
    );

    System.out.println("For product id " + product_id);
    System.out.println("Old price = " + old_price);
    System.out.println("New price = " + new_price);
    System.out.println("The price reduction is more than 25%");

    // insert row into the product_price_audit table
    myStatement.executeUpdate(
      "INSERT INTO product_price_audit " +
      "(product_id, old_price, new_price) VALUES (" +
      product_id + ", " + old_price + ", " +  new_price +
      ")"
    );

    // close the Statement and Connection objects
    myStatement.close();
    myConnection.close();

  } // end of triggerCode()

}
```

As you can see, the `triggerCode()` procedure performs the following major steps:

1. Uses the default database connection to access the database.

2. Sets up an output buffer to hold the output from the code.

3. Outputs the same messages as the original PL/SQL code of the `before_product_price_update` trigger.

4. Performs an `INSERT` statement to add a row to the `product_price_audit` table containing the product id, along with the old and new prices.

The following command compiles the JvmExample3.java file using javac:

```
javac JvmExample3.java
```

This produces the class file JvmExample3.class.

Step 2: Load the Java Class into the Database
The next step is to load the Java class into the database. The following command loads the JvmExample3 class into the database using the loadjava tool:

```
loadjava -user store_user/store_password JvmExample3.class
```

You can verify that the class was indeed successfully loaded into the database using a query against user_objects.

Step 3: Publish the Java Method
You publish the Java method by creating a call spec using PL/SQL. The following PL/SQL statement creates a call spec named trigger_code() for the JvmExample3.triggerCode() method:

```
CREATE OR REPLACE PROCEDURE trigger_code(
    product_id NUMBER,
    old_price  NUMBER,
    new_price  NUMBER
) AS
LANGUAGE JAVA
NAME 'JvmExample3.triggerCode(int, double, double)';
/
```

Notice that the trigger_code() call spec uses the PL/SQL NUMBER type to represent the Java int and double parameter types used by the JvmExample3.triggerCode() method.

Step 4: Recreate the Trigger Using the Call Spec
The final step is to recreate the trigger using an invocation of the call spec instead of the PL/SQL code in the trigger body. The following statement recreates the before_product_price_update trigger, replacing the PL/SQL trigger code with an invocation of the trigger_code() call spec:

```
CREATE OR REPLACE TRIGGER
    before_product_price_update
BEFORE UPDATE OF
```

```
  price
ON
  products
FOR EACH ROW
WHEN
  (new.price < old.price * 0.75)
CALL trigger_code(:old.id, :old.price, :new.price)
/
```

When the trigger fires, it will call the `trigger_code()` call spec, which in turn calls the `JvmExample3.triggerCode()` method. The following example performs an UPDATE statement to reduce the price of product #1 by 30 percent. This should cause the `before_product_price_update` trigger to fire and call `trigger_code()`:

```
SQL> SET SERVEROUTPUT ON
SQL> UPDATE products
  2   SET price = price * .7
  3   WHERE id = 1;
For product id 1
Old price = 19.95
New price = 13.97
The price reduction is more than 25%

1 row updated.
```

As you can see, the `before_product_price_update` trigger fires and calls `trigger_code()` as expected.

CHAPTER
11

Oracle9*i*AS Containers
for J2EE (OC4J)

ou can run Java 2 Enterprise Edition (J2EE) components using Oracle9iAS Containers for J2EE (OC4J). OC4J allows you to run J2EE components like Enterprise JavaBeans (EJB), servlets, and JavaServer Pages (JSP). You can then use JDBC statements within these components to access the database. In this chapter, you'll be introduced to OC4J, and you'll see how to deploy and run a servlet, a JSP, and an EJB using OC4J. These components will use JDBC to access the `products` table contained in the `store_user` schema.

You can download OC4J and its documentation from the Oracle Technology Network (OTN) website at `http://technet.oracle.com`. When I wrote this chapter, OC4J was available as a downloadable ZIP file (named `oc4j.zip`) from the OTN website.

NOTE
You should review any documentation for the version of OC4J you actually use, as the instructions for installing and running a particular version of OC4J may be different from the instructions shown in this chapter.

Overview of OC4J

OC4J may be run using a standard Java Virtual Machine, and OC4J is integrated with the Oracle9i Application Server (Oracle9iAS). OC4J forms the J2EE infrastructure for the Oracle9iAS product.

OC4J has the following features:

- OC4J may be run using the standard JVM that comes with the JDK (you should look on the OTN website for the exact version of the JDK supported by OC4J).

- OC4J is available for many operating systems, including Solaris, Linux, Windows, HP-UX, and AIX.

- OC4J is simple to install and use.

- OC4J is 100 percent compatible with the Tomcat Servlet Engine. This means that any servlets you already have running on Tomcat may also be run using OC4J.

OC4J supports the standard J2EE components; these components are shown in the following list:

- Java Database Connectivity (JDBC)

- JavaServer Pages (JSP)

- Servlets

- Enterprise JavaBeans (EJB) and Message-Driven Beans

- Java Transaction API (JTA)

- Java Messaging Service (JMS)

- Java Naming and Directory Interface (JNDI)

- Java Mail

- Java Authentication and Authorization Service (JAAS)

- J2EE Connector Architecture (JCA)

You should consult the OC4J documentation or the OTN website for details on the exact versions of these components supported by a particular version of OC4J. At the time of writing, OC4J 9.0.2 was the latest version; this version of OC4J supports J2EE 1.3.

Installing OC4J

Once you've obtained the OC4J ZIP file from the OTN website, you should unzip that file into your `ORACLE_HOME` directory (the directory where your other Oracle software is currently installed). Unzipping the OC4J file in that directory creates a directory named `j2ee\home`; this is where the OC4J files will be located once the OC4J ZIP file has been unzipped.

Next, using your OS command line, you must change directories to the `j2ee\home` directory. For example:

```
cd j2ee\home
```

NOTE
Windows uses back-slash characters (\), while Unix and Linux use forward-slash characters (/) in directories.

Finally, enter the following command to complete the installation:

```
java -jar oc4j.jar -install
```

This runs the `oc4j.jar` file using the Java tool. You will be prompted to set the password for the OC4J admin user. This user has the privileges to do things like shutdown OC4J. Enter **welcome** as the password and confirm that password when prompted; this password is assumed in the examples in this chapter, but you are free to pick your own password (if you do, you'll need to modify the examples in order to run them). Once you've set and confirmed the password, you should see the following message:

```
Installation done
```

This means the installation of OC4J is complete.

Starting, Restarting, and Shutting Down OC4J

In this section, you'll learn how to start and test OC4J and how to restart and shut down OC4J. Before running the commands described in this section, you must be in the j2ee\home directory.

Starting OC4J

To start OC4J, run the oc4j.jar file using the following command:

```
java -jar oc4j.jar
```

This runs the oc4j.jar file and starts OC4J.

You may use the -help option to view all the command-line options for starting OC4J. For example: java -jar oc4j.jar -help.

Restarting OC4J

As you'll see later in this chapter, when you deploy an application to OC4J, it automatically detects the application; therefore, you don't usually need to restart OC4J when deploying your applications. If, however, you change one of the OC4J configuration files (contained in the j2ee\home\config directory), you should restart OC4J. To restart OC4J, you use the -restart option, as shown in the following command, where *admin_password* is the password specified for the admin user when you installed OC4J:

```
java -jar admin.jar ormi://localhost/ admin admin_password -restart
```

For example, the following command uses the welcome password:

```
java -jar admin.jar ormi://localhost/ admin welcome -restart
```

Shutting Down OC4J

To shut down OC4J, you use the -shutdown option, as shown in the following command:

```
java -jar admin.jar ormi://localhost/ admin welcome -shutdown
```

When the -shutdown option is used on its own as shown in this command, it performs a graceful shutdown of OC4J. You can force a rapid shutdown of OC4J using the force option, for example:

```
java -jar admin.jar ormi://localhost/ admin welcome -shutdown force
```

If for some reason you cannot shut down OC4J, you may terminate the process using CTRL-C in Windows, or the kill command in Unix or Linux.

Defining a Data Source

Before running the examples in this chapter, you first need to define a JNDI *data source*. All the examples shown in this chapter will use the same data source; this data source will access the store_user schema using the Oracle Thin driver. To define a data source, you modify the data-sources.xml file located in the j2ee\home\config directory. Open the data-sources.xml file using a text editor and modify an existing data-source tag (or add a new data-source tag) to read as follows:

```
<data-source
    class="com.evermind.sql.DriverManagerDataSource"
    name="OracleDS"
    location="jdbc/OracleCoreDS"
    xa-location="jdbc/xa/OracleXADS"
    ejb-location="jdbc/OracleDS"
    connection-driver="oracle.jdbc.driver.OracleDriver"
    username="store_user"
    password="store_password"
    url="jdbc:oracle:thin:@localhost:1521:orcl"
    inactivity-timeout="30"
/>
```

This defines a data source named OracleDS (identified by the name parameter) that connects to the store_user schema with the password store_password (identified by the username and password parameters respectively). The database URL is jdbc:oracle:thin:@localhost:1521:orcl (identified by the url parameter).

A data source may be accessed by "looking up" its location using JNDI. The location is identified by the `location` parameter, which in this example is set to `jdbc/OracleCoreDS`. As you will see shortly, the examples connect to the database by calling the `lookup()` method of a `javax.naming.InitialContext` object.

Once you've made the change to the `data-sources.xml` file and saved it, you should restart OC4J as described earlier in this chapter.

Servlets

A *servlet* is a Java program that is typically used to dynamically generate HTML web pages. A servlet runs in a J2EE server such as OC4J. A servlet may be invoked using an Internet browser by specifying a URL containing the servlet class. The request to run the servlet is then sent to the server, which then runs the Java code contained in the servlet class; finally, any HTML output from the servlet is routed back to the browser.

NOTE
I'm not going to cover all the details of servlets in this section—for comprehensive coverage of servlets, I recommend the book Java Servlet Programming *by Jason Hunter and William Crawford (O'Reilly, 2001).*

A servlet is different from a stand-alone Java program in that a servlet doesn't contain a `main()` method. Instead, a servlet overrides certain access methods in the `javax.servlet.http.HttpServlet` class that the application server then invokes. For example, servlets typically override the `doGet()` and `doPost()` methods of the `HttpServlet` class to process the HTTP GET and POST requests from the browser.

In the rest of this section, I'll take you through an example of a servlet that connects to the database and displays the `id`, `name`, `description`, and `price` columns of the rows in the `products` table. Once I've shown you the listing for this servlet, I'll describe how to deploy it to OC4J and then invoke the servlet from a browser. The example servlet is defined in the `ServletExample.java` file (located in the `JDBC_book\programs` directory) and is shown in the following listing:

```
/*
  ServletExample.java illustrates how to include
  JDBC statements in a servlet
*/

// import the servlet, io, util, and naming classes
```

```java
import javax.servlet.*;
import javax.servlet.http.*;
import java.io.*;
import java.util.*;
import javax.naming.*;

// import the JDBC classes
import java.sql.*;
import javax.sql.*;

public class ServletExample extends HttpServlet {

  // handle get request
  public void doGet(
    HttpServletRequest req,
    HttpServletResponse res
  ) throws ServletException, IOException {

    // begin an HTML page
    res.setContentType("text/html");
    PrintWriter out = res.getWriter();
    out.println("<html><head><title>Products</title></head>");
    out.println("<body>");

    // declare Connection and Statement objects
    Connection myConnection = null;
    Statement myStatement = null;

    try {

      // locate the data source jdbc/OracleCoreDS defined in the
      // data-sources.xml file in the config directory of OC4J
      InitialContext myInitialContext = new InitialContext();
      DataSource myDataSource = (DataSource)
        (myInitialContext.lookup("jdbc/OracleCoreDS"));

      // connect to the database using the data source
      myConnection = myDataSource.getConnection();

      // initialize the Statement object
      myStatement = myConnection.createStatement();

      // create a ResultSet object, and populate it with the
      // results of a query that retrieves the
      // id, name, description, and price columns
      // for all the rows from the products table
      ResultSet productResultSet = myStatement.executeQuery(
        "SELECT id, name, description, price " +
```

```
      "FROM products " +
      "ORDER BY id"
    );

    // display the column values in an HTML table
    out.println("<table width=100% border=1>");
    out.println("<tr>");
    out.println("<th>Id</th>");
    out.println("<th>Name</th>");
    out.println("<th>Description</th>");
    out.println("<th>Price</th>");
    out.println("</tr>");

    int id;
    String name;
    String description;
    float price;

    while (productResultSet.next()) {
      id = productResultSet.getInt("id");
      name = productResultSet.getString("name");
      description = productResultSet.getString("description");
      price = productResultSet.getFloat("price");

      out.println("<tr>");
      out.println("<td>" + id + "</td>");
      out.println("<td>" + name + "</td>");
      out.println("<td>" + description + "</td>");
      out.println("<td>" + price + "</td>");
      out.println("</tr>");
    } // end of while

    // close the JDBC objects
    productResultSet.close();
    myStatement.close();
    myConnection.close();

    // finish the HTML page
    out.println("</table>");
    out.println("</body></html>");

  } catch (SQLException e) {

    out.println("SQLException " + e);

  } catch (NamingException e) {

    out.println("NamingException " + e);
```

```
      }
    }
  }
}
```

The doGet() method handles the HTTP GET requests, and in this example servlet the doGet() method performs the following steps:

1. Begins an HTML page by writing to a PrintWriter object named out. Anything sent to the out object is eventually displayed in the browser.

2. Declares Connection and Statement objects.

3. Locates the JDNI data source previously defined in the data-sources.xml file. This is done by creating a javax.naming.InitialContext object (named myInitialContext), then creating javax.sql.DataSource object (named myDataSource). The data source is located using the lookup() method of myInitialContext, specifying the location of the data source. The location passed to the lookup() method is jdbc/OracleCoreDS, the location parameter of the data source previously set in the data-sources.xml file described earlier.

4. Connects to the database using the data source by calling the getConnection() method of the Connection object.

5. Initializes the Statement object.

6. Creates a ResultSet object and populates it with the results of a query that retrieves the id, name, description, and price columns of the rows from the products table.

7. Displays the column values for each row in an HTML table.

8. Closes the JDBC objects, including the Connection object.

9. Finishes the HTML page.

You'll notice that most of the code for the doGet() method is placed in a try/catch statement. If a SQLException object is thrown, the details of the exception are displayed by OC4J and the output is sent to the output window from which you started OC4J. Similarly, if a NamingException occurs (when the data source cannot be located), the details of that exception are displayed by OC4J.

Deploying the Servlet

To deploy this servlet to OC4J, you can copy the ServletExample.java source file to the default-web-app\WEB-INF\classes directory where you installed

OC4J. You can get OC4J to automatically compile Java source files by adding `development="true"` to the `orion-web-app` tag in the `global-web-application.xml` file, which is contained in the `home\config` directory where you installed OC4J.

The following example shows the addition of `development="true"` to the `orion-web-app` tag:

```
<orion-web-app
   jsp-cache-directory="./persistence"
   servlet-webdir="/servlet"
   development="true"
>
```

NOTE
Setting `development` to `true` in your development servers helps you because you don't need to restart OC4J after you make a change to a servlet. However, for performance reasons, you'll want to set `development` to `false` in your production servers.

Once you've made the change to the `global-web-application.xml` file and saved it, you should restart OC4J as described earlier in this chapter. OC4J will now notice any new servlet source file (or changes to a source file) and automatically compile that source file into a class.

Invoking the Servlet

To invoke the servlet, point your Internet browser to `http://localhost:8888/servlet/ServletExample`, assuming you've installed OC4J on your local machine and haven't changed the default port setting of 8888. Figure 11-1 shows the result of invoking `ServletExample` using Internet Explorer. Notice in the figure that all the rows from the `products` table are displayed.

JavaServer Pages (JSP)

JavaServer Pages (JSP) are basically HTML pages that contain special tags that enable you to add Java statements embedded within the HTML. By using embedded Java statements, you can produce web pages that generate dynamic content. JSP files have an advantage over servlets: you embed your Java code within regular HTML statements, rather than embedding HTML within Java code; this makes JSP files easier to develop and understand than servlets.

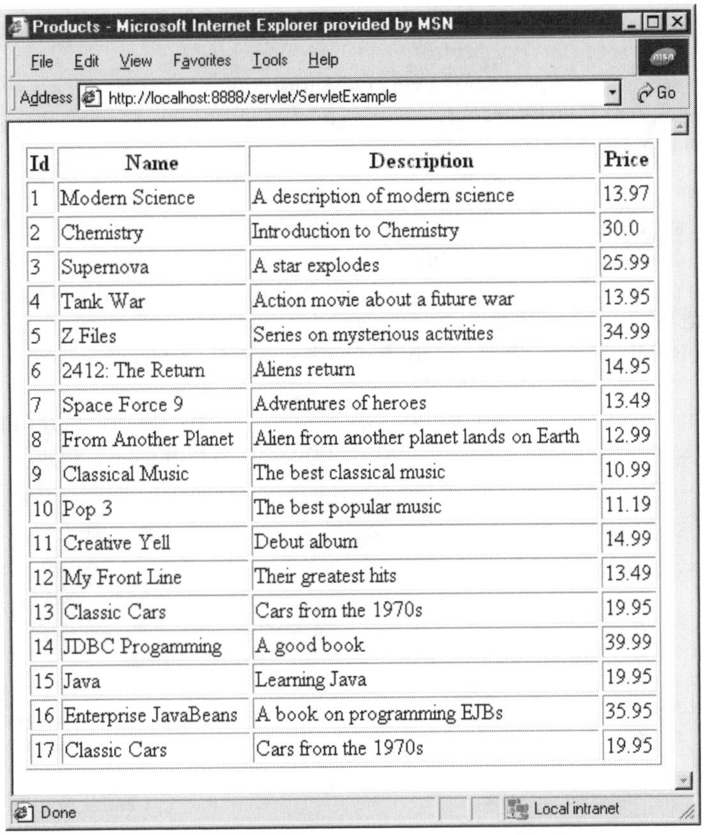

Id	Name	Description	Price
1	Modern Science	A description of modern science	13.97
2	Chemistry	Introduction to Chemistry	30.0
3	Supernova	A star explodes	25.99
4	Tank War	Action movie about a future war	13.95
5	Z Files	Series on mysterious activities	34.99
6	2412: The Return	Aliens return	14.95
7	Space Force 9	Adventures of heroes	13.49
8	From Another Planet	Alien from another planet lands on Earth	12.99
9	Classical Music	The best classical music	10.99
10	Pop 3	The best popular music	11.19
11	Creative Yell	Debut album	14.99
12	My Front Line	Their greatest hits	13.49
13	Classic Cars	Cars from the 1970s	19.95
14	JDBC Progamming	A good book	39.99
15	Java	Learning Java	19.95
16	Enterprise JavaBeans	A book on programming EJBs	35.95
17	Classic Cars	Cars from the 1970s	19.95

FIGURE 11-1. *ServletExample output*

Embedded Java statements are placed within your JSP file using special tags, such as the `<%` and `%>` tags. You may use the `<%=` and `%>` tags to specify expressions that are eventually sent to the browser along with the usual HTML tags. You may also use the `<%!` and `%>` tags for variable and object declarations, although you can also place declarations within `<%` and `%>` tags. In addition, classes are imported into a JSP source file using the `<%@` and `%>` tags.

When a JSP file is invoked, the application server compiles the JSP file into a servlet and then runs that servlet. JSP and servlets typically act as the front-end to your web-based applications, with the actual database access performed by an EJB that you call from within the JSP or servlet. You'll see an example of an EJB later in this chapter.

NOTE
I'm not going to cover all the details of JavaServer Pages in this section—for comprehensive coverage of JSP, I recommend the book Web Development with JavaServer Pages *by Duane Fields and Mark Kolb (Manning, 2000).*

In the rest of this section, I'll walk you through an example of a JSP that connects to the database using the same data source as the previous servlet example and displays the same columns and rows from the `products` table. The actual output of the example JSP is identical to that of the previous servlet. Once I've shown you the listing for this JSP, I'll describe how to deploy it to OC4J and then invoke the JSP from a browser.

The example JSP is defined in the `JSPExample.jsp` file (located in the `JDBC_book\programs` directory) and is shown in the following listing:

```
<!--
    JSPExample.jsp illustrates how to include
    JDBC statements in JavaServer Pages
-->

<!-- Import the required classes -->
<%@ page import="java.sql.*" %>
<%@ page import="javax.sql.*" %>
<%@ page import="javax.naming.*" %>

<html>
<head>
<title>Products</title>
</head>

<body>

<%
// declare Connection and Statement objects
Connection myConnection = null;
Statement myStatement = null;

try {

    // locate the data source jdbc/OracleCoreDS defined in the
    // data-sources.xml file in the config directory of OC4J
    InitialContext myInitialContext = new InitialContext();
    DataSource myDataSource = (DataSource)
      (myInitialContext.lookup("jdbc/OracleCoreDS"));
```

```
  // connect to the database using the data source
  myConnection = myDataSource.getConnection();

  // initialize the Statement object
  myStatement = myConnection.createStatement();

  // create a ResultSet object, and populate it with the
  // results of a query that retrieves the
  // id, name, description, and price columns
  // for all the rows from the products table
  ResultSet productResultSet = myStatement.executeQuery(
    "SELECT id, name, description, price " +
    "FROM products " +
    "ORDER BY id"
  );

%>

<!-- display the column values in an HTML table -->
<table width=100% border=1>
<tr>
<th>Id</th>
<th>Name</th>
<th>Description</th>
<th>Price</th>
</tr>

<%
  while (productResultSet.next()) {
%>
    <tr>
    <td><%= productResultSet.getInt("id") %></td>
    <td><%= productResultSet.getString("name") %></td>
    <td><%= productResultSet.getString("description") %> </td>
    <td><%= productResultSet.getFloat("price") %></td>
    </tr>
<%
  } // end of while
%>

</table>

<%
  // close the JDBC objects
  productResultSet.close();
  myStatement.close();
  myConnection.close();
```

```
} catch (SQLException e) {
%>
  SQLException <%= e %>
<%
} catch (NamingException e) {
%>
  NamingException <%= e %>
<%
}
%>

</body>
</html>
```

The main steps performed by this JSP are the same as the previous servlet and, not surprisingly, the actual Java code embedded in the JSP is similar to the code of the servlet. The bulk of the code lines in the JSP are placed within `<%` and `%>` tags, with the exception of the lines that write the column values to the HTML table rows: these lines use the `<%=` and `%>` tags. For example:

```
<td><%= productResultSet.getInt("id") %></td>
```

To deploy `JSPExample.jsp` to OC4J, you can copy this file to the `default-web-app\examples\jsp` directory where you installed OC4J.

To invoke `JSPExample.jsp`, point your Internet browser to `http://localhost:8888/examples/jsp/JSPExample.jsp`. The results displayed in the browser are identical to those shown in the servlet example and are therefore omitted from this book for brevity.

Enterprise JavaBeans (EJB)

Enterprise JavaBeans (EJB) is a standard server-side architecture for writing distributed Java components. In a three-tier architecture, the first tier is the presentation logic (servlets and JSP, for example), the second tier is the business logic (EJB), and the third tier is the backend (the database). An EJB is run using an EJB container, such as OC4J, which provides a number of services to the EJB, including:

- Persistence of object state
- Database transaction handling
- Security

As an EJB developer, you don't have to worry about providing these complicated pieces of code yourself for these services—you can just let the EJB container take care of them.

NOTE
I'm not going to cover all the details of EJB in this section—for comprehensive coverage of EJB, I recommend the book Enterprise JavaBeans *by Richard Monson-Haefel (O'Reilly, 2001).*

In the rest of this chapter, I'll refer to EJB simply as beans. There are two types of beans: *entity beans* and *session beans*. Entity beans are generally used to model things that exist in the real world—a customer, for example. Session beans are generally used to model tasks—a customer ordering a product, for example. Session beans are either *stateful* or *stateless*. Stateless beans don't maintain the same state between calls to the bean; stateful beans do maintain state.

In the rest of this section, I'll walk you through an example session bean that connects to the database using the same data source as the previous servlet and JSP examples and returns an object containing values for the `id`, `name`, `description`, and `price` columns of a specified row in the `products` table. I'll show you how to compile the bean, deploy the bean to OC4J, and subsequently use an instance of the bean using a stand-alone Java application. Finally, I'll show you a servlet that also uses an instance of the bean.

An Example Session Bean

The example bean shown in this section is a stateless session bean; all the files for this example are located in the `JDBC_book\programs\EJB` directory. The example bean retrieves the `name`, `description`, and `price` columns for a row with a specified `id` from the `products` table and returns an object of the `Product` class. The `Product.java` file defines this class and is shown in the following listing:

```
/*
  Product.java defines a class to represent a row from the
  products table
*/

package server;

public class Product implements java.io.Serializable {

  // declare the Product attributes
  public int id;
  public String name;
  public String description;
  public float price;

  // define the constructor
```

```
public Product(
  int id, String name, String description, float price
) {
  this.id = id;
  this.name = name;
  this.description = description;
  this.price = price;
}

}
```

The `Product` class declares four attributes: `id`, `name`, `description`, and `price`. An object of this class will use these attributes to store the respective column values from the `products` table, which are passed as parameters to the `Product` constructor. You'll notice that this class forms part of a package named `server`, which is used to group all the classes used in the bean together.

The Parts of a Bean

There are four parts that make up a bean:

■ The remote interface

■ The home interface

■ The bean class

■ The deployment descriptor

In the following sections you'll learn about these four parts.

The Remote Interface   The *remote interface* specifies the methods that users of the bean can call. The methods in the remote interface are "stubs" that tell the users of your bean which methods are available. The actual code for the stubbed methods is contained in the bean class. The remote interface for the example bean is contained in the `ProductRemote.java` file, shown in the following listing:

```
/*
  ProductRemote.java defines the remote interface for the bean
*/

package server;

// import the required classes
import java.rmi.RemoteException;
import javax.ejb.EJBObject;
```

```
import java.sql.SQLException;

public interface ProductRemote extends EJBObject {

  // the query() method is defined in the ProductBean class;
  // the method retrieves the name, description, and price columns
  // from the row in the products table that has the specified id
  // and returns a new Product object
  public Product query(int id) throws SQLException, RemoteException;

}
```

The `ProductRemote` interface extends the `javax.ejb.EJBObject` interface, as all remote interfaces must do. There is only one method stub in this class: `query()`. The `query()` method accepts an `int` parameter named `id` (the `id` parameter specifies the `id` of the row in the `products` table that is to be read) and returns a `Product` object. The `query()` method throws a `java.sql.SQLException` object if a database error occurs and throws a `java.rmi.RemoteException` object if a Remote Method Invocation (RMI) error occurs (RMI is used when calling a bean).

The Home Interface   The *home interface* defines the methods that are used to control the bean's life-cycle, and must, at a minimum, define a method named `create()`. The `create()` method is used to create an instance of the bean. The home interface for the example bean is contained in the `ProductHome.java` file, and is shown in the following listing:

```
/*
   ProductHome.java defines the home interface for the bean
*/

package server;

// import the required classes
import javax.ejb.EJBHome;
import javax.ejb.CreateException;
import java.rmi.RemoteException;

public interface ProductHome extends EJBHome {
  public ProductRemote create() throws CreateException,
  RemoteException;
}
```

The `ProductHome` interface extends the `javax.ejb.EJBHome` interface, as all home interfaces must do. When the `create()` method is called, the `ejbCreate()`

method defined in the bean class is automatically called. This call is done behind the scenes by the EJB container and is not explicitly shown in the create() method.

The Bean Class   The *bean class* contains the real "meat" of the bean: it declares the bean's attributes and defines the actual code for the bean's methods. The bean class must define the methods that are stubbed in the remote interface. You'll remember that the ProductRemote class contained a stub for the query() method, and so the bean class must actually define the code for this method. The bean class must also define any code for the ejbCreate() method, which is called automatically by the create() method in the home interface when an instance of the bean is created.

The bean class for the example bean is contained in the ProductBean.java file, and is shown in the following listing:

```
/*
  ProductBean.java defines the class that implements the methods
  defined in the ProductRemote class, plus the other standard methods
  that are required for a session bean
*/

package server;

// import the bean server classes
import server.*;

// import the JDBC classes
import java.sql.*;
import javax.sql.*;

// import the RMI, EJB, and JNDI classes
import java.rmi.RemoteException;
import javax.ejb.*;
import javax.naming.*;

public class ProductBean implements SessionBean {

  // declare the Connection attribute
  transient Connection myConnection;


  // define the ejbCreate() method
  public void ejbCreate() throws CreateException {

    try {

      // look up the data source and get the connection
      // to the database
```

```java
  InitialContext myInitialContext = new InitialContext();
  DataSource myDataSource =
    (DataSource)(myInitialContext.lookup("jdbc/OracleCoreDS"));
  myConnection = myDataSource.getConnection();

} catch(Exception e) {

  e.printStackTrace();
  throw new javax.ejb.CreateException(
    "Couldn't create JDBC connection"
  );

}

}


// define the query() method that retrieves the name, description,
// and price columns for a row in the products table with a
// specified id, and returns a Product object
public Product query(int id) throws SQLException, RemoteException {

  // declare a PreparedStatement object and a ResultSet object
  PreparedStatement myPrepStatement = null;
  ResultSet myResultSet = null;

  try {

    // prepare the SELECT statement that will retrieve the name,
    // description, and price columns for the specified row from
    // the products table
    myPrepStatement =
      myConnection.prepareStatement(
        "SELECT name, description, price " +
        "FROM products " +
        "WHERE id = ?"
      );

    // bind the id parameter to the PreparedStatement object
    // using the setInt() method
    myPrepStatement.setInt(1, id);

    // execute the query
    myResultSet = myPrepStatement.executeQuery();

    // if no row was retrieved then throw a RemoteException object
    if (!myResultSet.next()) {
      throw new RemoteException("No product with id of " + id);
```

```
        }

        // get the name, description, and price column values
        String name = myResultSet.getString("name");
        String description = myResultSet.getString("description");
        float price = myResultSet.getFloat("price");

        // create and return a new Product object
        Product myProduct = new Product(id, name, description, price);
        return myProduct;

      } catch(Exception e) {

        e.printStackTrace();

      } finally {

        try {

          // close the PreparedStatement object
          if (myPrepStatement != null) {
            myPrepStatement.close();
          }

          // close the ResultSet object
          if (myResultSet != null) {
            myResultSet.close();
          }

        } catch (SQLException e) {
          e.printStackTrace();
        }

      }

      return null;

    }


    // define stubs for the other bean methods
    public void ejbActivate() {}
    public void ejbPassivate() {}
    public void ejbRemove() {}
    public void setSessionContext(SessionContext sessionContext) {}

}
```

Because the `ProductBean` class implements the `javax.ejb.SessionBean` interface, it is a session bean. The `ejbCreate()` method looks up the data source previously defined in the `data-sources.xml` file and connects to the database using this data source. The `query()` method retrieves the `name`, `description`, and `price` columns for a row in the `products` table with a specified `id` and returns a `Product` object whose attributes are set to the row's column values; if the row was not found, the `query()` method returns `null`.

The `ProductBean` class also defines four method stubs, which are required by the `javax.ejb.SessionBean` interface. These stubs don't contain any code because the example bean itself doesn't call these methods. The `ejbActivate()` and `ejbPassivate()` methods are called when a bean instance is about to be activated or deactivated. The `ejbRemove()` method is called when the bean instance is no longer needed. The `setSessionContext()` method is used to set the context of the bean instance.

The Deployment Descriptor   The *deployment descriptor* is an XML file that describes the bean components and tells the EJB container how to manage the bean at runtime. I mentioned earlier that the EJB container provides services like database transaction handling and security—the deployment descriptor tells the EJB container how the bean is to use those services.

The deployment descriptor specifies the following details:

- The bean home and remote interfaces, along with the bean class

- Whether the bean is stateful or stateless

- How database transactions are handled for the bean

- The names of any data sources used by the bean

- The *security roles* that may use the bean—I'll talk more about security roles shortly

The deployment descriptor for the example bean is defined in the `ejb-jar.xml` file (located in the `JDBC_book\programs\EJB\META-INF` directory). The "jar" part of the filename comes from the fact that the bean interface and class files will be packaged together in a *Java Archive* (JAR) file—I'll show you how this is done later in this chapter. The `ejb-jar.xml` file for the example bean is shown in the following listing:

```
<?xml version="1.0"?>
<!DOCTYPE ejb-jar PUBLIC "-//Sun Microsystems Inc.//DTD
 Enterprise JavaBeans 1.1//EN" "ejb-jar.dtd">
<ejb-jar>
  <enterprise-beans>
```

```
<session>
  <description>no description</description>
    <ejb-name>ProductBean</ejb-name>
    <home>server.ProductHome</home>
    <remote>server.ProductRemote</remote>
    <ejb-class>server.ProductBean</ejb-class>
    <session-type>Stateless</session-type>
    <transaction-type>Container</transaction-type>
    <resource-ref>
      <res-ref-name>jdbc/DB1</res-ref-name>
      <res-type>javax.sql.DataSource</res-type>
      <res-auth>Application</res-auth>
    </resource-ref>
</session>
</enterprise-beans>
<assembly-descriptor>
  <security-role>
    <description>no description</description>
    <role-name>users</role-name>
  </security-role>
  <method-permission>
    <description>no description</description>
    <role-name>users</role-name>
    <method>
      <ejb-name>ProductBean</ejb-name>
      <method-name>*</method-name>
    </method>
  </method-permission>
  <container-transaction>
    <description>no description</description>
    <method>
      <ejb-name>ProductBean</ejb-name>
      <method-name>*</method-name>
    </method>
    <trans-attribute>Required</trans-attribute>
  </container-transaction>
</assembly-descriptor>
</ejb-jar>
```

The deployment descriptor is an XML file containing a number of tags. The
`session` tag contained in the Enterprise Beans tag indicates this descriptor is for
a session bean. The tags inside the `session` tag specify the home and remote
interfaces, the bean class, the session and transaction types, and the data source
reference used by the example bean.

The tags in the `assembly-descriptor` tag specify the security role allowed
to access the bean, along with the methods that the security role can access
(* indicates all methods are accessible). The name of the security role used by the

bean is specified using the role-name tag, and for this bean the security role used is called users. You'll see how this role is defined in the next section.

Additional XML Files Required to Deploy the Bean

There are three other XML files used during the deployment of the example bean:

- **application.xml** Lists the files that make up the bean

- **principals.xml** Defines the users and groups of users who may potentially access the bean

- **orion-application.xml** Defines the security roles, and maps the user groups to security roles—these mappings define which groups may actually create an instance of the bean

The following sections show the three XML files used for the example bean (these files are in the JDBC_book\programs\EJB\META-INF directory).

The application.xml File The application.xml file lists the files that make up the bean; the application.xml file for the example bean is shown in the following listing:

```
<?xml version="1.0"?>
<!DOCTYPE application PUBLIC "-//Sun Microsystems, Inc.//DTD
 J2EE Application 1.2//EN"
 "http://java.sun.com/j2ee/dtds/application_1_2.dtd">

<application>
  <display-name>Oracle JDBC EJB example</display-name>
  <module>
    <ejb>server.jar</ejb>
  </module>
</application>
```

The ejb tag in the module tag indicates that the server.jar file contains the interface and class files that make up the bean. You will see how the server.jar file is created shortly.

The principals.xml File The principals.xml file defines the users and groups of users who may potentially access the bean; the principals.xml file for the example bean is shown in the following listing:

```
<?xml version="1.0"?>
<!DOCTYPE principals PUBLIC "//Evermind - Orion Principals//"
```

```
 "http://xmlns.oracle.com/ias/dtds/principals.dtd">

<principals>
  <groups>
    <group name="users">
      <description>users</description>
      <permission name="rmi:login" />
      <permission name="com.evermind.server.rmi.RMIPermission" />
    </group>
  </groups>
  <users>
    <user username="store_user" password="store_password">
      <description>store_user</description>
      <group-membership group="users" />
    </user>
  </users>
</principals>
```

The group definitions are placed in the `groups` tag; this `principals.xml` file defines one group named `users`. The `users` group has two permissions: `rmi.login` and `com.evermind.server.rmi.RMIPermission`, which allow users in this group to perform remote method invocations. The users who make up a group are placed in the `users` tag; as you can see, the `store_user` is in the `users` group.

The orion-application.xml File   The `orion-application.xml` file defines the security roles and maps the user groups to security roles. These mappings define which groups may actually create an instance of the bean. The `orion-application.xml` file for the example bean is shown in the following listing:

```
<?xml version="1.0"?>
<!DOCTYPE orion-application PUBLIC "-//Evermind//DTD
 J2EE Application runtime 1.2//EN"
 "http://xmlns.oracle.com/ias/dtds/orion-application.dtd">

<orion-application deployment-version="1.4.5">
  <ejb-module remote="false" path="server.jar" />
  <persistence path="persistence" />
  <principals path="principals.xml" />
  <log>
    <file path="application.log" />
  </log>
  <namespace-access>
    <read-access>
      <namespace-resource root="">
        <security-role-mapping name="&lt;jndi-user-role&gt;">
          <group name="users" />
```

```
        </security-role-mapping>
      </namespace-resource>
    </read-access>
    <write-access>
      <namespace-resource root="">
        <security-role-mapping name="&lt;jndi-user-role&gt;">
          <group name="users" />
        </security-role-mapping>
      </namespace-resource>
    </write-access>
  </namespace-access>
</orion-application>
```

   This file maps the `users` group (defined in the `principals.xml` file) to the
`jndi-user-role` security role. The `jndi-user-role` has read and write access
to the bean namespace. This basically means that any members of the `users` group
can create an instance of the example bean; because `store_user` is a member of
the `users` group, `store_user` can create an instance of the example bean.

Compiling and Deploying the Bean

Compiling and deploying a bean is a somewhat involved process; to help you
deploy the example bean, I've provided a Windows script. This script is named
`bean.bat` and is located in the `JDBC_book\programs\EJB` directory; this script
is shown in the following listing:

```
REM Script for compiling and deploying the example bean

REM set the required environment variables
REM (you'll need to change the setting of OC4J_HOME,
REM and probably CLASSPATH)
set OC4J_HOME=E:\Oracle\iSuites\j2ee\home
set ORIGINAL_CLASSPATH=%CLASSPATH%
set CLASSPATH=.;..;%OC4J_HOME%\ejb.jar;%OC4J_HOME%\jndi.jar;
%OC4J_HOME%\lib\classes12.jar
set ADMIN_PASSWORD=welcome

REM compile the bean source files
javac server/*.java

REM build the JAR file containing the bean classes
jar -cf server.jar server/*.class META-INF/ejb-jar.xml

REM build the EAR file
jar -cf jdbcejb.ear server.jar META-INF/application.xml
 META-INF/orion-application.xml META-INF/principals.xml
```

```
REM deploy the EAR file to OC4J
copy jdbcejb.ear %OC4J_HOME%
java -jar %OC4J_HOME%\admin.jar ormi://localhost
 admin %ADMIN_PASSWORD%
 -deploy -file jdbcejb.ear -deploymentName JDBCEJB

REM set the classpath back to the original setting
set CLASSPATH=%ORIGINAL_CLASSPATH%
```

NOTE
Those of you using Linux or Unix can either type in
similar commands using one of the shells for your
operating system, or write a similar shell script.

The first thing `bean.bat` does is to set a number of environment variables—
you'll need to change the setting for the `OC4J_HOME` variable (this must be set to
the directory where you installed OC4J). You may also need to change `CLASSPATH`,
depending on your installation of OC4J and where the required JAR files are located.
The `ORIGINAL_CLASSPATH` variable records the current setting of the `CLASSPATH`
variable, and the `CLASSPATH` variable is then set with the required directories and
JAR files to compile and deploy the bean. The `ADMIN_PASSWORD` variable is set to
the password for the `admin` user.

The script then compiles all the Java source files for the bean and builds a JAR
file containing the bean class files and the `ejb-jar.xml` deployment descriptor
file; this JAR file is named `server.jar`. Next, an *Enterprise Archive* (EAR) file
named `jdbcejb.ear` is built, which contains the `server.jar` file, along with
the `application.xml`, `orion-application.xml`, and `principals.xml`
files. To deploy the `jdbcejb.ear` file to OC4J, this file is first copied to the
`OC4J_HOME` directory; the following command is then used by the script to perform
the deployment of the `jdbcejb.ear` file:

```
java -jar %OC4J_HOME%\admin.jar ormi://localhost
 admin %ADMIN_PASSWORD%
 -deploy -file jdbcejb.ear -deploymentName JDBCEJB
```

This command runs the `admin.jar` file using the `java` tool (`admin.jar`
forms part of OC4J). The location of the OC4J server is `ormi://localhost`.
The `admin` user (with the password specified in the `ADMIN_PASSWORD` variable)
is used to perform the deployment. The `-deploy` option indicates that an
application is being deployed; the `-file` option is used to specify the EAR file
to deploy (`jdbcejb.ear`); the `-deploymentName` option names the bean
(JDBCEJB)—this name will be used later to look up the bean.

At the end of the `bean.bat` script, the `CLASSPATH` variable is set back to what it was originally set to prior to the script being run.

To run the `bean.bat` script, enter the following command using the Windows command-line:

```
bean.bat
```

This will run the commands in the `bean.bat` script and compile and deploy the bean.

Using the Bean in a Stand-Alone Java Program

Once you've compiled and deployed the bean, you can create and use an instance of the bean using a client program. In this section, you'll see a stand-alone Java program that creates an instance of the bean shown in the previous section and uses that bean instance to retrieve the details of a specified row from the `products` table.

The files for this client program are contained in the `JDBC_book\programs\ EJB\client` directory. The Java class for the client program is contained in the `Client.java` file and is shown in the following listing:

```
/*
   Client.java is a stand-alone Java application that
   creates an instance of the bean
*/

// import the bean classes
import server.ProductHome;
import server.ProductRemote;
import server.Product;

// import the Java Naming and Directory Interface (JNDI) classes
import javax.naming.Context;
import javax.naming.InitialContext;

public class Client {

  public static void main(String args []) throws Exception {

    // the first argument in the args array is the id of the product
    int id = Integer.valueOf(args[0]).intValue();

    // create a JNDI Context object
    Context myInitialContext = new InitialContext();

    // create a ProductHome object and use the lookup() method
    // of the Context object to find the bean
```

```
ProductHome myProductHome = (ProductHome)
  myInitialContext.lookup("java:comp/env/JDBCEJB");

// create a ProductRemote object by calling the create() method
ProductRemote myProductRemote = myProductHome.create();

// create a Product object and use the query() method of the
// ProductRemote object to get the column values from the products
// table and copy those values to the Product object
// - the parameter to the query method is the id of the row in
// the products table to be read
Product myProduct = myProductRemote.query(id);

// if the Product object is not null (i.e. the row was found in
// the products table), then display the Product object's
// attributes
if (myProduct != null) {

  // display the Product object's variables
  System.out.println("myProduct details:");
  System.out.println("myProduct.id = " + myProduct.id);
  System.out.println("myProduct.name = " + myProduct.name);
  System.out.println("myProduct.description = " +
    myProduct.description);
  System.out.println("myProduct.price = " + myProduct.price);

} else {

  System.out.println("Product not found");

}
  }
}
```

The `id` of the row to retrieve from the `products` table is specified as an argument to the `main()` method. The `main()` method reads this argument and then creates a JNDI `javax.naming.Context` object named `myInitialContext`; this object is then used to look up the example bean using the following statement:

```
ProductHome myProductHome = (ProductHome)
  myInitialContext.lookup("java:comp/env/JDBCEJB");
```

This statement finds the bean named `JDBCEJB`, which you previously deployed. This statement also creates a `ProductHome` object, through which the bean's `create()` method is called using the following statement:

```
ProductRemote myProductRemote = myProductHome.create();
```

This statement creates an instance of the bean. Next, the bean's `query()` method is called:

```
Product myProduct = myProductRemote.query(id);
```

The `query()` method attempts to retrieve the specified row from the `products` table. If the row was found, the `Product` object returned by the `query()` method has attributes whose values are set to the column values of that row; if the row wasn't found, the `Product` object returned by the `query()` method is set to `null`. If the `Product` object is *not* set to `null`, then the object's attributes are displayed.

The jndi.properties File

In addition to the `Client.java` file, the program needs a *JNDI properties file*. This file indicates the JNDI context factory to use, the URL for the bean, and the user name and password to use when accessing the bean. The JNDI properties file for this example is in the `JDBC_book\programs\EJB\client` directory and is named `jdni.properties`; this file is shown in the following listing:

```
java.naming.factory.initial=
com.evermind.server.ApplicationClientInitialContextFactory
java.naming.provider.url=ormi://localhost/JDBCEJB
java.naming.security.principal=store_user
java.naming.security.credentials=store_password
```

The URL for the bean is `ormi://localhost/JDBCEJB`, and the `store_user` is used to access the bean.

The application-client.xml File

The final file required by the program is the `application-client.xml` file, located in the `JDBC_book\programs\EJB\client` directory. The `application-client.xml` file lists the name of the bean, along with the name of the home and remote interfaces for the bean; this file is shown in the following listing:

```
<?xml version="1.0"?>
<!DOCTYPE application-client PUBLIC "-//Sun Microsystems, Inc.//DTD
 J2EE Application Client 1.2//EN"
 "http://java.sun.com/j2ee/dtds/application-client_1_2.dtd">

<application-client>
  <display-name>Client</display-name>
  <ejb-ref>
    <ejb-ref-name>JDBCEJB</ejb-ref-name>
    <ejb-ref-type>Session</ejb-ref-type>
    <home>server.ProductHome</home>
```

```
   <remote>server.ProductRemote</remote>
 </ejb-ref>
</application-client>
```

To compile and run the Client program, I've supplied another Windows script. This script is named `client.bat` and is shown in the following listing:

```
REM Script for compiling and running the stand-alone
REM Java client program

REM set the required environment variables
REM (you'll need to change the setting of OC4J_HOME,
REM and probably CLASSPATH)
set OC4J_HOME=E:\Oracle\iSuites\j2ee\home
set ORIGINAL_CLASSPATH=%CLASSPATH%
set CLASSPATH=.;..;%OC4J_HOME%\ejb.jar;%OC4J_HOME%\jndi.jar;%OC4J_HOME%\oc4j.jar;
%OC4J_HOME%\lib\classes12.jar

REM compile the client source files
javac client/Client.java

REM run the client program with different argument values for the
REM product id (including a non-existent product id of 20)
cd client
java Client 1
java Client 2
java Client 20
cd ..

REM set the classpath back to the original setting
set CLASSPATH=%ORIGINAL_CLASSPATH%
```

The `client.bat` script compiles the `Client.java` file and then runs the resulting `Client` class three times with a different argument for the product `id` each time; the third run supplies a nonexistent product `id` of 20 to the class.

You may run the `client.bat` script using the Windows command-line tool. The output for the three runs of the `Client` class are shown in the following listing:

```
D:\JDBC_book\JDBC_book\programs\EJB\client>java Client 1
myProduct details:
myProduct.id = 1
myProduct.name = Modern Science
myProduct.description = A description of modern science
myProduct.price = 13.97

D:\JDBC_book\JDBC_book\programs\EJB\client>java Client 2
myProduct details:
myProduct.id = 2
myProduct.name = Chemistry
myProduct.description = Introduction to Chemistry
myProduct.price = 30.0
```

```
D:\JDBC_book\JDBC_book\programs\EJB\client>java Client 20
Product not found
```

The first two runs successfully retrieve and display the product details for products #1 and #2. The third run displays a message stating that the product was not found; this is as expected because there is no product with an id of 20.

Using the Bean in a Servlet

You can also use the bean in a servlet or a JSP. The servlet shown in this section is contained in the JDBC_book\programs directory, and the servlet source file is named ProductServlet.java. The contents of this file is shown in the following listing:

```java
/*
  ProductServlet.java illustrates how to use a bean in a servlet
*/

// import the required classes
import java.util.*;
import java.io.IOException;
import java.rmi.RemoteException;
import javax.servlet.*;
import javax.servlet.http.*;
import javax.ejb.*;
import javax.naming.*;
import javax.rmi.PortableRemoteObject;
import java.sql.*;

public class ProductServlet extends HttpServlet
{
  // declare a server.ProductHome object
  server.ProductHome myProductHome;

  public void init() throws ServletException {
    try {

      // create a Hashtable object to store the details
      // of how to look up the bean
      Hashtable env = new Hashtable();
      env.put(Context.INITIAL_CONTEXT_FACTORY,
          "com.evermind.server.rmi.RMIInitialContextFactory");
      env.put(Context.PROVIDER_URL, "ormi://localhost/JDBCEJB");
      env.put(Context.SECURITY_PRINCIPAL, "store_user");
      env.put(Context.SECURITY_CREDENTIALS, "store_password");

      // create a JNDI Context object
```

```
      Context myInitialContext = new InitialContext(env);

      // locate the bean using the lookup() method
      Object homeObject = myInitialContext.lookup("ProductBean");

      // narrow the reference to a ProductHome object
      myProductHome = (server.ProductHome)
        PortableRemoteObject.narrow(
          homeObject,
          server.ProductHome.class
        );

    } catch(NamingException e) {
      throw new ServletException("Error looking up home", e);
    }
  }


  // handle get request
  public void doGet(
    HttpServletRequest request, HttpServletResponse response
  ) throws ServletException, IOException {

    // begin an HTML page
    response.setContentType("text/html");
    ServletOutputStream out = response.getOutputStream();
    out.println("<html>");
    out.println("<head><title>Product</title></head>");
    out.println("<body>");

    // display an HTML table
    out.println("<table width=100% border=1>");
    out.println("<tr>");
    out.println("<th>Id</th>");
    out.println("<th>Name</th>");
    out.println("<th>Description</th>");
    out.println("<th>Price</th>");
    out.println("</tr>");

    try {

      // create a ProductRemote object by calling the create() method
      server.ProductRemote myProductRemote = myProductHome.create();

      // create a Product object and use the query() method of the
      // ProductRemote object
```

```
server.Product myProduct = myProductRemote.query(1);

// if the Product object is not null (i.e. the row was found in
// the products table), then display the Product object's
// attributes in the table
if (myProduct != null) {

  out.println("<tr>");
  out.println("<td>" + myProduct.id + "</td>");
  out.println("<td>" + myProduct.name + "</td>");
  out.println("<td>" + myProduct.description + "</td>");
  out.println("<td>" + myProduct.price + "</td>");
  out.println("</tr>");

}

// finish the HTML page
out.println("</table>");
out.println("</body></html>");

} catch(RemoteException e) {
out.println("Error communicating with EJB-server: " +
  e.getMessage());
} catch(CreateException e) {
out.println("Error creating EJB: " + e.getMessage());
} catch(SQLException e) {
out.println("SQL Exception: " + e.getMessage());
}
}

}
```

This servlet looks up the bean using a call to the `lookup()` method of the `InitialContext` object, creates an instance of the bean, and uses the `query()` method to retrieve the column values for product #1. These values are then displayed in an HTML table.

To deploy this servlet to OC4J, you copy the `ProductServlet.java` source file to the `default-web-app\WEB-INF\classes` directory where you installed OC4J.

To invoke `ProductServlet`, point your Internet browser to `http://localhost:8888/servlet/ProductServlet`, assuming you've installed OC4J on your local machine and you haven't changed the default port setting of 8888. Figure 11-2 shows the result of invoking `ProductServlet` using Internet Explorer.

As you can see, the details of product #1 are displayed by `ProductServlet`.

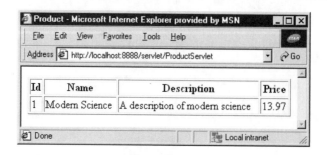

FIGURE 11-2. *ProductServlet output*

PART
IV

Performance

CHAPTER
12

Connection Pooling
and Caching

p until now, the programs you've seen have used separate connections to access the database. Creating a connection to the database is a very resource intensive operation, and therefore takes a relatively long time to complete. If you have a program that services many intermittent requests for access to the database, creating a new connection for each request is obviously undesirable because it takes a long time.

Rather than create a new connection for each database request, a better way is to initially create one connection to the database; this connection may then be used whenever your program needs to temporarily access the database. This is known as *connection pooling.*

Typically, you'll use a connection pool indirectly by creating a *connection cache*; a connection cache creates a connection pool and automatically creates additional connections for that connection pool as needed.

NOTE
You cannot use connection pooling or caching when using the server-side internal driver (this driver is used in Java stored procedures and triggers). This is because the server-side internal driver uses the default database connection.

Because connection caching is made possible by connection pooling, I'll discuss the details of connection pooling before describing the details of connection caching. This chapter will use the concept of a data source; data sources were discussed in Chapter 3. First off, I'll discuss the connection pooling and caching packages that your program must import.

Connection Pooling and Caching Packages

The JDBC 2.0 API comes with a package known as the Optional Package—also known as the Standard Extension—which defines the interfaces for connection pooling and caching. These interfaces may then be implemented by a third-party software vendor such as Oracle. The Optional Package also provides support for the Java Naming and Directory Interface (JNDI), among other things.

NOTE
You'll learn about JNDI in Appendix D.

The Optional Package is defined in the `javax` package provided by Sun Microsystems, and the JDBC parts of the Optional Package are located in the `javax.sql` package. The Oracle extensions to JDBC implement the connection pooling and caching interfaces defined in the Optional Package. The Oracle extensions for connection pooling and caching are located in the `oracle.jdbc.pool` package.

The following statements import the `javax.sql` and `oracle.jdbc.pool` packages:

```
import javax.sql.*;
import oracle.jdbc.pool.*;
```

Now that I've finished with the preamble, I'll describe the details of connection pooling with the Thin driver (connection pooling with the OCI driver is very similar to connection caching, and therefore I'll defer discussion of connection pooling with the OCI driver until the final section of this chapter).

Connection Pooling with the Thin Driver

When using connection pooling with the Thin driver, you initially create one physical connection to the database. When you need to access the database, you simply request a temporary connection from the connection pool. This temporary database connection is known as a *connection instance*, and you use a connection instance to access the database. When the connection instance accesses the database, it uses the connection pool's physical database connection.

When you're finished with your database operation, you close your connection instance. Closing the connection instance doesn't close the physical connection to the database maintained by the connection pool. You can therefore request another connection instance from the connection pool when you need to access the database again.

NOTE
You can request a connection instance from the connection pool many times, although you can only have one connection instance open at any time.

If you have a program that makes many intermittent requests to the database, using a connection pool can significantly improve the performance of your programs. You simply set up a connection pool at the start of your program and then access the database when you need to by requesting a connection instance.

Because requesting a connection instance is fast, unlike creating a physical database connection, the execution time of your program can be significantly reduced.

In order to use connection pooling with the Thin driver in your programs, you may perform the following steps:

1. Create a connection pool data source object.

2. Set the attributes for the physical database connection using the connection pool data source object.

3. Create a pooled connection object, which represents the physical connection to the database.

4. Request, use, and finally, close a connection instance. You use the connection instance to access the database. When you need to access the database again, you simply request another connection instance.

5. Close the pooled connection object.

The following sections describe these steps in detail.

Step 1: Create a Connection Pool Data Source Object

The first step is to create a connection pool data source object of the `OracleConnectionPoolDataSource` class. This object acts as the data source for your program (data sources were discussed in Chapter 3). The following statement creates an `OracleConnectionPoolDataSource` object named myOCPDS:

```
OracleConnectionPoolDataSource myOCPDS =
    new OracleConnectionPoolDataSource();
```

The `OracleConnectionPoolDataSource` class implements the `ConnectionPoolDataSource` interface (defined in the `javax.sql` package); the `OracleConnectionPoolDataSource` class also extends the `OracleDataSource` class. You'll see why this is important in the next step.

Step 2: Set the Attributes for the Physical Database Connection Using the Connection Pool Data Source Object

The second step is to set the attributes for the physical database connection using the connection pool data source object. Now, because the `OracleConnectionPoolDataSource` class extends the `OracleDataSource` class, it inherits all the attributes and methods for accessing those attributes that are defined in the `OracleDataSource` class. Also, because the `OracleDataSource` class implements the `DataSource` interface, the attributes of the `DataSource` interface are available to the `OracleConnectionPoolDataSource` class.

Table 3-1 in Chapter 3 shows the DataSource attributes, and Table 3-2 shows the additional attributes of the OracleDataSource class. Chapter 3 also describes the get and set methods that may be used to read from and write to the various attributes. Just as a reminder, some of these attributes and methods include:

- The name of the server on which the database is running. This is set using the setServerName() method.

- The database name (Oracle SID). This is set using the setDatabaseName() method.

- The port on which the Oracle Net listener is waiting for requests. This is set using the setPortNumber() method.

- The Oracle JDBC driver to use to communicate with the database. This is set using the setDriverType() method.

The following statements use the methods shown in this list to set the attributes of the OracleConnectionPoolDataSource object named myOCPDS, which was created in Step 1:

```
myOCPDS.setServerName("localhost");
myOCPDS.setDatabaseName("ORCL");
myOCPDS.setPortNumber(1521);
myOCPDS.setDriverType("thin");
```

You may also optionally specify the username and password for the database user that is to be used in the database connection. This is done using the setUser() and setPassword() methods, as shown in the following statements:

```
myOCPDS.setUser("store_user");
myOCPDS.setPassword("store_password");
```

If you don't specify the username and password in your OracleConnectionPoolDataSource object, you must specify them using your pooled connection object. I'll show you how to do that at the end of the next step.

Step 3: Create a Pooled Connection Object
The third step is to create a pooled connection object. The pooled connection object represents the physical connection to the database, and you use the pooled connection object to request database connection instances.

You can create a pooled connection object using either the PooledConnection interface (defined in the javax.sql package) or the OraclePooledConnection class (the OraclePooledConnection class implements the PooledConnection interface). The following statement creates a `PooledConnection` object named `myPooledConnection`:

```
PooledConnection myPooledConnection = myOCPDS.getPooledConnection();
```

Notice that the `getPooledConnection()` method for the `myOCPDS` object is called. This method returns a `PooledConnection` object, and this object is then stored in `myPooledConnection`.

In Step 2, I mentioned that you may omit the username and password for the database connection when setting the attributes for your `OracleConnectionPoolDataSource` object. Instead, you can supply the username and password when calling the `getPooledConnection()` method, as shown in the following statement:

```
PooledConnection myPooledConnection =
  myOCPDS.getPooledConnection("store_user", "store_password");
```

Your `PooledConnection` object represents the physical connection to the database. You can create multiple `PooledConnection` objects from your `OracleConnectionPoolDataSource` object using the `getPooledConnection()` method, and each `PooledConnection` object will represent a separate physical connection to the database.

Step 4: Request, Use, and Finally, Close a Connection Instance

The fourth step is to request, use, and finally, close a connection instance. You request a connection instance from your `PooledConnection` object using the `getConnection()` method. The `getConnection()` method returns a connection instance that you may then use to access the database. This connection instance actually uses the underlying physical database connection represented by the `PooledConnection` object.

The following statement requests a connection instance from `myPooledConnection` and stores the returned connection instance in `myConnection`:

```
Connection myConnection = myPooledConnection.getConnection();
```

You can now access the database using `myConnection`.

Once you're finished with your connection instance, you must close it using the `close()` method, as shown in the following statement:

```
myConnection.close();
```

When you need to access the database again, you simply request another connection instance using the `getConnection()` method of your `PooledConnection` object.

NOTE
You can only request and use one
connection instance at a time.

Step 5: Close the Pooled Connection Object

Before your program ends, you should close your PooledConnection object using
the close() method. The following statement closes myPooledConnection:

```
myPooledConnection.close();
```

The following section contains a complete program that illustrates the use of the
steps shown in this section.

Example Program: ConnectionPoolExample1.java

The ConnectionPoolExample1.java, program, shown in the following listing,
follows the five steps described in the previous sections to display the first_name
and last_name columns for customer #1 and customer #2. I've provided a
procedure named DisplayCustomer() that retrieves and displays the required
columns from the customers table.

```
/*
  ConnectionPoolExample1.java illustrates connection pooling
  with the Thin driver
*/

// import the JDBC packages
import java.sql.*;
import javax.sql.*;
import oracle.jdbc.pool.*;

public class ConnectionPoolExample1 {

  public static void main(String args [])
  throws SQLException {

    // step 1: create a connection pool data source object
    System.out.println("Creating an OracleConnectionPooDataSource " +
      "object");
    OracleConnectionPoolDataSource myOCPDS =
      new OracleConnectionPoolDataSource();

    // step 2: set the attributes for the physical database
```

```
    // connection using the connection pool data source object
    System.out.println("Setting the attributes of the " +
      "OracleConnectionPoolDataSource object");
    myOCPDS.setServerName("localhost");
    myOCPDS.setDatabaseName("ORCL");
    myOCPDS.setPortNumber(1521);
    myOCPDS.setDriverType("thin");
    myOCPDS.setUser("store_user");
    myOCPDS.setPassword("store_password");

    // step 3: create a pooled connection object
    System.out.println("Creating a PooledConnection object");
    PooledConnection myPooledConnection =
      myOCPDS.getPooledConnection();

    // step 4: request, use, and finally close a connection instance
    System.out.println("Requesting a Connection instance");
    Connection myConnection = myPooledConnection.getConnection();
    DisplayCustomer(myConnection, 1);  // display customer #1
    System.out.println("Closing the Connection instance");
    myConnection.close();

    // repeat step 4 to display customer #2
    System.out.println("Requesting a Connection instance");
    myConnection = myPooledConnection.getConnection();
    DisplayCustomer(myConnection, 2);  // display customer #2
    System.out.println("Closing the Connection instance");
    myConnection.close();

    // step 5: close the pooled connection object
    System.out.println("Closing the PooledConnection object");
    myPooledConnection.close();

  } // end of main()


  public static void DisplayCustomer(Connection myConnection, int id)
  throws SQLException {

    // create a Statement object
    Statement myStatement = myConnection.createStatement();

    // declare variables and objects used to represent
    // the column values retrieved from the customers table
    String firstName;
    String lastName;

    // create a ResultSet object
```

```
ResultSet customerResultSet = myStatement.executeQuery(
  "SELECT first_name, last_name " +
  "FROM customers " +
  "WHERE id = " + id
);

// retrieve and display the column values
while (customerResultSet.next()) {
  firstName = customerResultSet.getString("first_name");
  lastName = customerResultSet.getString("last_name");

  System.out.println("id = " + id);
  System.out.println("firstName = " + firstName);
  System.out.println("lastName = " + lastName);
} // end of while loop

// close the ResultSet and Statement objects
customerResultSet.close();
myStatement.close();

  } // end of DisplayCustomer()

}
```

The output from this program is as follows:

```
Creating an OracleConnectionPoolDataSource object
Setting the attributes of the OracleConnectionPoolDataSource object
Creating a PooledConnection object
Requesting a Connection instance
id = 1
firstName = John
lastName = Brown
Closing the Connection instance
Requesting a Connection instance
id = 2
firstName = Cynthia
lastName = Green
Closing the Connection instance
Closing the PooledConnection object
```

Connection Caching

A *connection cache* is a collection of one or more physical database connections that you may access using connection instances. Connection caching makes use of connection pooling: each physical database connection in the case is represented using a pooled connection object.

The main advantages of connection caching are:

- You can use a connection cache to establish more than one physical connection to a database once, and then access those physical connections using connection instances.

- You don't have to worry about creating and managing the various pooled connection objects required to represent all the physical connections. By default, a connection cache will dynamically create a pooled connection object for you when one is required.

The following sections describe the details of connection caching.

Creating a Connection Cache

To create a connection cache, you create an object of the `OracleConnectionCacheImpl` class, which implements the `OracleConnectionClass` interface. The `OracleConnectionCacheImpl` class extends the `OracleDataSource` class; therefore, the `OracleConnectionCacheImpl` class has access to all the attributes and methods defined in the `OracleDataSource` class.

The simplest way to create an `OracleConnectionCacheImpl` object is to use the default constructor, as shown in the following statement:

```
OracleConnectionCacheImpl myOCCI =
   new OracleConnectionCacheImpl();
```

This statement creates an `OracleConnectionCacheImpl` object named myOCCI.

To set the attributes for the physical database connections, you may use the various set methods inherited from the `OracleDataSource` class. The following statements show the use of the set methods of myOCCI:

```
myOCCI.setServerName("localhost");
myOCCI.setDatabaseName("ORCL");
myOCCI.setPortNumber(1521);
myOCCI.setDriverType("thin");
myOCCI.setUser("store_user");
myOCCI.setPassword("store_password");
```

You can also pass an existing `ConnectionPoolDataSource` object to the constructor of your `OracleConnectionCacheImpl` object. The resulting physical database connections will use the attributes that were previously set for your `ConnectionPoolDataSource` object. For example, if you had a `ConnectionPoolDataSource` object named myCPDS, the statement would be as follows:

```
OracleConnectionCacheImpl myOCCI =
    new OracleConnectionCacheImpl(myCPDS);
```

You can also use the setConnectionPoolDataSource() method of your OracleConnectionCacheImpl object; this method accepts an ConnectionPoolDataSource object and sets the database connection attributes for your OracleConnectionCacheImpl object. For example:

```
myOCCI.setConnectionPoolDataSource(myCPDS);
```

The myOCCI object then uses the physical database connection attributes that were previously set for myCPDS.

Requesting, Using, and Closing a Connection Instance

In order to access the database, you use a connection instance, which you request using the getConnection() method of your OracleConnectionCacheImpl object. For example, the following statement requests a connection instance from myOCCI using the getConnection() method and stores the returned connection instance in myConnection:

```
Connection myConnection = myOCCI.getConnection();
```

I mentioned earlier that a PooledConnection object represents a physical database connection. By default, when you call the getConnection() method for myOCCI, myOCCI checks if there are any PooledConnection objects already in its cache. If there aren't any such objects, myOCCI creates one for you.

The myOCCI object then checks if any of its PooledConnection objects have a free connection instance, and if so, returns that connection instance. If there aren't any free connection instances, myOCCI will create a new PooledConnection object (which will have a free connection instance) and return the connection instance for that new PooledConnection object.

In the previous example that calls the myOCCI.getConnection() method, we know this is the first time a connection instance has been requested, and therefore myOCCI doesn't have any PooledConnection objects. Thus, myOCCI creates a PooledConnection object and returns its connection instance, which is then stored in myConnection. You can then use myConnection to access the database.

The getActiveSize() and getCacheSize() Methods

You can get the number of PooledConnection objects that have connection instances in use by calling the getActiveSize() method of your

`OracleConnectionCacheImpl` object. For example, the following statement calls `myOCCI.getActiveSize()` and displays the result:

```
System.out.println(myOCCI.getActiveSize());
```

Because `myOCCI` created one `PooledConnection` object earlier in the previous section, `myOCCI.getActiveSize()` returns 1 at this point.

You can get the total number of `PooledConnection` objects using the `getCacheSize()` method of your `OracleConnectionCacheImpl` object; this total counts all of the `PooledConnection` objects, regardless of whether their connection instance is in use or not. For example, the following statement calls `myOCCI.getCacheSize()` and displays the result:

```
System.out.println(myOCCI.getCacheSize());
```

Because `myOCCI` only has one `PooledConnection` object at this point, `myOCCI.getCacheSize()` also returns 1.

Requesting Another Connection Instance

If you request another connection instance from `myOCCI` without first closing `myConnection`, `myOCCI` will create another `PooledConnection` object with a free connection instance. For example, the following statement requests another connection instance from `myOCCI`:

```
Connection myConnection2 = myOCCI.getConnection();
```

Because `myConnection` (created in the previous section) hasn't been closed yet, `myOCCI` creates *another* `PooledConnection` object to handle the request. This may be verified by calling `myOCCI.getCacheSize()`, which returns 2 because there are now two `PooledConnection` objects in the cache; `myOCCI.getActiveSize()` will also return 2 because the connection instances for both `PooledConnection` objects are now in use.

Closing a Connection Instance

Once you've finished with a connection instance, you close it using the `close()` method. The following statement closes `myConnection`:

```
myConnection.close();
```

Once the connection instance has been closed, the connection instance for the `PooledConnection` object in the cache is freed up, but the `PooledConnection` object itself will still remain in the cache. This may be verified by calling `myOCCI.getActiveSize()`, which will return 1 because the second

`PooledConnection` object has just had its connection instance closed; however, `myOCCI.getActiveSize()` will return 2 because there are still two `PooledConnection` objects in the cache. The connection instance that has just been closed is now available and will be returned if another request is made for a connection instance.

Closing a Connection Cache

Before your program ends, you should close your `OracleConnectionCacheImpl` object using the `close()` method. The following statement closes `myOCCI`:

```
myOCCI.close();
```

Closing `myOCCI` also closes all the `PooledConnection` objects in the cache. The following section contains a complete program that illustrates the use of a connection cache.

Example Program: ConnectionCacheExample1.java

The `ConnectionCacheExample1.java` program shown in the following listing, shows the use of the statements described in the previous sections.

```
/*
  ConnectionCacheExample1.java illustrates connection caching
*/

// import the JDBC packages
import java.sql.*;
import javax.sql.*;
import oracle.jdbc.pool.*;

public class ConnectionCacheExample1 {

  public static void main(String args [])
  throws SQLException {

    // create an OracleConnectionCacheImpl object
    System.out.println("Creating an OracleConnectionCacheImpl " +
      "object");
    OracleConnectionCacheImpl myOCCI =
      new OracleConnectionCacheImpl();

    // set the attributes for the physical database connections
    System.out.println("Setting the attributes of the " +
```

```
      "OracleConnectionCacheImpl object");
myOCCI.setServerName("localhost");
myOCCI.setDatabaseName("ORCL");
myOCCI.setPortNumber(1521);
myOCCI.setDriverType("thin");
myOCCI.setUser("store_user");
myOCCI.setPassword("store_password");

// request a connection instance from myOCCI and store
// the connection instance in myConnection
System.out.println("Requesting a Connection instance " +
  "and storing it in myConnection");
Connection myConnection = myOCCI.getConnection();

// display the values returned by the getActiveSize() and
// getCacheSize() methods; both methods return 1 at this point,
// since there is one PooledConnection object
// in the cache, and whose connection instance is in use
System.out.println("myOCCI.getActiveSize() = " +
  myOCCI.getActiveSize());
System.out.println("myOCCI.getCacheSize() = " +
  myOCCI.getCacheSize());

// keep myConnection open, so that further requests for
// connection instances require myOCCI to create a new
// PooledConnection object in the cache
// myConnection.close();

// request another connection instance from myOCCI
// and store the connection instance in myConnection2
System.out.println("Requesting another Connection instance " +
  "and storing it in myConnection2");
Connection myConnection2 = myOCCI.getConnection();

// display the values returned by the getActiveSize() and
// getCacheSize() methods; both methods return 2 at this point,
// since there are two PooledConnection objects
// in the cache, both of whose connection instances are in use
System.out.println("myOCCI.getActiveSize() = " +
  myOCCI.getActiveSize());
System.out.println("myOCCI.getCacheSize() = " +
  myOCCI.getCacheSize());

// close myConnection2 using the close() method, this frees the
// connection instance used by myConnection2
System.out.println("Closing myConnection2");
myConnection2.close();
```

```java
// request another connection instance from myOCCI
// and store the connection instance in myConnection3
System.out.println("Requesting another Connection instance " +
  "and storing it in myConnection3");
Connection myConnection3 = myOCCI.getConnection();

// display the values returned by the getActiveSize() and
// getCacheSize() methods; both return 2 at this point,
// because myConnection is still in use and
// myConnection3 uses the connection instance that was freed
// when myConnection2 was closed earlier
System.out.println("myOCCI.getActiveSize() = " +
  myOCCI.getActiveSize());
System.out.println("myOCCI.getCacheSize() = " +
  myOCCI.getCacheSize());

// close myConnection3 using the close() method
System.out.println("Closing myConnection3");
myConnection3.close();

// display the values returned by the getActiveSize() and
// getCacheSize() methods; getActiveSize() returns 1 at this
// point, since the connection instance used by myConnection3
// is now free; getCacheSize() still returns 2 since there
// are still two PooledConnection objects in the cache
System.out.println("myOCCI.getActiveSize() = " +
  myOCCI.getActiveSize());
System.out.println("myOCCI.getCacheSize() = " +
  myOCCI.getCacheSize());

// close the OracleConnectionCacheImpl object
System.out.println("Closing the OracleConnectionCacheImpl " +
  "object");
myOCCI.close();

// display the values returned by the getActiveSize() and
// getCacheSize() methods; both methods return 0 at this point,
// since both PooledConnection objects have been closed
System.out.println("myOCCI.getActiveSize() = " +
  myOCCI.getActiveSize());
System.out.println("myOCCI.getCacheSize() = " +
  myOCCI.getCacheSize());

} // end of main()

}
```

The output from this program is as follows:

```
Creating an OracleConnectionCacheImpl object
Setting the attributes of the OracleConnectionCacheImpl object
Requesting a Connection instance and storing it in myConnection
myOCCI.getActiveSize() = 1
myOCCI.getCacheSize() = 1
Requesting another Connection instance and storing it in
 myConnection2
myOCCI.getActiveSize() = 2
myOCCI.getCacheSize() = 2
Closing myConnection2
Requesting another Connection instance and storing it in
 myConnection3
myOCCI.getActiveSize() = 2
myOCCI.getCacheSize() = 2
Closing myConnection3
myOCCI.getActiveSize() = 1
myOCCI.getCacheSize() = 2
Closing the OracleConnectionCacheImpl object
myOCCI.getActiveSize() = 0
myOCCI.getCacheSize() = 0
```

Controlling the Number of PooledConnection Objects

By default, when you request a connection instance from your connection cache (and none of the PooledConnection objects have a free connection instance), a new PooledConnection object is created. Because creating (and closing) PooledConnection objects take a certain amount of time, you can control the number of PooledConnection objects present in your connection cache—and you might want to do this for performance reasons. You can set the maximum and minimum number of PooledConnection objects that are available in your connection cache. You'll see how to do that in the next two sections.

You can also specify what happens when you request a connection instance and your connection cache already has the maximum number of PooledConnections previously set: you do this using a *connection cache scheme*. You'll learn about connection cache schemes at the end of this section.

Setting the Maximum Number of PooledConnection Objects

By default, the maximum number of PooledConnection objects that may be created in a connection cache is ten. You change the maximum number of PooledConnection objects in your connection cache by using the setMaxLimit()

method of your `OracleConnectionCacheImpl` object. The following statement
sets the maximum number of `PooledConnections` in `myOCCI` to five:

```
myOCCI.setMaxLimit(5);
```

By default, when five `PooledConnection` objects have been created in the
cache and all of their connection instances are being used, a request for another
connection instance will cause `myOCCI` to create another `PooledConnection`
object. You can change this behavior by changing the connection cache scheme.
You'll learn how to do that shortly.

Setting the Minimum Number of PooledConnection Objects

You can set the minimum number of `PooledConnection` objects in
your connection cache by using the `setMinLimit()` method of your
`OracleConnectionCacheImpl` object. The following statement sets the
minimum number of `PooledConnections` in `myOCCI` to five:

```
myOCCI.setMinLimit(5);
```

This means that `myOCCI` always has at least five `PooledConnection`
objects in the cache.

Connection Cache Schemes

Connection cache schemes specify what happens when you've requested a connection
instance and the following conditions are true:

- All the existing connection instances are being used.

- The maximum number of `PooledConnection` objects have already
  been created in the cache.

There are three connection cache schemes:

- **Dynamic**   This is the default scheme, which you'll typically stick to, unless
  you want to limit the number of `PooledConnection` objects in your cache
  for performance reasons. When a connection instance is requested and the
  previous conditions are true, a new `PooledConnection` object is created
  to satisfy the request. When the connection instance is closed, the additional
  `PooledConnection` object created to handle the original request is closed.

- **Fixed wait**   When a connection instance is requested and the previous
  conditions are true, the request is forced to wait until a connection instance
  is available.

■ **Fixed with no wait** When a connection instance is requested and the previous conditions are true, the request is denied immediately (with no waiting for a response) and `null` is returned by the call to the `getConnection()` method.

Let's consider an example. Assume we have a connection cache that allows up to five `PooledConnection` objects to be created, and there are currently five `PooledConnection` objects in our cache. Further, assume that we've requested a connection instance. Because our cache already contains the maximum number of `PooledConnection` objects, what happens next depends on the connection cache scheme. Let's consider what happens with each of the three schemes: in the *dynamic* scheme (the default), a new `PooledConnection` object is created to handle the request; in the *fixed wait* scheme, the request waits until a connection instance is available; in the *fixed with no wait* scheme, the request is denied and `null` is returned.

You can change the scheme using the `setCacheScheme()` method of your `OracleConnectionCacheImpl` object. The `setCacheScheme()` method accepts one of the following constants that specifies the scheme to use:

```
OracleConnectionCacheImpl.DYNAMIC_SCHEME
OracleConnectionCacheImpl.FIXED_WAIT_SCHEME
OracleConnectionCacheImpl.FIXED_RETURN_NULL_SCHEME
```

The following statement sets the connection cache scheme to the *fixed with no wait* scheme:

```
myOCCI.setCacheScheme(
  OracleConnectionCacheImpl.FIXED_RETURN_NULL_SCHEME
);
```

The following section contains a complete program that illustrates the use of controlling the number of `PooledConnection` objects in a connection cache.

Example Program: ConnectionCacheExample2.java

The `ConnectionCacheExample2.java` program, shown in the following listing, shows the use of the statements described in the previous sections. This program performs the following major steps:

1. Creates a connection cache that uses the *fixed with no wait* scheme.

2. Sets the maximum limit of `PooledConnection` objects in the cache to five.

3. Creates an array of five `Connection` objects and populates each object with a connection instance requested from the connection cache (this causes the connection cache to contain the maximum number of five `PooledConnection` objects).

4. Requests another connection instance from the cache. Because the cache uses the *fixed with no wait* scheme, it returns a `null` connection instance.

```
/*
  ConnectionCacheExample2.java illustrates connection caching and
  shows how to control the number of PooledConnection objects
  created in the connection cache. The connection cache featured
  in this program uses the fixed with no wait scheme.
*/

// import the JDBC packages
import java.sql.*;
import javax.sql.*;
import oracle.jdbc.pool.*;

public class ConnectionCacheExample2 {

  public static void main(String args [])
  throws SQLException {

    // create an OracleConnectionCacheImpl object
    System.out.println("Creating an OracleConnectionCacheImpl " +
      "object");
    OracleConnectionCacheImpl myOCCI =
      new OracleConnectionCacheImpl();

    // set the attributes for the physical database connections
    System.out.println("Setting the attributes of the " +
      "OracleConnectionCacheImpl object");
    myOCCI.setServerName("localhost");
    myOCCI.setDatabaseName("ORCL");
    myOCCI.setPortNumber(1521);
    myOCCI.setDriverType("thin");
    myOCCI.setUser("store_user");
    myOCCI.setPassword("store_password");

    // set the connection cache scheme to fixed return null
    System.out.println("Setting cache scheme to fixed with no wait");
    myOCCI.setCacheScheme(
      OracleConnectionCacheImpl.FIXED_RETURN_NULL_SCHEME
```

```
);

// display the default maximum limit of PooledConnection objects
// using the getMaxLimit() method
System.out.println("myOCCI.getMaxLimit() = " +
  myOCCI.getMaxLimit());

// change the maximum limit of PooledConnection objects
int numPooledConnections = 5;
System.out.println("Setting maximum limit of PooledConnection " +
  "objects to " + numPooledConnections);
myOCCI.setMaxLimit(numPooledConnections);
System.out.println("myOCCI.getMaxLimit() = " +
  myOCCI.getMaxLimit());

// create an array of Connection objects
Connection[] myConnectionArray =
  new Connection[numPooledConnections];

// request all the Connection instances from myOCCI and
// store them in myConnectionArray
for (int loopCount = 0; loopCount < numPooledConnections;
  loopCount++) {

  System.out.println("Requesting a Connection instance, " +
    "storing it in myConnectionArray[" + loopCount + "]");
  myConnectionArray[loopCount] = myOCCI.getConnection();

} // end of for loop

// request another connection instance from myOCCI
// and store the connection instance in myConnection;
// since the maximum number of PooledConnection objects already
// exist in myOCCI, what happens next depends on the connection
// cache scheme in use - in this program, the fixed with no wait
// scheme is used, which means null is returned when another
// connection instance is requested
System.out.println("Requesting another Connection instance, " +
  "storing it in myConnection");
Connection myConnection = myOCCI.getConnection();
if (myConnection != null) {
  System.out.println("myConnection is valid (not null)");
} else {
  System.out.println("myConnection is invalid (null)");
}
```

```
        // close the OracleConnectionCacheImpl object
        System.out.println("Closing the OracleConnectionCacheImpl " +
          " object");
        myOCCI.close();

      } // end of main()

    }
```

The output from this program is as follows:

```
Creating an OracleConnectionCacheImpl object
Setting the attributes of the OracleConnectionCacheImpl object
Setting cache scheme to fixed with no wait
myOCCI.getMaxLimit() = 10
Setting maximum limit of PooledConnection objects to 5
myOCCI.getMaxLimit() = 5
Requesting a Connection instance, storing it in myConnectionArray[0]
Requesting a Connection instance, storing it in myConnectionArray[1]
Requesting a Connection instance, storing it in myConnectionArray[2]
Requesting a Connection instance, storing it in myConnectionArray[3]
Requesting a Connection instance, storing it in myConnectionArray[4]
Requesting another Connection instance, storing it in myConnection
myConnection is invalid (null)
Closing the OracleConnectionCacheImpl object
```

If you change the connection cache scheme used in this program to *fixed wait*, the program will wait indefinitely for a connection instance. If you change it to *dynamic* (the default), the cache will automatically create another `PooledConnection` instance to handle the request and return the connection instance for that `PooledConnection` object.

Connection Pooling with the OCI Driver

Connection pooling with the OCI driver is conceptually similar to connection caching in that you have a number of physical connections you can request connection instances for.

Connection pooling with the OCI driver has two main advantages over connection caching:

■ The number of physical connections that may be maintained by the connection pool can be dynamically configured while the program is running.

- Each connection instance (represented using an `OracleOCIConnection` object) can have a different username and password, so you can access different schemas using the same OCI connection pool.

In addition, connection pooling with the OCI driver allows you to have multiple pooled connections, whereas connection pooling with the Thin driver (described earlier in this chapter) allows you to have only one intermittent connection to the database.

Connection pooling with the OCI driver is performed using an object of the `OracleOCIConnectionPool` class, which extends `OracleDataSource` and implements `OracleDataSource`.

To use connection pooling with the OCI driver, you may import the `oracle.jdbc.oci.*` package into your program, as well as the other packages mentioned at the beginning of this chapter. The `oracle.jdbc.oci.*` package contains the `OracleOCIConnection` class. You'll see how to use this class shortly to represent connection instances.

Creating an OCI Connection Pool

To create an OCI connection cache, you create an object of the `OracleOCIConnectionPool` class. The following statement creates `OracleOCIConnectionPool` object named myOOCP:

```
OracleOCIConnectionPool myOOCP = new OracleOCIConnectionPool();
```

To set the attributes for the physical database connections, you may use the various set methods inherited from the `OracleDataSource` class. The following statements show the use of the set methods of myOOCP:

```
myOOCP.setServerName("localhost");
myOOCP.setDatabaseName("ORCL");
myOOCP.setDriverType("oci");
myOOCP.setPortNumber(1521);
myOOCP.setUser("store_user");
myOOCP.setPassword("store_password");
```

The OracleOCIConnectionPool Dynamic Attributes

You can also set a number of the optional attributes for your `OracleOCIConnectionPool` object; these optional attributes can be set dynamically while your program is running and can be used to improve performance.

There are five dynamic attributes you can set for your `OracleOCIConnectionPool` object:

- **CONNPOOL_MIN_LIMIT** Specifies the minimum number of physical connections that may be maintained by the connection pool. The default for this attribute is 1, and you may obtain its current value using the `getMinLimit()` method.

- **CONNPOOL_MAX_LIMIT** Specifies the maximum number of physical connections that may be maintained by the connection pool. The default for this attribute is 1, and you may obtain its current value using the `getMaxLimit()` method.

- **CONNPOOL_INCREMENT** Specifies the additional number of physical connections to be opened when all the existing connections are in use and a request for an additional connection instance has been made. The additional physical connections are only opened if the total number of connections will be less than the number specified by `CONNPOOL_MAX_LIMIT`. The default for this attribute is 0, and you may obtain its current value using the `getConnectionIncrement()` method.

- **CONNPOOL_TIMEOUT** Specifies the number of seconds before an idle physical connection is disconnected. The default for this attribute is 0, and you may obtain its current value using the `getTimeout()` method.

- **CONNPOOL_NOWAIT** This is a Boolean `true`/`false` value, and controls what happens when all of the physical connections are busy when a request for a connection instance is made. If this attribute is set to `true`, an error is returned. If this attribute is set to `false`, the request waits until a connection is available. Once this attribute is set to `true`, it cannot be set to `false`. The default for this attribute is `false`, and you may obtain its current value using the `getNoWait()` method.

These attributes are set using an object of the `java.util.Properties` class, so you'll need to either import that class, or use the full class name when creating your `Properties` object. The following statement creates a `Properties` object named `myProperties`:

```
Properties myProperties = new Properties();
```

Next, you use the `put()` method to populate your `Properties` object with the appropriate values for your dynamic attributes. The following statements use the `put()` method to populate `myProperties` with values for the five dynamic attributes:

```
myProperties.put(OracleOCIConnectionPool.CONNPOOL_MIN_LIMIT, "5");
myProperties.put(OracleOCIConnectionPool.CONNPOOL_MAX_LIMIT, "10");
myProperties.put(OracleOCIConnectionPool.CONNPOOL_INCREMENT, "2");
```

```
myProperties.put(OracleOCIConnectionPool.CONNPOOL_TIMEOUT, "30");
myProperties.put(OracleOCIConnectionPool.CONNPOOL_NOWAIT, "true");
```

The final step is to set the dynamic attributes of your
`OracleOCIConnectionPool` object using the `setPoolConfig()` method
and passing your `Properties` object containing the attribute values to this
method. The following statement passes `myProperties` to the `setPoolConfig()`
method of the `myOOCP` object, therefore setting the dynamic attributes of `myOOCP`
to the values supplied in the previous set of statements:

```
myOOCP.setPoolConfig(myProperties);
```

As I mentioned earlier, the five attributes described in this section
may be set dynamically; therefore, you can set these attributes for your
`OracleOCIConnectionPool` object anywhere, as long as your
`OracleOCIConnectionPool` and `Properties` objects are in scope.
In this way, you can tune your cache while using it in your program.
You may obtain the current values of the dynamic attributes using various
get methods. The following statements illustrate the use of these get methods:

```
System.out.println(myOOCP.getMinLimit());
System.out.println(myOOCP.getMaxLimit());
System.out.println(myOOCP.getConnectionIncrement());
System.out.println(myOOCP.getTimeout());
System.out.println(myOOCP.getNoWait());
```

You can also use the `getPoolSize()` and `getActiveSize()` methods to
display the total number of physical connections in the cache and the number of
physical connections that are busy. For example:

```
System.out.println(myOOCP.getPoolSize());
System.out.println(myOOCP.getActiveSize());
```

Requesting, Using, and Closing a Connection Instance

In order to access the database, you need a connection instance. You
request a connection instance using the `getConnection()` method of your
`OracleOCIConnectionPool` object. The following statement requests a
connection instance from `myOOCP` using the `getConnection()` method and
stores the returned connection instance in `myConnection`:

```
OracleOCIConnection myConnection =
    (OracleOCIConnection) myOOCP.getConnection();
```

Notice that the `Connection` object returned by the `getConnection()` method is cast to an `OracleOCIConnection` object. You can then use `myConnection` to access the database. Once you're finished with the connection instance, you should close it using the `close()` method, for example:

```
myConnection.close();
```

Closing the OCI Connection Pool

Before your program ends, you should close your `OracleOCIConnectionPool` object using the `close()` method. The following statement closes myOOCP:

```
myOOCP.close();
```

The following section contains a complete program that illustrates the use of an OCI connection cache.

Example Program: ConnectionPoolExample2.java

The `ConnectionPoolExample2.java`, program, shown in the following listing, shows the use of the statements described in the previous sections.

```
/*
   ConnectionPoolExample2.java illustrates connection pooling
   with the OCI driver
*/

// import the required packages
import java.sql.*;
import javax.sql.*;
import oracle.jdbc.pool.*;
import oracle.jdbc.oci.*;
import oracle.jdbc.*;
import java.util.*;

public class ConnectionPoolExample2 {

  public static void main(String args [])
  throws SQLException {

    // create an OracleOCIConnectionPool object named myOOCP
    System.out.println("Creating an OracleOCIConnectionPool object " +
      "named myOOCP");
    OracleOCIConnectionPool myOOCP = new OracleOCIConnectionPool();
```

```
// set the attributes for the physical database connections
System.out.println("Setting the attributes of myOOCP");
myOOCP.setServerName("localhost");
myOOCP.setDatabaseName("ORCL");
myOOCP.setDriverType("oci");
myOOCP.setPortNumber(1521);
myOOCP.setUser("store_user");
myOOCP.setPassword("store_password");

// set the values for the dynamic attributes of myOOCP
System.out.println("Setting the dynamic attribute values of " +
  "myOOCP");
Properties myProperties = new Properties();
myProperties.put(OracleOCIConnectionPool.CONNPOOL_MIN_LIMIT,
  "5");
myProperties.put(OracleOCIConnectionPool.CONNPOOL_MAX_LIMIT,
  "10");
myProperties.put(OracleOCIConnectionPool.CONNPOOL_INCREMENT,
  "2");
myProperties.put(OracleOCIConnectionPool.CONNPOOL_TIMEOUT,
  "30");
myProperties.put(OracleOCIConnectionPool.CONNPOOL_NOWAIT,
  "true");
myOOCP.setPoolConfig(myProperties);

// display the dynamic attributes values of myOOCP
System.out.println("myOOCP.getMinLimit() = " +
  myOOCP.getMinLimit());
System.out.println("myOOCP.getMaxLimit() = " +
  myOOCP.getMaxLimit());
System.out.println("myOOCP.getConnectionIncrement() = " +
  myOOCP.getConnectionIncrement());
System.out.println("myOOCP.getTimeout() = " +
  myOOCP.getTimeout());
System.out.println("myOOCP.getNoWait() = " +
  myOOCP.getNoWait());

// request a connection instance from myOOCP and store
// the connection instance in myConnection
System.out.println("Requesting connection instance from myOOCP");
OracleOCIConnection myConnection =
  (OracleOCIConnection) myOOCP.getConnection();

// display the values returned by the getPoolSize() and
// getActiveSize() methods
System.out.println("myOOCP.getPoolSize() = " +
  myOOCP.getPoolSize());
```

```
    System.out.println("myOOCP.getActiveSize() = " +
      myOOCP.getActiveSize());

    // close myConnection and myOOCP using the close() method
    System.out.println("Closing connection instance and myOOCP");
    myConnection.close();
    myOOCP.close();

  } // end of main()

}
```

The output from this program is as follows:

```
Creating an OracleOCIConnectionPool object named myOOCP
Setting the attributes of myOOCP
Setting the dynamic attribute values of myOOCP
myOOCP.getMinLimit() = 5
myOOCP.getMaxLimit() = 10
myOOCP.getConnectionIncrement() = 2
myOOCP.getTimeout() = 30
myOOCP.getNoWait() = true
Requesting connection instance from myOOCP
myOOCP.getPoolSize() = 5
myOOCP.getActiveSize() = 0
Closing connection instance and myOOCP
```

CHAPTER
13

Performance Tuning

n this final chapter, you'll learn how to reduce the amount of time it takes for your program to complete. This process is called *performance tuning* your program. You'll learn some of the standard JDBC performance tuning techniques, along with the Oracle performance extensions. Typically, the Oracle performance extensions offer an edge over standard JDBC.

You'll learn the how the following techniques can boost the performance of your program:

■ Disabling auto-commit mode

■ Batching SQL statements together and sending them to the database in one go

■ Fetching multiple rows at a time from the database using row prefetching

■ Defining the types of result set columns up front

■ Storing statements in a cache for re-use

In the final section of this chapter, I'll offer a couple of tips you can use to increase the performance of the SQL statements your program issues. You may combine the various techniques described in this chapter to make your programs really fly.

First, I'll describe the table used by the programs in this chapter.

The perf_test Table

The SQL*Plus script `store_user.sql` (which you should have run earlier) creates a table named `perf_test`; this table will be used by the programs in this chapter. The `perf_test` table is defined as follows:

```
CREATE TABLE perf_test (
  value INTEGER
);
```

As you can see, `perf_test` contains a single integer column named `value`.

Disabling Auto-Commit Mode

Back in Chapter 3, I mentioned that by default, any SQL `INSERT`, `UPDATE`, or `DELETE` statements your program issues will be committed automatically. This is known as *auto-commit mode*. Since it takes time to complete a commit, enabling auto-commit mode has a significant impact on the performance of your program (auto-commit mode is enabled by default). As I also mentioned in Chapter 3, you should only perform a commit at the end of an actual transaction—and your transactions will typically contain more than one SQL statement at a time. Refer back to Chapters 2 and 3 if you need to refresh your memory on transactions.

For these reasons, you should disable auto-commit mode by calling the `setAutoCommit()` method for your `java.sql.Connection` or `oracle.jdbc.OracleConnection` object. The following statement shows an example of this:

```
myConnection.setAutoCommit(false);
```

Let's take a look at a complete program that allows you to compare the performance impact of enabling and disabling auto-commit mode.

Example Program: AutoCommitExample.java

The program `AutoCommitExample.java`, shown in the following listing, shows the effect of auto-commit mode on program performance when inserting 2,000 rows into the `perf_test` table. This program performs the following major tasks:

1. Truncates the `perf_test` table. Truncating a table deletes any rows already in the table and prepares the table for a fresh set of rows.

2. Enables auto-commit mode.

3. Inserts 2,000 rows into the `perf_test` table and displays the total time taken to perform the inserts in milliseconds.

4. Truncates the `perf_test` table again.

5. Disables auto-commit mode.

6. Inserts 2,000 rows into the `perf_test` table again and shows the new time taken to perform the inserts.

```
/*
  AutoCommitExample.java shows how disabling auto-commit
  improves performance
*/

// import the JDBC packages
import java.sql.*;

public class AutoCommitExample {
```

```
// the TOTAL_NUM_ROWS constant is the total number of rows
// that will be inserted into the perf_test table
public static final int TOTAL_NUM_ROWS = 2000;

public static void main(String [] args)
throws SQLException {

  // register the Oracle JDBC drivers
  DriverManager.registerDriver(
    new oracle.jdbc.OracleDriver()
  );

  // create a Connection object and connect to the database
  // as store_user using the Oracle JDBC Thin driver
  Connection myConnection = DriverManager.getConnection(
    "jdbc:oracle:thin:@localhost:1521:ORCL",
    "store_user",
    "store_password"
  );

  // create a Statement object
  Statement myStatement = myConnection.createStatement();

  // truncate the perf_test table
  myStatement.execute("TRUNCATE TABLE perf_test");

  // enable auto-commit mode
  System.out.println("Enabling auto-commit mode");
  myConnection.setAutoCommit(true);

  // insert rows into the perf_test table
  insertRows(myConnection);

  // truncate the perf_test table again
  myStatement.execute("TRUNCATE TABLE perf_test");

  // disable auto-commit mode
  System.out.println("Disabling auto-commit mode");
  myConnection.setAutoCommit(false);

  // insert rows again
  insertRows(myConnection);
```

```
    // close the Statement and Connection objects
    myStatement.close();
    myConnection.close();

} // end of main()


private static void insertRows(Connection myConnection)
throws SQLException {

    // create a PreparedStatement object
    PreparedStatement myPrepStatement =
      myConnection.prepareStatement(
        "INSERT INTO perf_test " +
        "(value) VALUES (?)"
      );

    // record the start time
    long start_time = System.currentTimeMillis();

    // insert the rows
    for (int count = 0; count < TOTAL_NUM_ROWS; count++) {
      myPrepStatement.setInt(1, count);
      myPrepStatement.executeUpdate();
    }

    // record the end time
    long end_time = System.currentTimeMillis();

    // display the total time taken to insert the rows
    System.out.println("Total time for inserting " + TOTAL_NUM_ROWS +
      " rows was " + (end_time - start_time) + " milliseconds");

    // commit the SQL statements
    myConnection.commit();

    // close the PreparedStatement object
    myPrepStatement.close();

  } // end of insertRows()

}
```

The output from this program is as follows:

```
Enabling auto-commit mode
Total time for inserting 2000 rows was 11666 milliseconds
Disabling auto-commit mode
Total time for inserting 2000 rows was 3405 milliseconds
```

As you can see, disabling auto-commit mode results in a significant improvement in performance.

Batching

You can combine many SQL INSERT, UPDATE, and DELETE statements into a *batch*. You then send this batch of statements to the database in one go. This is faster than sending one SQL statement at a time. This is because each time you send a SQL statement to the database, the statement typically has to travel over a network; the database then receives the SQL statement, runs its, and sends a result back to your program. This entire process is known as a *round trip*. By batching multiple statements together, you reduce the number of round trips to the database, therefore decreasing your program's execution time.

There are two types of batching you can use in your programs:

- **Standard update batching** This code forms part of standard JDBC 2.0.

- **Oracle update batching** This code forms part of the Oracle JDBC extensions.

Typically, Oracle update batching will perform better than standard update batching. If, however, you want your code to be portable and run against multiple databases, you should use standard update batching.

There are some limitations to batching:

- You can only batch SQL INSERT, UPDATE, and DELETE statements. If you try to batch any other SQL statement, you'll get an exception.

- If you try to use any of the long or large object types (LONG, LONG RAW, CLOB, BLOB, or BFILE) in a batched SQL statement, batching is disabled and your SQL statements will be sent to the database one at a time.

- Oracle update batching only works with OraclePreparedStatement objects.

- You can only use one type of batching with the same OraclePreparedStatement object: either standard update batching or Oracle update batching. If you try to use both types of batching with the same object, you'll get a SQLException.

I'll discuss standard update batching first; then I'll discuss Oracle update batching.

Standard Update Batching

Standard update batching forms part of JDBC 2.0. You can use standard update batching to batch SQL statements issued by the following types of objects:

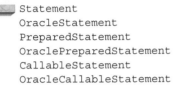

```
Statement
OracleStatement
PreparedStatement
OraclePreparedStatement
CallableStatement
OracleCallableStatement
```

To use standard update batching in your program, you may follow these five steps:

1. Disable auto-commit mode.

2. Prepare a statement object.

3. Add statements to the batch.

4. Execute the batch of statements.

5. Commit the executed statements.

I'll describe the details of these steps in the following sections.

Step 1: Disable Auto-Commit Mode

The first step is to disable auto-commit mode. You must do this to prevent each batch of SQL statements from being immediately committed after they are sent to the database. Also, by disabling auto-commit mode, if an error occurs while you are executing a batch, you can choose to either commit or rollback the statements in the batch that have already been executed.

The following statement shows an example of disabling auto-commit mode:

```
myConnection.setAutoCommit(false);
```

Step 2: Create a Statement Object

The second step is to create a statement object. You can use any of the types of statement objects listed at the beginning of this section; the example shown here will use a `PreparedStatement` object (named `myPrepStatement`) to add a row to the `perf_test` table:

```
PreparedStatement myPrepStatement = myConnection.prepareStatement(
    "INSERT INTO perf_test " +
```

```
  "(value) VALUES (?)"
);
```

The placeholder for this statement indicates that the `value` column of `perf_test` will be set, and I'll do that in the following step.

Step 3: Add Statements to the Batch

The third step is to add your statements to the batch. Depending on the number of SQL statements in your transaction, you can vary the number of statements in your batch. Although you can batch as many statements as you want, you don't necessarily want to flood the database with a huge number of statements all at once.

TIP

A batch containing ten SQL statements at a time is reasonable, but you can batch more if you really need to. A batch containing between 5 and 30 SQL statements is usually optimal.

You add a statement to the batch using the `addBatch()` method of your statement object. When you call this method for the first time, a batch is created and this first statement is added to the batch. Successive calls to the `addBatch()` method add another statement to this batch. After you execute the batch—as you'll see in Step 4—and later call `addBatch()` again, a new batch is created.

Let's look at an example of adding statements to a batch. The following example shows a `for` loop that adds ten statements to the batch using the `addBatch()` method, setting the `value` column for each statement to 0 through 9 using the `setInt()` method:

```
for (int count = 0; count < 10; count++) {
    myPrepStatement.setInt(1, count);
    myPrepStatement.addBatch();
}
```

At the end of this loop, the batch will contain ten `INSERT` statements that each add a row to the `perf_test` table.

NOTE

Because a batch is associated with a single statement object, you can only batch the same `INSERT`, `UPDATE`, or `DELETE` statement. You can, however, specify different values for any bind variables when batching a prepared statement, as shown in the previous `for` loop.

Step 4: Execute the Batch of Statements

The fourth step is to execute your batch of statements. You do this using the
executeBatch() method of your statement object. This method sends the batch
of statements to the database, which then executes each statement in the batch,
and returns an array of int elements.

The following example calls the executeBatch() method for the
PreparedStatement object myPrepStatement:

 `int [] rowsInserted = myPrepStatement.executeBatch();`

This statement sends the batch of INSERT statements previously added to
myPrepStatement to the database.

Depending on the type of statement object used in the batch, each int element
in the array returned by executeBatch() will represent something different. I'll
discuss what the int elements represent for the various statement objects—and
how you handle errors—shortly.

NOTE
*You can cancel a batch of SQL statements by calling
the clearBatch() method for your statement
object. You can also execute a nonbatched
statement between batches by calling the
executeUpdate() method. However, if you
already have some batched SQL statements, then
you must first execute or cancel that batch using the
executeBatch() or clearBatch() methods (if
you don't, you'll get a SQLException).*

Step 5: Commit the Executed Statements

The fifth and final step is to commit your executed statements. You do this
using the commit() method for your Connection object, as shown in the
following example:

 `myConnection.commit();`

This commits the ten INSERT statements that were executed in Step 4.

The example shown here assumes that the batched statements all executed
without any errors. In your own programs, you should handle errors gracefully.
I'll now describe how you might do this.

Handling Errors

You've seen how to send a batch of SQL statements to database for execution.
If an error occurs for any of the statements in the batch, a java.sql.
BatchUpdateException occurs. You can catch this exception in your

code and call the getUpdateCounts() method for your caught BatchUpdateException object; this method returns an int array containing the same values as the executeBatch() method described earlier. Typically, you should also perform a rollback in your catch block.

The following code illustrates how to catch a BatchUpdateException and call the getUpdateCounts() method; notice that the rollback() method is called within the catch block to rollback any executed SQL statements:

```
try {
  // ... code that executes a batch of SQL statements ...
} catch (BatchUpdateException e) {
  int [] updateCounts = e.getUpdateCounts();
  myConnection.rollback();
}
```

Depending on the type of statement object used in the try block, the int array will contain different values, as I'll describe in the next two sections. You can use these values as an additional check before deciding to rollback the successfully executed statements in your batch.

Array Values and the PreparedStatement and OraclePreparedStatement Objects
If you use a PreparedStatement or OraclePreparedStatement object, the int elements indicate if all the SQL statements in the batch succeeded or not. The JDBC driver cannot determine exactly which SQL statement in the batch failed, and therefore the int element values apply to all the SQL statements. A value of -2 for the int elements indicates that all the batched SQL statements were executed successfully, while a value of -3 indicates there was a problem with one or more of the batched SQL statements.

For example, say you had a batch of ten INSERT statements and assume that the first nine of those statements succeeded, but the tenth statement failed for some reason. If that were the case, all ten of the int elements in the array would contain -3. You can use the -3 value an additional check before deciding to rollback any successfully executed SQL statements in your batch.

Array Values and the Other Statement Objects
If you use a Statement, OracleStatement, CallableStatement, or OracleCallableStatement object, each int element in the array will represent the number of rows affected by each batched SQL statement.

For example, say you had a batch of two UPDATE statements and assume the first statement updated six rows, and the second one updated three rows. The returned int array would contain two elements: the first int would contain six, and the second int would contain three—the number of rows affected by each UPDATE statement in the batch. If the second UPDATE statement in the batch failed for some reason, the returned array would only contain one int element—and it corresponds to the first UPDATE statement that succeeded. Since the number of elements in the array comes up short when there's an exception, you can use this fact as an additional check when deciding whether to rollback any successfully executed SQL statements in your batch.

Example Program: BatchingExample1.java

The program BatchingExample1.java, shown in the following listing, illustrates how to use standard update batching—and shows the effect on performance when this technique is used. This program performs the following major tasks:

1. Truncates the perf_test table.

2. Inserts 2,000 rows into the perf_test table without using batching and displays the total time taken to perform the inserts in milliseconds.

3. Truncates the perf_test table again.

4. Inserts 2,000 rows into the perf_test table again, this time using standard update batching. The batch will be executed when the number of SQL statements in the batch reaches ten. The time taken to perform the inserts is again displayed.

```
/*
  BatchingExample1.java shows how to use standard update
  batching to improve performance
*/

// import the JDBC packages
import java.sql.*;

public class BatchingExample1 {

  // the TOTAL_NUM_ROWS constant is the total number of rows
  // that will be inserted; the BATCH_SIZE constant is the maximum
  // number of statements that may be batched at any one time
  public static final int TOTAL_NUM_ROWS = 2000;
  public static final int BATCH_SIZE = 10;

  public static void main(String [] args)
  throws SQLException {

    // register the Oracle JDBC drivers
    DriverManager.registerDriver(
      new oracle.jdbc.OracleDriver()
```

```
  );

  // create a Connection object and connect to the database
  // as store_user using the Oracle JDBC Thin driver
  Connection myConnection = DriverManager.getConnection(
    "jdbc:oracle:thin:@localhost:1521:ORCL",
    "store_user",
    "store_password"
  );

  // disable auto-commit mode
  myConnection.setAutoCommit(false);

  // create a Statement object
  Statement myStatement = myConnection.createStatement();

  // delete the rows from the perf_test table
  myStatement.execute("TRUNCATE TABLE perf_test");

  // insert rows without batching (as indicated by the
  // second parameter that is set to false)
  System.out.println("Inserting " + TOTAL_NUM_ROWS +
    " rows without batching");
  insertRows(myConnection, false);

  // insert rows with batching
  System.out.println("Inserting " + TOTAL_NUM_ROWS +
    " rows with standard update batching");
  insertRows(myConnection, true);

  // close the Statement and Connection objects
  myStatement.close();
  myConnection.close();

} // end of main()


private static void insertRows(
  Connection myConnection, boolean batching
) throws SQLException {

  // create a PreparedStatement object
  PreparedStatement myPrepStatement =
    myConnection.prepareStatement(
      "INSERT INTO perf_test " +
```

```
      "(value) VALUES (?)"
    );

  // record the start time
  long start_time = System.currentTimeMillis();

  // insert the rows
  int count2 = 0;
  for (int count = 0; count < TOTAL_NUM_ROWS; count++) {
    myPrepStatement.setInt(1, count);

    // if batching is true, then batch the SQL statements,
    // otherwise simply execute the statement
    if (batching) {

      myPrepStatement.addBatch();
      count2++;

      // execute the batch when there are a total of
      // BATCH_SIZE SQL statements in the batch
      if (count2 % BATCH_SIZE == 0) {
        int [] rowsInserted = myPrepStatement.executeBatch();
      }

    } else {
      myPrepStatement.execute();
    }
  }

  // record the end time
  long end_time = System.currentTimeMillis();

  // display the total time taken to insert the rows
  System.out.println("Total time for inserting " + TOTAL_NUM_ROWS +
    " rows was " + (end_time - start_time) + " milliseconds");

  // rollback the SQL statements
  myConnection.rollback();

  // close the PreparedStatement object
  myPrepStatement.close();

  } // end of insertRows()

}
```

The output from this program is as follows:

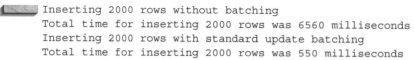
```
Inserting 2000 rows without batching
Total time for inserting 2000 rows was 6560 milliseconds
Inserting 2000 rows with standard update batching
Total time for inserting 2000 rows was 550 milliseconds
```

Notice the improvement in performance when using standard update batching.

Oracle Update Batching

Oracle update batching typically offers an additional performance boost when compared to standard update batching. A limitation of Oracle update batching is that it will only batch `OraclePreparedStatement` objects, but you can also cast `PreparedStatement` objects to an `OraclePreparedStatement` and then use that object with Oracle update batching.

Oracle update batching differs from standard update batching in that you set the maximum number of SQL statements allowed in the batch up front—this maximum value is known as the *batch value*.

When you call the `executeUpdate()` method for your `OraclePreparedStatement` object, the SQL statement is automatically added to the batch. When the number of SQL statements in the batch reaches the batch value, the batch is automatically sent to the database for execution. For example, if you set the batch value to 10 and then execute ten `INSERT` statements, then on the tenth `executeUpdate()` call, the batch of ten `INSERT` statements is sent to the database.

TIP

As I mentioned earlier, for standard update batching, a batch containing between 5 and 30 SQL statements is usually optimal. Therefore, you should set your batch value somewhere within this range.

The setting of the batch value up front is the reason why Oracle update batching is usually faster than standard update batching. This is because the JDBC driver knows how many SQL statements are to be batched at a time using the batch value, and can therefore make optimizations based on this batch value. With standard update batching, you don't set a batch value, so the JDBC driver doesn't know how many SQL statements you'll place in a batch before executing it; therefore, the JDBC driver can't make any additional optimizations.

To use Oracle update batching, you follow these four steps:

1. Disable auto-commit mode.

2. Set the batch value.

3. Batch the SQL statements.

4. Commit the executed statements.

Steps 1 and 4 are the same as Steps 1 and 5 for standard update batching—therefore, I'll only cover the details of Steps 2 and 3 in this section.

Step 2: Set the Batch Value

You can set the batch value for an OracleConnection object or an OraclePreparedStatement object. When you set the batch value for an OracleConnection object, any OraclePreparedStatement objects created using your OracleConnection will automatically use that batch value. If you set a batch value for an OraclePreparedStatement object, then that batch value will override a batch value previously set for your OracleConnection.

NOTE
By default, the batch value for an OracleConnection or OraclePreparedStatement object is 1— meaning that SQL statements are not batched: they are sent one at a time to the database.

Setting the Batch Value for an OracleConnection Object   You set the batch value for an OracleConnection object using the setDefaultExecuteBatch() method; this method accepts an int parameter containing your batch value. The following example sets the batch value to 10 for an OracleConnection object named myOracleConnection:

```
myOracleConnection.setDefaultExecuteBatch(10);
```

Of course, you can cast an existing Connection object to an OracleConnection object and then use the setDefaultExecuteBatch() method. The following example shows this; it casts a Connection object named myConnection to an OracleConnection and then calls the setDefaultExecuteBatch() method:

```
((OracleConnection) myConnection).setDefaultExecuteBatch(10);
```

You can check the current setting for the batch value of an OracleConnection object using the getDefaultExecuteBatch() method; this method returns an int value. The following example shows the use of the getDefaultExecuteBatch() method:

```
int batchSize = myOracleConnection.getDefaultExecuteBatch();
```

Since the batch value for myOracleConnection was set to 10 earlier, getDefaultExecuteBatch() will return ten.

Setting the Batch Value for an OraclePreparedStatement Object

You set the batch value for an OraclePreparedStatement object using the setExecuteBatch() method; this method accepts an int parameter containing the batch value. This batch value will override the batch value for your OracleConnection object.

For example, let's first assume you have the following OraclePreparedStatement object named myOraclePrepStatement:

```
OraclePreparedStatement myOraclePrepStatement =
  (OraclePreparedStatement) myConnection.prepareStatement(
    "INSERT INTO perf_test " +
    "(value) VALUES (?)"
  );
```

Next, the following statement sets the batch value to 20 for myOraclePrepStatement using its setExecuteBatch() method:

```
myOraclePrepStatement.setExecuteBatch(20);
```

The batch value for myOraclePrepStatement overrides the batch value previously set for myConnection, and so 20 SQL statements may be batched before they are sent to the database.

You can check the current batch value for an OraclePreparedStatement using its getExecuteBatch() method, for example:

```
System.out.println("Batch value = " +
  myOraclePrepStatement.getExecuteBatch());
```

The next step is to batch the SQL statements.

Step 3: Batch the SQL Statements

Once you've set the batch value, all you have to do to add a SQL statement to a batch is call the executeUpdate() method for your OraclePreparedStatement object. When the number of SQL statements in your batch reaches the batch value, your batch will be sent automatically to the database for execution.

The following example shows a for loop that adds 20 INSERT statements to the batch, setting the value column for each INSERT statement to 0 through 19:

```
for (int count = 0; count < 20; count++) {
  myOraclePrepStatement.setInt(1, count);
```

```
    int rowsInserted = myOraclePrepStatement.executeUpdate();
}
```

Earlier in Step 2, the batch value for `myOraclePrepStatement` was set to 20. Therefore, when the twentieth `INSERT` statement is added to the batch, the batch is automatically sent to the database for execution.

The `int` value returned by the `executeUpdate()` method is the number of rows affected by a SQL statement. Since the SQL statements are batched and then sent to the database, this `int` value will be 0 if the statement was simply added to the batch by the `executeUpdate()` method. If, however, the batch is actually sent to the database by this method, then the `int` value will contain the total number of rows affected by all the batched SQL statements. So, in the example `for` loop, the `int` value returned by `executeUpdate()` will be 0 for the first 19 iterations of the loop; on the twentieth iteration, the batch is sent to the database and the `int` value returned will be 20—the number of rows added to the database by the batched `INSERT` statements.

Forcing the Execution of a Batch   You can also force the execution of batch before the batch is filled by calling the `sendBatch()` method. Typically, you'll never need to use this method because even if your batch isn't full, the batch will still be sent to the database when you perform a commit.

Let's consider an example of using `sendBatch()`. Say you put three `INSERT` statements in a batch. You could then force the execution of those three statements by calling `sendBatch()` using your `OraclePreparedStatement` object; an example of using the `sendBatch()` method is shown in the following statement:

```
int rowsInserted = myOraclePrepStatement.sendBatch();
```

The `sendBatch()` method returns an `int` value that contains the number of rows affected by the SQL statements in the batch. In this example, `sendBatch()` will return 3—the number of rows inserted by the statements in the batch (assuming each `INSERT` statement only inserts one row).

Example Program: BatchingExample2.java

The program `BatchingExample2.java`, shown in the following listing, illustrates how to use Oracle update batching and the effect on performance when this technique is used. This program performs the following major tasks:

1. Truncates the `perf_test` table.

2. Inserts 2,000 rows into the `perf_test` table without using batching, and displays the total time taken to perform the inserts in milliseconds.

3. Truncates the `perf_test` table again.

4. Inserts 2,000 rows into the `perf_test` table again, this time using Oracle update batching. The batch value is set to 10 for an `OraclePreparedStatement` object.

```
/*
  BatchingExample2.java shows how to use Oracle
  update batching to improve performance
*/

// import the JDBC packages
import java.sql.*;
import oracle.jdbc.*;

public class BatchingExample2 {

  // the TOTAL_NUM_ROWS constant is the total number of rows
  // that will be inserted; the BATCH_SIZE constant is the maximum
  // number of statements that may be batched at any one time
  public static final int TOTAL_NUM_ROWS = 2000;
  public static final int BATCH_SIZE = 10;

  public static void main(String [] args)
  throws SQLException {

    // register the Oracle JDBC drivers
    DriverManager.registerDriver(
      new oracle.jdbc.OracleDriver()
    );

    // create a Connection object and connect to the database
    // as store_user using the Oracle JDBC Thin driver
    Connection myConnection = DriverManager.getConnection(
      "jdbc:oracle:thin:@localhost:1521:ORCL",
      "store_user",
      "store_password"
    );

    // disable auto-commit mode
    myConnection.setAutoCommit(false);

    // create a Statement object
    Statement myStatement = myConnection.createStatement();

    // delete the rows from the perf_test table
    myStatement.execute("TRUNCATE TABLE perf_test");
```

```java
  // insert rows without batching
  System.out.println("Inserting " + TOTAL_NUM_ROWS +
    " rows without batching");
  insertRows(myConnection, false);

  // inserted rows with batching
  System.out.println("Inserting " + TOTAL_NUM_ROWS +
    " rows with Oracle update batching");
  insertRows(myConnection, true);

  // close the Statement and Connection objects
  myStatement.close();
  myConnection.close();

} // end of main()


private static void insertRows(
  Connection myConnection, boolean batching
) throws SQLException {

  // create an OraclePreparedStatement object
  OraclePreparedStatement myOraclePrepStatement =
    (OraclePreparedStatement) myConnection.prepareStatement(
      "INSERT INTO perf_test " +
      "(value) VALUES (?)"
    );

  // if batching is true, then set the batch value to BATCH_SIZE
  if (batching) {
    System.out.println("Setting the batch value to " +
      BATCH_SIZE);
    myOraclePrepStatement.setExecuteBatch(BATCH_SIZE);
  }

  // display the current batch value
  System.out.println("Batch value = " +
    myOraclePrepStatement.getExecuteBatch());

  // record the start time
  long start_time = System.currentTimeMillis();

  // insert the rows
  for (int count = 0; count < TOTAL_NUM_ROWS; count++) {
    myOraclePrepStatement.setInt(1, count);
    int rowsInserted = myOraclePrepStatement.executeUpdate();
```

```
      }

      // record the end time
      long end_time = System.currentTimeMillis();

      // display the total time taken to insert the rows
      System.out.println("Total time for inserting " + TOTAL_NUM_ROWS +
        " rows was " + (end_time - start_time) + " milliseconds");

      // rollback the SQL statements
      myConnection.rollback();

      // close the PreparedStatement object
      myOraclePrepStatement.close();

    } // end of insertRows()

  }
```

The output from this program is as follows:

```
Inserting 2000 rows without batching
Batch value = 1
Total time for inserting 2000 rows was 4877 milliseconds
Inserting 2000 rows with Oracle update batching
Setting the batch value to 10
Batch value = 10
Total time for inserting 2000 rows was 391 milliseconds
```

Notice the improvement in performance when using Oracle update batching.

Row Prefetching

With *row prefetching*, you can specify the number of rows that are to be fetched into a result set during each round trip to the database. Retrieving multiple rows during each round trip is faster than retrieving one row at a time. The maximum number of rows prefetched during each round trip is known as the *fetch size.*

TIP
The default fetch size is 10. Typically, this fetch size will be adequate for most of your programs. If however, you have a very large number of rows to retrieve, you can increase the fetch size in order to further boost the performance of your program.

There are two types of row prefetching you can use in a program:

- **Standard row prefetching**   This forms part of JDBC 2.0.
- **Oracle row prefetching**   This forms part of the Oracle JDBC extensions.

Typically, Oracle row prefetching will have better performance than standard row prefetching. If, however, you want your code to be portable, you should use standard row prefetching.

CAUTION
Don't mix standard row prefetching and Oracle row prefetching with the same object: use one or the other type of row prefetching.

I'll discuss standard row prefetching first, and then I'll discuss Oracle row prefetching.

Standard Row Prefetching

As I mentioned, standard row prefetching comes with JDBC 2.0. You can set a fetch size for the following types of objects:

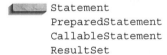
```
Statement
PreparedStatement
CallableStatement
ResultSet
```

I'll now cover the details of setting the fetch size; once I've done that, I'll show you how to check the fetch size.

Setting the Fetch Size

To set the fetch size for one of the objects in the previous list, you use the setFetchSize() method. The setFetchSize() method accepts an int parameter that specifies the fetch size. The following example creates a Statement object named myStatement and uses the setFetchSize() method to set myStatement's fetch size to 20:

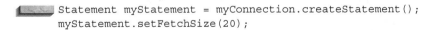
```
Statement myStatement = myConnection.createStatement();
myStatement.setFetchSize(20);
```

Any `ResultSet` objects returned by a `Statement` object get the same fetch size as that `Statement` object. The following example creates a `ResultSet` object named `myResultSet`:

```
ResultSet myResultSet = myStatement.executeQuery(
  "SELECT value " +
  "FROM perf_test"
);
```

Now, since the fetch size for `myStatement` was set to 20 earlier, this means that `myResultSet` also has a fetch size of 20. Therefore, 20 rows are retrieved each time `myResultSet` is used to read rows from the database.

You can override the fetch size for a `ResultSet` object by calling `setFetchSize()` for that object. For example, the following statement overrides the fetch size for `myResultSet` with a value of 50:

```
myResultSet.setFetchSize(50);
```

When `myResultSet` is used to retrieve rows, it will retrieve 50 rows each time.

Checking the Fetch Size

To check the current fetch size, you use the `getFetchSize()` method. This method returns an `int` parameter containing the fetch size for an object. For example, the following statement displays the fetch size for `myStatement`:

```
System.out.println(myStatement.getFetchSize());
```

Since the fetch size for `myStatement` was set to 20 earlier, this example will display 20. Similarly, the following statement displays the fetch size for `myResultSet`:

```
System.out.println(myResultSet.getFetchSize());
```

Since the fetch size for `myResultSet` was set to 50, this example will display 50.

Example Program: PrefetchingExample1.java

The program `PrefetchingExample1.java`, shown in the following listing, illustrates how to use standard row prefetching and the effect on performance when this technique is used. This program performs the following major tasks:

1. Truncates the `perf_test` table.

2. Inserts 2,000 rows into the `perf_test` table.

3. Sets the fetch size to 1 for a `Statement` object (that is, one row at a time is retrieved during each round trip).

4. Retrieves the 2,000 rows from the `perf_test` table and displays the total time taken to retrieve the rows in milliseconds.

5. Sets the fetch size to 10 for the `Statement` object (that is, ten rows at a time are retrieved during each round trip).

6. Retrieves the 2,000 rows from the `perf_test` table again.

7. Sets the fetch size to 20 for the `Statement` object.

8. Retrieves the 2,000 rows from the `perf_test` table once more.

```java
/*
  PrefetchingExample1.java shows how to use standard JDBC row
  prefetching to improve performance
*/

// import the JDBC packages
import java.sql.*;

public class PrefetchingExample1 {

  // the TOTAL_NUM_ROWS constant is the total number of rows
  // that will be inserted
  public static final int TOTAL_NUM_ROWS = 2000;

  public static void main(String [] args)
  throws SQLException {

    // register the Oracle JDBC drivers
    DriverManager.registerDriver(
      new oracle.jdbc.OracleDriver()
    );

    // create a Connection object and connect to the database
    // as store_user using the Oracle JDBC Thin driver
    Connection myConnection = DriverManager.getConnection(
      "jdbc:oracle:thin:@localhost:1521:ORCL",
      "store_user",
      "store_password"
    );

    // disable auto-commit mode
    myConnection.setAutoCommit(false);
```

```
      // create a Statement object
      Statement myStatement = myConnection.createStatement();

      // delete the rows from the perf_test table
      myStatement.execute("TRUNCATE TABLE perf_test");

      // insert a total of TOTAL_NUM_ROWS to the perf_test table
      System.out.println("Adding " + TOTAL_NUM_ROWS +
        " rows to perf_test table");
      for (int count = 0; count < TOTAL_NUM_ROWS; count++) {
        myStatement.executeUpdate(
          "INSERT INTO perf_test " +
          "(value) VALUES (" + count + ")"
        );
      }
      myConnection.commit();

      // retrieve the rows with a fetch size of 1
      retrieveRows(myStatement, 1);

      // retrieve the rows again, this time with a fetch size of 10
      retrieveRows(myStatement, 10);

      // retrieve the rows again, this time with a fetch size of 20
      retrieveRows(myStatement, 20);

      // close the Statement and Connection objects
      myStatement.close();
      myConnection.close();

    } // end of main()


    private static void retrieveRows(
      Statement myStatement, int fetchSize
    ) throws SQLException {

      // set the fetch size
      System.out.println("Setting the statement fetch size to " +
        fetchSize);
      myStatement.setFetchSize(fetchSize);

      // display the statement fetch size
      System.out.println("Statement fetch size = " +
        myStatement.getFetchSize());
```

```java
      // create a ResultSet object
      ResultSet myResultSet = myStatement.executeQuery(
        "SELECT value " +
        "FROM perf_test"
      );

      // display the result set fetch size
      System.out.println("Result set fetch size = " +
        myResultSet.getFetchSize());

      // record the start time
      long start_time = System.currentTimeMillis();

      // retrieve the rows from the ResultSet object
      while (myResultSet.next()) {
        // do nothing
      } // end of while loop

      // record the end time
      long end_time = System.currentTimeMillis();

      // display the total time taken to retrieve the rows
      System.out.println("Total time for retrieving " +
        TOTAL_NUM_ROWS + " rows was " + (end_time - start_time) +
        " milliseconds");

      // close the ResultSet object
      myResultSet.close();

    } // end of retrieveRows()

  }
```

The output from this program is as follows:

```
Adding 2000 rows to perf_test table
Setting the statement fetch size to 1
Statement fetch size = 1
Result set fetch size = 1
Total time for retrieving 2000 rows was 1642 milliseconds
Setting the statement fetch size to 10
Statement fetch size = 10
Result set fetch size = 10
Total time for retrieving 2000 rows was 161 milliseconds
Setting the statement fetch size to 20
Statement fetch size = 20
```

```
Result set fetch size = 20
Total time for retrieving 2000 rows was 91 milliseconds
```

Notice the improvement in performance when the fetch size is set to 10 and 20.

Oracle Row Prefetching

Oracle row prefetching typically offers an additional performance boost when compared to standard row prefetching. You can set the fetch size for the following types of objects:

```
OracleStatement
OraclePreparedStatement
OracleCallableStatement
OracleConnection
```

You can't override the fetch size for a result set as you can do with standard row prefetching. You can, however, set the fetch size for an `OracleConnection` object. This means that you can set the fetch size once for an `OracleConnection` object and have all your Oracle statement objects use this same fetch size; this saves you from having to set the fetch size for every statement object.

I'll now cover the details of setting the fetch size; once I've done that, I'll show you how to check the fetch size.

Setting the Fetch Size

To set the fetch size for an `OracleStatement`, `OraclePreparedStatement`, or `OracleCallableStatement` object, you use the `setRowPrefetch()` method. The `setRowPrefetch()` method accepts an `int` parameter that specifies the fetch size. For example, the following statements create an `OracleStatement` object named `myOracleStatement` and use the `setRowPrefetch()` method to set the fetch size to 20 for this object:

```
OracleStatement myOracleStatement =
    (OracleStatement) myConnection.createStatement();
myOracleStatement.setRowPrefetch(20);
```

You can, of course, cast an existing `Statement` object to an `OracleStatement` and then use the `setRowPrefetch()` method; for example:

```
((OracleStatement) myStatement).setRowPrefetch(20);
```

The following statement creates a `ResultSet` object named `myResultSet`:

```
ResultSet myResultSet = myStatement.executeQuery(
    "SELECT value " +
```

```
  "FROM perf_test"
);
```

Any `ResultSet` objects returned by a `Statement` object get the same fetch size as that `Statement` object. Similarly, any `OracleResultSet` objects returned by an `OracleStatement` object also get the same fetch size. Going back to my example, since the fetch size for `myStatement` was set to 20 earlier, this means that `myResultSet` also has a fetch size of 20.

Setting the Fetch Size for an OracleConnection Object   You can also set the fetch size for an `OracleConnection` object—and any statement objects created using that `OracleConnection` object will use that fetch size. To set the fetch size for an `OracleConnection` object, you use the `setDefaultRowPrefetch()` method. For example, the following statement sets the fetch size to 20 for an `OracleConnection` object named `myOracleConnection`:

```
myOracleConnection.setDefaultRowPrefetch(20);
```

You can also cast an existing `Connection` object to an `OracleConnection` object and then call the `setDefaultRowPrefetch()` method; for example:

```
((OracleConnection) myConnection).setDefaultRowPrefetch(20);
```

Checking the Fetch Size

To check the current fetch size for an `OracleStatement`, `OraclePreparedStatement`, or `OracleCallableStatement` object, you use the `getRowPrefetch()` method. This method returns an `int` that contains the fetch size for one of those objects. For example, the following statement displays the fetch size for `myOracleStatement`:

```
System.out.println(myOracleStatement.getRowPrefetch());
```

Since the fetch size for `myOracleStatement` was set to 20 earlier, this example will display 20.

You can also cast an existing `Statement` object to an `OracleStatement` and then use the `getRowPrefetch()` method; for example:

```
((OracleStatement) myStatement).getRowPrefetch();
```

Checking the Fetch Size for an OracleConnection Object   You can check the fetch size for an `OracleConnection` object using the `getDefaultRowPrefetch()` method. For example, the following statement displays the fetch size for `myOracleConnection`:

```
System.out.println(myOracleConnection.getDefaultRowPrefetch());
```

Since the fetch size for myOracleConnection was set to 20 earlier, this example will display 20.

You can also cast an existing Connection object to an OracleConnection object and then call the getDefaultRowPrefetch() method; for example:

```
System.out.println(
    ((OracleConnection) myConnection).getDefaultRowPrefetch()
);
```

Example Program: PrefetchingExample2.java

The program PrefetchingExample2.java, shown in the following listing, illustrates how to use Oracle row prefetching and shows the effect on performance when this technique is used. This program performs the following major tasks:

1. Truncates the perf_test table.

2. Inserts 2,000 rows into the perf_test table.

3. Sets the fetch size to 1 for a Statement object that is first cast to an OracleStatement object.

4. Retrieves the 2,000 rows from the perf_test table and displays the total time taken to retrieve the rows in milliseconds.

5. Sets the fetch size to 10 for the Statement object.

6. Retrieves the 2,000 rows from the perf_test table again.

7. Sets the fetch size to 20 for the Statement object.

8. Retrieves the 2,000 rows from the perf_test table once more.

```
/*
  PrefetchingExample2.java shows how to use Oracle JDBC row
  prefetching to improve performance
*/

// import the JDBC packages
import java.sql.*;
import oracle.jdbc.*;

public class PrefetchingExample2 {

  // the TOTAL_NUM_ROWS constant is the total number of rows
  // that will be inserted
  public static final int TOTAL_NUM_ROWS = 2000;
```

```java
public static void main(String [] args)
throws SQLException {

  // register the Oracle JDBC drivers
  DriverManager.registerDriver(
    new oracle.jdbc.OracleDriver()
  );

  // create a Connection object and connect to the database
  // as store_user using the Oracle JDBC Thin driver
  Connection myConnection = DriverManager.getConnection(
    "jdbc:oracle:thin:@localhost:1521:ORCL",
    "store_user",
    "store_password"
  );

  // disable auto-commit mode
  myConnection.setAutoCommit(false);

  // create a Statement object
  Statement myStatement = myConnection.createStatement();

  // delete the rows from the perf_test table
  myStatement.execute("TRUNCATE TABLE perf_test");

  // add a total of TOTAL_NUM_ROWS to the perf_test table
  System.out.println("Adding " + TOTAL_NUM_ROWS +
    " rows to perf_test table");
  for (int count = 0; count < TOTAL_NUM_ROWS; count++) {
    myStatement.executeUpdate(
      "INSERT INTO perf_test " +
      "(value) VALUES (" + count + ")"
    );
  }
  myConnection.commit();

  // retrieve the rows with a fetch size of 1
  retrieveRows(myStatement, 1);

  // retrieve the rows again, this time with a fetch size of 10
  retrieveRows(myStatement, 10);

  // retrieve the rows again, this time with a fetch size of 20
  retrieveRows(myStatement, 20);
```

```
    // close the Statement and Connection objects
    myStatement.close();
    myConnection.close();

  } // end of main()


  private static void retrieveRows(
    Statement myStatement, int fetchSize
  ) throws SQLException {

    // set the statement fetch size
    System.out.println("Setting the statement fetch size to " +
      fetchSize);
    ((OracleStatement) myStatement).setRowPrefetch(fetchSize);

    // display the statement fetch size
    System.out.println("Statement fetch size = " +
      ((OracleStatement) myStatement).getRowPrefetch());

    // create a ResultSet object
    ResultSet myResultSet = myStatement.executeQuery(
      "SELECT value " +
      "FROM perf_test"
    );

    // record the start time
    long start_time = System.currentTimeMillis();

    // retrieve the rows from the ResultSet object
    while (myResultSet.next()) {
      // do nothing
    } // end of while loop

    // record the end time
    long end_time = System.currentTimeMillis();

    // display the total time taken to retrieve the rows
    System.out.println("Total time for retrieving " +
      TOTAL_NUM_ROWS + " rows was " + (end_time - start_time) +
      " milliseconds");

    // close the ResultSet object
    myResultSet.close();
```

```
        } // end of retrieveRows()

    }
```

The output from this program is as follows:

```
Adding 2000 rows to perf_test table
Setting the statement fetch size to 1
Statement fetch size = 1
Total time for retrieving 2000 rows was 1532 milliseconds
Setting the statement fetch size to 10
Statement fetch size = 10
Total time for retrieving 2000 rows was 140 milliseconds
Setting the statement fetch size to 20
Statement fetch size = 20
Total time for retrieving 2000 rows was 80 milliseconds
```

Notice the improvement in performance when the fetch size is set to 10 and 20.

Defining the Types of Result Set Columns

A performance feature provided by the Oracle JDBC extensions is the ability to define the column types for a result set. When a query is sent to the database, one round trip is used to determine the Java types that should be used for the result set. By defining the Java types for the columns of your result set up front, you save a round trip to the database. If you have a lot of queries, then you might want to use this technique.

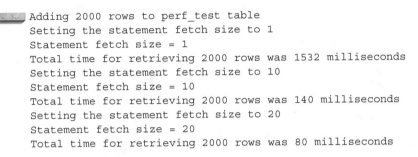

NOTE
If you're using the OCI driver, you won't save a round trip. This is because the OCI driver returns the column types along with the first row of a result set.

The defineColumnType() Method

To define the Java type for a column, you use the `defineColumnType()` method for objects of the following types:

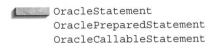

```
OracleStatement
OraclePreparedStatement
OracleCallableStatement
```

For example, let's say you want to retrieve the `value` column from the `perf_test` table (this column is defined as a database `INTEGER`). Assume that you already have an existing `Statement` object named `myStatement`. You can cast `myStatement` to an `OracleStatement`, and then use the `defineColumnType()` method; for example:

```
((OracleStatement) myStatement).defineColumnType(
  1, java.sql.Types.INTEGER
);
```

The first parameter to the `defineColumnType()` method is the numeric position of the column used in a query—in this example, position 1. The second parameter is the JDBC Java type code that you want to set for the column—in this example, `java.sql.Types.INTEGER`. This constant came from the `java.sql.Types` class, but you can also use the constants defined in the `oracle.jdbc.OracleTypes` class, which contains constants for the Oracle extended types. You can see the names of the constants in the `java.sql.Types` class in Table C-7 of Appendix C; Table C-8 of that appendix shows the names of the constants in the `oracle.jdbc.OracleTypes` class.

Next, the following statement creates a `ResultSet` object named `myResultSet`:

```
ResultSet myResultSet = myStatement.executeQuery(
  "SELECT value " +
  "FROM perf_test"
);
```

When `myResultSet` is populated with the rows from the `perf_test` table, the values for the `value` column are stored as integers. Because this type has already been defined earlier using the `defineColumnTypes()` method, one round trip is saved.

CAUTION

If you define the column type for one column in a result set using the `defineColumnType()` method, you must define column types for all the columns used in the result set. If you don't, you'll get a `SQLException`.

Defining the Length for a Column

For a database column type that has an associated length (a `VARCHAR2`, for example), you can also optionally specify the column length as the third parameter of the `defineColumnType()` method. For example, the following statement sets the length to 20 for a column that uses the `java.sql.Types.VARCHAR` constant:

```
defineColumnType(1, java.sql.Types.VARCHAR, 20);
```

Structured Objects, Object References, and Array Columns

For a database object, object reference, or array column, you can specify the type name as the alternative third parameter to the `defineColumnType()` method. The following example shows the use of a database object type named `PERSON_TYP`; notice the use of the `oracle.jdbc.OracleTypes.STRUCT` constant to specify that the column is a structured object:

```
defineColumnType(1, oracle.jdbc.OracleTypes.STRUCT, "PERSON_TYP");
```

The next example shows the use of an object reference type named `PERSON_REF_TYP`; notice the use of the `oracle.jdbc.OracleTypes.REF` constant to specify that the column is an object reference:

```
defineColumnType(1, oracle.jdbc.OracleTypes.REF, "PERSON_REF_TYP");
```

The final example shows the use of an array type named `PERSON_ARRAY_TYP`; notice the use of the `oracle.jdbc.OracleTypes.ARRAY` constant to specify that the column is an array:

```
defineColumnType(1, oracle.jdbc.OracleTypes.ARRAY, "PERSON_ARRAY_TYP");
```

NOTE
You cannot define the length for a structured object, object reference, or array column.

Example Program: DefineColumnTypeExample.java

The program `DefineColumnTypeExample.java`, shown in the following listing, illustrates how to define the column type for the `value` column of the `perf_test` table. This program performs the following major tasks:

1. Truncates the `perf_test` table.

2. Inserts a row into the `perf_test` table.

3. Defines a column as an integer using the `defineColumnType()` method.

4. Uses a result set to read the `value` column from the `perf_test` table.

```
/*
  DefineColumnTypeExample.java shows how to define a column type
*/

// import the JDBC packages
import java.sql.*;
import oracle.jdbc.*;

public class DefineColumnTypeExample {

  public static void main(String [] args)
  throws SQLException {

    // register the Oracle JDBC drivers
    DriverManager.registerDriver(
      new oracle.jdbc.OracleDriver()
    );

    // create a Connection object and connect to the database
    // as store_user using the Oracle JDBC Thin driver
    Connection myConnection = DriverManager.getConnection(
      "jdbc:oracle:thin:@localhost:1521:ORCL",
      "store_user",
      "store_password"
    );

    // disable auto-commit mode
    myConnection.setAutoCommit(false);

    // create a Statement object
    Statement myStatement = myConnection.createStatement();

    // delete the rows from the perf_test table
    myStatement.execute("TRUNCATE TABLE perf_test");

    // insert a row into the perf_test table
    System.out.println("Adding row to perf_test table");
    myStatement.executeUpdate(
      "INSERT INTO perf_test " +
      "(value) VALUES (1)"
    );
    myConnection.commit();
```

```
        // define the column type as Types.INTEGER for the first column
        // (the first column is the value column)
        System.out.println("Defining column type as Types.INTEGER for " +
          "first column");
        ((OracleStatement) myStatement).defineColumnType(
          1, Types.INTEGER
        );

        // create a ResultSet object
        ResultSet myResultSet = myStatement.executeQuery(
          "SELECT value " +
          "FROM perf_test"
        );

        // read the row from the ResultSet
        while (myResultSet.next()) {
          System.out.println("value = " + myResultSet.getInt("value"));
        } // end of while loop

        // close the ResultSet, Statement and Connection objects
        myResultSet.close();
        myStatement.close();
        myConnection.close();

      } // end of main()

    }
```

The output from this program is as follows:

```
Adding row to perf_test table
Defining column type as Types.INTEGER for first column
value = 1
```

Statement Caching

Each time you prepare a new statement using JDBC, that statement must be parsed
and created. These operations take a certain amount of time to complete. With
statement caching, you can store previously prepared statements in a cache and
then re-use those cached statements. Typically, using a cached statement reduces
the length of time to prepare a statement by half. Statement caching also prevents
new cursors from being created when using result sets. (I discussed cursors in
Chapter 2.)

TIP

Consider using statement caching if your program repeatedly executes SQL statements contained in a method or loop.

In this section, I'll show you how to enable statement caching and then store and re-use statements in the cache.

Enabling Statement Caching and Setting the Statement Cache Size

You can enable a statement cache for an `OracleConnection` object or an `OraclePooledConnection` object (I discussed `OraclePooledConnection` objects in Chapter 12). Each physical connection to the database has its own statement cache.

You set the number of statements allowed in the cache using the `setStmtCacheSize()` method. The first parameter to this method is an `int` that specifies the number of statements that may be stored in the cache. When you set this parameter to a number greater than zero, you both enable statement caching and you set the number of statements that may be stored in that cache. If you set this number to zero, no statements may be stored and you therefore disable the cache.

NOTE

The `setStmtCacheSize()` method accepts a second optional Boolean parameter that specifies if statement meta data is to be cleared when a statement is retrieved from the cache. Don't set this parameter: leave it in the default setting of `false` because there's no need to clear the statement meta-data. I discussed meta-data in Chapter 4.

Let's take a look at an example of enabling a statement cache. The following example casts an existing `Connection` object to an `OracleConnection` and then sets the number statements allowed in the cache to 20 using the `setStmtCacheSize()` method:

 `((OracleConnection) myConnection).setStmtCacheSize(20);`

Once you've done this, up to 20 statements can be stored in the cache.

Checking the Statement Cache Size

You can check the statement cache size using the `getStmtCacheSize()` method. This method returns an `int` containing the number of statements that may be stored in the cache. The following example shows the use of `getStmtCacheSize()`:

```
int myStatementCacheSize =
    ((OracleConnection) myConnection).getStmtCacheSize();
```

Since the cache size was set to 20 earlier, `getStmtCacheSize()` will return 20 in this example.

Types of Statement Caching

There are two types of statement caching you can use in your programs: *implicit statement caching* and *explicit statement caching*. With implicit statement caching, statements are automatically stored and retrieved from the cache. With explicit statement caching, you must first assign a key to a statement when storing it in the cache and later use this key to retrieve that statement. Explicit statement caching can have a slight edge in performance over implicit statement caching.

NOTE
Implicit and explicit statement caching use the same cache. You should therefore set your cache size large enough to accommodate the number of statements you want to store in your cache.

In the following sections, I'll describe how you use implicit and explicit statement caching, starting with implicit statement caching.

Using Implicit Statement Caching

With implicit statement caching, statements are automatically stored when you close them. When you then prepare another statement, the cache is automatically searched for an identical statement; if one is found, that statement is retrieved from the cache and re-used. The following types of objects are implicitly cached:

```
PreparedStatement
OraclePreparedStatement
CallableStatement
OracleCallableStatement
```

NOTE
Statement and OracleStatement objects are not implicitly cached. You can, however, explicitly cache these types of statements. I'll discuss explicit statement caching shortly.

To prepare a `PreparedStatement` or `OraclePreparedStatement` object, you use the `prepareStatement()` method; to prepare a `CallableStatement` or `OracleCallableStatement`, you use the `prepareCall()` method. When you close one of these objects using the `close()` method, your statement is automatically stored in the cache. Later, when you prepare an identical statement using the `prepareStatement()` or `prepareCall()` method, the statement previously stored in the cache is retrieved, and you can execute that same statement again.

In the following sections, I'll describe the details of using implicit statement caching, along with some concrete examples to help you understand the concepts.

Implicitly Storing a Statement in the Cache

The following example creates a `PreparedStatement` object (named `myPrepStatement`) and calls the `prepareStatement()` method for that object:

```
PreparedStatement myPrepStatement =
  myConnection.prepareStatement(
    "INSERT INTO perf_test " +
    "(value) VALUES (?)"
  );
```

Once you've executed this statement, you close it using the `close()` method. When you call the `close()` method, the statement will be stored automatically in the cache; for example:

```
myPrepStatement.close();
```

The details for `myPrepStatement` are now stored in the cache.

Implicitly Retrieving a Statement from the Cache

To retrieve a prepared statement from the cache, you call `prepareStatement()` again, using the same SQL string and object type; for example:

```
PreparedStatement myPrepStatement2 =
  myConnection.prepareStatement(
    "INSERT INTO perf_test " +
    "(value) VALUES (?)"
  );
```

You can then use `myPrepStatement2` to execute the same statement that was previously cached. You may, of course, provide a different value to the placeholder of `myPrepStatement2`.

Note that the SQL string and the object type must be *exactly* the same. This means that the SQL string's *characters* must be identical to those for the cached statement: that is, the letters must be the same and use the same case and the spaces in the string must also be the same. Also, the *statement object type* must be the same; for example, if you previously prepared a `PreparedStatement` object, you must also use another `PreparedStatement` object when calling `prepareStatement()` again; similarly, if you prepared a `CallableStatement` object, you must use another `CallableStatement` object when calling `prepareCall()`.

You can see why you'll typically want to use statement caching when using a method or loop: in a method or loop, you're executing exactly the same code repeatedly, and therefore you're using the same SQL string and object type.

Checking the Statement Creation State

You can check whether or not your statement was retrieved from the cache by checking the *creation state* for your statement. You do this using the `creationState()` method; this method returns an `int`. The use of this method is shown in the following example:

```
int myCreationState =
    ((OracleStatement) myPrepStatement).creationState();
```

The `int` returned by `creationState()` corresponds to one of three possible constants; these constants are shown in the following table.

Constant	Integer Value	Meaning
`OracleStatement.NEW`	0	The statement is new: the statement was not retrieved from the cache.
`OracleStatement.IMPLICIT`	1	The statement was retrieved using implicit statement caching.
`OracleStatement.EXPLICIT`	2	The statement was retrieved using explicit statement caching.

You can compare the `int` returned by `creationState()` to these constants and determine whether a statement was retrieved from the cache and, if so, what type of caching was used. You'll see an example of doing this shortly in an example program.

Disabling Implicit Caching for a Statement

You can choose not to implicitly store a statement in the cache using the
setDisableStmtCaching() method. You might want to do this because
the cache can only store a certain number of statements, and you should only
store statements that are repeatedly executed by your program.

Let's take a look at an example of disabling implicit caching for a specific
statement. The following examples create a new PreparedStatement object,
and then disable caching for this object using the setDisableStmtCaching()
method:

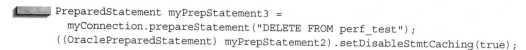

```
PreparedStatement myPrepStatement3 =
    myConnection.prepareStatement("DELETE FROM perf_test");
((OraclePreparedStatement) myPrepStatement2).setDisableStmtCaching(true);
```

When myPrepStatement3 is later closed, it will not be stored in the cache.

Closing Cached Statements

Because you use the close() method to implicitly cache a statement, this method
doesn't actually close your statement object. How then, do you close a statement?
The answer is, you don't! Cached statements are automatically closed for you when
one of the following conditions occurs:

■ You close your connection to the database. This closes all statements in the
  cache for that connection.

■ Your cache is already full and you've just called the close() method for a
  new statement. Because the cache is full, the least recently used statement
  in the cache is closed to make room for the new statement.

The following section contains a complete program that shows the use of implicit
statement caching.

Example Program: StatementCacheExample1.java

The program StatementCacheExample1.java, shown in the following listing,
shows the use of implicit statement caching. This program performs the following
major tasks:

1. Truncates the perf_test table.

2. Sets the statement cache size to 1: one statement may be stored in the cache.

3. Displays the cache size.

4. Calls the `insertRows()` method (defined in the program) to insert 2,000 rows into the `perf_test` table. This method creates a `PreparedStatement` object named `myPrepStatement` and displays the creation state for `myPrepStatement`; `insertRows()` then executes and closes `myPrepStatement`. When `myPrepStatement` is closed, it is implicitly cached.

5. Truncates the `perf_test` table again.

6. Calls the `insertRows()` method again. This time, when `myPrepStatement` is prepared, the original statement is retrieved from the cache; this is verified by displaying the creation state for `myPrepStatement`.

```java
/*
  StatementCacheExample1.java shows the use of
  implicit statement caching
*/

// import the JDBC packages
import java.sql.*;
import oracle.jdbc.*;

public class StatementCacheExample1 {

  // the TOTAL_NUM_ROWS constant is the total number of rows
  // that will be inserted
  public static final int TOTAL_NUM_ROWS = 2000;

  public static void main(String [] args)
  throws SQLException {

    // register the Oracle JDBC drivers
    DriverManager.registerDriver(
      new oracle.jdbc.OracleDriver()
    );

    // create a Connection object and connect to the database
    // as store_user using the Oracle JDBC Thin driver
    Connection myConnection = DriverManager.getConnection(
      "jdbc:oracle:thin:@localhost:1521:ORCL",
      "store_user",
      "store_password"
    );

    // disable auto-commit mode
```

```java
    myConnection.setAutoCommit(false);

    // create a Statement object
    Statement myStatement = myConnection.createStatement();

    // delete the rows from the perf_test table
    myStatement.execute("TRUNCATE TABLE perf_test");

    // set the statement cache size to 1
    ((OracleConnection) myConnection).setStmtCacheSize(1);

    // get and display the statement cache size
    int myStatementCacheSize =
      ((OracleConnection) myConnection).getStmtCacheSize();
    System.out.println("Statement cache size = " +
      myStatementCacheSize);

    // insert rows
    insertRows(myConnection);

    // delete the rows from the perf_test table
    myStatement.execute("TRUNCATE TABLE perf_test");

    // insert rows again (implicitly cached statement is used)
    insertRows(myConnection);

    // close the Statement and Connection objects
    myStatement.close();
    myConnection.close();

  } // end of main()


  private static void insertRows(
    Connection myConnection
  ) throws SQLException {

    System.out.println(
      "Inserting " + TOTAL_NUM_ROWS + " rows"
    );

    // create a PreparedStatement object
    PreparedStatement myPrepStatement =
      myConnection.prepareStatement(
        "INSERT INTO perf_test " +
        "(value) VALUES (?)"
```

```
      );

      // get and display the creation state
      int creationState =
        ((OracleStatement) myPrepStatement).creationState();
      System.out.println("creationState = " + creationState);

      // display the meaning of the creation state
      switch (creationState) {
        case OracleStatement.NEW:
          System.out.println("New statement created");
          break;
        case OracleStatement.IMPLICIT:
          System.out.println("Using implicitly cached statement");
          break;
        case OracleStatement.EXPLICIT:
          System.out.println("Using explicitly cached statement");
          break;
      } // end of switch

      // insert the rows
      int count2 = 0;
      for (int count = 0; count < TOTAL_NUM_ROWS; count++) {
        myPrepStatement.setInt(1, count);
        myPrepStatement.execute();
      }

      // commit the SQL statements
      myConnection.commit();

      // close the PreparedStatement object
      myPrepStatement.close();

    } // end of insertRows()

  }
```

The output from this program is as follows:

```
Statement cache size = 1
Inserting 2000 rows
creationState = 0
New statement created
Inserting 2000 rows
creationState = 1
Using implicitly cached statement
```

Using Explicit Statement Caching

Using explicit statement caching is a little more complicated than implicit statement caching. With implicit statement caching, all you had to do was call the `close()` method to store your statement in the cache; then when you later prepare an identical statement, your original statement is automatically retrieved from the cache. With explicit statement caching, you must assign a key to a statement when storing it in the cache. You then use this key to later retrieve your statement from the cache.

The following types of objects may be explicitly cached:

```
Statement
OracleStatement
PreparedStatement
OraclePreparedStatement
CallableStatement
OracleCallableStatement
```

As you can see from this list, you can explicitly cache `Statement` and `OracleStatement` objects. These objects are in addition to those listed earlier that may be implicitly cached.

In the following sections, I'll describe the details of using explicit statement caching.

Explicitly Storing a Statement in the Cache Using the Key

To explicitly store a statement in the cache you use the `closeWithKey()` method. This method accepts a `String` parameter that specifies a key for your statement. Let's take a look at an example; the following statement creates a `PreparedStatement` object named `myPrepStatement`:

```
PreparedStatement myPrepStatement =
    myConnection.prepareStatement(
      "INSERT INTO perf_test " +
      "(value) VALUES (?)"
    );
```

To explicitly store this statement in the cache, you use the `closeWithKey()` method, as shown in the following example:

```
((OracleStatement) myPrepStatement).closeWithKey(
    "myCachedStatement"
);
```

As you can see, the key for this statement is set to `myCachedStatement`. This key must be used to retrieve the statement from the cache later.

Explicitly Retrieving a Statement from the Cache Using the Key

To explicitly retrieve a statement from the cache, you must supply the same key that you set earlier using the `closeWithKey()` method. To do this, you must use a method that accepts a key when creating or preparing your statement. The following table shows the methods you use for each statement object.

Statement Object	Method
`Statement` or `OracleStatement`	`createStatementWithKey(String key)`
`PreparedStatement` or `OraclePreparedStatement`	`prepareStatementWithKey(String key)`
`CallableStatement` or `OracleCallableStatement`	`prepareCallWithKey(String key)`

Each of these methods is used with an `OracleConnection` object (you can also cast an existing `Connection` object to an `OracleConnection` prior to using the appropriate method). The following example shows the use of the `prepareStatementWithKey()` method; this example retrieves the statement that was previously cached using the `myCachedStatement` key:

```
PreparedStatememt myPrepStatement2 =
  ((OracleConnection) myConnection).prepareStatementWithKey(
    "myCachedStatement"
  );
```

You can then use `myPrepStatement2` to execute the same statement that was previously cached. You can, of course, provide a different value for the placeholder of `myPrepStatement2`.

NOTE
If you supply a key for a nonexistent statement, the `prepareStatementWithKey()` method will return `null`. This also applies to the other "WithKey" methods.

You can check the creation state for your statement using the `creationState()` method described earlier. The following section contains a complete program that shows the use of explicit statement caching.

Example Program: StatementCacheExample2.java

The program `StatementCacheExample2.java`, shown in the following listing, shows the use of explicit statement caching. This program performs the following major tasks:

1. Truncates the `perf_test` table.

2. Sets the statement cache size to 1: one statement may be stored in the cache.

3. Displays the cache size.

4. Calls the `insertRows()` method (defined in the program) to insert 2,000 rows into the `perf_test` table. This method accepts a Boolean parameter named `firstTime`, which indicates whether it is the first time that `insertRows()` has been called. When `firstTime` is set to `true`, `insertRows()` creates a `PreparedStatement` object named `myPrepStatement`. This object is closed at the end of `insertRows()` using the `closeWithKey()` method, setting the key to `myCachedStatement`.

5. Truncates the `perf_test` table again.

6. Calls the `insertRows()` method again with `firstTime` set to `false`. This time, `insertRows()` uses the `prepareStatementWithKey()` method, passing the key `myCachedStatement` to this method. This retrieves the statement that was previously stored in the cache in Step 4.

```
/*
  StatementCacheExample2.java shows the use of
  explicit statement caching
*/

// import the JDBC packages
import java.sql.*;
import oracle.jdbc.*;

public class StatementCacheExample2 {

  // the TOTAL_NUM_ROWS constant is the total number of rows
  // that will be inserted
  public static final int TOTAL_NUM_ROWS = 2000;
```

```java
public static void main(String [] args)
throws SQLException {

  // register the Oracle JDBC drivers
  DriverManager.registerDriver(
    new oracle.jdbc.OracleDriver()
  );

  // create a Connection object and connect to the database
  // as store_user using the Oracle JDBC Thin driver
  Connection myConnection = DriverManager.getConnection(
    "jdbc:oracle:thin:@localhost:1521:ORCL",
    "store_user",
    "store_password"
  );

  // disable auto-commit mode
  myConnection.setAutoCommit(false);

  // create a Statement object
  Statement myStatement = myConnection.createStatement();

  // delete the rows from the perf_test table
  myStatement.execute("TRUNCATE TABLE perf_test");

  // set the statement cache size to 1
  ((OracleConnection) myConnection).setStmtCacheSize(1);

  // display the statement cache size
  System.out.println("Statement cache size = " +
    ((OracleConnection) myConnection).getStmtCacheSize());

  // call insertRows() for the first time (as specified by
  // second parameter which is set to true)
  insertRows(myConnection, true);

  // delete the rows from the perf_test table
  myStatement.execute("TRUNCATE TABLE perf_test");

  // call insertRows() again
  insertRows(myConnection, false);

  // close the Statement and Connection objects
  myStatement.close();
```

```
    myConnection.close();

} // end of main()


private static void insertRows(
  Connection myConnection,
  boolean firstTime
) throws SQLException {

  System.out.println(
    "Inserting " + TOTAL_NUM_ROWS + " rows"
  );

  // declare a PreparedStatement object
  PreparedStatement myPrepStatement = null;

  // if its the first time insertRows() was called, then
  // set the INSERT statement for the PreparedStatement;
  // otherwise, use the key to retrieve the previously
  // cached statement
  if (firstTime) {
    System.out.println("First time insertRows() was called: " +
      "creating a new statement");
    myPrepStatement =
      myConnection.prepareStatement(
        "INSERT INTO perf_test " +
        "(value) VALUES (?)"
      );
  } else {
    System.out.println("insertRows() has been called before: " +
      "using the explicitly cached statement");
    myPrepStatement =
      ((OracleConnection) myConnection).prepareStatementWithKey(
        "myCachedStatement"
      );
  }

  // get and display the creation state
  int creationState =
    ((OracleStatement) myPrepStatement).creationState();
  System.out.println("creationState = " + creationState);

  // display the meaning of the creation state
  switch (creationState) {
```

```
    case OracleStatement.NEW:
      System.out.println("New statement created");
      break;
    case OracleStatement.IMPLICIT:
      System.out.println("Using implicitly cached statement");
      break;
    case OracleStatement.EXPLICIT:
      System.out.println("Using explicitly cached statement");
      break;
  } // end of switch

  // insert the rows
  int count2 = 0;
  for (int count = 0; count < TOTAL_NUM_ROWS; count++) {
    myPrepStatement.setInt(1, count);
    myPrepStatement.execute();
  }

  // commit the SQL statements
  myConnection.commit();

  // close the PreparedStatement object using the
  // closeWithKey() method to set the key for the cached statement
  System.out.println("Closing the statement and setting the key");
  ((OracleStatement) myPrepStatement).closeWithKey(
    "myCachedStatement"
  );

  } // end of insertRows()


}
```

The output from this program is as follows:

```
Statement cache size = 1
Inserting 2000 rows
First time insertRows() was called: creating a new statement
creationState = 0
New statement created
Closing the statement and setting the key
Inserting 2000 rows
insertRows() has been called before: using the explicitly
 cached statement
creationState = 2
Using explicitly cached statement
Closing the statement and setting the key
```

Tuning SQL Statements

In addition to tuning your JDBC code, you can also tune the SQL statements that your program issues. SQL tuning is very large subject, and in this section I'll just offer a couple of tips to improve the performance of your SQL statements.

NOTE
For detailed information on SQL tuning, I recommend the book Oracle High-Performance SQL Tuning *by Donald Burleson (McGraw-Hill/Osborne, 2001).*

Use a WHERE Clause to Restrict the Rows

Many novice programmers retrieve all the rows from a table into a result set, and then examine every row in that result set to find the row they actually want. This is very wasteful. A better approach is to use a WHERE clause in your SELECT statements. That way, you restrict the rows retrieved to just those you actually need.

Add Additional Indexes

A database index is conceptually similar to an index in a book. A book index allows you to look up the page number of a particular topic alphabetically. A database index is used by the database software to find a particular row in a table; adding database indexes can improve the performance of your SELECT statements.

Indexes are typically added to tables by a DBA, but you can provide valuable feedback to your DBA about the SELECT statements issued by your program. After all, only you know the details of how your program works. If you're not happy with the performance of your SELECT statements, you might want to talk with your DBA about adding indexes.

A Final Note

You are now at the end of the final chapter. I hope you found this book informative and useful, and I hope I've held your interest! As you've seen in this book, JDBC programming with Oracle9i is a very large subject. But armed with this book, I have every confidence you will master this subject.

PART

V

Appendixes

APPENDIX
A

Oracle and Java Type Mappings

his appendix contains three tables that document the mappings between the Oracle database types and the compatible Java types.

JDBC 2.0 Type Mappings

Table A-1 shows the mappings between the Oracle database types and the standard JDBC 2.0 types. You should use the standard JDBC 2.0 types when you want to make your code as portable as possible.

Oracle Type	Java Type
BLOB	java.sql.Blob
CHAR	java.lang.String
CLOB	java.sql.Clob
DATE	java.sql.Date
DATE	java.sql.Time
DATE	java.sql.Timestamp
JAVA_STRUCT	java.sql.SQLData
LONG	java.lang.String
LONGRAW	byte[]
NUMBER	boolean
NUMBER	byte
NUMBER	double
NUMBER	float
NUMBER	int
NUMBER	java.math.BigDecimal
NUMBER	long
NUMBER	short
RAW	byte[]

TABLE A-1. *Standard JDBC 2.0 Type Mappings*

Oracle Type	Java Type
TIMESTAMP	`java.sql.Timestamp`
User-defined Collection	`java.sql.Array`
User-defined Object	`java.sql.Struct`
User-defined Object Reference	`java.sql.Ref`
VARCHAR2	`java.lang.String`

TABLE A-1. *Standard JDBC 2.0 Type Mappings* (continued)

Oracle Extended JDBC Type Mappings

Table A-2 shows the mappings between the Oracle database types and the Oracle extended JDBC types. You should use the Oracle extended JDBC types when you want to use any Oracle database type not supported by a standard JDBC 2.0 type (BFILE, for example), or you want to take advantage of the additional functionality and performance offered by the Oracle extended JDBC types.

Oracle Type	Java Type
BFILE	`oracle.sql.BFILE`
BLOB	`oracle.sql.BLOB`
CHAR, NCHAR VARCHAR2, NVARCHAR2	`oracle.sql.CHAR`
CLOB	`oracle.sql.CLOB`
DATE	`oracle.sql.DATE`
NUMBER	`oracle.sql.NUMBER`
OPAQUE	`oracle.sql.OPAQUE`
RAW	`oracle.sql.RAW`
ROWID	`oracle.sql.ROWID`
TIMESTAMP	`oracle.sql.TIMESTAMP`
TIMESTAMPTZ	`oracle.sql.TIMESTAMPTZ`

TABLE A-2. *Oracle Extended JDBC Type Mappings*

Oracle Type	Java Type
User-defined collection	`oracle.sql.ARRAY`
User-defined object	`oracle.sql.STRUCT`
User-defined object reference	`oracle.sql.REF`

TABLE A-2. *Oracle Extended JDBC Type Mappings* (continued)

Java Wrapper Type Mappings

Table A-3 shows the mappings between the Oracle database NUMBER type and the various Java wrapper types. You may use the Java wrapper types when you want to retrieve a database NULL from a NUMBER column (you can also use an Oracle JDBC extended `oracle.sql.NUMBER` to retrieve a database NULL, but if you want to keep your code portable, you can use the Java wrapper types instead).

NOTE
Oracle's NUMBER type doesn't comply with an IEEE 754 float.

Oracle Type	Java Type
NUMBER	`java.lang.Boolean`
NUMBER	`java.lang.Byte`
NUMBER	`java.lang.Double`
NUMBER	`java.lang.Float`
NUMBER	`java.lang.Integer`
NUMBER	`java.lang.Long`
NUMBER	`java.lang.Short`
NUMBER	`java.math.BigDecimal`

TABLE A-3. *Java Wrapper Type Mappings*

APPENDIX
B

Oracle Java Tools
Reference

his appendix documents the syntax and command-line options for the following Oracle Java tools:

- **JPublisher** Allows you to automatically generate custom Java classes from your database object types and object references (covered in Chapter 6), along with collections (covered in Chapter 7).

- **loadjava** Allows you to load Java classes and JAR files into the database. A loaded Java class can then form part of a Java stored program (covered in Chapter 10).

- **dropjava** Allows you to drop previously loaded Java classes from the database.

- **ncomp** Allows you to compile your Java classes into native machine code for your platform. This tool generates a deployment JAR file that may then be loaded into the database. A loaded Java class can then form part of a Java stored program.

- **deploync** Allows you to load a deployment JAR file (previously created by the ncomp tool) into the database.

- **statusnc** Allows you to check the status of previously compiled and loaded classes in the database.

The following sections discuss each of these tools.

JPublisher

JPublisher (jpub) allows you to automatically generate custom Java classes from your database object types, object references (REFs), and collections (varrays and nested tables). JPublisher can even generate Java wrapper methods that will invoke your database object's methods. The syntax for running jpub from the command line is as follows:

```
jpub <options>
```

The options are supplied from the command line (you can also pass a number of options to jpub using a file). The various options are shown in Table B-1. The following example shows the use of jpub:

```
jpub -user=store_user/store_password -sql=my_database_type
```

In this example, jpub connects to the local database as store_user and generates a custom Java class for a database object type named my_database_type. In the next example, jpub connects to the database at a specified location (specified using the -url option), and the custom classes will implement the SQLData interface (specified using the -usertypes=jdbc option) with no Java wrapper methods for the database objects (-methods=none):

```
jpub -user=object_user/object_password
 -url=jdbc:oracle:thin:@localhost:1521:ORCL
 -usertypes=jdbc -methods=none
```

Chapter 6 contains other examples of running JPublisher.

loadjava

The loadjava tool allows you to load Java classes into the database. You can load your Java class files individually, or you can package your files together into a JAR file (Java Archive) and then load that JAR file. The syntax for running loadjava from the command line is as follows:

```
loadjava <options> files
```

Option	Description
-access	Sets the Java access modifiers for the generated methods. The default is public.
-builtintypes	Specifies the data type mappings for all *nonnumeric* and *non-LOB* built-in data types. May be set to jdbc (the default) or oracle. If set to jdbc, the various character database types (CHAR and VARCHAR2, for example) are mapped to java.lang.String; RAW and LONG RAW are mapped to byte arrays; DATE is mapped to java.sql.Timestamp. See Table A-1 of Appendix A for a full list of the mappings. If set to oracle, the various character database types are mapped to oracle.sql.CHAR; RAW and LONG RAW are mapped to oracle.sql.RAW; DATE is mapped to oracle.sql.DATE. See Table A-2 of Appendix A for a full list of the mappings.
-case	Specifies the case for the generated Java identifiers. May be set to mixed (the default), same, lower, or upper.

TABLE B-1. *JPublisher Options*

Option	Description
-compatible	Specifies either the Oracle8i compatibility mode or the interface to implement in the generated classes for your database object types.
	May be set to ORAData (the default) or CustomDatum (CustomDatum is supported for backward compatibility). This option modifies the behavior of -usertypes=oracle.
-context	Specifies the connection context used by JPublisher. May be set to the SQLJ DefaultContext class (the default), a user-specified class, or an inner class previously generated by JPublisher.
-dir	Specifies the base directory to which your generated files are saved. An empty directory saves all generated files in the current directory.
-driver	Specifies the driver class that JPublisher uses for JDBC connections to the database.
	The default is oracle.jdbc.OracleDriver.
-encoding	Specifies the Java encoding of the JPublisher input and output files. The default comes from the System property file.encoding.
-help	Displays the usage message on how to use JPublisher and its options.
-input	Specifies a file that lists the mappings for your database types and Java types.
-lobtypes	Specifies the data type mappings that JPublisher uses for BLOB and CLOB types.
	May be set to oracle (the default) or jdbc.
	If set to oracle, CLOB and BLOB columns are mapped to oracle.sql.CLOB and oracle.sql.BLOB, respectively.
	If set to jdbc, CLOB and BLOB columns are mapped to java.sql.CLOB and java.sql.BLOB, respectively.
-methods	Determines whether JPublisher generates wrapper methods for your database object's methods and PL/SQL package methods. May be set to all (the default), none, or named.

TABLE B-1. *JPublisher Options* (continued)

Option	Description
-numbertypes	Specifies the data type mappings that JPublisher uses for numeric database types.
	May be set to `objectjdbc` (the default), `jdbc`, `bigdecimal`, or `oracle`.
	If set to `objectjdbc`, most numeric database types are mapped to various Java wrapper classes contained in java.lang.* (for example, `java.lang.Int`). You can use these classes to represent database NULL values. See Table A-3 of Appendix A for the full mappings.
	If set to `bigdecimal`, all numeric database types are mapped to `java.math.BigDecimal`.
	If set to `jdbc`, most numeric database types are mapped to the standard Jdbc Mappings (`Int`, `Float`, For Example). See Table A-1 of Appendix A for the full mappings.
	If set to `oracle`, all numeric database types are mapped to `oracle.sql.NUMBER`.
	For further details, see the sections "Handling Numbers" and "Handling Database NULL Values" in Chapter 3 for advice on handling numbers and NULL values.
-omit_schema _names	Indicates that the generated Java types and packages will not include the schema names.
-package	Specifies the name of the Java package for the generated Java code.
-props	Specifies a file that contains any additional options you want to send to JPublisher.
-sql	Specifies your database object types and packages for which JPublisher will generate custom Java classes.
-url	Specifies the URL that JPublisher will use to connect to the database. The default is `jdbc:oracle:oci:@` (notice that this default uses `oci`; if you're using Oracle8i, you can use `oci8`; if you're using Oracle7, you can use `oci7`).
-user	Specifies a database username and password.

TABLE B-1. *JPublisher Options* (continued)

Option	Description
-usertypes	Specifies the type mappings that JPublisher will use for your database types.
	May be set to oracle (the default) or jdbc.
	If set to oracle, JPublisher generates ORAData classes for your objects, collections, and object references.
	If set to jdbc, JPublisher generates SQLData classes for your objects.

TABLE B-1. *JPublisher Options* (continued)

The options are supplied from the command line and are shown in Table B-2. The files are the Java files you want to load into the database. You can specify .java, .class, .sqlj, .ser, .zip, .jar, and resource file names on the command line in any order. The following example shows the use of loadjava:

```
loadjava -user store_user/store_password MyClass.class
```

This example connects to the database as store_user and loads the Java class MyClass.class.

Option	Description
-andresolve	Causes the files to be compiled or resolved at the time that they are loaded, instead of in a separate pass (as the -resolve option does). This option may be used instead of -resolve. Resolving at the time of loading the class will not invalidate any dependent classes.
	This option should only be used to replace classes that were previously loaded. If you changed the code only for existing methods within your class, you should use this option instead of the -resolve option.
-debug	Turns on SQL logging and is equivalent to using javac -g.

TABLE B-2. *loadjava Options*

Option	Description
-definer	By default, any class schema objects run with the privileges of their *invoker*—the user who calls the Java schema objects. This option changes the runtime privileges to those set for the *definer*—the user who invoked loadjava.
-encoding	Specifies the file encoding of a Java source for the compiler, overriding the matching value, if any, in the JAVA$OPTIONS database table. Values are the same as for the javac -encoding option. If you do not specify an encoding on the command line or in a JAVA$OPTIONS table, the encoding is assumed to be that returned by calling the following Java code: System.getProperty("file.encoding"); This option is only relevant when you're loading a Java source file.
-fileout <file>	Sends all messages from loadjava to the specified file.
-force	Forces all your files to be loaded.
-grant	Grants the EXECUTE privilege on your loaded classes to the listed database users; to call the methods of the class, the users must have the EXECUTE privilege. Any number and combination of user names can be specified, and they must be separated by commas (but not spaces); For example: -grant SCOTT,STORE_USER You cannot grant to a database role: you can only grant to users, and you must uppercase the schema name. The -grant option is cumulative: users are added to the list of those users that already have the EXECUTE privilege. To remove privileges from a user, you can either drop and reload the schema object and set your new privileges, or change the privileges with the SQL REVOKE command. If you want to grant the EXECUTE privilege on an object in someone else's schema, you must have CREATE PROCEDURE privilege (that privilege must have been granted with the WITH GRANT option).
-help	Displays the usage message on how to use the loadjava tool and its options.

TABLE B-2. *loadjava Options* (continued)

Option	Description
-jararesource	Causes the whole JAR file to be loaded into the schema as a resource instead of unpacking the JAR file and loading each individual class.
-oci | -oci8	Specifies that loadjava is to communicate with the database using the OCI JDBC driver. -oci and -thin are mutually exclusive; if neither option is specified, -oci is used by default.
-resolve	Compiles (if necessary) and resolves any external class references after all classes on the command line have been loaded. If you don't specify -resolve, loadjava loads your files but doesn't compile or resolve them.
-schema	Specifies the schema where your schema objects are created. If you don't supply a schema, the database logon schema is used. To create a schema object in a schema that you don't own, you must have the CREATE ANY PROCEDURE and CREATE ANY TABLE privileges. You must also have the JServerPermission.loadLibraryInClass for the class.
-stdout	Causes the output from loadjava to be directed to stdout, rather than to stderr.
-synonym	Creates a PUBLIC synonym for your loaded classes; this makes them accessible outside of the schema where you loaded them. To specify this option, you must have the CREATE PUBLIC SYNONYM privilege. If -synonym is specified for source files, the classes compiled from your source files are treated as if they had been loaded with -synonym.
-tableschema <schema>	Creates the loadjava internal tables within this specified schema rather than in the Java file destination schema.
-thin	Directs loadjava to communicate with the database using the Thin JDBC driver. The -oci and -thin options are mutually exclusive; if neither option is specified, -oci is used by default.

TABLE B-2. *loadjava Options* (continued)

Option	Description
-time	Adds a timestamp to every message displayed by loadjava.
-unresolvedok	When this option is combined with -resolve, loadjava will ignore any unresolved errors.
-user	Specifies the database username, password, and database connect string. The argument for the -user option has the form <username>/<password>[@<database>], where database is the URL location for the database (formatted appropriately for the driver used for the database connection).
-verbose	Causes loadjava to display detailed status messages while running.

TABLE B-2. *loadjava Options* (continued)

NOTE
You must have CREATE PROCEDURE and CREATE TABLE database privileges to load items into your schema; you must have CREATE ANY PROCEDURE or CREATE ANY TABLE privileges to load items into any schema.

dropjava

The dropjava tool allows you to drop previously loaded Java classes from the database. The dropjava tool transforms command-line file names and JAR or ZIP file contents to schema object names and then drops the schema objects from the database.

You can also specify a schema object name (the full name schema object name, not the short name) directly using dropjava. Any command-line argument that does not end in .jar, .zip, .class, .java, or .sqlj is presumed to be a schema object name and will be removed from the database. If you specify a schema object name that applies to multiple schema objects (such as a source schema object named MyClass and a class schema object named MyClass), all the schema objects will be removed. In addition, dropping a class invalidates any classes that depend on it. Finally, dropping a source file also drops any classes that derived from that source file.

You must remove Java schema objects in the same way that you first loaded them. For example, if you previously loaded a .jar file, you must run dropjava for the same .jar file.

The syntax for running dropjava from the command line is as follows:

```
dropjava <options> files
```

The options are supplied from the command line and are shown in Table B-3. The files are the Java files containing items you want to drop from the database. You can specify .java, .class, .sqlj, .ser, .zip, .jar, and resource file names on the command line in any order. The following example shows the use of dropjava:

```
dropjava -user store_user/store_password MyClass.class
```

This example connects to the database as store_user and drops MyClass.class from the database.

Option	Description
-encoding	Specifies the file encoding of a Java source file.
-help	Displays the usage message on how to use the dropjava tool and its options.
-jararesource	Drops the whole JAR file that was previously loaded from the schema.
-oci | -oci8	Specifies that dropjava is to communicate with the database using the OCI JDBC driver.
	-oci and -thin are mutually exclusive; if neither option is specified, -oci is used by default.
-schema	Specifies the schema from which the schema objects are to be dropped. If you don't supply a schema, the database logon schema is used.
	To drop a schema object from a schema that you don't own, you must have DROP ANY PROCEDURE and UPDATE ANY TABLE privileges.

TABLE B-3. *dropjava Options*

Option	Description
-stdout	Causes the output from dropjava to be directed to stdout, rather than to stderr.
-synonym	Drops a previously created PUBLIC synonym.
-thin	Directs dropjava to communicate with the database using the Thin JDBC driver. The -oci and -thin options are mutually exclusive; if neither option is specified, then -oci is used by default.
-time	Adds a timestamp to every message displayed by dropjava.
-user	Specifies the database username, password, and database connect string. The argument for the -user option has the form <username>/<password>[@<database>], where database is the URL location for the database (formatted appropriately for the driver used for the database connection).
-verbose	Causes dropjava to display detailed status messages while running.

TABLE B-3.   *dropjava Options* (continued)

ncomp

The ncomp tool allows you to compile your Java classes into native machine code for your platform; this gives your Java stored programs an additional performance boost. Before you can use ncomp, you must perform the following steps (your System Administrator and DBA can assist you with these steps):

1. Install a C compiler for your platform on your development machine.

2. Check and, if necessary, modify the compiler and linker executables referenced in one of the property setting files; these files are located in the System*.properties file; this file is located in the ORACLE_HOME\ javavm\jahome directory. Because the compiler and linker details are specific to your platform, you should consult the README file for your platform.

3. Set the directory of your JDK to your JAVA_HOME environment variable.

4. If you're using JDK 1.2, add the JAVA_HOME\lib\tools.jar and JAVA_HOME\lib\dt.jar files to your CLASSPATH environment

variable. If you're using JDK 1.1, add `JAVA_HOME\lib\classes.zip` to your `CLASSPATH`.

5. Add the `JAVA_HOME\bin` directory to your `PATH` environment variable (this directory contains the JDK binaries).

6. Set the `JAVA_HOME\lib` directory to your `LD_LIBRARY_PATH` environment variable (this directory contains the JDK libraries).

7. Grant the following database roles to the database user through which the ncomp tool is run: `JAVA_DEPLOY` and `JAVASYSPRIV`.

The syntax for running the `ncomp` tool from the command line is as follows:

```
ncomp <options> files
```

The `options` are supplied from the command line and are shown in Table B-4. The `files` are the Java files containing the classes that you want to natively compile. You can specify Java class files or ZIP and JAR files containing multiple classes. The ncomp tool will compile your classes and generate a deployment JAR file containing the natively compiled version of your classes. You can also have ncomp invoke the loadjava tool to load the resulting deployment JAR file into the database (you do this using the `-load` option, described in Table B-4). The following example shows the use of ncomp:

```
ncomp -user store_user/store_password MyClass.class
```

This example connects to the database as `store_user` and compiles `MyClass.class` into native code.

Option	Description
`-force`	Specifies that native compilation is to be performed on all your classes, even if they've already been natively compiled.
`-lightweightDeployment`	Allows you to deploy shared libraries and native compilation information separately.
`-load`	Causes ncomp to also execute `loadjava` to load the deployment JAR file into the database.

TABLE B-4. *ncomp Options*

Option	Description
`-noDeploy`	Specifies that `ncomp` is to produce only a deployment JAR file and is not to deploy that JAR file to the database. You can then use the `deploync` tool to deploy the JAR file later (the `deploync` tool is described later in this appendix).
`-oci	-oci8`	Specifies that `ncomp` is to communicate with the database using the OCI JDBC driver. `-oci` and `-thin` are mutually exclusive; if neither option is specified, `-oci` is used by default.
`-outputJarFile` `<JAR filename>`	Causes all natively compiled classes to be stored in a JAR file. This option specifies the name of the deployment JAR file and its destination directory. If you omit this option, the `ncomp` tool names the JAR file with the same name as your input with `_depl.jar` appended to it. If you omit the directory, the JAR file is stored in your project directory (specified by the `-projectDir` option).
`-projectDir` `<full directory>`	Specifies the full directory for your project (this is where your deployment JAR file will be stored). If you omit this option, the directory from which `ncomp` was invoked is used as the project directory.
`-thin`	Directs `ncomp` to communicate with the database using the Thin JDBC driver. The `-oci` and `-thin` options are mutually exclusive; if neither option is specified, `-oci` is used by default.
`-user`	Specifies the database username, password, and database connect string. The argument for the `-user` option has the form `<username>/<password>[@<database>]`, where `database` is the URL location for the database (formatted appropriately for the driver used for the database connection).

TABLE B-4. *ncomp Options* (continued)

Option	Description
-update	If you add more classes to a JAR or ZIP file that has already been natively compiled, you can use this option to tell ncomp to update the deployment JAR file with the new classes; ncomp will then compile your new classes and add them to the appropriate shared libraries.
-verbose	Causes ncomp to display detailed status messages while running.

TABLE B-4. *ncomp Options* (continued)

 deploync

The deploync tool allows you to load a deployment JAR file (previously created by the ncomp tool) into the database. The syntax for running the deploync tool from the command line is as follows:

```
deploync <options> deployment_JAR_file
```

The options are supplied from the command line and are shown in Table B-5. The deployment_JAR_file is the JAR file previously generated by ncomp. The following example shows the use of deploync:

```
deploync -user store_user/store_password MyJarFile.jar
```

This example connects to the database as store_user and loads MyJarFile.jar.

Option	Description
-oci | -oci8	Specifies that deploync is to communicate with the database using the OCI JDBC driver. -oci and -thin are mutually exclusive; if neither option is specified, -oci is used by default.
-projectDir <full directory>	Specifies the full directory containing your deployment JAR file. If you omit this option, the directory from which deploync was invoked is used.

TABLE B-5. *deploync Options*

Option	Description
-thin	Directs `deploync` to communicate with the database using the Thin JDBC driver. The `-oci` and `-thin` options are mutually exclusive; if neither option is specified, `-oci` is used by default.
-user	Specifies the database username, password, and database connect string. The argument for the `-user` option has the form `<username>/<password>[@<database>]`, where `database` is the URL location for the database (formatted appropriately for the driver used for the database connection).

TABLE B-5.   *deploync Options* (continued)

statusnc

The `statusnc` tool allows you to check the status of your Java classes; the status of each class can be any of the following:

- **ALREADY_NCOMPED**   Indicates that the class has been natively compiled.

- **NEED_NCOMPING**   Indicates that you must natively compile the class.

- **INVALID**   Indicates that the class wasn't successfully loaded into the database. You should load the class into the database.

The syntax for running the `statusnc` tool from the command line is as follows:

```
statusnc <options> deployment_JAR_file
```

The `options` are supplied from the command line and are shown in Table B-6. The `deployment_JAR_file` is the JAR file that you previously loaded into the database. The following example shows the use of `statusnc`:

```
statusnc -user store_user/store_password MyJarFile.jar
```

This example connects to the database as `store_user` and checks the status of `MyJarFile.jar`.

Option	Description
-oci | -oci8	Specifies that deploync is to communicate with the database using the OCI JDBC driver. -oci and -thin are mutually exclusive; if neither option is specified, -oci is used by default.
-output <filename>	Specifies that the output from statusnc is to be sent to filename instead of the screen.
-projectDir <full directory>	Specifies the full directory containing your deployment JAR file. If you omit this option, the directory from which statusnc was invoked is used.
-thin	Directs statusnc to communicate with the database using the Thin JDBC driver. The -oci and -thin options are mutually exclusive; if neither option is specified, -oci is used by default.
-user	Specifies the database username, password, and database connect string. The argument for the -user option has the form <username>/<password>[@<database>], where database is the URL location for the database (formatted appropriately for the driver used for the database connection).

TABLE B-6. *statusnc Options*

APPENDIX
C

Selected JDBC
Interface and Class
Reference

his appendix documents the following:

- The get and update methods of the java.sql.ResultSet interface that allow you to read from and write to values in a ResultSet object.

- The get and update methods of the oracle.jdbc.OracleResultSet interface that allow you to read from and write to values in an OracleResultSet object.

- The set methods of the java.sql.PreparedStatement interface that allow you to supply values to placeholders of a PreparedStatement object.

- The set methods of the oracle.jdbc.OraclePreparedStatement interface that allow you to supply values to placeholders of an OraclePreparedStatement object.

- The integer constants of the java.sql.Types class.

- The integer constants of the oracle.jdbc.OracleTypes class.

The methods and constants for the interfaces and classes were obtained using javap; you can use javap to see the definition of any Java class and interface. For example, to see the definition of java.sql.ResultSet, you use the following command:

```
javap java.sql.ResultSet
```

This example will list all the methods and constants in the java.sql.ResultSet interface. Similarly, the following command shows the definition of oracle.jdbc.OracleResultSet:

```
javap oracle.jdbc.OracleResultSet
```

NOTE
To see the options for javap, you can enter javap -help.

Get and Update Methods of the java.sql.ResultSet Interface

The java.sql.ResultSet interface declares a number of get and update methods. The get methods are used to retrieve values and the update methods are used to set values. You can learn about result sets in Chapter 3 and updatable result sets in Chapter 4.

The Get Methods of java.sql.ResultSet

The get methods of `java.sql.ResultSet` and their return types are shown in Table C-1.

Method	Return Type
getString(int)	java.lang.String
getBoolean(int)	boolean
getByte(int)	byte
getShort(int)	short
getInt(int)	int
getLong(int)	long
getFloat(int)	float
getDouble(int)	double
getBigDecimal(int, int)	java.math.BigDecimal
getBytes(int)[]	byte
getDate(int)	java.sql.Date
getTime(int)	java.sql.Time
getTimestamp(int)	java.sql.Timestamp
getAsciiStream(int)	java.io.InputStream
getUnicodeStream(int)	java.io.InputStream
getBinaryStream(int)	java.io.InputStream
getString(java.lang.String)	java.lang.String
getBoolean(java.lang.String)	boolean
getByte(java.lang.String)	byte
getShort(java.lang.String)	short
getInt(java.lang.String)	int

TABLE C-1. *java.sql.ResultSet Get Methods*

Method	Return Type
getLong(java.lang.String)	long
getFloat(java.lang.String)	float
getDouble(java.lang.String)	double
getBigDecimal(java.lang.String, int)	java.math.BigDecimal
getBytes(java.lang.String)[]	byte
getDate(java.lang.String)	java.sql.Date
getTime(java.lang.String)	java.sql.Time
getTimestamp(java.lang.String)	java.sql.Timestamp
getAsciiStream(java.lang.String)	java.io.InputStream
getUnicodeStream(java.lang.String)	java.io.InputStream
getBinaryStream(java.lang.String)	java.io.InputStream
getObject(int)	java.lang.Object
getObject(java.lang.String)	java.lang.Object
getCharacterStream(int)	java.io.Reader
getCharacterStream(java.lang.String)	java.io.Reader
getBigDecimal(int)	java.math.BigDecimal
getObject(int, java.util.Map)	java.lang.Object
getRef(int)	java.sql.Ref
getBlob(int)	java.sql.Blob
getClob(int)	java.sql.Clob
getArray(int)	java.sql.Array
getObject(java.lang.String, java.util.Map)	java.lang.Object

TABLE C-1. *java.sql.ResultSet Get Methods* (continued)

Method	Return Type
getRef(java.lang.String)	java.sql.Ref
getBlob(java.lang.String)	java.sql.Blob
getClob(java.lang.String)	java.sql.Clob
getArray(java.lang.String)	java.sql.Array
getDate(int, java.util.Calendar)	java.sql.Date
getDate(java.lang.String, java.util.Calendar)	java.sql.Date
getTime(int, java.util.Calendar)	java.sql.Time
getTime(java.lang.String, java.util.Calendar)	java.sql.Time
getTimestamp(int, java.util.Calendar)	java.sql.Timestamp
getTimestamp(java.lang.String, java.util.Calendar)	java.sql.Timestamp

TABLE C-1. *java.sql.ResultSet Get Methods* (continued)

The Update Methods of java.sql.ResultSet

The `java.sql.ResultSet` interface declares a number of update methods; these methods are shown in Table C-2 (the methods all return `void`).

Method
updateNull(int)
updateBoolean(int, boolean)
updateByte(int, byte)

TABLE C-2. *java.sql.ResultSet Update Methods*

Method

```
updateShort(int, short)

updateInt(int, int)

updateLong(int, long)

updateFloat(int, float)

updateDouble(int, double)

updateBigDecimal(int, java.math.BigDecimal)

updateString(int, java.lang.String)

updateBytes(int, byte[])

updateDate(int, java.sql.Date)

updateTime(int, java.sql.Time)

updateTimestamp(int, java.sql.Timestamp)

updateAsciiStream(int, java.io.InputStream, int)

UpdateBinaryStream(int, java.io.InputStream, int)

updateCharacterStream(int, java.io.Reader, int)

updateObject(int, java.lang.Object, int)

updateObject(int, java.lang.Object)

updateNull(java.lang.String)

updateBoolean(java.lang.String, boolean)

updateByte(java.lang.String, byte)

updateShort(java.lang.String, short)

updateInt(java.lang.String, int)

updateLong(java.lang.String, long)

updateFloat(java.lang.String, float)

updateDouble(java.lang.String, double)

updateBigDecimal(java.lang.String, java.math.BigDecimal)

updateString(java.lang.String, java.lang.String)
```

TABLE C-2. *java.sql.ResultSet Update Methods* (continued)

Method

```
updateBytes(java.lang.String, byte[])

updateDate(java.lang.String, java.sql.Date)

updateTime(java.lang.String, java.sql.Time)

updateTimestamp(java.lang.String, java.sql.Timestamp)

updateAsciiStream(java.lang.String, java.io.InputStream, int)

updateBinaryStream(java.lang.String, java.io.InputStream, int)

UpdateCharacterStream(java.lang.String, java.io.Reader, int)

updateObject(java.lang.String, java.lang.Object, int)

updateObject(java.lang.String, java.lang.Object)
```

TABLE C-2. *java.sql.ResultSet Update Methods* (continued)

Get and Update Methods of the oracle.jdbc.OracleResultSet Interface

The `oracle.jdbc.OracleResultSet` interface extends `java.sql.ResultSet`; `oracle.jdbc.OracleResultSet` declares a number of get and update methods. The get methods are used to retrieve values, and the update methods are used to set values. You can learn about result sets in Chapter 3 and updatable result sets in Chapter 4.

The Get Methods of oracle.jdbc.OracleResultSet

The get methods of `oracle.jdbc.OracleResultSet` and their return types are shown in Table C-3.

Method	Return Type
getARRAY(int)	oracle.sql.ARRAY
getARRAY(java.lang.String)	oracle.sql.ARRAY

TABLE C-3. *oracle.jdbc.OracleResultSet Get Methods*

Method	Return Type
getBFILE(int)	oracle.sql.BFILE
getBFILE(java.lang.String)	oracle.sql.BFILE
getBLOB(int)	oracle.sql.BLOB
getBLOB(java.lang.String)	oracle.sql.BLOB
getBfile(int)	oracle.sql.BFILE
getBfile(java.lang.String)	oracle.sql.BFILE
getCHAR(int)	oracle.sql.CHAR
getCHAR(java.lang.String)	oracle.sql.CHAR
getCLOB(int)	oracle.sql.CLOB
getCLOB(java.lang.String)	oracle.sql.CLOB
getCursor(int)	java.sql.ResultSet
getCursor(java.lang.String)	java.sql.ResultSet
getCustomDatum(int, oracle.sql.CustomDatumFactory)	oracle.sql.CustomDatum
getCustomDatum(java.lang.String, oracle.sql.CustomDatumFactory)	oracle.sql.CustomDatum
getDATE(int)	oracle.sql.DATE
getDATE(java.lang.String)	oracle.sql.DATE
getNUMBER(int)	oracle.sql.NUMBER
getNUMBER(java.lang.String)	oracle.sql.NUMBER
getOPAQUE(int)	oracle.sql.OPAQUE
getOPAQUE(java.lang.String)	oracle.sql.OPAQUE
getORAData(int, oracle.sql.ORADataFactory)	oracle.sql.ORAData

TABLE C-3. *oracle.jdbc.OracleResultSet Get Methods* (continued)

Method	Return Type
getORAData(java.lang.String, oracle.sql.ORADataFactory)	oracle.sql.ORAData
getOracleObject(int)	oracle.sql.Datum
getOracleObject(java.lang.String)	oracle.sql.Datum
getRAW(int)	oracle.sql.RAW
getRAW(java.lang.String)	oracle.sql.RAW
getREF(int)	oracle.sql.REF
getREF(java.lang.String)	oracle.sql.REF
getROWID(int)	oracle.sql.ROWID
getROWID(java.lang.String)	oracle.sql.ROWID
getSTRUCT(int)	oracle.sql.STRUCT
getSTRUCT(java.lang.String)	oracle.sql.STRUCT
getTIMESTAMP(int)	oracle.sql.TIMESTAMP
getTIMESTAMP(java.lang.String)	oracle.sql.TIMESTAMP
getTIMESTAMPLTZ(int)	oracle.sql.TIMESTAMPLTZ
getTIMESTAMPLTZ(java.lang.String)	oracle.sql.TIMESTAMPLTZ
GetTIMESTAMPTZ(int)	oracle.sql.TIMESTAMPTZ
GetTIMESTAMPTZ(java.lang.String)	oracle.sql.TIMESTAMPTZ

TABLE C-3. *oracle.jdbc.OracleResultSet Get Methods* (continued)

The Update Methods of oracle.jdbc.OracleResultSet

The update methods of oracle.jdbc.OracleResultSet are shown in Table C-4 (these methods all return void).

Method

```
updateARRAY(int, oracle.sql.ARRAY)

updateARRAY(java.lang.String, oracle.sql.ARRAY)

updateArray(int, java.sql.Array)

updateArray(java.lang.String, java.sql.Array)

updateBFILE(int, oracle.sql.BFILE)

updateBFILE(java.lang.String, oracle.sql.BFILE)

updateBLOB(int, oracle.sql.BLOB)

updateBLOB(java.lang.String, oracle.sql.BLOB)

updateBfile(int, oracle.sql.BFILE)

updateBfile(java.lang.String, oracle.sql.BFILE)

updateBlob(int, java.sql.Blob)

updateBlob(java.lang.String, java.sql.Blob)

updateCHAR(int, oracle.sql.CHAR)

updateCHAR(java.lang.String, oracle.sql.CHAR)

updateCLOB(int, oracle.sql.CLOB)

updateCLOB(java.lang.String, oracle.sql.CLOB)

updateClob(int, java.sql.Clob)

updateClob(java.lang.String, java.sql.Clob)

updateCustomDatum(int, oracle.sql.CustomDatum)

updateCustomDatum(java.lang.String, oracle.sql.CustomDatum)

updateDATE(int, oracle.sql.DATE)

updateDATE(java.lang.String, oracle.sql.DATE)

updateNUMBER(int, oracle.sql.NUMBER)

updateNUMBER(java.lang.String, oracle.sql.NUMBER)

updateORAData(int, oracle.sql.ORAData)

updateORAData(java.lang.String, oracle.sql.ORAData)
```

TABLE C-4. *oracle.jdbc.OracleResultSet Update Methods*

Method

updateOracleObject(int, oracle.sql.Datum)

updateOracleObject(java.lang.String, oracle.sql.Datum)

updateRAW(int, oracle.sql.RAW)

updateRAW(java.lang.String, oracle.sql.RAW)

updateREF(int, oracle.sql.REF)

updateREF(java.lang.String, oracle.sql.REF)

updateROWID(int, oracle.sql.ROWID)

updateROWID(java.lang.String, oracle.sql.ROWID)

updateRef(int, java.sql.Ref)

updateRef(java.lang.String, java.sql.Ref)

updateSTRUCT(int, oracle.sql.STRUCT)

updateSTRUCT(java.lang.String, oracle.sql.STRUCT)

TABLE C-4. *oracle.jdbc.OracleResultSet Update Methods* (continued)

Set Methods of the java.sql.PreparedStatement Interface

The java.sql.PreparedStatement interface extends java.sql.Statement; java.sql.PreparedStatement declares a number of set methods, which are used to set placeholder values. These methods are shown in Table C-5 (the methods all return void). You can learn about prepared statements in Chapter 3.

Method

setNull(int, int)

setBoolean(int, boolean)

setByte(int, byte)

TABLE C-5. *java.sql.PreparedStatement Set Methods*

Method

setShort(int, short)

setInt(int, int)

setLong(int, long)

setFloat(int, float)

setDouble(int, double)

setBigDecimal(int, java.math.BigDecimal)

setString(int, java.lang.String)

setBytes(int, byte[])

setDate(int, java.sql.Date)

setTime(int, java.sql.Time)

setTimestamp(int, java.sql.Timestamp)

setAsciiStream(int, java.io.InputStream, int)

setUnicodeStream(int, java.io.InputStream, int)

setBinaryStream(int, java.io.InputStream, int)

setObject(int, java.lang.Object, int, int)

setObject(int, java.lang.Object, int)

setObject(int, java.lang.Object)

setCharacterStream(int, java.io.Reader, int)

setRef(int, java.sql.Ref)

setBlob(int, java.sql.Blob)

setClob(int, java.sql.Clob)

setArray(int, java.sql.Array)

setDate(int, java.sql.Date, java.util.Calendar)

setTime(int, java.sql.Time, java.util.Calendar)

setTimestamp(int, java.sql.Timestamp, java.util.Calendar)

setNull(int, int, java.lang.String)

TABLE C-5.   *java.sql.PreparedStatement Set Methods* (continued)

Set Methods of the oracle.jdbc.OraclePreparedStatement Interface

The `oracle.jdbc.OraclePreparedStatement` interface extends the `java.sql.PreparedStatement` and `oracle.jdbc.OracleStatement` interfaces; `oracle.jdbc.OraclePreparedStatement` declares a number of set methods, which are used to set placeholder values. These methods are shown in Table C-6 (the methods all return void). You can learn about prepared statements in Chapter 3.

Method

setARRAY(int, oracle.sql.ARRAY)

setBFILE(int, oracle.sql.BFILE)

setBLOB(int, oracle.sql.BLOB)

setBfile(int, oracle.sql.BFILE)

setCHAR(int, oracle.sql.CHAR)

setCLOB(int, oracle.sql.CLOB)

setCursor(int, java.sql.ResultSet)

setCustomDatum(int, oracle.sql.CustomDatum)

setDATE(int, oracle.sql.DATE)

setFixedCHAR(int, java.lang.String)

setNUMBER(int, oracle.sql.NUMBER)

setOPAQUE(int, oracle.sql.OPAQUE)

setORAData(int, oracle.sql.ORAData)

setOracleObject(int, oracle.sql.Datum)

setPlsqlIndexTable(int, java.lang.Object, int, int, int, int)

setRAW(int, oracle.sql.RAW)

setREF(int, oracle.sql.REF)

TABLE C-6.   *oracle.jdbc.OraclePreparedStatement Set Methods*

Method

```
setROWID(int, oracle.sql.ROWID)

setRefType(int, oracle.sql.REF)

setSTRUCT(int, oracle.sql.STRUCT)

setStructDescriptor(int, oracle.sql.StructDescriptor)

setTIMESTAMP(int, oracle.sql.TIMESTAMP)

setTIMESTAMPLTZ(int, oracle.sql.TIMESTAMPLTZ)

setTIMESTAMPTZ(int, oracle.sql.TIMESTAMPTZ)
```

TABLE C-6. *oracle.jdbc.OraclePreparedStatement Set Methods* (continued)

Integer Constants of the java.sql.Types Class

The `java.sql.Types` class defines a number of `int` constants that are used to specify the type of a column in a `PreparedStatement` or `OraclePreparedStatement` object; these int constants are shown in Table C-7.

Int Constant

```
BIT

TINYINT

SMALLINT

INTEGER

BIGINT

FLOAT

REAL

DOUBLE
```

TABLE C-7. *java.sql.Types Constants*

Int Constant

NUMERIC

DECIMAL

CHAR

VARCHAR

LONGVARCHAR

DATE

TIME

TIMESTAMP

BINARY

VARBINARY

LONGVARBINARY

NULL

OTHER

JAVA_OBJECT

DISTINCT

STRUCT

ARRAY

BLOB

CLOB

TABLE C-7.   *java.sql.Types Constants* (continued)

Integer Constants of the oracle.jdbc.OracleTypes Class

The `oracle.jdbc.OracleTypes` class defines the same constants as those in `java.sql.Types` plus the additional constants shown in Table C-8. These additional constants are used to specify the type of a column in an `OraclePreparedStatement` object.

Int Constant

TIMESTAMPNS

TIMESTAMPTZ

TIMESTAMPLTZ

ROWID

CURSOR

BFILE

OPAQUE

JAVA_STRUCT

PLSQL_INDEX_TABLE

NUMBER

RAW

FIXED_CHAR

TABLE C-8. *oracle.jdbc.OracleTypes Constants*

APPENDIX
D

JNDI and Data Sources

The Java Naming and Directory Interface (JNDI) is an API (Applications Programming Interface) that provides naming and directory functionality to your Java programs. Using JNDI with JDBC is very useful because it allows you to register, or *bind*, data sources, and then look up those data sources in your program without having to provide the exact database connection details. Therefore, if the database connection details change, only the JNDI object must be changed, rather than your program.

JNDI is not limited to data sources: JNDI may be used to store and retrieve named Java objects of any type and to perform standard directory operations like searching for objects that have been bound to JNDI. For thorough coverage of JNDI, I recommend the book *JNDI API Tutorial and Reference: Building Directory-Enabled Java Applications* by Rosanna Lee and Scott Seligman (Addison-Wesley, 2000).

In this appendix, you'll learn how to bind a data source to JNDI and then look up that data source from within a program.

NOTE
The program examples in this appendix use the JNDI file system. In order to use the JNDI file system, you must download the `fscontext1_2beta3.zip` *file from the JNDI pages of Sun's Java website. Once you have this file, you must unzip it and add the resulting* `fscontext.jar` *and* `providerutil.jar` *files to your* `ClassPath` *environment variable.*

Binding a Data Source to JNDI

Binding a data source to JNDI may be done programmatically using Java statements, although typically, your DBA or system administrator should be responsible for binding data sources to JNDI.

When binding a data source using Java statements in your program, you follow these steps:

1. Create an `OracleDataSource` object (these were covered in Chapter 3).

2. Set the attributes for the `OracleDataSource` object.

3. Create a `Properties` object.

4. Add the JNDI properties to the `Properties` object.

5. Create a JNDI `Context` object.

6. Bind the `OracleDataSource` object to JNDI using the `Context` object.

The following sections describe these steps in detail.

Step 1: Create an OracleDataSource Object

The first step is to create an `OracleDataSource` object. The following statement creates an `OracleDataSource` object named myODS:

```
OracleDataSource myODS = new OracleDataSource();
```

This `OracleDataSource` object will later be bound to JNDI in Step 6.

Step 2: Set the Attributes for the OracleDataSource Object

The second step is to set the attributes of your `OracleDataSource` object using the various set methods. These attributes specify the details of the database connection. The following statements set the attributes for the myODS object created in the previous step:

```
myODS.setServerName("localhost");
myODS.setDatabaseName("ORCL");
myODS.setPortNumber(1521);
myODS.setDriverType("thin");
myODS.setUser("store_user");
myODS.setPassword("store_password");
```

Step 3: Create a Properties Object

The third step is to create an object of the `java.util.Properties` class; this object will later be used to initialize a JNDI `Context` object in Step 5. The following statement creates a `Properties` object named myProperties (assuming the `java.util.Properties` class has been previously imported):

```
Properties myProperties = new Properties();
```

This `Properties` object is used in the next step to hold two JNDI properties.

Step 4: Add the JNDI Properties to the Properties Object

The fourth step is to add the JNDI properties to your `Properties` object using the `setProperty()` method. The following statements show this:

```
myProperties.setProperty(Context.INITIAL_CONTEXT_FACTORY,
  "com.sun.jndi.fscontext.RefFSContextFactory");
myProperties.setProperty(Context.PROVIDER_URL,
  "file:C:/TEMP");
```

The `Context.INITIAL_CONTEXT_FACTORY` property specifies that the JNDI file system is to be used to store the JNDI binding information file. The `Context.PROVIDER_URL` property specifies the directory in the file system in which that binding file is to be stored; in this case, the directory is set to the Windows directory `C:/TEMP` (if you are using Unix or Linux, you would omit `C:` from the directory name).

Step 5: Create a JNDI Context Object

The fifth step is to create a JNDI object of the `javax.naming.Context` class. This object is used in Step 6 to bind your `OracleDataSource` object to JNDI. The following statement creates a `Context` object named `myContext`, passing in the `myProperties` object created in Step 3 to the constructor (assuming the `javax.naming.Context` class has been previously imported):

```
Context myContext = new InitialContext(myProperties);
```

The `InitialContext` constructor creates a `Context` object that references the initial JNDI naming context.

Step 6: Bind the OracleDataSource Object to JNDI Using the Context Object

The sixth and final step is to bind your `OracleDataSource` object to JNDI using your `Context` object. You do this using the `bind()` method of your `Context` object. The `bind()` method accepts two parameters: a `String` containing the name you want to use for your JNDI object and the Java object you want to bind.

NOTE
You can bind many different classes of objects to JNDI, including `ConnectionPoolDataSource` objects. Connection pools were covered in Chapter 12.

The following statement binds the `OracleDataSource` object named myODS (created in Step 1) to a JNDI object named myBoundODS:

```
myContext.bind("myBoundODS", myODS);
```

Once this statement has been executed, you'll find a file named `.bindings` in the directory specified in the `Context.PROVIDER_URL` property (set in Step 4). The `.bindings` file contains the details of your data source. You may then look up the JNDI object using the name myBoundODS and use it to connect to the database. You'll see how to do that later in this appendix.

Example Program: JNDIExample1.java

The `JNDIExample1.java` program, shown in the following listing, uses the six program steps described in the previous sections to bind a data source to JNDI. This data source will be looked up and used to connect to the database in the next section.

```
/*
   JNDIExample1.java illustrates how to bind a data source
   to JNDI
*/

// import the required packages
import java.util.*;
import java.sql.*;
import oracle.jdbc.pool.*;
import javax.naming.*;

public class JNDIExample1 {

  public static void main(String args [])
  throws SQLException, NamingException {

    // step 1: create an OracleDataSource object
    System.out.println("Creating an OracleDataSource object");
    OracleDataSource myODS = new OracleDataSource();

    // step 2: set the attributes for the OracleDataSource object
    System.out.println("Setting the attributes of the " +
      "OracleDataSource object");
    myODS.setServerName("localhost");
    myODS.setDatabaseName("ORCL");
    myODS.setPortNumber(1521);
    myODS.setDriverType("thin");
    myODS.setUser("store_user");
    myODS.setPassword("store_password");
```

```
// step 3: create a Properties object
System.out.println("Creating a Properties object");
Properties myProperties = new Properties();

// step 4: add the JNDI properties to the Properties object
System.out.println("Adding the JNDI properties");
myProperties.setProperty(Context.INITIAL_CONTEXT_FACTORY,
    "com.sun.jndi.fscontext.RefFSContextFactory");
myProperties.setProperty(Context.PROVIDER_URL,
    "file:C:/TEMP");

// step 5: create a JNDI Context object
System.out.println("Creating a JNDI Context object");
Context myContext = new InitialContext(myProperties);

// step 6: bind the OracleDataSource object to JNDI
System.out.println("Binding the OracleDataSource object to " +
    "JNDI using the name 'myBoundODS'");
myContext.bind("myBoundODS", myODS);

} // end of main()

}
```

The output from this program is as follows:

```
Creating an OracleDataSource object
Setting the attributes of the OracleDataSource object
Creating a Properties object
Adding the JNDI properties
Creating a JNDI Context object
Binding the OracleDataSource object to JNDI using the name
 'myBoundODS'
```

Looking Up a Data Source Using JNDI

Once a data source has been bound using JNDI, you may look up that data source using JNDI. You perform the following four steps to do this:

1. Create a `Properties` object.

2. Add the JNDI properties to the `Properties` object.

3. Create a JNDI `Context` object.

4. Look up the data source using JNDI.

Steps 1 through 3 are identical to Steps 3 through 5 shown earlier for binding a data source using JNDI: only Step 4 in this list is new. The following section describes Step 4 in detail.

Step 4: Look Up the Data Source Using JNDI

To look up a data source using JNDI, you use the `lookup()` method of your `Context` object. The `lookup()` method accepts a `String` parameter containing the name of the JNDI object that was previously bound. The `lookup()` method returns a Java `Object`, which you must cast to the required class. The following statement calls the `lookup()` method, passing `myBoundODS` as the parameter, which is the name of the JNDI data source object previously bound in the earlier examples:

```
OracleDataSource myODS =
  (OracleDataSource) myContext.lookup("myBoundODS");
```

The `Object` returned by the `lookup()` method is cast to an `OracleDataSource` object, which is then stored in `myODS`. You can then request a database connection from `myODS`, as shown in the following statement:

```
Connection myConnection = myODS.getConnection();
```

You may then use `myConnection` to connect to the database.

The following section contains a complete program that illustrates all four steps in the previous list.

Example Program: JNDIExample2.java

The `JNDIExample2.java` program, shown in the following listing, uses the program steps outlined earlier to look up the data source named `myBoundODS`. This is the data source that was previously bound by the `JNDIExample1.java` program. The `JNDIExample2.java` program requests a database connection from this data source and uses it to display the details of customer #1. I've supplied a procedure named `DisplayCustomer()` that retrieves and displays the customer details.

```
/*
  JNDIExample.java illustrates how to lookup a data source
  using JNDI, and uses that data source to connect to
  the database
*/

// import the required packages
import java.util.*;
import java.sql.*;
```

```java
import oracle.jdbc.pool.*;
import javax.naming.*;

public class JNDIExample2 {

  public static void main(String args [])
  throws SQLException, NamingException {

    // step 1: create a Properties object
    System.out.println("Creating a Properties object");
    Properties myProperties = new Properties();

    // step 2: add the JNDI properties to the Properties object
    System.out.println("Adding the JNDI properties");
    myProperties.setProperty(Context.INITIAL_CONTEXT_FACTORY,
      "com.sun.jndi.fscontext.RefFSContextFactory");
    myProperties.setProperty(Context.PROVIDER_URL,
      "file:C:/TEMP");

    // step 3: create a JNDI Context object
    System.out.println("Creating a JNDI Context object");
    Context myContext = new InitialContext(myProperties);

    // step 4: lookup the data source using JNDI
    System.out.println("Looking up the data source with " +
      "the name 'myBoundODS' using JNDI");
    OracleDataSource myODS =
      (OracleDataSource) myContext.lookup("myBoundODS");

    // request, use, and finally close a Connection object
    // from the OracleDataSource object
    System.out.println("Requesting a connection from the " +
      "OracleDataSource object");
    Connection myConnection = myODS.getConnection();
    DisplayCustomer(myConnection, 1);  // display customer #1
    myConnection.close();

  } // end of main()


  public static void DisplayCustomer(Connection myConnection, int id)
  throws SQLException {

    // create a Statement object
    Statement myStatement = myConnection.createStatement();
```

```
    // declare variables and objects used to represent
    // the column values retrieved from the customers table
    String firstName;
    String lastName;

    // create a ResultSet object
    ResultSet customerResultSet = myStatement.executeQuery(
      "SELECT first_name, last_name " +
      "FROM customers " +
      "WHERE id = " + id
    );

    // retrieve and display the column values
    while (customerResultSet.next()) {
      firstName = customerResultSet.getString("first_name");
      lastName = customerResultSet.getString("last_name");

      System.out.println("id = " + id);
      System.out.println("firstName = " + firstName);
      System.out.println("lastName = " + lastName);
    } // end of while loop

    // close the ResultSet and Statement objects
    customerResultSet.close();
    myStatement.close();

  } // end of DisplayCustomer()

}
```

The output from this program is as follows:

```
Creating a Properties object
Adding the JNDI properties
Creating a JNDI Context object
Looking up the data source with the name 'myBoundODS' using JNDI
Requesting a connection from the OracleDataSource object
id = 1
firstName = John
lastName = Brown
```

Index

Q

INTERNATIONAL CONTACT INFORMATION

AUSTRALIA
McGraw-Hill Book Company Australia Pty. Ltd.
TEL +61-2-9417-9899
FAX +61-2-9417-5687
http://www.mcgraw-hill.com.au
books-it_sydney@mcgraw-hill.com

CANADA
McGraw-Hill Ryerson Ltd.
TEL +905-430-5000
FAX +905-430-5020
http://www.mcgrawhill.ca

GREECE, MIDDLE EAST,
NORTHERN AFRICA
McGraw-Hill Hellas
TEL +30-1-656-0990-3-4
FAX +30-1-654-5525

MEXICO (Also serving Latin America)
McGraw-Hill Interamericana Editores S.A. de C.V.
TEL +525-117-1583
FAX +525-117-1589
http://www.mcgraw-hill.com.mx
fernando_castellanos@mcgraw-hill.com

SINGAPORE (Serving Asia)
McGraw-Hill Book Company
TEL +65-863-1580
FAX +65-862-3354
http://www.mcgraw-hill.com.sg
mghasia@mcgraw-hill.com

SOUTH AFRICA
McGraw-Hill South Africa
TEL +27-11-622-7512
FAX +27-11-622-9045
robyn_swanepoel@mcgraw-hill.com

UNITED KINGDOM & EUROPE
(Excluding Southern Europe)
McGraw-Hill Education Europe
TEL +44-1-628-502500
FAX +44-1-628-770224
http://www.mcgraw-hill.co.uk
computing_neurope@mcgraw-hill.com

ALL OTHER INQUIRIES Contact:
Osborne/McGraw-Hill
TEL +1-510-549-6600
FAX +1-510-883-7600
http://www.osborne.com
omg_international@mcgraw-hill.com

GET YOUR FREE SUBSCRIPTION
TO ORACLE MAGAZINE

Oracle Magazine is essential gear for today's information technology professionals. Stay informed and increase your productivity with every issue of *Oracle Magazine*. Inside each free bimonthly issue you'll get:

- Up-to-date information on Oracle Database, E-Business Suite applications, Web development, and database technology and business trends
- Third-party news and announcements
- Technical articles on Oracle Products and operating environments
- Development and administration tips
- Real-world customer stories

Three easy ways to subscribe:

① Web

Visit our Web site at www.oracle.com/oraclemagazine. You'll find a subscription form there, plus much more!

② Fax

Complete the questionnaire on the back of this card and fax the questionnaire side only to +1.847.647.9735.

③ Mail

Complete the questionnaire on the back of this card and mail it to P.O. Box 1263, Skokie, IL 60076-8263

IF THERE ARE OTHER ORACLE USERS AT YOUR LOCATION WHO WOULD LIKE TO RECEIVE THEIR OWN SUBSCRIPTION TO ORACLE MAGAZINE, PLEASE PHOTOCOPY THIS FORM AND PASS IT ALONG.

Oracle Publishing

ORACLE®

FREE SUBSCRIPTION

signature (required)   date

X

name   title

company   e-mail address

street/p.o. box

city/state/zip or postal code   telephone

country   fax

YOU MUST ANSWER ALL NINE QUESTIONS BELOW.

① WHAT IS THE PRIMARY BUSINESS ACTIVITY OF YOUR FIRM AT THIS LOCATION? (check one only)

- ☐ 01 Application Service Provider
- ☐ 02 Communications
- ☐ 03 Consulting, Training
- ☐ 04 Data Processing
- ☐ 05 Education
- ☐ 06 Engineering
- ☐ 07 Financial Services
- ☐ 08 Government (federal, local, state, other)
- ☐ 09 Government (military)
- ☐ 10 Health Care
- ☐ 11 Manufacturing (aerospace, defense)
- ☐ 12 Manufacturing (computer hardware)
- ☐ 13 Manufacturing (noncomputer)
- ☐ 14 Research & Development
- ☐ 15 Retailing, Wholesaling, Distribution
- ☐ 16 Software Development
- ☐ 17 Systems Integration, VAR, VAD, OEM
- ☐ 18 Transportation
- ☐ 19 Utilities (electric, gas, sanitation)
- ☐ 98 Other Business and Services

② WHICH OF THE FOLLOWING BEST DESCRIBES YOUR PRIMARY JOB FUNCTION? (check one only)

Corporate Management/Staff
- ☐ 01 Executive Management (President, Chair, CEO, CFO, Owner, Partner, Principal)
- ☐ 02 Finance/Administrative Management (VP/Director/ Manager/Controller, Purchasing, Administration)
- ☐ 03 Sales/Marketing Management (VP/Director/Manager)
- ☐ 04 Computer Systems/Operations Management (CIO/VP/Director/ Manager MIS, Operations)

IS/IT Staff
- ☐ 05 Systems Development/ Programming Management
- ☐ 06 Systems Development/ Programming Staff
- ☐ 07 Consulting
- ☐ 08 DBA/Systems Administrator
- ☐ 09 Education/Training
- ☐ 10 Technical Support Director/Manager
- ☐ 11 Other Technical Management/Staff
- ☐ 98 Other

③ WHAT IS YOUR CURRENT PRIMARY OPERATING PLATFORM? (select all that apply)

- ☐ 01 Digital Equipment UNIX
- ☐ 02 Digital Equipment VAX VMS
- ☐ 03 HP UNIX
- ☐ 04 IBM AIX

- ☐ 05 IBM UNIX
- ☐ 06 Java
- ☐ 07 Linux
- ☐ 08 Macintosh
- ☐ 09 MS-DOS
- ☐ 10 MVS
- ☐ 11 NetWare
- ☐ 12 Network Computing
- ☐ 13 OpenVMS
- ☐ 14 SCO UNIX
- ☐ 15 Sequent DYNIX/ptx
- ☐ 16 Sun Solaris/SunOS
- ☐ 17 SVR4
- ☐ 18 UnixWare
- ☐ 19 Windows
- ☐ 20 Windows NT
- ☐ 21 Other UNIX
- ☐ 98 Other
- ☐ 99 None of the above

④ DO YOU EVALUATE, SPECIFY, RECOMMEND, OR AUTHORIZE THE PURCHASE OF ANY OF THE FOLLOWING? (check all that apply)

- ☐ 01 Hardware
- ☐ 02 Software
- ☐ 03 Application Development Tools
- ☐ 04 Database Products
- ☐ 05 Internet or Intranet Products
- ☐ 99 None of the above

⑤ IN YOUR JOB, DO YOU USE OR PLAN TO PURCHASE ANY OF THE FOLLOWING PRODUCTS? (check all that apply)

Software
- ☐ 01 Business Graphics
- ☐ 02 CAD/CAE/CAM
- ☐ 03 CASE
- ☐ 04 Communications
- ☐ 05 Database Management
- ☐ 06 File Management
- ☐ 07 Finance
- ☐ 08 Java
- ☐ 09 Materials Resource Planning
- ☐ 10 Multimedia Authoring
- ☐ 11 Networking
- ☐ 12 Office Automation
- ☐ 13 Order Entry/Inventory Control
- ☐ 14 Programming
- ☐ 15 Project Management
- ☐ 16 Scientific and Engineering
- ☐ 17 Spreadsheets
- ☐ 18 Systems Management
- ☐ 19 Workflow

Hardware
- ☐ 20 Macintosh
- ☐ 21 Mainframe
- ☐ 22 Massively Parallel Processing

- ☐ 23 Minicomputer
- ☐ 24 PC
- ☐ 25 Network Computer
- ☐ 26 Symmetric Multiprocessing
- ☐ 27 Workstation

Peripherals
- ☐ 28 Bridges/Routers/Hubs/Gateways
- ☐ 29 CD-ROM Drives
- ☐ 30 Disk Drives/Subsystems
- ☐ 31 Modems
- ☐ 32 Tape Drives/Subsystems
- ☐ 33 Video Boards/Multimedia

Services
- ☐ 34 Application Service Provider
- ☐ 35 Consulting
- ☐ 36 Education/Training
- ☐ 37 Maintenance
- ☐ 38 Online Database Services
- ☐ 39 Support
- ☐ 40 Technology-Based Training
- ☐ 98 Other
- ☐ 99 None of the above

⑥ WHAT ORACLE PRODUCTS ARE IN USE AT YOUR SITE? (check all that apply)

Software
- ☐ 01 Oracle9i
- ☐ 02 Oracle9i Lite
- ☐ 03 Oracle8
- ☐ 04 Oracle8i
- ☐ 05 Oracle8i Lite
- ☐ 06 Oracle7
- ☐ 07 Oracle9i Application Server
- ☐ 08 Oracle9i Application Server Wireless
- ☐ 09 Oracle Data Mart Suites
- ☐ 10 Oracle Internet Commerce Server
- ☐ 11 Oracle interMedia
- ☐ 12 Oracle Lite
- ☐ 13 Oracle Payment Server
- ☐ 14 Oracle Video Server
- ☐ 15 Oracle Rdb

Tools
- ☐ 16 Oracle Darwin
- ☐ 17 Oracle Designer
- ☐ 18 Oracle Developer
- ☐ 19 Oracle Discoverer
- ☐ 20 Oracle Express
- ☐ 21 Oracle JDeveloper
- ☐ 22 Oracle Reports
- ☐ 23 Oracle Portal
- ☐ 24 Oracle Warehouse Builder
- ☐ 25 Oracle Workflow

Oracle E-Business Suite
- ☐ 26 Oracle Advanced Planning/Scheduling
- ☐ 27 Oracle Business Intelligence
- ☐ 28 Oracle E-Commerce
- ☐ 29 Oracle Exchange
- ☐ 30 Oracle Financials

- ☐ 31 Oracle Human Resources
- ☐ 32 Oracle Interaction Center
- ☐ 33 Oracle Internet Procurement
- ☐ 34 Oracle Manufacturing
- ☐ 35 Oracle Marketing
- ☐ 36 Oracle Order Management
- ☐ 37 Oracle Professional Services Automation
- ☐ 38 Oracle Projects
- ☐ 39 Oracle Sales
- ☐ 40 Oracle Service
- ☐ 41 Oracle Small Business Suite
- ☐ 42 Oracle Supply Chain Management
- ☐ 43 Oracle Travel Management
- ☐ 44 Oracle Treasury

Oracle Services
- ☐ 45 Oracle.com Online Services
- ☐ 46 Oracle Consulting
- ☐ 47 Oracle Education
- ☐ 48 Oracle Support
- ☐ 98 ther
- ☐ 99 None of the above

⑦ WHAT OTHER DATABASE PRODUCTS ARE IN USE AT YOUR SITE? (check all that apply)

- ☐ 01 Access
- ☐ 02 Baan
- ☐ 03 dbase
- ☐ 04 Gupta
- ☐ 05 IBM DB2
- ☐ 06 Informix
- ☐ 07 Ingres
- ☐ 98 Other
- ☐ 99 None of the above
- ☐ 08 Microsoft Access
- ☐ 09 Microsoft SQL Server
- ☐ 10 PeopleSoft
- ☐ 11 Progress
- ☐ 12 SAP
- ☐ 13 Sybase
- ☐ 14 VSAM

⑧ DURING THE NEXT 12 MONTHS, HOW MUCH DO YOU ANTICIPATE YOUR ORGANIZATION WILL SPEND ON COMPUTER HARDWARE, SOFTWARE, PERIPHERALS, AND SERVICES FOR YOUR LOCATION? (check only one)

- ☐ 01 Less than $10,000
- ☐ 02 $10,000 to $49,999
- ☐ 03 $50,000 to $99,999
- ☐ 04 $100,000 to $499,999
- ☐ 05 $500,000 to $999,999
- ☐ 06 $1,000,000 and over

⑨ WHAT IS YOUR COMPANY'S YEARLY SALES REVENUE? (please choose one)

- ☐ 01 $500, 000, 000 and above
- ☐ 02 $100, 000, 000 to $500, 000, 000
- ☐ 03 $50, 000, 000 to $100, 000, 000
- ☐ 04 $5, 000, 000 to $50, 000, 000
- ☐ 05 $1, 000, 000 to $5, 000, 000

123101